HOUSTON BASEBALL

THE EARLY YEARS
1861-1961

2365 Rice Blvd., Suite 202
Houston, Texas 77005

ISBN: 978-1-939055-74-3

10 9 8 7 6 5 4 3 2 1

Library of Congress Cataloging-in-Publication Data on file with publisher.

Editorial Direction, Lucy Herring Chambers
Creative Direction, Ellen Peeples Cregan
Editor, Eva J. Freeburn
Design, Marla Y. Garcia

Printed in Canada through Friesens

HOUSTON BASEBALL

THE EARLY YEARS 1861-1961

A project of the Larry Dierker Chapter –
The Society for American Baseball Research

Edited by **MIKE VANCE**
Afterword by **MICKEY HERSKOWITZ**

TABLE OF CONTENTS

CHAPTER ONE

IN THE BIG INNING 1836–1861

BY MIKE VANCE & BOB DORRILL

Much like the birthday of baseball itself, it's impossible to put an exact date on the first game ever played in the Bayou City, but it definitely happened sometime prior to April 1861. That was the month when two small items in the *Houston Weekly Telegraph* reported on a piece of local business, a story that might have gotten a front page mention partially because it involved the newspaper's publisher/editor, Edward Hopkins Cushing.

Baseball was being referenced as America's National Game even before the Civil War, and that passion included parts of Texas.

Courtesy Library of Congress

"Base Ball Club. – A meeting for the purpose of organizing a Base Ball Club was held over J.H. Evans' store on Thursday night. After the organization meeting, and the adoption of the name "Houston Base Ball Club," a ballot per permanent officers was had, with the following result: President F.A. Rice; Vice-President, E.H. Cushing; Secretary, W.H. Campbell; Treasurer, J.H. Evans; Corresponding Secretary, John S. Clute; Directors, G.A. Ellsworth; J.C. Baldwin and C.C. Clute."

The date of this Thursday organizational meeting was April 11, 1861, a matter of weeks after Texas had voted to secede from the United States of America and mere hours before rebels fired on Fort Sumter. The timing here probably speaks less to the priority that Houstonians may have been giving to "base ball" and more to their gross underestimation of how secession was going to impact manpower and leisure time activity for years to come.

Ball games of one sort or another had been occurring in the Bayou City well before the formation of this club. Diarists and Houston historians commented on local youngsters playing various ball games going back to the second San Jacinto Celebration in 1838.[1] Dr. Samuel O. Young, who wrote newspaper pieces about the old days for the *Houston Post*, recalled playing town ball games with his friends while growing up in the 1850s.[2] Other Houston newspapers also reported stories of ball teams and games played before the Civil War, although they lacked almost all details.[3]

Pure English cricket had been known to provide enjoyment in Texas, if not to actual Texans. In the decade prior to the Civil War, Galveston, the most populous city in Texas, was home to consular officials representing 11 foreign governments. With the commercial interests between the Texas cotton growers and English cotton mills, the British were the best represented among them.[4] Those buyers sometimes staged cricket matches on the island.[5]

Certainly town ball, a predecessor to the game that we would more closely identify with modern baseball, could be found all over Texas. There were accounts of Mexican War soldiers in Zachary Taylor's army playing ball at Corpus Christi in 1846.[6] The earlier game seemed to have lingered even after sports-minded Texans could readily distinguish it from the most modern form of baseball. An Austin editor reported on a "real old fashioned game of base or town ball" being played by government and store clerks on the open prairie north of the state Capitol.[7] He wrote that it made him feel almost like a young man.[8] Clearly, baseball-like games went back a long way in Texas.

In the broadest historical context, the roots of baseball go back many centuries beyond this state or any of the other 49. Evidence exists of games using balls and clubs, sticks or bats going back thousands of years on multiple continents. There were illustrations of them on ancient Egyptian temples and among 14th century nuns and monks.[9]

Early America had many versions of the game we recognize today, dating to Jamestown and Plymouth. Barn ball, stool ball, round ball, chermany, Dutch long and Old Cat were just a few that varied widely in duration, shape, execution and number of players. Getting to our modern game has been a long evolutionary process, albeit one that isn't very scientific.

The British, in particular, insisted that baseball was simply a derivative of their games of cricket or rounders. Americans, however, didn't want a national pastime that came from someplace else. That obsession for United States purity would eventually create misinformation about baseball's origins that linger to this day. Fortunately for nationalism, most of the important refinements are indeed all-American.

John Thorn, the Historian of the Baseball Hall of Fame and a foremost authority on the game's origins, suggests that, if pressed for a date that "baseball took root in America," it might be around 1735 in the Berkshires and Housatonic Valley. A history of Pittsfield, Massachusetts, states that not only were ball games played there, but that they were played so often that the town passed an ordinance prohibiting any game with a ball being played within a distance of 80 yards from the Meeting House. [10]

The annals of the American Revolution itself contain plenty of ball-playing references. New Hampshire officer Henry Dearborn complained of northern Pennsylvania that, "we are oblige'd to walk four miles today to find a place leavel enough to play ball."[11] In 1778, a Continental soldier named George Ewing wrote of a "game of base" being played at Valley Forge.[12]

The frequency and urgency of these records suggests that the games contained elements of serious competition as opposed to merely being a way to idle away time in camp.

There are Revolutionary era mentions of ball playing by patriots and loyalists alike. Even captured British officers are reported to have played "at almost all hours of the day," and they proved ready customers for a Pennsylvania teen who fashioned new balls from old stockings wrapped and bound in white leather.[13]

A forerunner of baseball was being played on college campuses like Princeton to the point that it was banned in 1787 as "low and unbecoming gentlemen students…an exercise attended with great danger." Their alarm was likely aimed at the custom of "soaking" players by hitting them with the ball as they ran the bases.[14] Yale, Dartmouth, the University of Pennsylvania and others issued similar bans, some suggesting that the colleges also feared for their windows.[15]

Ball games were not exclusive to the North, with mentions of them in South Carolina by the dawn of the 19th century.[16] Even the legal prohibitions meant to placate the non-fans spread southward. There were laws on the books in Fayetteville, North Carolina, in 1797 specifically prohibiting organized play of baseball on Sundays by African Americans.[17]

As the nineteenth century developed, so did two distinct games of baseball, each with its own set of rules. Differences were major, including the number of bases and the distance between them, the way a hurler delivered the ball, how many outs would prompt a change of sides, the ability to "plug" a runner for an out and even the very existence of baselines and foul territory. They would eventually come to be known as the Massachusetts game and the New York game.

The merits of each might be debated, but one would become relegated to historical minutia while the other lives on as the progenitor of our modern game.

Early baseball is often imagined as a game for pastoral village greens enjoyed in crisp, fresh country air. And though some of the early players might have first learned their skills in those rural settings, the game we know today began developing in New York City in the 1830s.

Though there were certainly earlier clubs with the same rule changes and innovations, the first highly organized and highly publicized baseball team was the Knickerbockers, some of whom were former members of other New York City teams. In 1845, they recruited new members, codified rules and formed an exclusive social club, the purpose of which was to play the game with the right sort of compatriots.[18]

They styled their ballgames as a vehicle for genteel exercise and fellowship. The ball was pitched and not thrown, the number of innings was unimportant and punctuality for the contest was required. Post game banquets were an integral part of the ritual, and some measure of social standing was compulsory. Annual dues were five dollars, and the initiation fee was two.

By the latter half of the 1850s, Manhattan had seen several rival clubs: the New Yorks, Gothams, Magnolias, Eagles and Empires. Brooklyn had the Excelsiors, Eckfords, Putnams and Atlantics and Philadelphia had the Olympics. The Knickerbockers, though, are the ones best remembered by history. Their books of organization and rules became generally accepted as the "New York Game," the direct ancestor of baseball today.[19]

The cynic might enjoy another milestone from the late 1850s. In 1858 an all-star game, though that term had not yet been coined, was played between the top players from New York and Brooklyn. It holds the distinction of the first baseball game for which admission was charged.[20]

In the earliest years of the 20th century, famous baseballist and equipment manufacturer Albert Spalding sought to establish pure American roots for the National Game. This purity mattered greatly to people like Spalding, who dismissed English cricket as lacking the manliness and vitality of baseball. He wrote, "Cricket is a gentle game. Baseball is war. Cricket is an athletic sociable, played in a conventional, decorous and English manner. Baseball is played in an unconventional, enthusiastic American manner."[21]

Spalding led the formation of a distinguished commission comprised of seven of the game's power brokers and headed by National League President, A. G. Mills. They were tasked with documenting the origins of baseball. In 1907, they credited General Abner Doubleday, a longtime friend of Mills, as the "Father of Baseball," a conclusion that was rather quickly disproved. Numerous people with knowledge of both Doubleday and the early game put forth their own theories, most of which were no better than the one they debunked.

Doubleday was, though, involved in the beginning of something even more momentous: the Civil War. Then a Captain of artillery, he was second in command at Fort Sumter in April of 1861, and is credited with supervising the first Union cannon shot in response to the Southern volley that opened the long and brutal hostilities. He wrote later

It didn't take long before American commercial interests sought to capitalize on baseball's popularity. Tobacco, along with beer, was among the first products successfully advertised through a connection to the game.

Courtesy Library of Congress

Charleston toward the island fort "penetrated the masonry and burst near my head," and he "aimed the first gun on our side in reply to the attack."[22]

Another Doubleday myth had credited him with bringing baseball to Texas, a state where he served extensively after the war, including command of the 24th Colored Infantry and, prior to that, a post on Galveston Island. The popular story was that he organized a game for Washington's Birthday celebrations in the Oleander City in 1866. Once again, evidence proves that he had no association with developing baseball on the island or in the state in general, but grow and flourish it did.[23]

The first printed record of baseball

The first printed record of baseball taking hold in Texas was when a club formed at Galveston on February 24, 1859, several years before Abner Doubleday was stationed there.[24] A majority of club members did, however, share at least one thing with Doubleday: they were New Yorkers. The rules under which they played were specified as being the same as those used "at the North."[25] Those rules had gone through a major upgrade just two years prior, so that could have made these Texas sportsmen quite cutting edge.[26]

The club president was Ira M. Freeman, a man almost two decades older than the other officers named.[27] Freeman had come from New York to Marshall, Texas, by the early 1840s, later moving to Galveston where he partnered in the cotton business with the young Newton Squire.[28] Squire, who wrote a regular item on cotton prices in Galveston for a local paper, had come from New York City much more recently. Elected secretary of the new baseball club, Squire was in his late twenties. So were vice president A. Davidson and treasurer Edwin, or Edmund, Van York.[29]

These were not the only relocated New Yorkers bringing baseball to Galveston, either. Just weeks later, the Rochester, New York, newspaper reported that one of their own, Francis A. Schoeffel, had led formation of the Empire Base Ball Club in Galveston where he was working for a railroad. He had previously been "one of the most forward of the ball players" at Rochester, founding a club there most interestingly named the Lone Star.[30]

Elsewhere along the Gulf Coast, baseball was doing fine, too. Though the surviving record of baseball clubs forming in New Orleans indicates that Galveston might have gotten a two or three month jump on them in that regard, the Crescent City caught up with a vengeance. By the end of 1859, the city had seven teams whose names have survived history. A year later they could boast 15 clubs. By comparison, Chicago had only four at the end of 1860.[31] It caused notice in New York City where one paper reported that "baseball is now being played in New Orleans almost daily."[32]

Even some of the small Texas locales had noticed baseball by 1859. The editor of the *Belton Independent* wrote that he would like to "see a base ball club started in" their town.[33]

All of this goes to suggest that the lack of specific baseball news from Houston might reflect more on the surviving record than on the lack of local interest in the game in the late 1850s. Not all newspapers from the time period are still extant. Often a paper's editor was the primary writer, focusing on topics that were brought to his attention.

From a business standpoint, the city of Houston was remarkably similar to both Galveston and New Orleans. All had bustling port operations. Whereas Galveston outpaced Houston in terms of large ocean going vessels, Houston was the unquestionable rail center of Texas and the Southwest. Goods from around the region arrived by rail near the foot of Main Street where they were loaded onto steamboats and barges to travel down Buffalo Bayou to Galveston Bay and beyond.[34] By far the biggest commodity leaving the area was cotton, a balance that continued until the end of the century.[35]

Travel between Houston/Galveston and New Orleans was an almost daily occurrence. The one-way fare seldom rose above five dollars.

More important to the rise of baseball, though, was the fact that the cotton trade was hottest between this trio of Gulf Coast ports and the City of New York. Passage could be booked several times a week. The Morgan Line led the way, operating four steamboats and eight barks between Galveston and New York.[36]

Some of the New York-born players who comprised those first Galveston teams were working as clerks for cotton and transportation brokers such as Wm. Hendley and Company, a firm with offices in New York and in a brand new, spacious building on Galveston's Strand.[37] Newspapers from the time period show many businesses in both Texas cities advertising close ties to New York.

It is only natural that the young up-and-comers who followed their jobs to Texas would bring their passion for a favored pastime along with them.

The thriving cotton, railroad and shipping industries in Houston and Galveston could at times be both familial and cutthroat. Undoubtedly, almost all the business players knew one another, yet they spared nothing in the quest to get a leg up. City leaders used everything from railroad track right of way to yellow fever quarantine as weapons against the other.

The rivalry would also play out on the diamond, with a variety of Houston ball clubs considering their island counterparts as the most familiar and fierce of opponents for the next hundred years.

1 Bartholomew, Ed. *The Houston Story.* (Frontier Press, 1951)
2 Young, Samuel O. *True Stories of Old Houston and Houstonians.* (Oscar Springer,1913)
3 *Houston Daily Union*, April 25, 1871.
4 Carroll, John M. *The Doubleday Myth and Texas Baseball.* Southwestern Historical Quarterly, Vol. 92, No. 4, April 1989.
5 Ziegler, Jesse. *Wave of the Gulf.* (Naylor & Co., 1938)
6 Gomez, Cesar Gonzalez. *March, Conquest and Play Ball: The Game in The Mexican American War, 1846-1848.* Base Ball, Fall 2011
7 Austin Southern Intelligencer, 23 February 1859
8 Colorado Citizen (Columbus, TX), 5 March 1859
9 Thorn, John. *Origins of the New York Game.* Base Ball. Fall 2009; Altherr, Thomas. *A Place Leavel Enough to Play Ball: Baseball and Baseball-type Games in the Colonial Era, Revolutionary War and Early American Republic.* Nine: A Journal of Baseball History and Culture. Number 8. 2000.
10 Thorn, John. *Baseball in the Garden of Eden, The Secret History of the Early Game.* (Simon and Schuster, 2011)
11 Altherr, Thomas. *A Place Leavel Enough to Play Ball: Baseball and Baseball-type Games in the Colonial Era, Revolutionary War and Early American Republic.* Nine: A Journal of Baseball History and Culture. Number 8. 2000.
12 Thorn, John, Editor. *Total Baseball.* 7th Edition. (Sport Media Publishing, 2004)
13 John Smith Hanna, ed., *A History of the Life and Services of Captain Samuel Dewees, A Native of Pennsylvania, and Soldier of the Revolutionary and Last Wars,* (Robert Neilson, 1844)
14 Ward, Geoffrey C.. *Baseball: An Illustrated History.* (Knopf, 1994)
15 Altherr, Thomas. *A Place Leavel Enough to Play Ball: Baseball and Baseball-type Games in the Colonial Era, Revolutionary War and Early American Republic.* Nine: A Journal of Baseball History and Culture. Number 8. 2000.
16 Altherr, Thomas. *A Place Leavel Enough to Play Ball: Baseball and Baseball-type Games in the Colonial Era, Revolutionary War and Early American Republic.* Nine: A Journal of Baseball History and Culture. Number 8. 2000.
17 Thorn, John, Editor. *Total Baseball.* 7th Edition. (Sport Media Publishing, 2004)
18 Thorn, John. *Baseball in the Garden of Eden, The Secret History of the Early Game.* (Simon and Schuster, 2011)
19 Thorn, John. *Baseball in the Garden of Eden, The Secret History of the Early Game.* (Simon and Schuster, 2011); Thorn, John, Editor. *Total Baseball.* 7th Edition. (Sport Media Publishing, 2004)
20 Bruce, H. Addington. Outlook Magazine. 17 May 1913.
21 Spalding, Albert. *America's National Game.* (American Sports , 1911)
22 Doubleday, Abner. *Reminiscences of Forts Sumter and Moultrie, 1860-'61*(Harper & Brothers, 1876); Thorn, John. *Baseball in the Garden of Eden, The Secret History of the Early Game.* (Simon and Schuster, 2011)
23 Carroll, John M. *The Doubleday Myth and Texas Baseball.* Southwestern Historical Quarterly, Vol. 92, No. 4, April 1989.
24 (Galveston) Civilian and Gazette Weekly, 1 March 1859
25 (Galveston) Civilian and Gazette Weekly, 1 March 1859
26 Thorn, John. *Baseball in the Garden of Eden, The Secret History of the Early Game.* (Simon and Schuster, 2011)
27 Allardice, Bruce. *The Inauguration of this Noble and Manly Game Among Us: The Spread of Baseball in the South Prior to 1870.* Base Ball. Fall 2012
28 United States Census 1850, Harrison County, TX; Galveston City Directory 1859; Allardice, Bruce. *The Inauguration of this Noble and Manly Game Among Us: The Spread of Baseball in the South Prior to 1870.* Base Ball. Fall 2012
29 United States Census 1860, Galveston County, TX
30 Rochester (NY) Democrat and American, 6 April 1859
31 Somers, Dale. *The Rise of Sport in New Orleans, 1850-1900.* (Pelican, 1972)
32 New York Sunday Mercury, 30 Dec 1860
33 Houston Weekly Telegraph, 28 September 1859
34 McComb, David G. *Galveston A History* (University of Texas, 1986)
35 Hall, Andrew. *Galveston-Houston Packet: Steamboats on Buffalo Bayou* (The History press, 2012)
36 Fornell, Earl Wesley. The Galveston Era: The Texas Crescent on the Eve of Secession. (University of Texas, 1961)
37 Allardice, Bruce. *The Inauguration of this Noble and Manly Game Among Us: The Spread of Baseball in the South Prior to 1870.* Base Ball. Fall 2012

KEY

GDN – *Galveston Daily News*
HI – *Houston Informer*
HP – *Houston Post*
CD – *Chicago Defender*
HC – *Houston Chronicle*

CHAPTER TWO

THE CLIMB TO THE PROS 1861–1887

BY MIKE VANCE & JOSEPH THOMPSON

Though the game was clearly being played in Houston beforehand, a meeting above J.H. Evans' dry goods store survives as the earliest printed record of baseball activity in the Bayou City. It was held on April 11, 1861, in the Palmer Building at what would now be 315 Main Street, midway between Congress and Preston.[1]

Soldiers on both sides of the Civil War played lots of baseball during slack hours in camp. The same was true of prisoners of war such as these Union captives in Salisbury, NC. Conditions at the prison camps were never this bucolic, however.
Courtesy Library of Congress

The news item furnished only the eight names of the club officers, leaving the identities of the other young ball players to the vagaries of history.

As in the Galveston ball club that had been documented two years earlier, the presence of many Northerners among the members is indisputable.[2]

Compared to most other places in the South, early Houston had more than its share of Yankees. The founding Allen family were New Yorkers. A good number of early residents came from the Northeastern states, and some undoubtedly brought knowledge of "base ball" with them to Texas. New York and Massachusetts, especially, were states where clubs had been actively refining the working rules of the game we know today as baseball.

The first club's president, Frederick Allyn Rice, was a native of Springfield, Massachusetts, who moved to Houston in 1850 to join the booming business enterprises of his older brother, William Marsh Rice.[3] The elder Rice had parlayed interests in cotton, railroads, shipping, banking and real estate into the greatest fortune in town, and young Fred anxiously moved southwest to help run things.[4] F. A. Rice would call Houston home for the rest of his life, and one of his 10 children would become a notable Houston mayor. Brother William Rice moved to New York, but in his will, of which Frederick would be the first executor, W.M. Rice bequeathed money to start the institute that is today Rice University.

Jonas C. Baldwin, Rice's brother-in-law and next door neighbor, came from an even more connected Houston family. His Aunt Charlotte was the wife of Augustus Allen, one of the city's founders, and his father, Horace Baldwin, served a term as Houston mayor in 1844. At the time of the ball club's formation, the newly married J. C. sold furniture in the establishment of his brother-in-law, Fred Rice. Later he would own a grocery and a livery stable.[5]

Edward Hopkins Cushing was in the newspaper business. He had come to Texas fresh out of Dartmouth College to become a teacher. Gravitating to journalism in Brazoria County, he ended up as owner of the *Houston Telegraph* newspaper by 1856. Just over 30 when the baseball team formed, Cushing had already found success on the bayou. He would eventually own a large stationary and book store, publish poetry and become recognized as a horticulturist.[6]

Three other club directors, George A. Ellsworth and brothers John S. and Charles C. Clute, were newer to town, brought to Houston by jobs in the emerging technology sector. The Ontario-born Clutes had come far south to become officers in the new Texas Telegraph Company. Fellow Canadian Ellsworth had learned telegraphy as a teenager and was said to have been exceptionally good at it. Charlie Clute, superintendant of the telegraph company headquartered in Houston, brought him to town as an operator.[7]

Joseph H. Evans and William H. Campbell were the only southern-born officers of the first Houston Base Ball Club, though Evans' father was a druggist from Massachusetts.[8] Campbell was a 21-year-old native Texan. He was listed in the 1860 census as a non-property owning clerk who lived in a large hotel. Tennessee-born Evans was a definite up-and-comer. At 24, he already owned a mercantile business on Main Street and had a young wife and an infant son, Henry.[9]

Even prior to the meeting on Main Street, the players had agreed to be on hand at five o'clock on Monday, Wednesday, and Friday mornings, for "field exercise" in Academy Square, the block bounded by Austin, Caroline, Capitol and Rusk streets[10] and home to the city's largest school, the Houston Academy. The bird's eye map of 1873 drawn by Augustus Koch shows a vacant city block immediately to the west of the Academy, so it is possible that the dawn practices took place there instead, though the school grounds were ample for a small ball field.

There was surely throwing, batting and running, but whether games were held is not known. Aside from the formation of this team and the practices held, not much else survives concerning Houston's first attempt at the organization of a ball club.

The 1861 meeting at J.H. Evans Store offers important evidence to dispel the common notion that baseball only spread to the South after Confederate soldiers learned the game as Civil War prisoners.

The truth is that baseball already enjoyed varying degrees of familiarity across a good portion of the Southern states, and nowhere was it known better than in the Gulf Coast ports of New Orleans, Galveston and Houston.

In fact, that first Houston Base Ball Club was joined by a second within weeks, despite secession and growing military service. *The Galveston News* reported on June 11 of that year that there were then two base ball clubs organized in Houston.[11] Both ball clubs soon became secondary to the Civil War that had enveloped the United States.

Though the biggest battles raged far to the north and east, Houston was hardly a town abandoned during the war. The city served as the headquarters of the District of Texas, New Mexico and Arizona, making it a bustling center for Confederate military activity. On a national scale, the sheer numbers of American families directly affected by the Civil War would be approached only during World War II.

Many young Houston men stayed in the area and did their Confederate service in largely local units. Frederick Rice, for example, the president of the first Houston Base Ball Club, entered Southern service in spite of his Northern birth, as did his brother-in-law J. C. Baldwin.[12] Most of their time was spent in the quartermaster corps in Fort Bend, Wharton, Brazoria and Matagorda Counties. Among Rice's duties was impressing slaves from local landowners for work on the Galveston, Houston and Henderson Railroad.[13] Many Houstonians referred to the popular Rice by his honorific of Captain until his untimely death on a train near La Marque in 1901.[14]

E. H. Cushing, another Yankee who felt strongly about Southern rights, stayed in Houston during the war, rallying the citizenry with the *Telegraph's* support for the Confederate cause.[15] At times the shortage of newsprint became so acute that the paper was published on alternate media including some issues printed on the back of wallpaper or wrapping paper.[16]

Other charter members of the early ball clubs went off to war, as well. Charlie Clute joined the rebels as a "telegraphic superintendant," reaching the rank of captain. His brother, John, chose to return to Canada when hostilities began. William Campbell reached the rank of sergeant with the Texas unit, Waul's Legion, a combined arms unit that included infantry, cavalry and artillery. He was captured at Vicksburg.[17]

Among the founders of the first two Galveston clubs, Newton Squire and E. Van York would stay to join the Confederates, both remaining near the island. Squire was a lieutenant with the Galveston Guards by mid-April 1861, just days after the war began.[18] He later appeared among junior officers proffering an honorary dinner to General Sterling Price upon his visit to the Island City.[19] Van York was in Cook's Regiment of heavy artillery which served along the coast and took part in the battle to retake Galveston on New Year's Eve 1863.[20] He would also appear to be the man listed as New Yorker Edmund Van York who was captured while serving as supercargo for the blockade running Confederate schooner, Uncle Mose.[21]

The Empire Base Ball Club founder, Frank Schoeffel, returned to Rochester, New York, and a commission with the 13th New York Infantry, seeing action at Bull Run, the Peninsular Campaign and Fredericksburg. By the time the regiment was mustered out, Schoeffel was the commanding officer. He would spend his career with the New York Railroad, also serving time as sheriff of Monroe County, New York.

Among the known ball players, George Ellsworth made the biggest name in military service. Joining the Bayou City Guards at the outbreak of the war, Ellsworth chafed at the idea of serving as a mere infantry private. He resolved to put his telegraphic skills to work. Fleeing Houston on a hand car under the pretext of "going out to repair the telegraph line in the direction of Sabine Pass," he ran all the way to Mobile with the plan to offer his services to the famously daring Confederate raider John Hunt Morgan.

Re-enlisted, this time in the 2nd Kentucky (Confederate) Cavalry, Ellsworth soon became indispensible to his new commanding officer. Cutting into telegraph lines, he proved adept at imitating other operators and sending reports that placed Morgan's raiders many miles from their actual location. Ellsworth's great speed at the key earned him the nickname "Lightning."[22]

After the war, Ellsworth continued to amass notoriety. Wanted for drunkenly murdering a barkeeper in Kentucky, he dropped from public view only to possibly reemerge as a train robber and desperado in Montgomery County, Texas. Mentioned as being a telegraph operator in Houston, he was reported to have been one of the men captured for robbing the Texas Express office in Willis. He eventually surfaced at New Orleans where the *Times-Democrat* would publish his memoirs.[23] Ellsworth died at the telegraph key in Antonia, Louisiana.[24]

The most touching story connected to pre-war baseball in the area was that of J. H. Evans. He entered Confederate service as an officer, becoming a lieutenant in Waul's Legion, the same unit that took William Campbell. Serving as an adjutant, the newly promoted Evans went with the Legion, by then downsized to 12 companies of infantry only, to Mississippi, where it would participate in the defense of Vicksburg.

Captain Evans, though, did not survive to witness that city's fall and the capture of all but one company of the Legion. He died of illness early in 1863.

When E.H. Cushing wrote in his obituary that Evans was "an exemplary and noble hearted man" and that "few, if any, of our young men could be more missed by our people," he did so from the position of personal friend.[25]

The Civil War didn't suspend baseball around Houston entirely, it just changed the uniforms. Texas housed its share of Union prisoners during the war, and one of the pastimes afforded them was the game of baseball. Camp Ford at Tyler was the largest Confederate prison facility west of the Mississippi, housing about 5,300 captured U.S. soldiers and sailors at its peak. A regular baseball club operated there, though the improvised equipment was a bit lacking.[26]

Close to Hempstead at Camp Groce, ball playing almost proved fatal for one inmate. A rebel militia guard "deliberately fired at a sailor-boy, whose offense was, in the excitement of sport, pursuing a runaway ball to the guard-line. Without challenge or caution, the cowardly fellow drew up his gun, and discharged it at our sailor lad; and the bullet, whizzing past the latter, sped toward our barracks in dangerous closeness to the ball-players."[27]

To see Union prisoners playing at baseball, however, some citizens didn't even have to leave home. Following the rebels' victory at the Battle of Galveston, United States prisoners were brought to downtown Houston. Captured Union officers were confined in Kennedy's Building at the corner of Travis and Congress while enlisted men were kept at a cotton warehouse along the bayou. In February and March of 1863, prior to their being sent to Camp Groce, the officers were allowed two hours a day under guard to "play ball upon the prairie land, free of annoyance from citizens."[28]

Regimental histories show that the Southern soldiers away at war frequently spent down time playing baseball, too. One main difference was that, just as with other equipment, they had a much tougher time getting quality gear than the United States Army. Oftimes the "bat might be a board, a section of some farmer's rail, or a slightly trimmed hickory limb; the pellet might be nothing better than a yarn-wrapped walnut."[29]

When the Civil War ended in 1865, thousands of soldiers returned home, but life in the Lone Star State was different than it had been four years earlier. Among the required adjustments was living with the fact that Houston and the rest of Southeast Texas were now occupied by United States troops. The transition did not always go smoothly for the defeated rebels.

Galveston's Union occupiers definitely found baseball to be one welcome diversion from local resentment. Their first reported game was in 1865 at a stretch of unoccupied land on Avenue N between 25th and 27th streets just north of the Ursuline Convent. Some Galvestonians hooted at the Federals for claiming the game as their own, saying that it was merely Southern town-ball to which the Yankees had "substituted a few additional features."[30]

With the coming of the new year, local residents also saw the game as a means to move closer to normality. E.H. Cushing, still running the *Telegraph*, noted that baseball was returning to other towns around the country and urged a revival of the club that "we had here before the war."[31] Whether his call for Houston was heeded in 1866 is not known.

The likely answer is that Galvestonians beat them to the punch. In the first days of 1867, meetings were held and games were being played on grounds located directly in front of City Hospital.[32] By the end of that January, though, Houston ball clubs had joined them, as had teams in other Texas locales. Even San Antonians had written to Galveston in search of an official book of the game's regulations.[33]

Not surprisingly, the close ties between all things Houston and Galveston had been infused into the world of baseball. One celebrated meeting in particular has been routinely described using a series of "firsts." In truth, it is doubtful the game was the first of its kind in almost any way whatsoever, but the Stonewalls of Houston met Galveston's Lees on San Jacinto Day with the former winning by a score of 35-2.[34]

In spite of the promising start, the baseball season that year was shortened at both ends of Galveston Bay due to the worst epidemic of yellow fever in the area's history. Both cities had been prone to outbreaks of Yellow Jack since their beginnings. One of the worst had been the summer of 1839 when the disease killed over 10% of the population in both cities.[35]

The hot weather in 1867, though, brought suffering that surpassed them all. Quarantines and efforts to improve sanitation to rid the air of miasmas did nothing to alleviate the deaths. Entire families perished, over 725 people in Galveston alone.[36] Many Northern soldiers died, too, including General Charles Griffin, the head of the Freedmen's Bureau in Texas.

One memoir described Houston as a town "reeking of carbolic acid" where "a great number of people died during this terrible plague." Still not realizing that mosquitoes spread the epidemic, both cities nonetheless rejoiced when the first cold weather stopped the disease dead in its tracks.[37] From a baseball standpoint, that joy included a Christmas Day game in Galveston between the Stonewall and R.E. Lee Base Ball Clubs, the latter being made up largely of the island's volunteer fire company number five.[38]

The annual San Jacinto Day game was repeated in 1868. Its onset, as played out in the press, was indicative of the mindset and circumstances of inter-club baseball contests immediately following the Civil War. If the newspapers are to be believed, it was also very much a last minute affair.

On Saturday, April 18, 1868, two different Houston teams played intra-squad games on their respective grounds. The Stonewalls, who like their island namesakes honored a Civil War hero, were in the rear of the rail depot that served the Galveston line and the Bayou City Club "at the terminus of the McKinney Street Railroad." Both teams invited the public to attend, with the Stonewalls proudly specifying that they would be in uniform.[39]

Much like dueling, baseball contests of the period often required a public challenge. The Stonewalls of Houston had previously issued one to the Robert E. Lee Baseball Club of Galveston, sending it to that city's newspaper some days prior. The Lees had been busy that week themselves, playing a Sunday match against another island team, the St. Elmo's, so perhaps that delayed an answer.[40]

The response from the Lee club's secretary was written the very afternoon that the Stonewalls were entertaining the Houston public. The most salient point in the brief missive was the notation that the Stonewalls claimed to be champions of the state, a claim the Lees made, too. The Galveston team happily accepted the demand to meet at San Jacinto on April 21st to help commemorate the vaunted battle. In other words, it was on![41]

The Houston team, wearing uniforms of red caps, white flannel shirts and black pants, boarded the steamboat *Whitelaw* on their way to the match. As the vessel left the Houston port, the sounds of a German band filled the air. The *St. Clair*, bringing the Galveston team, beat the Houston boat to the San Jacinto landing by over half an hour. As one wag remarked, it was the only thing they won all day.

One description of the game went as follows:

"Captain Doswell of the 'Stonewall' team and Captain Forrest of the 'Lees' tossed for innings, and the latter won. W. J. McKernan of the Empire Base Ball Club of St. Louis was umpire; Jack White was scorer for the 'Stonewalls,' while L. W. Hertz acted in that capacity for the 'Lees.' The first nine of Houston's club consisted of Doswell, Paulson, Williamson, Van Patton, Myer, Robinson, Noble, Sterne, and Hogan." The story continued:

"The contest now commenced in good earnest ... but from the first innings it was apparent to the most disinterested looker on that the Lees (although the vaunted champions of the State) had at last met more than their match. ... At the conclusion of the eighth inning, the Lees disheartened by the success of their antagonists, gave up the game and acknowledged themselves beaten, fairly and squarely. The runs being counted, it was found that the score stood, Stonewalls 34, the Lees 5. Mr. McKernan, the umpire then declared the Stonewalls the Champions of the State of Texas. Three cheers were then given for the Lee Club, three for the Stonewall, three for the umpire and scorers, and three for San Jacinto, when the bases were taken up, everything gathered together, and all started for Lynchburg, for the ball."[42]

Baseball matches, from the codification of the New York rules in the 1840s well into the 1870s and beyond, were often surrounded by dinners and social events. Top clubs in New York, Philadelphia and Boston sometimes put more effort into the after-party than the main event. Sharing chowder became de rigueur for many teams.[43] Others allied themselves with a particular dining and drinking establishment where they could always be found for post-game toasts.

The celebrants on that San Jacinto Day certainly did their best to uphold those traditions. Following the game and the awarding of a golden ball to the Stonewalls, there were rousing remarks to the crowd of perhaps a thousand, including words from Texas Army hero Dr. Ashbel Smith who had spoken prior to the match, too. An abundant supply of barbeque "and other edibles" was served near the San Jacinto cemetery, and then, with dark coming on, the party, including several San Jacinto veterans and ex-Governor Francis Lubbock, boarded the two steamboats and sailed the short distance downstream to Lynchburg. There they all danced to fine music, both on shore and aboard the steamers, until well past midnight. The excursionists arrived back in their respective cities shortly after daybreak.[44]

That one heavily celebrated game at the Battleground is only part of the story, however. Newspapers of the day show that the baseball scene in the two Texas cities was already thriving by Spring of 1868. In the weeks immediately after San Jacinto Day, the Stonewalls met the Island City Club, a new team having been constructed of the best players from several other Galveston teams.[45] It was a best of three series with each team winning at home and the Galvestonians taking the final game and the prize of "a splendid bat and ball."[46]

That last contest was originally planned for a neutral site at Clear Creek, where a Mr. Wren was to have provided barbeque,[47] but was instead played at the ball park on McKinney Street in Houston, served by the mule-drawn streetcars and described as a beautiful place where "the shade is abundant." Festivities also included "a grand pic-nic, at which all the ladies of the city are respectfully invited to assist."[48]

The gentlemanly expectations of the baseballists were underscored in an exchange of items between the newspapers of the two cities. *The Houston Telegraph* complained of ill-mannered remarks aimed against the Stonewall players by some Island City fans. *The Daily News* countered that the taunts must have come from "mere boys, whom the Stonewalls should not have noticed," adding for good measure that the *Telegraph* was being a bit too sensitive.[49]

The monopolization of the game of baseball by the upper-middle and merchant classes was beginning to shift, though. At least some budding athletes refused to let a six-day work-week block their participation in the nation's hottest pastime. Galveston's lofty Island City club refused a challenge from the upstart Grey Jackets because they were "mostly mechanics who have... no time to play a match game except on Sundays."[50] As late as 1872, the Galveston Lees were forced to remind the Island Citys that they were working men and could play during the week only at "risk of losing their situations."[51]

There was even the occasional team that, on the surface at least, seemed to have been quite out of place in the area. Two Galveston games in 1868 pitted the McClellans against the R.E. Lees and the Island Citys.[52] Given the general ill-will between Unionists and rebels, it seems a surprising pairing. McClellan was, though, a Democrat who favored compromise with the South. The games might not have taken place at all had the other team been nicknamed the Lincolns.

Another change in the game locally was that a majority of players were now southern born as opposed to the large percentage of northerners who helped start the Houston and Galveston clubs before the war. The name players in Houston included working class immigrants from states such as Virginia and Alabama and many locally born sons of top merchants who had moved to the burgeoning city prior to the Civil War. The players were also very young. The most common ages of the baseballists on the top local teams were squarely in the late teens and very early twenties.[53]

The next boon to inter-city competition in Texas was the formation of the Agricultural, Mechanical, and Blood Stock Association of Texas in 1869. The following May, this group joined with other local merchants and businessmen to help support an exposition of farm products, machinery and various contests in Houston. They dubbed it the State Fair of Texas.[54]

Houston ball players would organize to their best advantage in a bid for the state crown. On April 15, 1870, a call went out for the formation of a new baseball club within the city. At the office of W.B. Bonner, Esq., a constitution and bylaws were drawn and officers were elected. A.W. Robinson became the captain of the new team, called the "Pioneer Base Ball Club of Houston." After selection of a group of nine from the large number of men attending the meeting, Robinson, a local iron worker and a Stonewall B.B.C. alum, scheduled a practice for the next Sunday on the grounds above the Magnolia Warehouse at 2 p.m.[55] The purpose of the club was for participation in the upcoming state championship at the Fair.[56]

Teams from multiple Texas towns journeyed to the Bayou City to compete for the title. One three-hour match saw the Houston Pioneers take the Merry Nines of Calvert by the mark of 49-22.[57] The locals beat Bastrop and the dreaded Island City Club with the latter acknowledging themselves as "handsomely defeated" but vowing to try again soon.[58]

Having bested all comers at the State Fair, the Houston Pioneers found themselves challenged by the Austin Unknowns later that year.

The Austinites agreed to play a series

The Fairgrounds was an active spot for diversion and entertainment in Houston throughout the 1870s. Here Mechanic Fire Company Number 6 poses in front of the Agricultural Hall in 1878.

Houston Metropolitan Research Center, Houston Public Library

of match games against the Pioneers starting in Houston on July 4, the second game in the latter part of July in Austin, and, if necessary, a third game played on neutral grounds to decide the series.[59]

Before the games with the Unknowns, the Pioneers played a few warm up games with other local teams. The box score of one game showed a picked nine of the city besting the Pioneers by a tally of 14-13 in what the paper reported as "the closest (game) that has ever been played in Houston."[60]

Scoring in the 1870s and before tended to be quite high, and for another 20 years, a big tally often brought jibes about flashing back to the old days. The reasons behind these large sums were several. Players did not use gloves, so even with a well-worn and somewhat softer ball, fielding was not as sure as modern equipment allows. The playing surfaces themselves were often irregular, inviting unexpected hops. Umpires were not professionals, and perhaps as important as any other reason, the art of the breaking ball was still developing. The vast majority of pitchers in the decade didn't employ "curves and shoots."[61]

Many games of Houston's top club were described as being held "on the new grounds of the Pioneers at the head of Prairie Street."[62] An unsubstantiated reminiscence from the mid-20th century told of the city's first baseball field being located in the played out brick yard of S.W. Young which was indeed located very near the spot mentioned. The ground where the bayou clay had been excavated for brick making was a hard and level surface and therefore was suited to playing the game.[63]

In September, the Island City Club made good on their promise to again challenge the Pioneers for the ubiquitous "championship of Texas." Led by their shortstop, Tony Cleveland, the Island City Club won the first installment of the three game series 39-24. It was the Pioneers of Houston, though, who would end the year still claiming the title.[64] Buoyed by success, the fair organizers expanded the following year, purchasing their own property south of town.

Though the year 1871 was kind to the fair, it was rough on the Pioneers. Perhaps a bit cocksure after their success of the previous season, the team awaited challengers. The local press scolded the Pioneers for not practicing.[65] Meanwhile, teams looking to take their championship away from them were hard at work. Galveston alone had two clubs with eyes on the prize, the Robert E. Lees and the Island Citys.[66]

When competition at the fair began, Houstonians flocked to see the local heroes decked out in their new uniforms: white shirt trimmed with blue, pants of blue flannel to the knee, blue and white stockings, caps of blue and white, belts of the same color, and regular baseball shoes.[67] The makeup of the crowd was exhilarating, packed with a large portion of "Houston beauties, who of course were in attendance to encourage the Houston Base Ballers with their smiles."[68]

On the field, however, the results were dampening. The Houston Pioneers lost to Galveston's Robert E. Lees 21-15, followed closely by defeat at the hands of the Island City team who took home the state championship.[69] They also took home a good share of loot, as wagering on the game had exceeded $800 in gold several days earlier, and speculation had that being a proverbial drop in the bucket.[70] As for the local boys, Houston's press remarked the next day that the Pioneers were "not disheartened by their defeat, but keep spirits up wonderfully."[71]

And why not? State title or not, baseball was booming in Houston. Sports pages were filled with matches involving newly formed teams. In late July, the Harrisburg Athletics beat the Dexter baseball club 53-19, and in a match near the city park, the Buckeye Nines took the Athletics in a 35-31 squeaker. Soon the Silver Stars would enter the mix, and by September it was the Mutuals dusting the Prairie Flowers by the mark of 57 to 22.[72]

The formation of teams in the early 1870s was fluid, to say the least. Pioneers stalwart T.W. Whitmarsh would show up on the roster of the Houston Robert E. Lees by 1874 while the Pioneer name disappeared from the printed record. The aptly named Bayou City B.B.C. sprung up again, while to the southeast the Lees of Galveston would be replaced by clubs such as the Pastimes and Flyaways. When Galveston crushed Houston at the Volksfest of 1872 by the "modest score" of 59-7, the newspapers didn't even bother to record the teams' nicknames.[73]

Across the state, other cities were jumping on the baseball bandwagon. Only one year after being described as of poor quality, the Denison Blue Stockings were proudly touring the state.[74] New clubs had emerged in towns such as Sherman, Denton, Ft. Worth, Hillsboro, Waco, Paris, Corsicana, Corpus Christi and Cleburne.[75]

For the Fourth of July 1874, a true state tournament was staged in Dallas, a city that fielded two teams in the competition. Local papers reported the preparations of Houston's Lees and their departure on the train north. Galveston's nine passed up the road the same day.[76]

The tournament started well for Houston, as they defeated the Southerns of Shreveport, the team many considered the best of the lot. Next up was Denison, reported to be another worthy foe. The Lees, however, would suffer a baseball calamity that showed the perils of being a "nine" and belied the much-ballyhooed term "amateur." It was supremely illustrative of America's passion for gambling.

Sometime prior to the game with the Blue Stockings, infielder William Harvey, one of the "old members, and best and most skillful player on the club," not only accepted a bribe, he refused to play at all unless the Lees would pay him an amount higher than the bribe. The club demurred, and Harvey was out.

Because many teams at that time were literally comprised of nine players, a controversy arose over whether or not the Lees could substitute someone new. A request to add "an honorary member from Houston" was denied, and that spelled the end of Houston's shot at a title. The incident was the talk of Texas sporting types everywhere. A letter from the Lees' president, William Glass, appeared in the newspaper not only spelling out the particulars of William Harvey's betrayal, but also warning teams everywhere to shun "this cowardly and rascally villain."[77] Libel be damned.

Almost a footnote in the Bayou City was the news that the Denison Blue Stockings went on to defeat the Dallas Trinity B.B.C. in the championship game.

In September of that same year, the Robert E. Lee Base Ball Club of New Orleans visited both Galveston and Houston. The visitors were known on a national level, having played the venerable Cincinnati Red Stockings a few years previous. The local team that faced them was called the Comets, and it included at least one player each from the Lees, the Bayou Citys and the Pioneers. None of that seemed to matter, as the Louisiana bunch walloped them by a score of 61 to 6.[78]

The teams from Houston and Galveston continued to play each other throughout the decade, but travel for matches in other areas of the state became more common, as well. Houston and Waco made nine innings stretch for four hours with Waco squeaking out a 42-41 victory.[79] The Island Citys traveled to Austin to play, and lose to, the Colorado City club; and, in 1875, the Lees left Houston for a game at San Antonio against that city's Ben Milams.[80] Two years later, the Lees had an ugly and public exchange with the Palestine Hoxies when they dared make light of the upstarts in the press following a one-sided victory, joking that they were a town ball club.[81] Civil or not, these were more small steps toward the formation of a Texas League.

Professional baseball leagues can trace their history to the start of the National Association of Professional Base Ball Players in 1871. Teams in that circuit stretched across the Northern United States from Boston to Chicago and Rockford, Illinois. Five years later, baseball saw the start of the National League, the same circuit that continues to this day. In spite of any salaries the players might draw, however, much of their income was earned by barnstorming around the hinterlands. Texas soon became noted as a place worth stopping.

Early in 1876, Houston papers ran stories of the professional Louisville ball club, one month in advance of their start in the National League, planning a Southern tour. It would include stops at Houston and Galveston in the middle of March.[82] As time approached, and as the Lees fought to get into baseball playing shape, the arrival date was postponed, a rather common occurrence in those days.[83]

Ultimately there would be only disappointment among local fans. There is no record that the visit ever actually took place. If any South Texans harbored a grudge about being stood up, they may have been pleased to note that the Louisville team left the new National League after at least three of their players threw games for money the following season.

In 1877, the Indianapolis Blues did make the trip. They would join the National League the following year. Indy, known as the Irish Team, made short work of the Galveston Amateurs to the tune of 59-0. They went on to defeat the Pastimes the following day. For their part, the *Daily News* tried to buck up the whitewashed Galveston players, writing that they should not get discouraged, and "no matter how good a club, you should go on with the determination of playing."[84]

Of particular note was the pitching of Edward "The Only" Nolan, the mound star of the Blues. "The ball leaves his hand apparently straight," the island scribe reported. "but shoots off from a curve line made by a radius of 3 or 4 feet, and then, with a regularity seldom ever seen, passes over the home plate every time, also very swift."[85] Nolan compiled a losing record over his big league career, was suspended more than once for leaving his team to go drinking and was later blacklisted by the league for general "dissipation and insubordination;" yet contemporaries described him as having noticeably better stuff than his peers.[86]

Much more equally contested were the continuing games between Galveston and their rivals in Houston. The custom of the day was for the Lees to be at the docks or depot to meet the visiting clubs and their fans, 200 or more travelling for the game not being uncommon when the two cities met. A large dinner was often furnished before the match, sometimes at the fashionable Exchange Hotel at Main and Texas. On one visit, the Pastimes of Galveston found "great bottles of champagne, ice, goblets" both pre and post game.[87] Notwithstanding the bitter accusations with Palestine, the general feelings between Houston and Galveston in the 1870s appears to have been one of mutual respect.

In April of 1877 an interesting melee occurred in Galveston when the Muldoons hosted the Mashers for a series of games. During one contest, an 8-7 win by the Muldoons, several Mashers converged on a high pop foul. Though none of them got the baseball, they were successful in knocking over and crushing all the fruit belonging to "an old Italian orange peddler." Following the game, he swore out a complaint and had the appropriately named Mashers hauled off to jail. The Muldoons kindly pooled their money to bail them out.[88]

As the 1870s gave way to the 1880s, the frequency of inter-city baseball games continued to increase. The Missouri-Pacific club of St. Louis visited Houston in October 1883 complaining of over-exertion on their tour. They faced a Houston Nationals team that had substituted a couple of the rival Lees and even a trio of players from Galveston for Nationals players who were absent the city. In spite of morning rain that dampened both playing field and attendance, the contest was a close one. The visitors emerged with a 5-3 win even though they employed their substitute pitcher and catcher for most of the game.[89]

An interesting side note from the St. Louis–Houston tilt is that one newspaper report opined that the substitutes employed by the Nationals did not diminish the ability of the team. That is except for one player who committed several of the club's nine errors on the day. In what might be considered an act of great chivalry, the writer does not name the culprit. It should be considered, though, that three of the subs were from Galveston and so was the writer.[90]

Though not all of them toured as the St. Louis bunch did, other company ball teams of note were beginning to spring up. Ft. Worth boasted a Missouri-Pacific team of their own, and nines composed of railroaders or fire fighters were particularly commonplace.[91]

One certainty in Texas was that there was no worry or pretense over maintaining amateur status for their baseball operations. Over the following winter, the big city teams around the state were openly advertising their players from the pro ranks as a major drawing card. A case in point was a series in which the Dallas Browns visited the Galveston Gulf City team. The six professionals per side outnumbered the three amateurs.[92]

The professionals included top National Leaguers and American Association players who were earning extra money playing winter ball in Texas. The idea was carried out in spite of the occasional blue norther that kept attendance low and even brought a rare suspension of a game after six innings due to extreme cold. Three members of the Chicago White Stockings were playing: George Gore and Silver Flint for Galveston and Ned Williamson for Dallas. Future Hall of Famer Bid McPhee of Cincinnati and Providence catcher Sandy Nava were also playing for Dallas, and right-handed pitcher Guy Hecker, who would compile a league leading 52 wins for Louisville later that year, was twirling for the Gulf Citys.

In mid June of 1884, two of Houston's top teams, the Nationals and the Lees, met to consolidate their best players into one club consisting of an active and a reserve nine. The expectation was that as a representative of the city, they would soon be crossing bats with Galveston and San Antonio.[93] This was a harbinger of the formation of a new Texas League.

The teams around the state had been playing each other with regularity that year. Ft. Worth had defeated all comers, and had already declared themselves season's champion after winning a grand tournament at Waco around Independence Day.[94] The promise of a new league over the remainder of the summer, however, might provide more structure, and therefore greater profits.

The concept of minor leagues was a relatively new one. The National League certainly dominated, but in 1882 it had been joined by the American Association. Two years later, a one-season Union Association formed as part of the first "player's revolt." With player contract guarantees at $1000 a year and higher, these three were all considered the major leagues at the time.[95]

In 1883, the Northwestern League began play with teams in places like Peoria, Quincy and Springfield, Illinois, and Saginaw and Bay City, Michigan. In a move that spoke volumes about the tenuous grip that early teams and leagues held on financial viability, the league's first champion, the Toledo Blue Stockings, would fold before the following season. But the Northwestern League was notable in the respect that it set a lower minimum salary limit of $750 for players, making it a true professional minor league by comparison.

Further establishing a solid structure for the game of baseball, the Northwestern League joined with the National League and the American Association that same year to form what would be known as the National Agreement, an evolving document that would soon govern all the prime leagues in America. Most importantly to the business of baseball were provisions for things such as assignment rights and controls on player transfers between teams. By 1900, 14 leagues would be signatories, including the Texas League.[96]

Undoubtedly echoing conversations being held in all regions of the country, a group of enterprising baseball men felt that the developments in Eastern and Midwestern cities meant that the year 1884 was the right time for a league in Texas. The Lone Star baseball community was certainly more sophisticated. The first box score in the state's history had appeared in the *Houston Post* in 1883 for a game between the local Nationals and the Red Stockings of Austin.[97]

The driving force behind the Texas league was Samuel L. Hain, a railroad brakeman who had moved to Houston from North Central Pennsylvania at the start of the decade. He also brought with him a background in semi-pro baseball. One of his first actions upon arrival in Houston was to connect with one of the top amateur clubs in town.

Sam Hain was joined by his brother, George, in playing for, and later becoming captain of, the Nationals, the team that would consolidate with the Lees to become the Houston entry in the new league.[98] Meanwhile, Sam's personal life was going well, too. He was promoted to work in the land department for the Texas & New Orleans Railroad. His success established, he would soon bring a wife back from Pennsylvania.[99]

Meeting people around the state in his work as a land man, Hain became well-liked around Texas. He would live part time in Beaumont and spend extensive time traveling. Sam Hain was also active in politics, a passion which he would continue for much of his life even though he was something that was anathema to most Houstonians of the era: a Republican.[100]

Hain joined with Alex Easton of Galveston to whip up support around the state for the new league. Texas Association delegates met on the Fourth of July at the Pacific Hotel in Waco with Hain and J.C. Clark being the Houston delegates.[101] In addition to Houston, representatives were also there from teams in Galveston, San Antonio, Ft. Worth, Dallas, Austin and the host city of Waco.[102] The 30-game schedule, which ultimately excluded Austin, ran from mid-July until mid-October.[103]

An initial plan was that each team would follow the example said to have been set by Houston: using professional pitchers and catchers and fill out the remainder of the roster with local talent. With no particular prohibition against it, however, teams seemed to do what they could afford to field a winning roster.[104] Within days, the list of teams bringing in more paid players would also include Houston.

By the mid-1880s, baseball had been around Houston long enough to see the development of a few elder statesmen, men whose participation on the field may have dwindled, but who wished to remain involved with the game. William Hunter Coyle had been a bookbinder with the A.C. Gray Company when he played for the exalted Pioneers team of 1870. He later became a well-off job printer in town, with a steam-powered press, advertising as a lithographer who could create top notch work "at figures as can be had at St. Louis, Chicago and New York."[105]

His success hadn't dulled his interest in baseball, however. Coyle was one of the members of the executive committee that had overseen formation of the new Texas League, and more importantly, was listed as manager of the Houston team.[106]

League play got underway when the Houston Nationals visited Galveston on Sunday, July 13th.[107] Since the two cities were but a short train ride apart, the four game series went home and home with each team holding serve through the first three. The third game, played in Galveston, had been notable for a bad call that almost caused a row. The Galveston paper complimented the Nationals players for their restraint.[108]

When the fourth game of the series was held the following Sunday at the Fair Grounds in Houston, however, restraint was lost. The umpire was H.W. Bailey, said to have been an old veteran ballplayer from Chicago. After calling the Galveston catcher, Jules Pujol, out for running well inside the first base line and failing to touch the bag, the backstop led a mutiny on the grounds that Pujol had beaten the ball back to the bag. Ignoring the pleas of the Galveston captain, Rebenac, Pujol and the rest of the team stormed off the field "much to the disgust of the crowd." Umpire Bailey, who was defended as "perfectly impartial" by the island newspaper, ruled the game forfeited to Houston by a score of nine to nothing.[109]

The islanders didn't fare any better when they went to play the Sunsets of San Antonio at the start of August. In a last minute recalibration, the first game of the series "was played with an American Association ball as no league ball could be procured."[110]

Houston was next up at the Sunsets grounds at San Pedro Springs. Though the Nationals won the game, it proved a rough outing for right fielder George Hain who broke his ankle sliding safely into home. He was replaced by an Alamo City youth, J.C. Maybry, who was even gracious enough to score a run for the visitors in their 11-4 triumph. Another nick was suffered in the game when the Sunsets' catcher took a hard foul tip to the forehead. He shook it off and kept playing.[111]

As the league season progressed, so did difficulties for some of the teams. Waco had already left the league by the first of August. Teams sometimes scrambled to fill suddenly open dates. After a series in San Antonio, Galveston tried to get up a match at Austin, and they openly advertised that when they finished the series at Dallas, they were open to exhibitions at "Sherman, Denison, Paris, Shreveport or any club that had enclosed grounds."[112]

Another problem for the islanders was ticket prices. The tariff for the opener against Houston at Beach Park was advertised as 50 and 25 cents. By the second game of the year two weeks later, that price had been reduced in hopes of enticing the freeloaders who watched from the balcony at the Beach Hotel next door to "come inside and contribute to the support of the enterprise."[113]

Teams in the league were operating on much the same shoestring as they were when they made their own schedule. Aside from newspaper stories about the formation, shared marketing didn't appear to be part of the league offerings. Crowds reported in Houston were considered good at three to four hundred. Typical of many of the contests, when league-leading Dallas came to Houston late in September, the "attendance was not as large as expected."[114]

The end to the short Texas Association season was quite anti-climactic. Galveston dropped out of the circuit before it ended, forfeiting the final two games to Houston. In the end, the two North Texas teams proved to be the class of the league. Dallas won at San Antonio on September 28 to secure the championship.[115] The lines defining the league season of inter-city baseball in Texas were rather blurry, though, as the same teams continued to play one another through the end of the year.

By November, after some of the professional players had moved on to be replaced by others, Sam Hain was back at second base for the Nationals.[116] This indicates that he was not only a mover in the league, but still possessed some baseball chops on the diamond, even at the age of 30.

Baseball rosters in the 1880s were much more mercurial than they are today. New players had been added only a week into the season, and most Texas teams upgraded their players again after the 1884 major league seasons ended.[117] In October, Dallas added three journeymen: George Fisher from Cleveland and Len Stockwell and Bill Hunter from Louisville. Stockwell was not new to Dallas. He had been with the Browns the previous winter.

The Houston Nationals employed a pitcher who had been one of the top hurlers in the Union Association just weeks before.[118] Billy Taylor, also known as Bollicky Bill, had jumped from the Pittsburgh Alleghenys of the American Association (A.A.) to the upstart St. Louis Maroons. Playing five positions, he had been better known as a hitter than a hurler, but for the Maroons, he went 25-4 with a tiny ERA of 1.68, that was just through July. In midsummer, he jumped to the Philadelphia A's of the A.A. where he was the pitcher of record in 30 more games.[119]

By November, he was being paid to throw the ball for Houston, the city where he decided to spend the winter before returning to Philly and a nice new contract.[120] All those innings, approaching at least 600 for 1884, took their toll on his arm. He won only one game in each of the next two seasons, and his batting average dropped all the way down to .100.[121]

Perhaps the biggest challenge to professional baseball in Texas, and across America, was the constant presence of gamblers willing to pay to influence the outcome of a game. These payoffs dated back to at least 1865, four years before the Cincinnati Red Stockings toured the country as the first openly all-professional ball club. With the onset of the National Association, rules were put in place, but when sanction hearings were called, the clubs to be punished largely circumvented or ignored them.[122]

Like everywhere else, the instances of baseball hijinks across Texas were legion. A few weeks before the start of the official league season in 1884, the Navasota Blues accused the San Antonio Sunsets of bribing their catcher, McKale, to throw a game. They complained loudly in Austin, the next stop on their road trip, and one they made with McKale still catching. The Sunsets ridiculed the idea of any payoff, yet a few days later, McKale was the catcher in San Antonio.[123]

The new league was supposed to bring order and put a stop to money that was ruining baseball integrity in Texas, but of course, that didn't happen. Less than a month into the new season, the Houston Nationals sent five of their six professional players packing.[124]

The catalyst had been a pitcher,

Smith, and a catcher, Hanlon, who were thought to have acted in "bad faith," throwing a game at Dallas. There was no "proof positive," but the team strongly suspected money had changed hands. For good measure, Manager Coyle also released Messrs. Tennyson, Bothner and Shea who, though not guilty of accepting bribes, were due to leave the team for greener pastures in a few days anyway. Acting on behalf of the Association, Sam Hain was sent to New Orleans to secure the best pitcher, catcher and second baseman he could find for Houston to finish the season.[125]

The outlook for a reorganized league in 1885 was solid. A stock company was formed, and Sam Hain was reaching out to other cities to compile a top team for Houston.[126] One target was veteran Tricky Nichols who had pitched for Houston before and was then toiling much closer to his Connecticut home.[127] The papers made note of Nationals players who had returned to town from their home in Corsicana in February 1885 in preparation for the upcoming season.[128]

The organized schedule never materialized, however, and Houston teams scheduled their opponents on a mostly game-by-game basis. Action was hot-and-heavy in the rest of the state, too. The hottest months of summer saw Bastrop beat Austin, the Dallas Blue Stockings face the Corsicana Eclipse and the Belton Blues beat the Waco Browns with $100 on the line for each side.[129]

One novelty of the period that had been trumpeted for several days prior was a visit from an all female baseball club in 1885. The New Orleans-based club was perhaps a self contained act in the style of the Harlem Globetrotters, as indicated by the fact that the manager of Pillot's Opera House booked their Houston appearance.[130]

Though no histories of Texas baseball report a league for the years 1886 and 1887, the term continued to be used. The late May game that was the inaugural contest at Galveston's Gulf City Park in 1887 was billed as "the first base ball game for the Texas league of the season." It featured the Crescents of Houston defeating Galveston's Uhrig's Cave team by a score of 24 to 14, though only 15 of the total runs in the game were earned.[131]

The story of the "Texas league" of 1887 becomes clearer with the notation that the next league game would be between the Uhrig's Caves and the Island Citys, another Galveston team, indicating this was hardly a statewide loop.[132]

Houston also worked to maintain meaningful games between its teams that year. The Crescents were joined by the amateur Metropolitans and the semi-pro Heralds, a squad named for a short-lived Houston newspaper which also garnered naming rights for the ballpark.

Box scores indicate that there was even some player movement between the city's teams when circumstances warranted it. Joseph Lohbeck, who would be a part of Houston's all-professional team the following year, caught for the Heralds in October and for the Metropolitans two weeks later.[133]

Frederick C. "Tricky" Nichols was one of the earliest professional players imported to Houston merely to play baseball. A New Englander, he bounced from the big leagues to minor league clubs around the nation for over a dozen years.
Private Collection

"Handsome Dan" Murphy was a member of the inaugural Texas League. A native of Brooklyn, NY, he spent only one season on the Gulf Coast before returning to his Northeastern stomping grounds.

Courtesy Library of Congress

Much like fellow ringers in 1884, Lohbeck and pitcher Robert Pender had come to Houston in the fall of 1887 after playing a season for Ft. Smith and Springfield in the Southwestern League. An Arkansas colleague of theirs, Thomas Flood, would bring his talents to Houston a year later. Frank Motz and one of the Berkery brothers of New Orleans were also paid players on the Heralds in 1887.[134]

Pender and his teammates drew some complaints for dogging it during his time with the Heralds. Facing the "spunky" Mets, a team most Houston fans believed they could have shut out, the Heralds began with "careless and indifferent" play before Pender "got down to business" and struck out seven of the next nine Metropolitan batters. One sportswriter strongly lamented the slow start since most spectators had placed their bets expecting a more one-sided contest.[135]

In spite of any minor complaints about the locals, Houston ball fans were thrilled to see three teams of major leaguers pass through town during Texas tours in mid-November. Charlie Comiskey and the St. Louis Browns were traveling with a Chicago White Stockings team that also included players from Pittsburgh and Cincinnati. The promoter who brought them to Houston and a sold-out crowd was none other than Sam Hain.[136] At the same time, the New York Giants were playing in all the major markets of the state. These meetings raised Texas baseball fever yet a few more degrees.[137]

A fitting end to the era came at the close of the 1887 season. An old-timers game was planned that would pit by-gone stars of Houston and Galveston against one another at the ballpark at Travis and McGowen. The novel feature was that a box of crackers would be placed by first base, a box of cheese by second and a keg of beer was iced down at third. The players were obliged to partake at the station at which they stopped. With third base an "oasis in the form of a tankard of foaming, icy beer," the incentive to cross the pay station was scant. One small catalyst might have existed, however. The losing club was to pay for the cheese, crackers and beer.[138]

On April 1, 1888, a new league got under way, promising greater capitalization and stability. The first game was a contest between the Houston Babies and the Galveston Giants at Travis and McGowen. Semi-pro and amateur baseball would remain a vital part of the local sports scene for many decades, but a corner had been turned. The new Texas League had brought a full-time professional baseball team to the growing Bayou City.

1 Houston Weekly Telegraph 9 April 1861, Houston Weekly Telegraph 16 April 1861
2 Galveston News, 1 March 1859
3 Johnson, Frank W. *A History of Texas and Texans, Vol III.* (American Historical Association, 1914)
4 Dow, Christopher. *William Marsh Rice: A Centennial Portrait.* Rice News, 28 September 2000
5 Johnston, Marguerite. *Houston, the unknown city, 1836-1946.* (Texas A & M University Press,1991); GDN 19 April 1905; Allardice, Bruce. SABRpedia entry on First Houston Baseball Club; Houston City Directories; Biographical History of the Cities of Houston and Galveston. (Lewis Publishing Co. Chicago. 1895)
6 Reynolds, Donald E.. *Cushing, Edward Hopkins.* Handbook of Texas Online. Texas State Historical Association; Cushing, E.B. *Edward Hopkins Cushing.* Southwestern Historical Quarterly, April 1922
7 Towne and Heiser. *Everything is Fair in War: The Civil War Memoir of George A. "Lightning" Ellsworth, Telegraph Operator for John Hunt Morgan.* Register of the Kentucky Historical Society. Vol 108. Nos. 1 & 2. Winter/Spring 2010; Allardice, Bruce. SABRpedia entry on First Houston Baseball Club
8 United States Census 1850, Harris County, TX
9 United States Census 1860, Harris County, TX
10 Wood map of Houston, 1869
11 GDN, 11 June 1861
12 Biographical History of the Cities of Houston and Galveston. (Lewis Publishing Co. Chicago. 1895)
13 William Marsh Rice Collection. MSS 140. Houston Metropolitan Research Center. Personal Correspondence of Frederick Allyn Rice.
14 Dallas Morning News, 7 April 1901
15 Cushing, E.B. *Edward Hopkins Cushing.* Southwestern Historical Quarterly, April 1922
16 Sibley, Marilyn McAdams. *Lone Stars and State Gazettes: Texas Newspapers Before the Civil War.* (Texas A&M Press, 1983)
17 Towne and Heiser. *Everything is Fair in War: The Civil War Memoir of George A. "Lightning" Ellsworth, Telegraph Operator for John Hunt Morgan.* Register of the Kentucky Historical Society. Vol 108. Nos. 1 & 2. Winter/Spring 2010; Allardice, Bruce. SABRpedia entry on First Houston Baseball Club
18 (Galveston) Civilian and Gazette Weekly, 30 April 1861
19 Galveston Tri-Weekly News, 22 February 1864
20 GDN 9 April 1896, 29 March 1899; Cotham, Edward. *Battle on the Bay: The Civil War Struggle for Galveston* (University of Texas, 1998)
21 *Official Record of the Union and Confederate Navies in the War of the Rebellion.*
22 Towne and Heiser. *Everything is Fair in War: The Civil War Memoir of George A. "Lightning" Ellsworth, Telegraph Operator for John Hunt Morgan.* Register of the Kentucky Historical Society. Vol 108. Nos. 1 & 2. Winter/Spring 2010
23 Towne and Heiser. *Everything is Fair in War: The Civil War Memoir of George A. "Lightning" Ellsworth, Telegraph Operator for John Hunt Morgan.* Register of the Kentucky Historical Society. Vol 108. Nos. 1 & 2. Winter/Spring 2010
24 Fort Wayne (IN) Sentinel 30 November 1899
25 Houston Tri-Weekly Telegraph, 9 March 1863
26 Chase, Freeman H. *A Story of Adventures and Incidents in a Rebel Prison in Texas.* Maine Bugle IV. 1897
27 Duganne, A.J.H.. Twenty Months in the Department of the Gulf. (J.P. Robens , 1865)
28 Regimental History of 42nd Massachusetts; Duganne, A.J.H.. *Twenty Months in the Department of the Gulf.* (J.P. Robens , 1865)
29 New York Times 24 October 2012; Wiley, Bell. *The Life of Johnny Reb: The Common Soldier of the Confederacy.* (LSU Press, 1943)
30 Zeigler, Jesse. *Wave of the Gulf.* (Naylor & Co, 1938); Carroll, John M. *The Doubleday Myth and Texas Baseball.* Southwestern Historical Quarterly, Vol. 92, No. 4, April 1989.
31 Houston Tri-Weekly Telegraph, 11 April 1866
32 GDN 19 January 1867
33 GDN 28 January 1867
34 HP 10 July 1904
35 Johnston, Marguerite. *Houston, the Unknown City, 1836-1946.* (Texas A & M University Press, 1991) 45.
36 Burns, Chester R.. *Epidemic Diseases.* Handbook of Texas Online. Texas State Historical Association.
37 Red, Ellen Robbins and Taylor, Horace Dickinson. *Early Days on the Bayou, 1838-1890: the Life and Letters of Horace Dickinson Taylor, Houston, Texas.* (E.R. Red, 1986)
38 GDN 25 December 1867
39 DHT 18 April 1868
40 GDN 21 April 1868
41 GDN 19 April 1868
42 Writers' Program of the Work Projects Administration in the State of Texas. *Houston, A History and Guide.* (Anson Jones Press, 1942) 215-216.
43 Thorn, John. *Magnolia Club Predates Knickerbocker.* Base Ball. Spring 2011
44 Flake's Daily Bulletin, 23 April 1868
45 GDN 5 May 1868
46 Flake's Daily Bulletin, 30 May 1868, from the Houston Telegraph
47 GDN 3 May 1868; GDN 13 May 1868; GDN 14 May 1868; GDN 23 May 1868
48 Flake's Daily Bulletin, 30 May 1868, from the Houston Telegraph
49 GDN 5 May 1868
50 GDN 14 July 1868
51 GDN 26 July 1872
52 GDN 4 February 1868; GDN 14 June 1868
53 United States Census 1870, Harris County, Texas; Houston City Directories
54 Aulbach, Louis F.. *Buffalo Bayou: An Echo of Houston's Wilderness Beginnings.*
55 Houston City Directory 1873
56 Houston Daily Union, April 15, 1870.
57 Galveston Daily News, May 20, 1870.
58 GDN 21 May 1870
59 Houston Daily Union, 3 June 1870.
60 Houston Daily Union, 5 June 1870.
61 Galveston Tribune, 16 March 1928
62 Houston Daily Union 5 June 1870

63 Told to Janet Wagner, JK Wagner& Associates

64 Houston Daily Union, 23 September 1870. Houston Daily Union, 26 September 1870. Houston Daily Union, 27 September 1870. Galveston Times, 28 September 1870. Houston Daily Union, 15 March 1871. Records for the remaining games in the series are not available although the March 15, 1871 edition of the Houston Daily Union reported that the Pioneers won all their match games and were champions of the state.

65 Houston Daily Union 3 May 1871

66 *Houston Daily Union*, May 15, 1871.

67 *Galveston Times*, April 7, 1871. *Houston Daily Union*, April 10, 1871,

68 *Houston Daily Union*, May 24, 1871.

69 McComb, David G. *Houston, The Bayou City*. (University of Texas, 1969); *Galveston Tri-Weekly News*, 14 June 1871.

70 GDN 6 June 1871

71 Houston Daily Union 15 June 1871

72 *Houston Daily Union*, 19 July 1871; *Houston Daily Union*, 24 July 1871; *Houston Daily Union*, 10 August 1871; Houston Daily Union 25 September 1871

73 *Galveston Tri-Weekly News*, 17 June 1872.

74 GDN 14 November 1873; GDN 18 Nov 1874

75 Protoball website. Early Baseball in Texas. http://www.protoball.org/TX

76 DHT 1 July 1874; DHT 3 July 1874

77 DHT 7 July 1877

78 GDN 5 September 1874;

79 Houston Telegraph 21 May 1874

80 GDN 19 December 1873; San Antonio Express 2 September 1875

81 GDN 2 September 1877; GDN 6 September 1877

82 DHT 26 February 1876

83 DHT 4 March 1876

84 GDN 11 March 1877

85 GDN 11 March 1877

86 New York Times, 19 May 1913; James, Bill and Neyer, Rob. *The Neyer/James Guide to Pitchers: An Historical Compendium of Pitching, Pitchers and Pitches*. (Simon and Schuster, 2004)

87 DHT 24 June 1874; GDN 20 October 1874; GDN 3 August 1875

88 GDN 17 April 1877

89 GDN 23 October 1883

90 GDN 23 October 1883

91 GDN 16 June 1884

92 GDN 6 January 1884

93 GDN 16 June 1884

94 GDN 6 July 1884

95 Burk, Robert F.. Never Just a Game: Players, Owners and American Baseball to 1920. (University of North Carolina Press, 1994)

96 Spink, Alfred H.. The National Game. (National Game Publishing Co., 1911)

97 HP 10 July 1904

98 GDN 16 June 1884;

99 GDN 7 April 1907; GDN 7 June 1885

100 United States Census 1900, Jefferson County, Texas; GDN 27 April 1889; GDN 6 Dec 1887; GDN 2 Aprilm1922; Houston City Directories

101 GDN 5 July 1884

102 GDN 1 July 1884

103 San Antonio Light 11 July 1884

104 San Antonio Light 11 July 1884

105 Glenwood Cemetery Burial Records; Houston Herald 27 May 1885

106 GDN 5 July 1884

107 GDN 11 July 1884

108 GDN 28 July 1884

109 GDN 2 August 1884; http://www.baseball-reference.com

110 San Antonio Light 3 August 1884

111 San Antonio Light 12 August 1884

112 GDN 5 August 1884

113 GDN 27 July 1884

114 GDN 21 September 1884

115 GDN 28 September 1884

116 GDN 13 November 1884

117 GDN 27 July 1884

118 GDN 21 September 1884; http://www.baseball-reference.com; Thorn and Palmer, ed. *Total Baseball. 3rd Edition*. (Harper Collins, 1993)

119 http://www.baseball-reference.com; Thorn and Palmer, ed. *Total Baseball. 3rd Edition*. (Harper Collins, 1993)

120 GDN 13 November 1884

121 Thorn and Palmer, ed. *Total Baseball. 3rd Edition*. (Harper Collins, 1993)

122 Burk, Robert F.. Never Just a Game: Players, Owners and American Baseball to 1920. (University of North Carolina Press, 1994)

123 San Antonio Light 1 July 1884

124 GDN 27 August 1884

125 GDN 27 August 1884

126 GDN 24 September 1884; GDN 13 November 1884

127 http://www.baseball-reference.com

128 GDN 8 February 1885

129 GDN 13 September 1885; GDN 5 July 1885; GDN 2 June 1885

130 GDN 7 March 1885

131 GDN 23 May 1887

132 GDN 23 May 1887

133 HP 11 October 1887; HP 1 November 1887

134 HP 14 November 1887; http://www.baseball-reference.com

135 HP 11 October 1887

136 Ruggles, William B.. (Texas Baseball League, 1951)

137 HP 14 November 1887; GDN 13 November 1887

138 GDN 4 September 1887

KEY

GDN – *Galveston Daily News*
HI – *Houston Informer*
HP – *Houston Post*
CD – *Chicago Defender*
HC – *Houston Chronicle*

CHAPTER THREE

THE BALL PARK AT TRAVIS & McGOWEN

BY MIKE VANCE

The story of this ball park began with the First Annual State Fair that was held on the north bank of Buffalo Bayou in mid-May of 1870 under the auspices of the Agricultural, Mechanical, and Blood Stock Association of Texas. Many of the prominent men in Houston were behind the effort, and it was so well received that they determined to upgrade after only one year. They decided that "larger grounds must be purchased, suitable buildings and sheds erected, the grounds beautified," and with a can-do approach, they made it so.[1]

The ballpark blocks where Travis dead-ended into McGowen were a hotbed of activity on game days.
Original artwork courtesy of Patrick Lopez

By the following year organizers had laid out the groundwork for new fairgrounds located near where Main Street petered out onto the prairie south of town. In terminology that is somewhat confusing to modern Houstonians, this was called the head of Main, with the foot being to the north, where the street intersected Buffalo Bayou, the location of the city docks. To put a finer point on it, they were just past Hadley, at the southern edge of town, and the grounds spread away from that intersection to the southwest.

As the new complex neared completion, and as eager crowds toured the grounds in anticipation of the upcoming festivities, the town leaders expected a "State Fair such as Texas has never experienced before."[2] Based on the contemporary descriptions, they were right.

The fairgrounds had a one-mile racetrack, grandstand, and permanent exhibition halls.[3] They sat on 80 plus acres of smooth level prairie, but the improvements were great. "Beautiful fountains, grassy knolls, clumps of shrubbery and beds of flowers, along which the hard rolled gravel walks and carriage ways wind in graceful curves, while floral hall, pagodas and booths are so tastefully arranged as to present to the eye of the gazer a most picturesque appearance."[4]

During the Fair each May, exhibitions of farm implements and new machinery were numerous, and competitions were held for items that included canned meats, cakes, crochet work, stoves, jewelry, dentistry, beer, fruit and flowers. There was a livestock show for horses, mules, cattle and "milch cows." There was dancing and music in the pavilion.[5] Visitors could even see taxidermied ducks and prize winning terriers.[6] And there was baseball.

Some of the most highly anticipated events at the State Fair were the contests in which Houston's top nine defended the city's honor against teams from other Texas towns. It was the occasion for the frequent renewal of the rivalry with Galveston, and the earliest baseball competitions in Texas that could be thought of as statewide took place at the Houston Fair Grounds ball field.

Exactly where on the grounds the ball games took place is not clear. Observers mentioned the "luxuriantly green and thickly sewn" Bermuda grass, so it is easy to imagine a pastoral setting.[7] The historic location of the ball field certainly sat inside the boundaries of the Fair Grounds, but the precise configuration of the diamond in those first few years has not made itself known.

It is possible that the field sat on the very land that would serve as the home of Houston's first professional baseball team a decade later. The intersection most often used as the waymark for that 1880s ball park was Travis and McGowen, and as early as 1877, it was listed as the location of the Houston Agricultural Grounds and Driving Park, the latter being a late nineteenth century term for a horse racing track.[8]

Baseball, horse racing and other events kept the Fair Grounds lively and popular throughout the decade of the 1870s. When the Fair first moved to its new location, stable owner Michael Westheimer ran horse drawn omnibusses for the public at the fare of a quarter, but within a few years, city leaders were trumpeting the new streetcars which ran on tracks and were drawn by mules. Leaving the center of town every 10 minutes during the run of the fair, the cost for riders was a nickel, and the mile and a half trip took only 15 minutes.[9]

Thousands of people came to town each spring to attend the event, though by 1877 some attendees, many of whom were heavily engaged in betting on the races, complained of rampant pick-pockets.[10] The fair had been a sure-fire financial success until its final year in 1878 when it was plagued by bad weather and a brief yellow fever scare. Faced with the first monetary loss on the venture, the citizens of Houston did not see enough reason to continue it.[11] The state fair concept remained dormant in Texas until the city of Dallas took it up in 1886, and it has remained there to this day.

The demise of the State Fair did not mean the total abandonment of the Fair Grounds. Editorials calling to make the grounds public year round had gleaned a result, for the city of Houston entered a five-year lease agreement in March of 1876 to let the populace use the grounds as a city park, the first such public effort in the town's history.[12]

By the time the original city lease expired, Houston's boundaries had pushed out past the Fair Grounds, a sprinkling of development could be seen to the south, and suburban farms of 10 to 14 acres completely surrounded the original complex.[13]

Of all the varied uses of the Fair

property, the one that had established the firmest hold by this time was baseball. Since its beginnings, it had been the go-to diamond for important matches even when the State Fair was not underway. Occasionally, however, other Fair Grounds bookings got in the way.

In the case of one particular contest with Galveston, the culprit was "a religious revival being conducted at the Fair Grounds, which debarred the boys from playing there."[14] Instead, the game was moved to the home practice grounds of the Houston R.E. Lees which was described variously as behind or next to the International & Great Northern depot. Those grounds had previously been home to the Stonewalls all the way back to the end of the Civil War.[15] Located approximately where Congress Avenue dead-ended into the tracks east of downtown, it was as convenient as it got for someone coming from the island since those were the tracks between the two cities.

After the failure of the Fair, the ball yard at Travis and McGowen remained vibrant with competition. Newspapers in both Houston and Galveston still referred to the place as "the Fair Grounds" when those cities met.[16] This is further suggestion that it might have been the approximate location of the State Fair's baseball field since the outset.

Travis and McGowen was most definitely the spot used for the start of the professional Texas Association of 1884, the state's first attempt at establishing an intercity league. Sam Hain, owner of the team and one of the driving forces behind the league, paid to build out the grounds which was the site of a storied first game between Hain's Houston Nationals and the league entry from Galveston.

The year after the first foray into statewide league baseball in Texas, the Fair Grounds continued to offer public entertainment options. Messrs. J. Raphael and Whitrock managed an ambitious

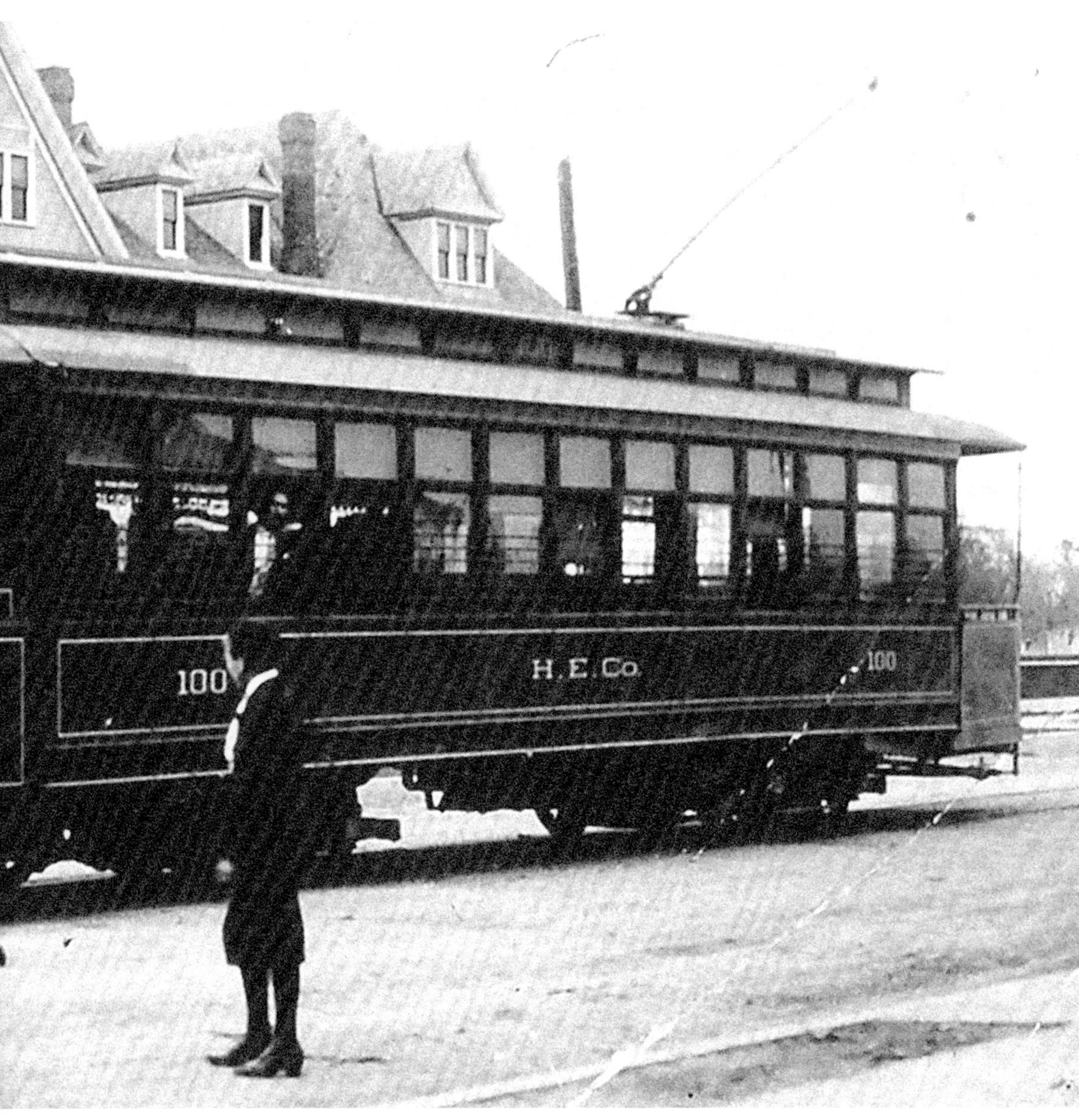

"Base Ball To-Day" is advertised on the Heights Streetcar, stopped here at 19th and Ashland. Public transportation was crucial to attendance at Houston ball games.

Houston Metropolitan Research Center, Houston Public Library

operation there. "They propose to make the grounds a place of summer resort, and are now putting the track, pavilion, baseball and cricket fields in first class order. The place will be free to all, except on special days, the management, no doubt, expecting to get a return for their outlay in the sale of refreshments. Sunday is the day for the opening. A band will be in attendance."[17]

The Mr. Raphael in question was Joseph Raphael, and he was running the venue under the name Fair Grounds Park. It was going "full blast every afternoon and night" in the summer of 1885.[18] Another attraction at the park that year was a skating rink operated by Messrs. Bailey and Skinner.[19]

Eventually, as with all property of value, money talked. By the late 1880s, most of the old State Fair grounds was being platted for residential development, marketed under the name of Fair Grounds Addition. One small exception remained mostly open land, a six-square block parcel bounded by McGowen, Main, Drew and Milam that was of utmost importance because that would remain the home to premier baseball in Houston for years to come.

As difficult as it might be for a modern head to wrap around, ball parks in the late nineteenth century did not always have official names. "The Fair Grounds" continued as one popular moniker as long as a large number of Houstonians had a recollection of the State Fair itself, but in a town growing as fast as any in the region, recent history might as well be ancient to the newcomers.

When the Cincinnati Red Stockings faced the local Babies on March 6, 1888, it was identified as the "Houston Base Ball Park." It was also regularly referenced in print as "League Park," "Travis Street Park," and the "Base Ball Park at Travis at McGowen" just to list a few. In the mid-1890s, with Houston Herald editor William H. Bailey as part of the ownership group, a sort of naming rights situation appeared, with even the rival *Post* referring to the action at "Herald Park."

The grandstand of the ball park on Travis burned in 1889, and the cause was never discovered. It certainly didn't crimp the play of the Houston ball club. They rolled to the city's first ever league championship there, dominating opponents to the degree that the park earned the nickname of the Slaughter Pen Grounds.[20]

For some years, the land on which the ball park sat had been owned by the firm that ran the city's streetcars. Though they were essential public transportation, they were not publicly held.[21] It was a business model that could be found with similar enterprises across the United States in the late nineteenth century, owning and promoting an attraction that made people want to pay to ride the streetcar.

Seeking to revive pro baseball after one of the Texas League's dark years, former Houston manager John McCloskey was back in town in April 1892. Trying to create a bidding war, McCloskey let it be known that he was entertaining options for a venue. E. L. Coombs who owned property on the southern edge of the Heights, was rumored to be courting McCloskey. So, too, was Henry F. MacGregor, president of the street railway company which still owned the ball park.[22]

After briefly floating a story that the streetcar folks proposed to turn the old ball park site into an "immense wigwam" for the meeting of state Democratic convention, flirtations ended and a deal was reached with the Heights left out in the cold.[23] Just two weeks after his arrival, McCloskey could smile about a story that had hit the national press. The Sporting Life reported that "The old park will be remodeled and new fences built... The Houston City Railway Company, who control the grounds, have given McCloskey carte blanche to make any improvements he may think necessary, and the public can rest assured that everything will be done to make the patrons of the game feel comfortable and at home. Electric cars in abundance will be placed on the line running to the park, and the crowds will have no cause to complain as they did heretofore when the mules balked and kicked."[24]

Just how much money and attention to detail went into the remodel of the grandstands is open to debate. On San Jacinto Day 1894, during exhibition drills by the Houston Light Guard, Houston Light Artillery, Rutherford Rangers and other drill companies from Galveston and Brenham, a section of the stands "on which several hundred people sat gave way with a terrible crash." Fortunately, two doctors were on hand to help with the aid and check the casualties, determining that there were three minor injuries.[25]

There was one post script to the story which came in the possible form of someone sniffing deep pockets. Two weeks later, the *Post* reported that "Mrs. Charles Herring of 2401 La Branch is confined to her bed in very bad condition after being injured in the collapse of seats at the baseball park on San Jacinto Day. At the time it was thought that Mrs. Herring was not badly hurt."[26]

In 1895, a block away from the ball park, at the northeast corner of Main and McGowen, the city opened a large municipal auditorium with great fanfare. It filled a large need for Houston, but the immediate catalyst was the Confederate Veterans Convention to be held in the city. Reports of construction and other preparations filled the newspapers daily. The world famous John Philip Sousa and his band were brought in as the opening day entertainment.[27]

By far the most honored guest in town for the huge event was Winnie Davis, the daughter of the late Confederate President, Jefferson Davis. Miss Davis's every curtsy, smile and titter was breathlessly reported along with the roll call of those lucky enough to be allowed into her presence.[28]

One group that was not hanging around McGowen Street in 1895 was the baseball team. Finally giving in to an offer which had first presented itself three years prior, they had opened the season with plans to make their home at the new Coombs Park near where Heights Boulevard crossed White Oak Bayou. Less than five years old, the planned community of Houston Heights was booming with new housing, business, heavy industry and a nearby military encampment. Still, it was a bold move to relocate to the city's suburban neighbor, though they were no doubt prompted by attractive promises from the park's owner, E. L. Coombs.

On Opening Day, Houston hosted, and lost to, Galveston at Coombs Park in front of "a crowd that was by no means large, considering it was the opening of the season's league contest."[29]

It took less than 24 hours for the

E.L. Coombs built a park at Heights Boulevard and White Oak Bayou and enticed, at least briefly, the Houston ball club to come play in the suburbs. The popular Heights Natatorium was the longest lasting vestige of Coombs Park.

Houston Metropolitan Research Center, Houston Public Library

nay-sayers to single out the reason for the sparse crowd. "The distance of the grounds from the city, rendering them inaccessible to the foot brigade and the fear of inadequate transportation facilities, particularly at the close of the game, undoubtedly kept many away who would have otherwise been on hand. Some of the old timers and most enthusiastic cranks were missed yesterday."[30]

The experiment with suburban baseball lasted all of four days. On the 26th of April, the *Post* reported a new deal. "Manager Hepworth finds the distance from Camp Houston to the business portion of the city is too great to draw crowds which will make the patronage supporting. Yesterday he signed a lease with the International and Great Northern for the old Lee grounds at the foot of Congress Street and today the lumber to fence in the park and build the grand stands will be on the grounds. ...This new park will be convenient for several reasons. it is not only accessible by streetcars, but people can walk back from the park if car service is short. Besides the trains from Galveston can unload their passengers right at the grounds."[31]

No one could accuse management of being unresponsive to its fan base. One day later, dirt was broken on the east edge of downtown with manager Hepworth digging the first post hole. Dubbed International Park, it was promised to be ready by May 5.[32] Even as the club continued to play games in the Heights, workers got after it at the team's new home. All the fence posts were set just one day following the ground breaking.[33]

And open on time it did. With the team's brief sojourn in the burbs behind him, Billy Hepworth summed up the episode nicely when he said, "the park at Houston Heights was too far removed to make baseball profitable."[34]

The team continued to be responsive to complaints and comments even after swapping field bosses in July. New Houston manager Jack Garson promised new walks from the streetcar stops. He said he would do everything possible to make patrons comfortable. "No hoodlumism; no overly boisterous conduct." He vowed to make it pleasant for ladies and

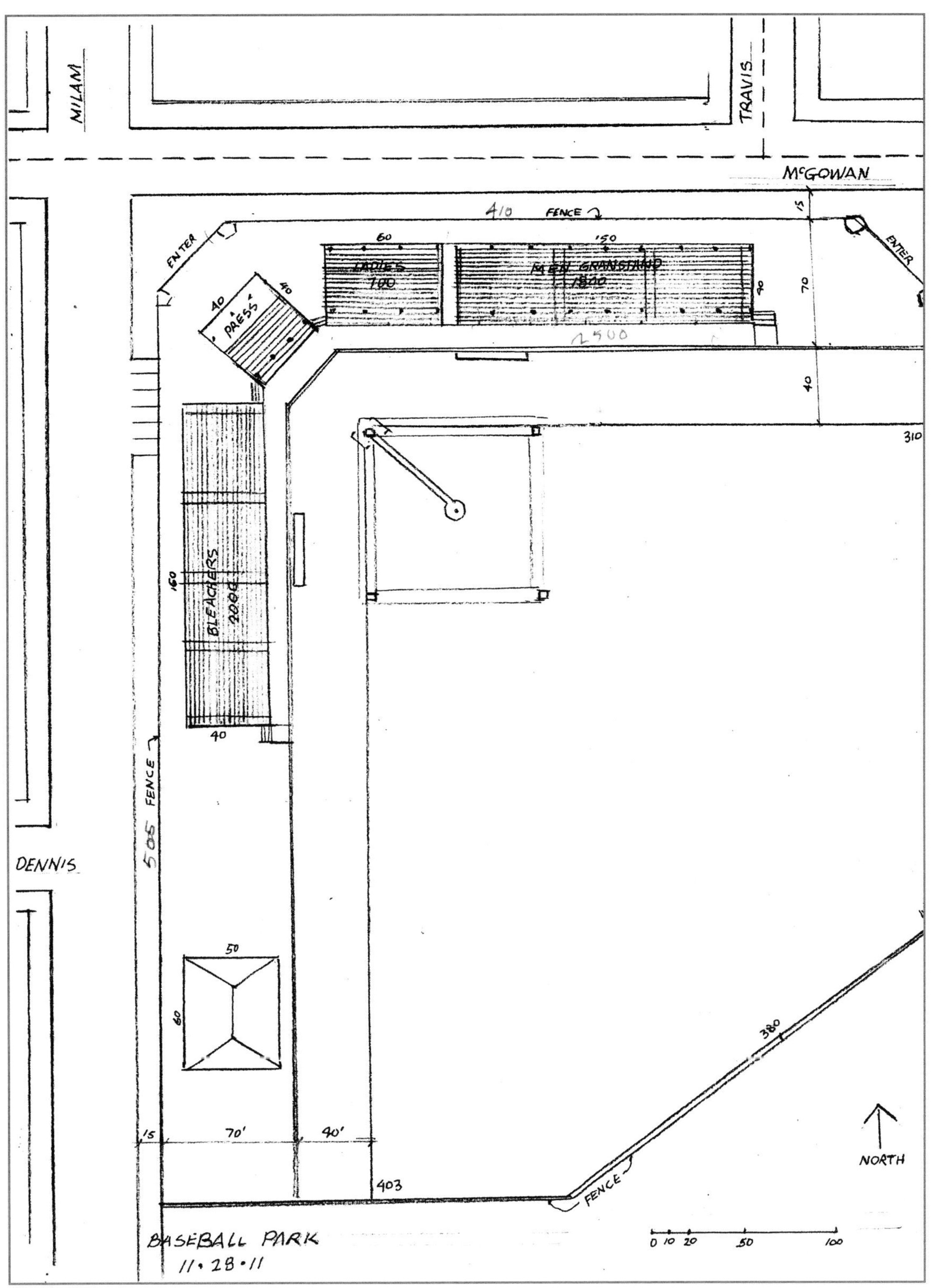

***This drawing is based on dimensions for the baseball park renovations that were published in the* Houston Post.** Original artwork courtesy of Patrick Lopez

A legend of overnight success grew up around Ollie Pickering's arrival in Houston. He would become a popular player in the Bayou City.

Courtesy Library of Congress

gentlemen "if I have to hire half a dozen policemen to do it."[35]

Meanwhile, the area around what was now referred to as the old ball park continued to become more urbanized, and that included all the sad drama of big city life. A boy named Ardie Lee wandering on the prairie beyond the Fair Grounds Addition, past the corner of Francis and Smith, found the body of "a male child, which had probably been killed at birth. Police determined that it was a white child, fully developed. It had probably been lying where found for four or five days."[36]

As often happens, larger events had a direct influence on smaller things, and in this case, one of those things was the ball park at Travis and McGowen. When the Houston City Street Railway Company got into serious financial trouble, local lumber magnate John Henry Kirby was appointed receiver of the company.[37] Over the next several weeks, Kirby inspected all of the company's properties which no doubt included the ball park. It might well be at least part of reason Kirby had gotten involved in team ownership by the end of the year.

The indisputable result was that much brighter times were in store for the ball park on Travis and McGowen in 1896. With a new, highly organized ownership syndicate in place, the decision was made to revamp the grounds, still referred to as "old" despite it possibly having not yet reached its teens. By the first of the year, workers were on hand clearing away brush and debris.[38]

Two days after the incorporation of the ownership group was filed, Jack Garson was personally supervising the rebuilding of the ball park. A new fence was constructed along the McGowen and Milam street sides, and the old fence in other spots was being repaired. "The trees have been cut down and thus the space between them and the right field fence, which was formerly unused, will be utilized. The grounds are 403 feet long and about 310 feet wide."

Seating was ample. "The two grand stands, one for ladies and their escorts and the other for gentlemen only, will be at the Milam Street and McGowen Avenue corner of the park and will be entirely of modern construction. The combined seating capacity of the two grandstands will be about 2500. The bleachers will be erected along the side of the right field fence and will be able to accommodate about 200 persons." Wire netting was in place to prevent fouls from hitting the grand stand occupants.[39]

A gate and ticket office was built at the head of Travis Street, and conveniences were put in for the press and scorer on top of the grand stand.[40]

With great concern for propriety among the fans high on their agenda, the directors agreed that "under no circumstances will there be sale of intoxicants at the ball park."[41]

Even for a wooden ball park, work progressed rapidly. By mid-February, the papers could report that "the grand stand at Herald Park is rapidly nearing completion, everything with the exception of the roof now being in place." Manager Garson asked that the published reports of completion by April 2 be corrected to March 1 since he was trying to get the Cincinnati club into town for an exhibition later in March.[42]

For those who had not journeyed to the South End to see for themselves, the public could get updates from the print media. On February 24, 1896 the *Post* ran a column written by Joe Emmich, longtime league umpire and one of the directors of the original Texas League team from 1888. "To say I would be surprised at the changes would be mildly expressing it." He conveyed his thanks to both manager Jack Garson and the directors of the ball club.

The old club house was moved to the southwest corner of the property, putting it out of the way. Garson had just finished water connections into the club house for a nice shower bath "which will be quite a treat, indeed." Considering how a player would feel after experiencing a nine inning ball game wearing flannel during August in Houston, Emmich was likely right.

He also commented on the removal of the trees, intimating that they had been a hazard. The old umpire said that with the trees back of first base gone, there was "no danger of getting hurt going after foul hits." In addition, the entire ground was being filled and leveled.

Emmich also recounted a conversation he had with "Wiley Hubert, barber, preacher and poet, and a representative of the colored people of this city, has requested that I get the directors to furnish a separate, as well as suitable, location for his people. They are good patrons and deserve some consideration." Hubert promised that if Houston won the season opening game the African-American stands would promise to show "the pandemonium existing in the late republican convention."[43]

Perhaps the crowds at the Fair Grounds were a bit too enthusiastic for some of the neighbors. Judge J.M. Smither of the 12th judicial district court sitting at Anderson, Texas, issued a temporary injunction against club president W.H. Bailey to stop the playing of ball at the Travis St. Park. It was issued "at the request of W.S. Latting who resides near the ball park, who complains that those attending the game disturb the residents of that locality with their applause." Much like some similar suits today, no mention was made of the fact that the ball park had occupied the site for over 12 years, well before the nearby houses were built.[44]

Admission for ball games was normally charged at the gate with an additional charge if one wished to sit in the covered grandstand. Otherwise the fan could find a place in the bleachers which were farther down the foul lines or stand. Advanced tickets could also be bought downtown at Otto Taub's cigar stand.

True to human nature, those attending the games had no trouble voicing displeasure over some practices. One complaint concerned the Milam Street gate not being opened in the late innings.

Patrons wishing to exit that direction had to wait for someone to come around and unlock it.

There were plenty of would be patrons who chose to save their money and scam the system. *Houston Post* writer James Quarles wrote an entire article on the freeloaders. Circling the yard, he first remarked on those along the right field fence along Milam.

"There is a motley crowd. I counted no less than a dozen animals, the owners standing on the saddles and looking over the fence being given an opportunity to see what transpires within. Some of the horses had as many as two to carry. Boys ranging in age from 8 to 15 are seen all along the fence looking through convenient cracks or holes that have been whittled. They watch through these cracks for a foul ball, and when one happens off the high fence—as is often the case—there is a scramble, whites and blacks joining in the rush to recover the sphere, the possession of which gives them free entry into the park."

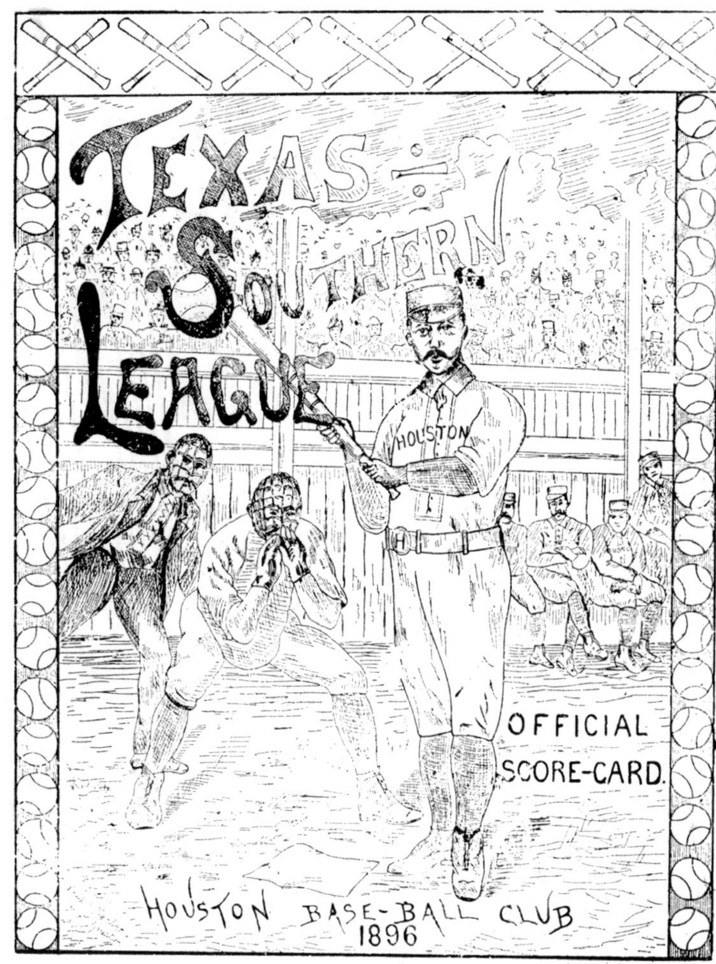

Players sat on uncovered benches in front of the grandstand as depicted in this 1896 score card.

Courtesy Special Collections, University of Houston Libraries

Along the outfield wall, where Dennis Avenue would one day cut through, was another crowd. "The first seen is a number of buggies—old ones, new ones, dilapidated ones, some with tops and some without, each having from three to a half dozen occupants who are perched about on the wheels and tops anxiously watching each successive play of the game... Next is seen a delivery wagon carrying upon the side the familiar sign of a well-known Houston business house. Upon the roof of this wagon, which should be used for the more legitimate purpose of distributing its cargo of fine silks, laces and dress goods, is roosting the driver and his friends."

Quarles offered descriptions of "portable grand stands" placed upon the back of an uncovered buggy and occupied by two grown men holding umbrellas to keep the sun off their heads during the two hour ballgame.

Some of those sponging off the team owners had even managed to avoid paying for devices upon which to sit. "Nature

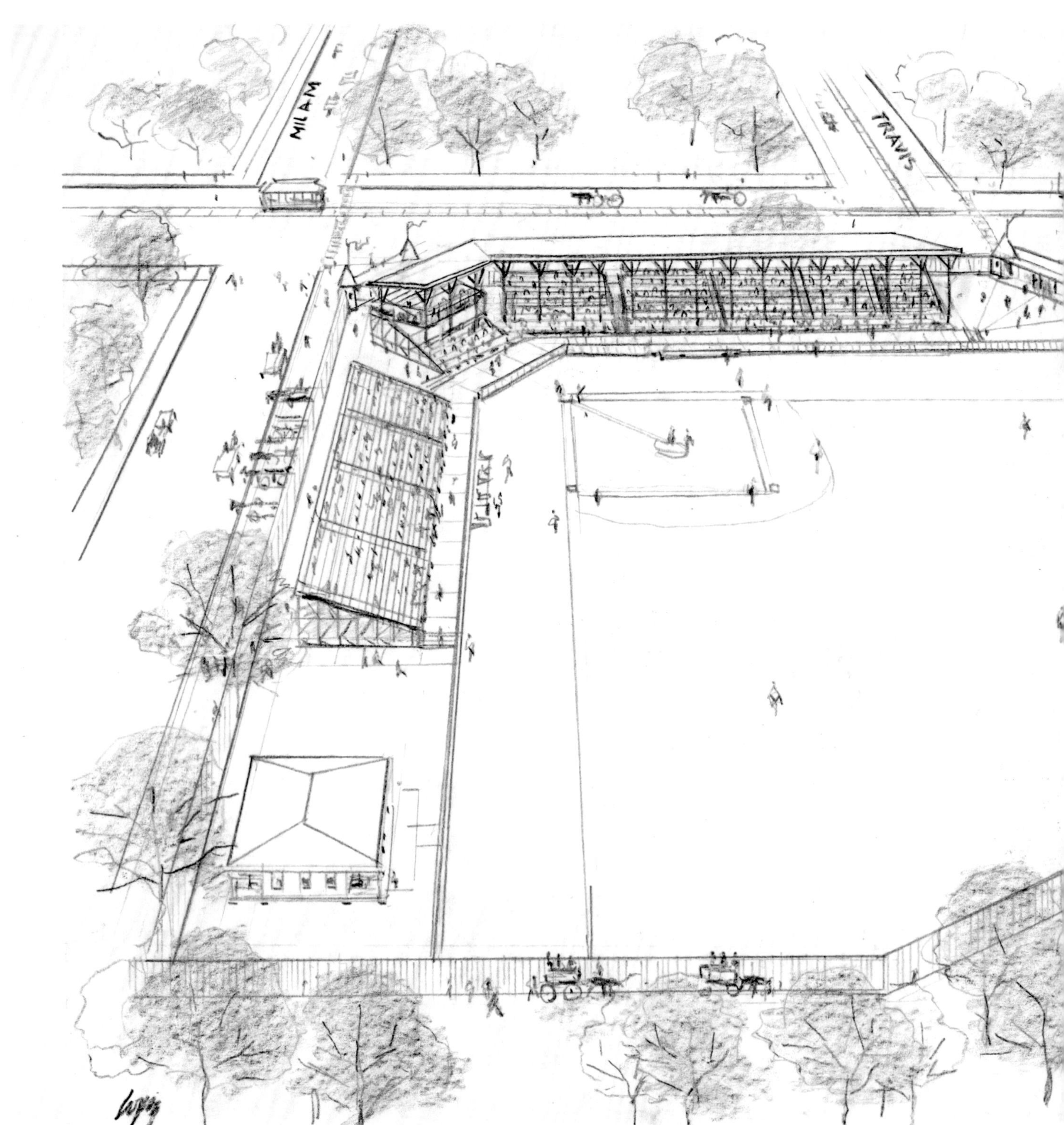

Freeloaders who parked their wagons against the outfield fences were a costly annoyance to the owners of the Houston ball club in the 1890s. Original artwork courtesy of Patrick Lopez

has assisted others. Just behind the portable grand stand is a large tree, a gnarled oak, which has grown throughout the time of many years... Its spreading branches have a seating capacity of about twenty-five, and the limbs are crowded. Men and boys, white and black, congregate among its foliage every afternoon and watch the game."

Other fans employed a bit of daring with their mooching. "Out in McGowen avenue I saw a small boy at the point of a deserted telegraph pole. A seat had been arranged on this pole and he was comfortably ensconced upon it."

Much as one can see today at parks like Wrigley Field, nearby rooftops were another bastion to avoid ticket charges as "a newly erected residence on McGowen avenue, which is yet unoccupied, affords a place of vantage for some of them."[45]

Quarles also wrote of some of the regular patrons including city engineer Louis Gueringer who sat in the bleachers along first base where "he can hear Shaffer kick," and Judge E. P. Hill who occupied the same seat every game, in one of the boxes at the rear.

He named Slim the score card vendor who sells for a nickel and mentioned unnamed boys who rent cushions for the seats.[46]

Football, rapidly growing in popularity across Texas, was also to be found at Travis and McGowen during the fall. By the time the Oregons and the Stogies played in September of 1897 the game was an expected norm in the city. The paper remarked that it was the "first football game at League park for the year."[47]

With the wooden structure exposed to Houston's heat, sun and rain, it was due a sprucing up every year or two. In preparation for the 1898 season, modernity was addressed. "Turnstiles have been ordered for the gates, and in the future Herald Park will have a regular bonafide National League ground appearance."[48]

The paint scheme for the year was described by the local press as "gaudy" with the seats of the grandstand painted orange and the inside of the grandstand painted red and orange. In addition the "ground has been packed and the steam roller will be put on this week so that grounds will be in good shape for the games with Cincinnati on March 19 and 20."[49]

Outfield fences were covered in signage advertising Houston merchants. Railroads were especially generous with 100 feet going to International & Great Northern and 40 feet to Galveston, Houston and Henderson.[50]

One final improvement was aimed at solving the issue of the freeloaders. "A barbed wire fence will be built about 25 feet east of the left field fence. This will keep the rabble away from the fence."[51]

Other activities continued to use the ball park at Travis and McGowen. Following the season of 1899, it was the Fruit, Flower and Vegetable Festival. Several canvas-roofed exhibit buildings were set up on the ball field and livestock pens were placed on two or more sides of the park. The "intermediate vacant block" that sat between the Auditorium and the ball park would be used for a midway filled with attractions.[52]

Amateur games were often held on the grounds between 1900 and 1902, years that the city had no Texas League entry, but with such a lengthy lapse, the ball park received only the most basic maintenance.[53]

The inevitable came two years later. Otto Witte bought the land from the Houston Electric Streetcar Company in February 1904 with the intention of developing the six blocks.[54] He granted the ball club a stay of execution until June.

Judging by the chaotic and sparsely attended season of 1904, nostalgia for the team was not running rampant. The business interests that ran the growing young city, not yet even 70 years old, put up nary a cry at the demise of the Travis Street grounds, but at least one local writer took the time to pen a paean to the park. It covered most of a page in the *Houston Post* a few weeks after the last game had been played there.

The byline was Harry M. Johnston, 20-year-old son of the head of the *Post*, Rienzi Johnston, who had once been an owner of the ball club.[55] Given the age and situation of the two at the time, at least some consideration is due as to which Johnston actually wrote the article. Or perhaps it was a collaboration and an assignment from father to son. Either way, he began his piece with these words:

> "The old league park, after many years service to the sunkissed athletes of the National game, has

faded into the dim past. The dull sombre roar of the base hit, the wild and thrilling yell of the fanatic, and the spicy field play, which have marked a period of 20 years at the famous old park will no longer be looked forward to, but, instead, will be remembered only as seen in the fast fleeting past.

There will always be something about the old park that holds one's attention as he passes there, although handsome residences will occupy the space once used as the diamond—a diamond on which the greatest ballplayers of the country have played."[56]

Less than a year after baseball moved away, the blocks at Travis and McGowen had been subdivided and sold. Substantial houses soon sprung up, yielding over the next decades to upscale apartments, a car dealership and then high end Midtown restaurants. A final reminder of its first use lives on, however, in every deed record for the six square blocks. Anyone looking at the official description will find the tiny neighborhood south of downtown was platted and developed under the name Ball Park Addition.[57]

1 Houston city directory 1870
2 *Houston Daily Union*, May 9, 1871.
3 McComb, David G. *Houston, The Bayou City*. (University of Texas, 1969) 62.
4 Official Report of the Third Annual State Fair, May 1872
5 DHT 23 May 1874
6 Official Report of the Third Annual State Fair, May 1872
7 DHT 27 October 1871
8 Houston City Directory 1877-78
9 HWT 24 May 1871; DHT 2 May 1874
10 GDN 26 May 1877
11 Aulbach, Louis. *Buffalo Bayou: Echoes of Houston's Wilderness Beginnings*. (Aulbach, 2012)
12 DHT 30 May 1874; Aulbach, Louis. *Buffalo Bayou: Echoes of Houston's Wilderness Beginnings*. (Aulbach, 2012)
13 Morrison and Fourmy Map of Houston 1882; Porter Map of Houston 1890
14 GDN 3 August 1875
15 DHT 18 April 1868
16 GDN 8 October 1883; GDN 23 October 1883
17 GDN 12 March 1885
18 HP 9 May 1885
19 Houston City Directory 1885
20 Sporting Life 30 November 1895
21 American Street Railway Convention program 1893-94; Commercial & Financial Register 1897; Case, Josephine Young and Case, Everett Needham. Owen D. Young and American Enterprise: A Biography. (David R. Godine, 1982)
22 GDN 8 April 1892
23 GDN 18 April 1892
24 Sporting Life 23 April 1892
25 HP 22 April 1894
26 HP 6 May 1894
27 HP 7 April 1895; HP 3 May 1895; HP 5 May 1895; HP 8 May 1895
28 HP 23 May 1895; HP 24 May 1895; HP 25 May 1895
29 HP 23April 1895
30 HP 23 April 1895
31 HP 26 April 1895
32 HP 27 April 1895
33 GDN 29 April 1895; HP 28 April 1895
34 HP 6 May 1895
35 HP 11 July 1895
36 HP 27 Nov 1895
37 HP 12 July 1895
38 HP 3 January 1896
39 HP 2 August 1896
40 HP 5 January 1896
41 HP 11 January 1896
42 GDN 18 February 1896
43 HP 24 February 1896
44 HP 7 June 1896
45 HP 2 August 1896
46 HP 9 August 1896
47 HP 7 September 1897
48 Sporting Life 1 January 1898
49 HP 8 March 1898; HP 10 March 1898
50 HP 13 February 1898
51 HP 8 March 1898
52 HP 21 November 1899
53 HP 22 July 1900; HP 16 August 1900; HP 30 June 1901
54 Harris County Deeds. Volume 160. Pages 381-383. 29 February 1904.
55 United States Census 1900 Harris County, TX; United States Census 1910 Harris County, TX
56 HP 10 July 1904
57 Block Books, Harris County Archives

KEY

GDN – *Galveston Daily News*
HI – *Houston Informer*
HP – *Houston Post*
CD – *Chicago Defender*
HC – *Houston Chronicle*

HOUSTON
HOUSTON

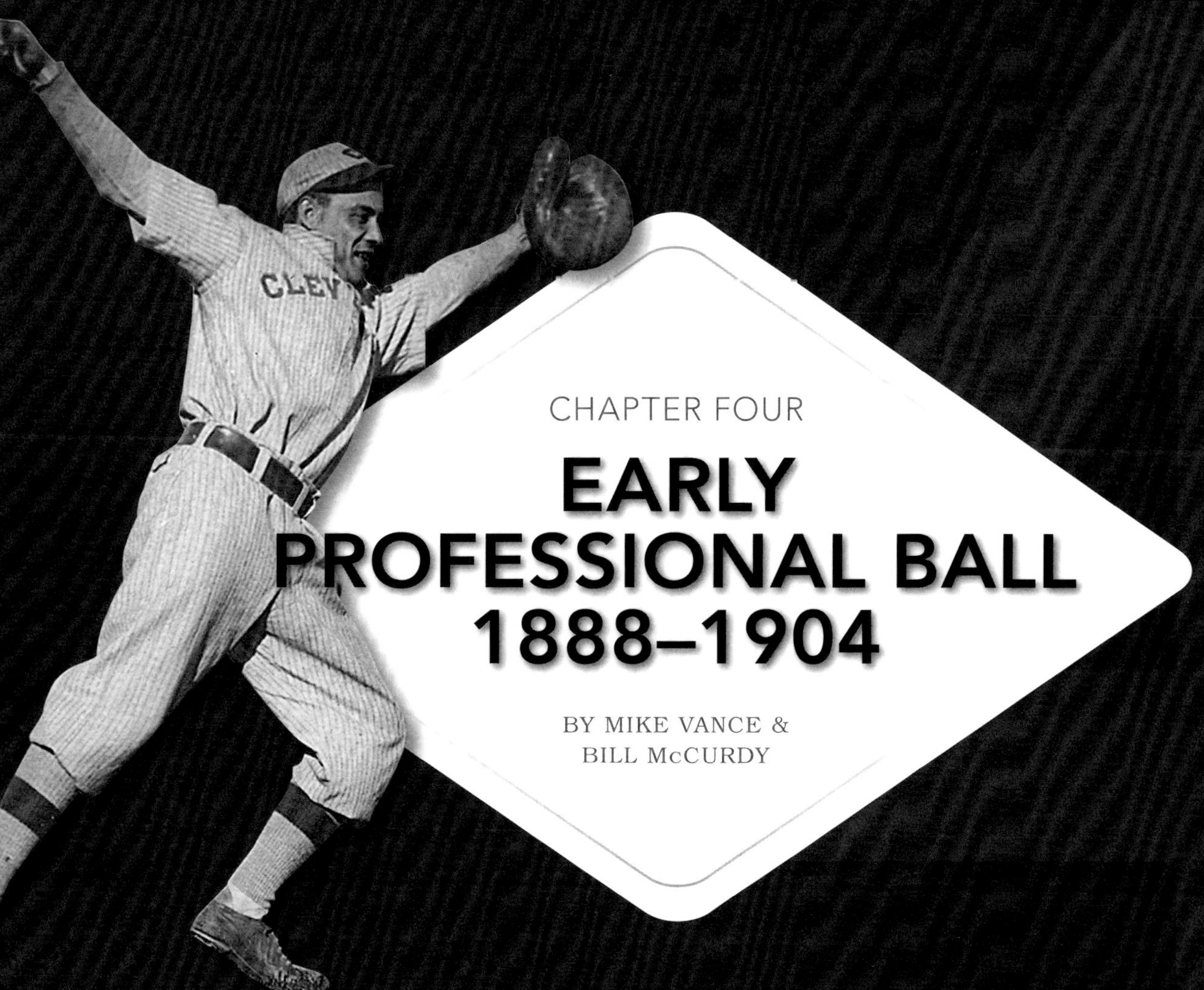

CHAPTER FOUR

EARLY PROFESSIONAL BALL 1888–1904

BY MIKE VANCE & BILL McCURDY

Though the first attempt at a Texas league had failed after a short 1884 season, the hunger among the state's baseball men for such an entity was still strong. Attempts at a restart were made almost every spring. Around the nation, other leagues were also trying to get steady on their feet. The year 1885, one season after the initial Texas Association experiment, saw the start of the Southern League[1], the Western League and the California League.[2] It was only a matter of time before Texas revitalized its own circuit.

The 1889 Houston team brought the first professional sports championship to the Bayou City.
Private Collection

The popularity of baseball as entertainment had grown steadily since the Civil War, not only in Texas, of course, but in every corner of the Union. It certainly had the attention of the sporting public, a term that often meant gamblers, but others were going simply because they liked the game. Newspapers reported that women were often in attendance. In fact, many teams advertised ladies days and ladies sections of the grandstands where the fairer sex and their escorts could observe the game unsullied by any vulgar and low single men who might be congregating.[3]

Another factor in baseball's popularity was a revolution in mass communication. Following the Civil War, the nation was united not just by law, but by a universal communications network in the form of the telegraph. Add to that the advent of wire services like the Associated Press, and baseball news and results from the East Coast could be sent almost instantly to hinterlands like Texas. At the same time, large rotary printing presses fed with rolls of newsprint were becoming more common, allowing American newspapers to drastically increase their circulation.[4] All this made certain baseball teams famous and created the first star athletes.

When The New York Giants passed through Texas in November 1887 with Boston's Mike "King" Kelly in tow, the state's press referred to him as the most famous baseball player in America and cooed over the $10,000 price tag the Bostons had paid to get him.[5]

The Giants had come from New Orleans to Texas, playing games in Houston, Galveston and Austin as they worked their way west to California. At the same time, the St. Louis Browns and a collection of Chicago White Stockings were playing through the state, as well. After an active Texas baseball season, it was major league icing on the cake.

From a marketing standpoint, the timing was impeccable. The *Houston Post* reported on November 15, 1887, that the "movement to organize a base ball association for next season is progressing finely. A prominent citizen has been asked to head it as president and has taken the matter under advisement."[6] Adding to the baseball talk that week was somewhat of a David vs. Goliath story with the Giants playing the part of the big guy.

The previous day the New Yorkers had suffered their first loss of the barnstorming tour, bowing to an Austin team by the score of 5 to 4.[7] Literally a week before, the Austins had been playing in Ft. Worth and Waco under the name of Joplin, Missouri.[8]

John J. McCloskey, shown here much later in life, was a driving force behind the establishment of the Texas League. He managed in multiple league cities over the course of his career.

National Baseball Hall of Fame Library, Cooperstown, NY

The team was led by John J. McCloskey, a 26-year-old Louisville native, who had brought a collection of Midwestern professionals to do a little ball playing through Texas. They were mostly young men who had played ball in the Western League earlier that year. Harry Dooms was the star pitcher, having thrown for three different Kansas teams already in 1887, and Harry Raymond, Farmer Weaver and Frank Hoffman would eventually see the major leagues themselves.[9]

Thanks to McCloskey's 1931 reminiscences shared with Texas League chronicler William Ruggles, a good deal of mythology has grown up around his Joplin/Austin squad. Spinning his tale almost 44 years after the fact, McCloskey put great importance on the series. He told of beating the Giants twice before New York slinked out of town prior to the promised third game. He credited the sweep and himself with being the prime catalysts for the new league.[10]

The fact of the matter was that the Giants came back to beat McCloskey's "Austin" team of Midwesterners by a count of 19 to 13 in front of "an immense crowd" on the second day, but the invigorating idea that Texas players could compete with anyone had indeed been sewn.[11]

Far from sneaking out in the dead of night, the New Yorkers had planned that their time in Texas would end at that point all along. They were due in El Paso where they would meet up with the St. Louis and Chicago aggregate to head to Los Angeles and two games scheduled for the 19th and 20th. The prospect of an exhibition on the border was squelched by the Giants because of "the fact that Kelly had been on a big tear for three days."[12]

Meanwhile, the Joplin/Austin team that had beaten the Giants and their possibly tipsy star player hooked up with two Austin businessmen and made plans to remain in the Capitol City as the local squad. Sam French and Ed Byrne had been running a pro team of their own, but with "kindred spirit" McCloskey, they saw dollars to be made in a Texas baseball enterprise.[13]

So, too, did other men around the state. On the 25th of the month, the *Houston Daily Post* published the following:

> *"Pursuant to notice the first meeting of the stockholders of the Houston Base Ball association was held last night at the Light Guard armory. The amount of stock to be issued is $5000, and this amount has about been taken. A number of gentlemen interested in base ball matters were present and the meeting was characterized by perfect harmony and sufficient enthusiasm to foretell the success of the association. It is the intention to have a league in the State embracing clubs in the principal cities of the State. The following officers were selected: Judge E.P. Hill, president; Captain F. A. Reichhart, vice-president; Sam L. Hain, corresponding secretary; Robert Adair, financial secretary; W.O. Ellis, treasurer. Board of*

Directors—H.T. Kellar, J.A. Baker, Jr., S. Hutchins, M. Rosenthal, Z.T. Hogan, John Cross, W.A. Childress, Sam Alexander, Gus Fredericks, C. Richmond, J. Emmick, Pat Farrell. The association starts out under the most favorable auspices, and it will accomplish no doubt what it intends—to give Houston the best club in the State. It is understood that the current ball park will be enlarged or a new one obtained."[14]

The list of directors for the Houston team includes men who had a history with Bayou City baseball. At least two names were men who had been crack players 15 years prior, but were now prominent local businessmen. Zach T. Hogan had played on the Stonewalls in the late 1860s while he was working for the firm of T.W. House. Gus Fredericks, a star with the powerful Lees of 1874, had moved from the position of clerk at J.J. Sweeney's jewelry store to being a partner in both the business and the turreted Main Street building in which it was housed. Joe Emmich was a frequent local umpire.

Other directors were among the city's business elite, including James A. Baker, Jr., better known as Captain Baker, the powerful lawyer who saved the estate on which Rice Institute was founded.[15] E.P. Hill was another influential lawyer, banker and railroad director.[16] Reichhardt, Hutchins and Childress were all officers of the Houston Light Guard, a combination military reserve unit and social club which was a close order drill champion of national note at the time.[17]

Things moved quickly after Houston formalized its ball club. Representatives of four teams met in Austin in December, and one month later, Dallas, Houston, Austin and Fort Worth formed what was to be known as "The Texas League of Baseball Clubs."[18] Galveston and San Antonio soon followed. The intention had been to become an eight team league, but they would start with six the first season.

The group chose Fred W. Turner of Austin to serve as their first league president. Robert Adair of Houston got the nod as vice-president, and W.L. Reynolds of Dallas drew the vote as the Texas League's first secretary-treasurer.[19]

Bob Adair was 34 at the time. Having grown up in Buffalo and Chicago, he came to Houston in 1875 to work for the Houston & Texas Central. He had also served as foreman of Hook and Ladder Company #1, part of the city's volunteer fire department. The year the baseball league was formed, Adair was in a seven year run as Houston's City Tax Assessor and Collector as well as belonging to the Light Guard, the Turnverein and the Left Handed Fishing Club.[20]

On the baseball side, Adair had joined Houston's R.E. Lee Base Ball Club almost as soon as he arrived in the city, bringing with him decent talent as a catcher.[21] Still playing almost a decade later, he had been the captain of the Crescents in Houston back in 1884 when that team joined with Sam Hain's

The Cincinnati club of the American Association made a much publicized tour through Texas in March of 1888. Courtesy Library of Congress

P. KAPPEL–3RD B.
KEENAN–C. VIAU–P
BALDWIN–C.

Nationals to create the city's entry in the Texas Association. Before the 1888 season was through, Adair would assume the league's executive spot after Turner resigned.[22]

Under this league leadership, rules and by-laws were agreed upon. A salary limit of $1000 was set for players on each team. Uniform ticket prices of 25 cents for adults and 15 cents for children were set for all league contests. It was also agreed that there would be no "free list" of complimentary tickets except for members of the working press and the grounds and gate crews.[23] No longer booking on a series-by-series basis, teams sought to get lower group rates from Texas railroads.[24] Operating costs would be scrutinized, and every dollar counted.

The concept of official names for teams and ballparks in the 19th century was a tenuous one. Rather than being assigned and marketed by the team ownership, nicknames were often dreamt up by local baseball writer. "Babies" seems to have been a title that the news media reserved, however informally, for any club that may have been the newest kid on the block. In Houston's case, they may not have been the final team to form, but it is possible they were the last to sign off on the particulars of the new Texas League. Whatever the reason, they played the 1888 season as the Houston Babies.

The Babies roster was a mixture of young and old with the widest possible range of future prospects. At the age of 20, Lew Whistler was looking forward to a long career that would soon include four years of major league service. John Godar, Pat Flaherty and Brooklyn-born Handsome Dan Murphy would each see the bigs, though for less than season.

Frank Weikart was a 26-year-old second baseman and pitcher, another transplant from the Southwestern League in Missouri and Arkansas. Playing primarily in the Texas League and Southern Association, Weikart would remain on active rosters for another two plus decades. Moving exclusively to the field after his pitching arm gave out, he earned the nickname of "Pop."[25] On the 1910 census, at the age of 48, his occupation was still listed as ball player.[26]

One man whose prime was already behind him was Babies pitcher Doc Landis. He had split the 1882 season between Philadelphia and Baltimore in the American Association where he amassed a league leading 29 losses. Another former National League pitcher was Dupee Shaw, a veteran of Detroit, Boston and Providence. When the Washington Nationals released him in July 1888, it marked his final appearance in the show. He promptly signed with Houston.

There were also returnees from previous Houston pro teams. Catcher Joseph Lohbeck, 20 years old, and 37-year-old hurler Tricky Nichols were two of the familiar faces that had graced the Bayou City box scores in previous years.

One rarity on the roster was the historically named outfielder Pizarro Douthett. Born in Virginia in 1857, Douthett was a Phi Kappa Psi fraternity boy who had played a few years of college ball at Wooster in Ohio. After that, he mixed four years of pro ball in with an additional year of schooling at Lafayette College. Professionally, Douthett had stints at New Brighton, Pennsylvania in the Iron and Oil League; Hartford in the Southern New England League; St. Paul and Oshkosh in the Northwestern League; Hastings in the Western League and with independent clubs in Decatur, Illinois and Little Rock, all before he came to Houston.[27]

The question of exactly who was managing this motley collection remains somewhat unanswered. Different sources list Douthett, Whistler, Frank Traut, Fred Carroll, Spencer Hutchins and Sam Hain as having been the field boss.[28] Douthett, sporting the nickname of Doc and credited with the first put out in Texas League history, was recalled by one old-time sports writer almost two decades later as having been the team captain as opposed to manager.[29]

On March 6th, prior to the start of the inaugural Texas League season, the Babies, clad in their new green flannel uniforms[30], played their first professional foe at the Travis Street Park. The opponents were the Cincinnati Red Stockings, a bona fide big league team. The Cincinnatians proved it by drubbing Houston on a rain-puddled field by a whopping count of 22-3, with Babies pitcher Thomas Flood going all the way and making six of the club's 13 errors. An anonymous *Houston Daily Post* writer offered that the locals might have fared better if only pitcher Flood had been able to maintain "better control of his balls."[31]

The first real game for Houston was also the inaugural game for the Texas League. It took place on Sunday, April 1, 1888, at the Fair Grounds park in Houston. About 600 Galveston fans paid the $1.50 round trip fare to journey from the island to the game, and they "literally bet everything except their team's classy new blue and maroon uniforms on the game."[32] It did not go well for them.

Meanwhile, it was a tense day for the winners, too. Director Joe Emmich recalled years later that "Sam Alexander had bet about $400 on Houston and he had me down in the grass up against the left field fence, and would not let me budge until the last man was out in the ninth inning. He was afraid I would change his luck."[33]

The starter for Houston was New Orleans native, Mike Shea. His two game run in the show had come the previous season at Cincinnati where he went 1-1. Coming up as a teenager with the Robert E. Lees of New Orleans, Shea spent most of his career bouncing around the Southern Association and the Texas League. He had done a stint with the city's Nationals in the Texas Association of 1884. In addition to Houston, he would later log Texas time in Galveston and Ft. Worth.[34]

But that first opening day, Shea was Houston's, and he was considered the top pitcher in the nascent Texas League. He didn't disappoint, and the Babies took it 4-1. A wild pitch in the fourth allowed the islanders' only tally, and Galveston's own News called Houston the stronger team, saying they won "with apparent ease."[35]

Galveston's Vanishing Scoreboard

The *Galveston Daily News* of April 22, 1889, opined that, "there should be a score board on the base ball grounds," adding that the press box needed to be enlarged and reserved for the exclusive use of reporters. The newspaper was referring to the fact that the scoreboard of the previous season had been removed, and the island's ball fans would suffer through the entire year without it being replaced. As the start of the season approached in 1890, the paper was still lamenting that there was no sign of a scoreboard being put up yet, and that "it was very popular in '88."

The decision to remove the feature, commonly referred to as a "bulletin board," was done by team management in order to encourage the sale of more score cards at the ball park. Galveston's press protested on behalf of the fans, pointing out that the score card would not help with getting scores from other concurrent Texas League games, either. At the same time, the team also forbade the wiring of inning-by-inning updates from Beach Park to outlets in downtown Galveston, saying that practice also discouraged patronage. The city's *Evening Tribune* flatly said that the team should be more accommodating to their visitors, "particularly the ladies, who are not acquainted with the mysterious workings of a score card."

Shea was not the only ball player who would play for multiple Texas league teams in a short span. Being well travelled was almost the norm. One fine example was infielder Gus Shearinghausen who came to the state as part of John McCloskey's barnstorming Joplin team. He would remain with Austin/San Antonio in 1888. The next year he played for Houston. The season after that he had three homes, seeing time in Dallas, Ft. Worth and Austin. When the Texas League revived in 1892, he was again in Houston. He would have another turn with San Antonio and two more in Austin before the decade was out.[36]

Keeping the Texas League operating turned out to be quite a task. The Houston club ownership actually reorganized in the midst of the season with E.P. Hill stepping away to be replaced as team president by the town's old baseball stalwart, W.H. Coyle.[37]

In the end, the Texas League of 1888 was perhaps even less successful than its 1884 counterpart had been. Four of the six original clubs, including Houston, were forced to disband before season's end, while another moved from Austin to San Antonio after the first Alamo City entry folded. New Orleans had been active in pre-season discussions before casting its 1888 lot with the Southern Association. It then came back to the Texas League to help pick up the slack when its Southern league disbanded in mid-July. For much of the Texas season, play was between a five-team league with one club forced to be idle for several days in a row.

Fitting a team into a championship season in mid-July defies common sense on the face of things, but by the time New Orleans came into the Texas group in 1888, the league's survivors were simply trying to fill game dates as best they were able. Selling a pennant race between only two or three teams was too tall an order.

By September, all that was left were Dallas and the Austin turned San Antonio team. Thus there would be no finish to the season or an official pennant awarded for the 1888 season. The disparity in total games played by each team ranged from 87 to 26.

The Dallas Hams (55-29) finished with the best record of all teams, whereas, the Houston Babies (39-46) finished fifth with their club disbanding before the league faded into oblivion at the start of September.[38] Some publications honor the Dallasites as the unofficial first league champions, but it is arguable that they were only a champion by attrition.

It was all a far cry from the efficiency that would eventually come to Texas League baseball, but it was a start. While mostly professional baseball had been going on in the larger Texas cities for some time, the Texas League in 1888 eliminated the remaining amateur spots on the teams. It also offered the most ambitious schedule ever undertaken in the Lone Star State.

For minor league baseball across the United States to succeed, greater commitment would be required from the team owners who organized the circuits, and it would come gradually. In the late 1880s, teams that ran out of money either cancelled road trips at the last minute, failed to show up or simply shut down operations entirely. Moving to another city as the Austin team did in 1888 was not something in which the municipal authorities had a say, and the idea of the wealthier teams supporting those that struggled was a rare one. The result was often chaos and financial losses across the board.

As for the baseball-going public, they were being asked to support regular weekday games for the first time ever. In the late nineteenth century, the average worker's week was six days, not five. The population of any given city was a fraction of what it is today. If the most popular player in town jumped ship in mid-year to make more money someplace else, or the hometown club began to lose heavily, fans simply did the most obvious thing: they stopped going to their team's games.

Another missing element was continuity. With the failed season behind them, the Texas League needed to be reorganized for 1889. This time it was representatives from Waco, Fort Worth, Houston and Galveston who assembled to discuss the particulars. Two weeks before the start of the 1889 season, Dallas and Austin joined the group. As the newcomer, it was Waco's team that was sometimes called the Babies that season.[39]

The Houston ball club of 1889 was led on the field by John McCloskey who had been lured away from San Antonio along with several of his players. The president of the reorganized team was Si Packard, a local laundry owner and city alderman who would be a main force pushing for a professional city fire department following the St. Joseph's Infirmary fire in 1894. Packard would remain active in Bayou City baseball doings until his death ten years later.[40]

Some Texans continued to apply the name Babies, but there was also a new nickname for the club in most circles: The Houston Mud Cats. It was an historical moniker for Houstonians dating back at least into the 1870s. With busy unpaved streets and a rainy, semi-tropical climate since its founding, the city had an ongoing problem with mud. Along with the heat, humidity and vermin, it was the most popular topic in the diaries of most early visitors.

The 1889 Houston team was talented. They started strong and would never be out of first place the entire season. Art Sunday (.344) led the team in hitting. This would be the first season that the league would keep batting averages, though the information and box scores provided to league secretary C.H. Thatcher were not always complete.

Emmett Rogers and Bill Peeples each had 50 stolen bases, and holdover Frank Weikart hit what was said to be the longest ball in the history of the ball park on Travis.[41] He also took his pitching to another level. After going a combined 4-4 in his appearances for two teams the prior year, Weikart won 27 games with an ERA of 2.18. It would be the next to last year of pitching for Weikart in a long minor league career.

Of all the Mud Cats, William "Scrappy Bill" Joyce, a 21-year-old infielder from St. Louis, would enjoy the most productive life in professional baseball. He led the league in home runs with 18, and when Houston's 1889 campaign was over, Joyce, along with Rogers and Sunday, were sold to Toledo in the International League.[42] The following year, Joyce was on Ward's Wonders in the short-lived Players League. Before he was out of his twenties, Scrappy Bill, "a bold and manly fellow," would manage the New York Giants for three seasons.[43]

One incident of note during the 1889 campaign was the mobbing of an umpire at the Houston park by fans upset with his calls. Mr. McLaughlin required the protection of most of the ballplayers to get him into the clubhouse where he stayed until the police arrived to "escort him from the grounds and see him safely home."[44]

As in the previous season, teams still faced financial difficulties. First Dallas and then Houston were forced to solicit new backing a few months into the season. Between August 9th and 14th, all six teams announced they had disbanded. Only Galveston, Austin and Fort Worth paid their league dues in full.

Thus started a debate which played out in the state's newspapers over whether Houston should be awarded the league pennant. Austin claimed that since they had paid their dues in full and were ahead of the other teams that had done likewise, they should be declared the league champion. It took until the meeting to organize the next season, but Houston was awarded the pennant.[45] It was the first professional sports championship in the history of the city.

Coming off their first taste of success, and with John McCloskey returning as manager, Houston's outlook was quite optimistic for 1890, but once again, the Texas League would have to be reorganized. This time Houston, Galveston, Dallas and Fort Worth formed the nucleus, followed eventually by Waco and Austin.[46]

Though it could be said that the Houston Mud Cats made it through the entire 1890 season, it lasted only two months. Any bright outlook was quickly dashed. On Opening Day, Austin was without a full roster or a manager. Harry "Bird Eye" Truby had signed two contracts, one to manage in Austin, where he had played the previous year, and one to play for Ft. Worth. Under orders from the league president, he was barred from the Ft. Worth lineup on opening day. The team forfeited as a matter of principle. The following day, with honor satisfied, the Panthers were back on the field sans Truby who had been placed on the Texas League blacklist.[47] Though he bounced around both minors and majors through 1904, Truby never again played in Texas.[48]

By late May, Austin was asking that other clubs transfer players to make their club more competitive. McCloskey considered sending Pat Flaherty to the Capital City, but an intervening tragedy necessitated keeping him on the Bayou.[49]

Harry Eliff, from Dayton, Ohio, was to be the regular catcher and backup first baseman for the Houston Mud Cats. Typical of many players, he spent1889 splitting time between Waco, Colorado and California. Coming to Houston the following year, he was touted as a good hitter. Eliff would only play in 16 games that season, however. After a scant mention of illness in mid-May, he was dead of typhoid or malaria, the first in-season death in Texas League history. Out of respect, the League took the following day off.[50]

In early June, with no reinforcements in sight, Austin folded. They were immediately followed by Fort Worth and then the Waco club. With only three teams left, the Texas League was officially disbanded on June 8th.[51] It was so dispiriting, that little discussion even took place about trying again in 1891.

The phenomenon of teams and leagues drifting in and out of existence was not confined to Texas. In fact, it was almost de rigueur among the nation's minor leagues. One of many examples was the Western League which would eventually become a rival to the National League itself. First formed in 1885, the Western League failed within months only to reform the following season. It failed and reformed again in 1888 and repeated the cycle in 1892 and 1893.[52]

Another, and geographically closer, example was the Southern League that brought the professional game to Louisiana and Arkansas, Texas' fellow Confederate states immediately to the east. In spite of the best efforts of several southern businessmen, the league failed to finish the season seven times between its 1885 founding and the turn of the century, and there were four seasons when the circuit never even left the gate.[53]

The Texas League would mirror those ups and downs through the last decade of the nineteenth century. The year 1891 was the first to come with no season at all. The destabilizing effect of teams disbanding brought what national baseball historians write off as a dark year of play, but the ballpark in Houston remained in steady use by both white and black semi-pro and amateur teams.[54]

Among the amateur ranks was Ed Kiam's department store team, clad in their all black uniforms, and a squad of employees of the *Post* which was not surprisingly well covered in the newspaper.[55] League or not, Houston and Galveston still had semi-pro clubs representing their respective cities. A pitcher named McCormick earned the honor of throwing a no-hitter against the city's island rivals, but it was far from a perfect game. Houston did win by a tally of 13-2 with both of Galveston's runs scoring in the first on a dropped third strike, two wild pitches and a muffed fly ball.[56]

With no league in which to play, many of the Texas ball players looked elsewhere to make a living in 1891. John McCloskey had headed to Peoria after the previous season ended early. In '91 he surfaced in Sacramento in the four team California

League with almost a dozen former Texas Leaguers.

Not yet ready to give up on the Lone Star State, McCloskey was back in Houston to manage the Mud Cats in 1892, bringing some of his old players back with him. He didn't arrive, though, until April, when he himself had to take a hand in forming the league.[57]It was an example of the drive that made him a favorite of many other baseball men.

Player and manager Ted Sullivan wrote of him, "John McCloskey has for years entered barren baseball fields, and by his hustling energy and enthusiasm has brought baseball to life in sections of the country where it has laid dormant for years."[58]

The game wasn't exactly dormant in Texas, but it would take all that McCloskey mojo to get the league up and running for 1892. After so many previous financial difficulties, rosters were limited and total salary capped at only $750 a month for each team.[59] Collusion to keep costs down would become an institution in the state. Twelve years later, it would even be codified that there was a $50 fine for any club allowing players to take sleeper cars or stay in high priced hotels.[60]

The salary caps would remain in the Texas League for many years, but cheating on them was equally institutionalized. Eventually some players would complain openly to the sporting press that they were not receiving "$100 a month not called for in his contract, as is often done" in such cases.[61]

The year 1892 would be the first time that the Texas League played a split season, though it didn't go off exactly as planned. Starting as a four-team circuit on May 7, the Dallas and Ft. Worth entries dropped out two months later. After a two week lull, Waco and San Antonio took over the spots, and a new season started. The entire affair ended a month shy of the initial plans, and no playoff between the first and second half winners was needed.[62]

By any measure, the Bayou City nine soared to their second official pennant with a 65-31 record that included eight successive games with Galveston while the league retooled. None of the other five teams who took part in either half season was able to post a winning record.[63]

The highlight of the Mud Cats' year was a 21 game winning streak early in the season, as other clubs were still getting their footing. Local papers rejoiced in the feat, which they said had only been surpassed by the legendary 1869 Cincinnati Red Stockings.[64]

Much of the league's futility is understandable. Unlike Houston which welcomed some old pros like Mike Shea back to the fold, other clubs in the loop had to rely on amateurs on occasion. When Dallas opened the season at Ft. Worth, neither club had all of their regulars in town yet.[65]

Many lineups looked like revolving doors. Probably owing to the low salaries and mid-season uncertainty, the list of players who saw time with Houston that year is especially long, numbering as many as 43 players. It is an amazing tally considering the rosters were supposed to be limited to 11 players at a time. Statistically there were several stars on the Houston roster, but it is difficult to know how much the numbers were reflective of league upheaval and inferior competition.

Harrison Peppers, one of three Mud Cats who would see time with the National League Louisville Colonels in 1894, posted 21 wins for Houston against only four defeats. Dudley Payne, in his only year of professional pitching, added 17. He also got six wins for Galveston that year.

Another soon to be Colonel, outfielder Ollie Smith, led the tiny Texas league in every major offensive category. Smith tallied 139 hits in the short season for a .355 average. He scored 136 runs, and just for good measure, led the league in homers with six.[66]

Another Ollie, this one named Pickering, was the subject of one of the most colorful tales in baseball history and one that would forever cement the fame of the Texas League. The story was told by *Houston Post* writer, Harry Johnston.

One day a young "fellow named Pickering," Johnston wrote, "floated into town in a box car and so impressed the manager of the Houston team that he took the new arrival down town, got him a hair cut, shave and a suit of clothes and put him in the game that afternoon."

The writer claimed that Pickering, who would later compile eight seasons in the majors, got seven hits in seven at bats that first day, all blooped between the

Telegraphing the Pitches

Radio didn't carry a baseball game until 1921, and there wouldn't be a televised game until almost two decades later. That did not mean that fans in the early part of the century didn't want play-by-play, however. The task fell to telegraph operators, the same gentlemen who had been disseminating accounts of major baseball games to newspapers around the nation.

As big league teams gained a national following, the public wanted more. They got it through a variety of cutting edge mechanical contraptions, with the earliest patent coming in 1888. Newspaper buildings, including the *Houston Chronicle*, were already equipped to receive up-to-the-minute reports over the telegraph wires, so many added display boards to their facades. The boards, with either hand-placed numbers or lights, reported pitch-by-pitch updates and drew crowds in the thousands for the biggest games. The *Chronicle*'s board was also used for prize fights, and was once the scene of altercations between African-American fans of heavyweight Jack Johnson and white fans of his opponent.

As time went on, theaters offered seats to watch the posted results at a price. Enterprising inventors fashioned lavish displays with giant arrays of colored lights and small movable pegs or cut outs of batters and base runners. Some early versions even dressed boys in baseball uniforms and had them run around the stage in front of a painted ballpark backdrop to represent the action. The paying crowds found it all quite exciting and often booed and cheered just as they would at a live contest, with some fans preferring the instant surprises offered by the recreations. New York sportswriter Heywood Broun wrote of overhearing two newsboys attending a World Series game in person at the Polo Grounds remarking, "Gee, what would you give to be at Times Square right now?"

infielders and outfielders. According to more than one version, that was the origin of the baseball idiom Texas Leaguer.[67]

Pickering did indeed arrive in Houston in 1892, staying for parts of two seasons, though the method of his arrival is not further documented. According to the official records of the Texas League, Ollie Pickering does indeed still hold the record for most singles in one game with seven on May 21, 1892.[68] No description of the hits could be found, but he struggled at catcher that day, yielding four passed balls and two errors. Pickering also had a reappearance in Houston in 1896, though not for long since that was the season he made his debut in the show with Louisville.[69]

As if that is not eventful enough, this was also the year of the first night game in the history of Texas or southern baseball. It took place at the park at Travis and McGowen. Houston had gotten electricity more than a dozen years before, and when the between-the-halves series with Galveston had ended, John McCloskey cooked up a plan to follow the lead of several other cities around the nation and try an exhibition under the lights.

The momentous evening came on July 22, 1892. For three days previous, workers had been installing nine arc lights on poles at "different parts of the field" to make the diamond as bright as daytime.[70] Herb's Light Guard Band, one of the top musical acts in town, was hired, and numerous other entertainments were planned for the circus-like event.

About a thousand people bought tickets for the extravaganza. They were treated to multiple foot races between well-matched players from each team, including a 50-yard dash by the two beefiest of the lot, first baseman Charley Isaacson of Galveston and Houston's catcher, Tub Welch. There was a goat race, a potato race, a watermelon eating contest in which James H. Bostick consumed his entire melon in 28 seconds, and of course, a brief baseball game.

The Sand Crabs wore their normal uniforms, but the Mud Cats were attired in the widest variety of garb. There were ball players clad as clowns, vaudevillians and jockeys. Manager McCloskey was dressed as the Uncle Sam-like cartoon character Brother Jonathan, and utility man Neil Donahue was decked out as Annie Rooney, a character from a popular song, complete with a dress and blond wig, which didn't slow him down in a 100-yard race. Deemed a success, the whole affair was repeated in Galveston later in the year.[71]

Unfortunately, the league found itself literally back in the dark the next season as financial instability threatened to kill the enterprise permanently. It would be two years before another collection of baseball loving businessmen would get together to reform the Texas League.

In the absence of a pro team, amateur clubs proliferated in Houston. Almost every business in town sponsored a ball club. Prominent among them were the breweries. The American Brewery, a gigantic enterprise that St. Louis' Adolphus Busch opened on the north side of the bayou, fielded one of the top teams in town. Over the next few years, this team frequently tangled with the Christian Moerleins, a Cincinnati-based brewer who operated a large branch in Galveston.

In addition to baseball, revivals and tent shows, including one particularly popular show from Japan, often rented the ballpark grounds.

The Texas League's second comeback in seven years unfolded with the resumption of league play in 1895. The plans were grand, if not contentious and confused. Eight teams were recruited, including a reach across the border for Shreveport and New Orleans. To accommodate the Louisiana clubs, the name Texas-Southern League was selected.

From the first meeting there was trouble. Galveston objected to the idea of traveling out of state. New Orleans dropped out while Shreveport stayed. Trouble in Waco led to it being replaced by Austin.

Ted Sullivan had agreed to manage the Houston club, now dubbed the Magnolias, but just prior to Opening Day, he suddenly accepted an offer to take the same job in Dallas. Bayou City fans were outraged. Billy Hepworth, who controlled the lease on the ballpark, stepped in to temporarily fill the position in spite of having to spend time away from his primary business as owner of the Jewel Saloon on Market Square. He had managed one of the city's top semi-pro teams during 1894 when there had been no league.[72]

There were at least a few good ball players on the Houston club. Harry Steinfeldt, who would later become a trivia answer as the infield partner to Tinker, Evers and Chance, played short for the locals. Ollie Pickering, on the eve of almost a decade in the bigs, roamed centerfield and even managed part of the season.

Scores and batting averages ran abnormally high including the still-intact league record .444 average posted by Austin's Algie McBride. Still, Houston fans and writers thought the team was Jonahed.[73]

Houston's club had been bad in the first half, and it turned pitiful in the second, winning only 5 of the 35 games it played. In what may be a unique, or certainly rare, move in baseball annals, they made an umpire their manager. W. G. "Jack" Garson took over the club on the same day that he'd officiated one of their games against Galveston.[74]

The Magnolias were not alone in their desperation. Most Austin players had gone on strike for a game in July just to get their back pay.[75] On August 6, 1895, Austin, Houston and San Antonio all disbanded citing failed financial situations. The league met, and Shreveport, never popular in some quarters to begin with, was dropped.

Adding insult to Houston's injury, the semi-pro team from the American Brewery challenged the city's professionals and beat them 8-1 behind the pitching of Albert Roper whose later career would be that of a machinist with the fire department.[76]

The remaining four Texas-Southern League clubs continued in spite of what was very much an unbalanced

For the Chicago Cubs, he was the infielder excluded from the famous "Tinker to Evers to Chance" refrain, but Harry Steinfeldt was a top player for the Houston Buffs.

National Baseball Hall of Fame Library, Cooperstown, NY

geographical situation. They called it a season on September 2, two weeks shy of the mark. Dallas and Ft. Worth had each won a half of the season, and a 15 game playoff was arranged for the championship. With Ft. Worth leading 7 games to 6, and with the next contest slated for Cowtown, Ted Sullivan, the Dallas manager and Houston pariah, backed out. Both teams and their rooters claimed the title throughout the next few months. It was ultimately given to Ft. Worth at the January league meeting.[77]

No matter what chaos was thrown at them, some Texas baseball men continued to deem it possible to make a few bucks off the game. Jack Garson launched an interesting scheme for the post-season. He proposed bringing the entire Sherman team south to play 30 games against Galveston and be "in all respects be a Houston club ... and the lost laurels of Houston regained." When pencil met paper, however, the idea was scrapped.[78]

In spite of a humiliating 1895, good things were brewing for the city's baseball community. In fact, it was such a hopeful atmosphere that two different factions angled to own the Houston league entry for 1896. Billy Hepworth wanted another opportunity, but he was beaten out by a collection of the city's top businessmen.[79]

The new Houston Baseball Association was walking on untrodden ground. Nine men with a common interest in the game had formed a corporation, duly registered with the Texas Secretary of State on January 3, 1896. Timber and lumber magnate John Henry Kirby headed a group of directors who stepped up to the plate with capital of $3,000 for another run at the reorganized Texas-Southern League.[80]

Also listed prominently among the team's backers was Rienzi M. Johnston, the publisher of the *Post* and eventual U.S. Senator for a month. Former league president Si Packard was a stockholder along with John Trentem, the sportswriter who was still acting as official scorer.

The director who was most notable for his long term, hands-on team leadership was Sam Taub who would be associated with the business side of the operation for several seasons. At the time he became a director, he was a nineteen-year-old, Hungarian-born merchant in the tobacco and cigar business with his father. In later years, Taub would become a director of Jesse Jones' National Bank of Commerce and Gus Wortham's American General Insurance Company; and, like his younger brother, Ben, Sam Taub would be a Houston philanthropist.[81]

New grandstands were constructed at Travis and McGowen, the old park which had evidently fallen deeply into disrepair. It was a substantial undertaking and included a portion that was double decked.[82]

Also new for 1896 was the team's nickname. They had suffered through 1895 as the Houston Magnolias. They would return in the new year bearing the name that would become their iconic minor league identity, the Houston Buffaloes.

Winning teams are always the ones remembered most fondly, and the 1896 Buffaloes were no exception. Harry Johnston described them as "the most popular team which ever represented Houston."[83] The well-liked Jack Garson stayed on as manager.

Flush with new money and energy, the '96 Buffs were loaded on the field, as well. Henry Cote, heralded as a catcher extraordinaire, was returning to the minors after spending most of two seasons with National League Louisville. John Roach, a pitcher who had enjoyed a cup of coffee with the New York Giants almost a decade prior, was brought in as the mound ace.

It was trumpeted that Harry Steinfeldt was back on board, but there was a small glitch. He had somehow managed to sign contracts with both Houston and Ft. Worth, the team he had joined after

John Henry Kirby is most notable in Texas as a lumber magnate who owned more timber land than anyone else in Texas. For a brief time, he was also the chief financial backer of the Houston baseball club.

Houston Metropolitan Research Center, Houston Public Library

COTE, PORTSMOUTH

Henry Cote was already 33 years old when he played in Houston. He would continue hopping around the minor leagues until his late forties.

Courtesy Library of Congress

the Magnolias had folded the year before. Sam Taub swore in the press that the infielder would either be in a Buffaloes uniform or be suspended since Taub was holding a receipt for advance money that Steinfeldt had already collected.

The decision on which signature would be honored came down to league president John L. Ward of Ft. Worth. Not surprisingly, his pick of his own team prompted loud and fruitless howls from South Texas.

If Steinfeldt had been awarded to Houston, it would have given the Buffs three of the eight starting position players who would comprise the talented Chicago Cubs teams of the early twentieth century. The other two were a couple of phenoms: 20-year-old Johnny Kling and 22-year-old outfielder Jimmy Slagle.

Kling, usually referred to in the box scores as Kline for his few months on the team, was the one who would gain the greater fame in Chicago, but it was Slagle who shined brightest for Houston in 1896.

Kling, who would become famous as a catcher, mostly played shortstop and had a few turns at pitcher with the Buffs. He was doing some catching while Cote was injured, earning him respect as "the best all around player" in Houston, when he inexplicably "packed his little grip… and silently left the city."[84] He surfaced at Chanute in the Kansas State League, close to his hometown.[85]

Outfielder Slagle, who would earn the nickname "Rabbit," garnered ample notice for making hard-running catches and pounding out 216 hits over the course of the season. He also scored 171 runs and stole 86 bases, a terrific number that was matched exactly by his teammate, first baseman Charles "Jugger" Shaffer.[86]

Even if he was not the best player on the Buffaloes, Shaffer was plenty talented and outspoken enough to be the team's lightning rod. A verbal altercation at Sherman got him arrested in the middle of the game. To hear Jack Garson's side of the story, Jugger was coaching first and trying his best to ignore some vicious hecklers when a foul ball was returned to the field at high velocity and aimed at Shaffer's head. Men and boys from the grandstand climbed onto the field and surrounded Shaffer with violence ensuing and a knife being flashed.

It was certainly in Shaffer's nature to rile opposing fans and players. He was described as "quite a comedian on the lines. Always funny—never tough or vulgar." But it was said that his commentary had made at least two players at St. Joseph, Missouri want to fight him while he played with Peoria in 1894, and the "people in the grandstand threw cushions at him to chase him off the lines."[87]

Manager Ryan of Sherman told the sportswriters that the foul ball had been returned harmlessly by the vendor at a lemonade stand along the foul line, and that it was Houston's Shaffer who had called an imagined culprit a "son of a bitch." It was at that point that he was mobbed by outraged husbands. Houston played the game under protest and received police protection the following day.[88]

By the end of June, team captain and speed demon Charles Shaffer had taken over as manager of the ball club. The catalyst was a baseball staple, the long losing streak. After dominating at home, the Buffs were swept at Austin and then had major trouble against the tough Panthers at Ft. Worth, and "Manager Garson's head was demanded and taken in forfeit."[89]

The more bizarre change at the helm took place in Galveston where the performance and attendance had both been flagging. Manager Billy Work refused to pay the guarantee to the visiting Dallas team and started circulating rumors that he wanted to sell the island ball club. The largest problem with that scenario was that he didn't own the team. Two longtime boosters of pro baseball on the island, men whose names were actually on the ball club, came to the rescue. Alex Easton made good on the visitors' portion of the gate receipts and future league president George Dermody took over as field boss of the Sand Crabs.[90]

Not to be outdone by the neighbor on the coast, the Buffs struck up another managerial controversy of its own. John McCloskey had been dismissed by the Louisville Colonels in early May,[91] and he turned to his old haunt of Houston for another job. The Buffs players went so far as to write "Honest John" saying they didn't want him, and that if he returned it would be against their wishes. Spurned, McCloskey went instead to Dallas to try to prevent them from quitting the league. In the end, he briefly returned to the Buffs as a player[92]

After a quirky three-part league schedule in which only the four southern teams crossed the finish line, it fell to Houston and Galveston to play for the championship. The original proposal of a 30 game playoff series was dropped for the more sane number of seven. The Buffaloes took the first five with Galveston winning the final two to avoid a skunking.[93]

John Henry Kirby didn't remain in the foreground for long. Once he had helped save the day financially, he stepped away from baseball. By the league meetings of 1897, it was Rienzi Johnston who represented his city's interests.

Charles Shaffer and George Reed were back, and each would have turns as player-manager during the season. Also returning was star catcher Henry Cote and outfielder Charlie Becker. Robert Pender, who had done a turn in Houston way back in 1887, was brought in, and the pitching staff featured ex-big leaguers George Stultz and Billy Crowell.[94] In spite of management's efforts, the team never captured the spark of the 1896 Buffaloes.

For its part, the Houston public started the year as in love with the national game as ever. It seemed the fans just couldn't get enough baseball. Like many years before and since, the months of March and April were filled with great hope and interest. By 1897, the papers were carrying stories and box scores of all the Texas League games, not just the ones involving the local team.

One notable game during the year was played on June 6 when Galveston visited the Houston ball park. An enormous crowd was on hand: 3300 fans, over 1000 of them up from Galveston, filled the grandstand and bleachers, stood along the foul lines and peered over the fences. Houston's management had Police Chief Heim and Deputy O'Leary on hand with a squad of men to keep the crowd off the diamond.

Adding to the festivities was King Wilhelm, the rooter-in-chief for the Sand Crabs. He was personally accompanied to town by a royal party of 160, many wearing red ribbons and badges sporting his picture, who marched from the train to the Capitol Hotel where they adjourned for lunch before the ball game. The game itself ended in a 4-4 tie, called due to darkness, but a good time seemed to have been had by all. One indication that it was perhaps too much fun is that the Houston ownership banned tin horns from being brought into the park starting the next day.[95]

As convoluted as many of the nineteenth century Texas League seasons were, some of the occurrences in 1897 might well have taken the cake. An eight team circuit was created with owners turning down applications from Shreveport and New Orleans due to concerns about travel. Sherman and Denison were admitted as a twin-city concept.

The San Antonio Bronchos won the first half with Houston as their closest pursuer. It went quickly downhill from there. Two weeks into the second half, the dual-city entry disbanded, "as usual without advance notice." John McCloskey, who was managing at Dallas, arranged for a Waco businessman to take over the team through a series of long distance phone calls. The one concession was that since Sunday baseball was illegal in Waco, those games would be played in Hillsboro or Corsicana. It was working well until their manager jumped ship, taking four other starters with him.[96]

Johnny Kling would soon become one of the top catchers in baseball, but in Houston, he was a young man who was homesick enough to leave the team entirely.

National Baseball Hall of Fame Library, Cooperstown, NY

Austin quit the first week of August, and San Antonio was dropped from the league, over the loud protests of its ownership, in order to even things out. The league then upgraded Houston from second place to winner of the first half. The Buffs, however, were behind on paying player salaries, so the running of the club was handed over to the players, with George Reed moving from field manager to executive, and Charlie Shaffer resuming managerial duties. The arrangement lasted for less than a week, until a Houston game netted only $20 at the gate. Their season was now over, too.

That left Galveston in first place, but with no other South Texas team to play. John L. Ward of Ft. Worth and McCloskey at Dallas promptly announced their clubs would play for the league title, that in spite of the fact that they had finished the first half in sixth and seventh place respectively. In the fall, it was decided that San Antonio and Galveston would be crowned co-champions in the record books. It was the first time any of the Texas League clubs played all the way until the scheduled finish.[97]

In 1898, things for the league went from bad to worse, but this time it was primarily because of political events. The six team circuit began play on April 9. Two days later, President McKinley wrote to Congress asking that war be declared against Spain. At first, the teams attempted to continue playing baseball amid the national upheaval and obsession with the fighting.

Ft. Worth dropped out on the first of May. Once again, in an attempt to level the games and expenses, the league shut down another team. This time it was John McCloskey's Dallas club. "Honest John" squawked, but the previous year's precedent, which he had supported, won out. The four southernmost teams soldiered on with ball playing, but it was a losing fight when competing with real battles in the news. On May 16, as Teddy Roosevelt arrived in San Antonio to begin training with the Rough Riders, the remaining ball clubs shut down.[98]

The team president for the year had been *Houston Herald* editor W.H. Bailey, yet another of the nine directors from the incorporated Houston Baseball Association. Bailey brought upgrades to the park in the form of a new fence and shifting the grounds slightly closer to Main Street. The uniforms in that era changed almost annually, but the ones ordered for 1898 showed that there was already an established look for the ball club. They were "navy blue with black stockings and grey cap. The Buffaloes would hardly look natural in anything but blue, and president Bailey has stuck to the color."[99]

When the aborted campaign came to a close, the Buffaloes were sitting at .500. In spite of the winter prognostications, George Reed's team was not one that held promise of greatness.[100] The leading hitter on the team was first sacker Bill Kemmer, one of the players who had been briefly blacklisted for jumping off the Waco team the year before. The only other Buff with major league experience

Diminutive outfielder Jimmy Slagle was one of the most popular players in town during his time in Houston.

National Baseball Hall of Fame Library, Cooperstown, NY

was George Keefe, a left-handed hurler who had amassed a losing record over seven big league seasons, the last of which was in 1891.[101]

Keefe would be back in Houston for 1899 along with five other players who had or would see action in the bigs. With the North Texas teams unable to get it together, the league consisted of only Austin, San Antonio, Houston and Galveston, the latter of which overtook Austin and moved to the head of the four-team pack.

Meanwhile the Southern Association was enduring an equally small field with Dallas taking over the place of Montgomery, Alabama.[102] After talk of combining the two went nowhere, the teams to the east folded. Sand Crabs executive George Dermody wired Jack Huston, the manager of the league leading Mobile Blackbirds, and talked him into bringing his whole club to Houston to literally become the Buffaloes.

Huston accepted. Keeping only a handful of the team with which Billy Crowell had been toiling, the Mobile squad did indeed improve the baseball fortunes in the Bayou City. It meant the return of old faces like Frank Weikart and Joe Dowie and new ones like Brownie Chamberlain.

Sam McMackin, who had gone 7-8 with the Montgomery/Dallas team also came to Houston where he would put up a 6 and 5 record. McMackin would later have a cup of coffee with the White Sox and Tigers in the young American League.[103]

The best numbers on the Buffaloes for 1899, though, belonged to the 21-year-old Galveston native Jim Murray. Before moving to San Antonio when the Mobile contingent arrived, Murray had put up 12 doubles, 6 triples and 4 home runs, all good enough to lead the team.[104]

Once again the season would be cut shorter than planned due to widespread financial difficulty. A June attempt to generate more interest by splitting the season didn't work, and things shut down immediately after the Fourth of July holiday with Galveston winning the second half just as it had won the first. Houston did manage to improve from last place to second after the break.

So dominant were the Sand Crabs that the *Galveston Tribune* even saw fit to do a little taunting of its close neighbor to the north. "Our fellows are not even getting good practice," the paper whined after a thrashing of the Buffs.

Regrettably, the *Post*'s best counter was "There's no chivalry in kicking a fellow when he's down."[105]

Some of the saddest local baseball news in 1899 was the death of Bob Adair, a man who had supported the sport in Houston for 25 years. Only a few days shy of his 45th birthday, Adair had been battling "galloping consumption," more modernly known as acute tuberculosis, for some time. Among his pallbearers were two of his old teammates with the Lees: L. J. Tuffly and Gus Fredericks.[106]

A good measure of the turbulence of Texas League baseball in the nineteenth century would transfer over to the twentieth. The continued pounding of heads against the wall of profitability had taken its toll. So much so that the entire notion of a professional league in the state would be pushed into the background in 1900. Once again, semi-pro and amateur ball would rule the roost in Houston.

There was still the occasional contest to preserve the honor of the city, however. In mid-August, 1900, a game between Houston firemen and the Beaumont team was hyped but ultimately cancelled due to rain.[107] Former league umpire Ed Clark, back from Army service in both Cuba and the Philippines, arranged for contests between the top amateurs of Houston and Galveston.[108]

By the late summer, the attention of

sports fans was squarely focused on the two other pastimes that had inspired Houstonians for decades. Newspapers in the weeks prior to the Great Storm of 1900 had a great deal of news about the long run-up to boxing matches between Gentleman Jim Corbett and Kid McCoy and between Bob Fitzsimmons and the tattooed Sailor Tom Sharkey.[109] The papers religiously covered horse racing around the country just as they had for years, publishing results from Saratoga, Hawthorne, St. Louis and Brighton Beach. Baseball news consisted of the standings and occasional notes from the distant National and American Leagues.

Through much of 1900, several of the state's baseball men were talking up a vibrant eight-team circuit for 1901. Galveston's George Dermody even dropped into other cities to keep the fires stoked, but in the end, Texas would endure a second consecutive dark season.[110]

It was not from a total lack of interest. Meetings took place early in the year, and representatives from six cities met and announced that there would be a state league beginning on May 3. Houston's man was Charles W. Eisenfelder who was actually a German-born furniture merchant from Galveston.[111] Two days later, Galveston was being talked up for an entry into the league which was already down to just four confirmed teams and three maybes.[112]

In the end, it played out like most other so-called dark years. Houston would have a team to carry the city's banner on a per game basis, but they were a mostly amateur bunch left to fend for themselves.

One series with Waco was informative of the situation. Following the first of three contracted games, the home club's management not only insisted that all expenses be deducted solely from the losing team's 40% share of receipts, they refused to provide an accounting of the expenses. They also wanted Houston to wait till all the games were played before handing over a dime. Smelling a rat, and unwilling to accept such last minute revisions to their agreement, manager Jack P. Arto loaded his players back on the train and headed for the Bayou City with his squad out all their costs.[113]

As early as November of 1901, ten Texas cities were already meeting to plan a league revival for the following spring. For the first time, there were feelers about El Paso being part of the circuit, a surprising fact since the consensus has always been that Shreveport was too far.[114] Ted "High Class" Sullivan, the Irish-born baseball scout and promoter who would run the Ft. Worth entry, made an exploratory trip to the southern cities and concluded that the "section is not prepared to go into the Texas league on account of the big mileage due to the crippled condition of Austin and Galveston."[115]

Sullivan's pronouncement proved to be correct, as the Texas League's return in 1902 would find Houston and the other southern clubs still sitting out. The six teams that did form in the north part of the state included two of the strangest

Bill Abstein was only twenty-one and on his way up the ladder to the Majors when he played in Houston.
Courtesy Library of Congress

team nicknames in league history. In early May the Sherman-Denison Students moved east and became the Texarkana Casket Makers.

The team from Paris, Texas, owned by the same Galvestonian who had attempted to back a Houston entry a year previously, played the second half under the moniker of Eisenfelder's Homeseekers after he tried to move his team to Houston. Not drawing in Paris and not allowed to relocate, they played primarily on the road.[116]

After a three-year gap in which the city was off of the professional baseball ledger, the South Texas League opened for business in 1903. Though there would be more ups and downs to come, Houston would field a real team from here on out, with the exception of the heart of World War II when the Texas League shut down altogether.

The men who brought the league back together were a mixture of old names and new. C.W. Eisenfelder took the lead in promoting the enterprise and also owned the Galveston club. His baseball involvement at home would be short lived, however. In June, he sold out to Marsene Johnson.

The Houston franchise was owned and operated by Claud Rielly, the 29-year-old son of an English carpenter and a Louisiana-born mother who had operated the Casino roller rink in Houston in the 1880s. Claud's father, James E Rielly, had previously been manager of the city's top notch Pillot's Opera House and was the man who had booked a group of female baseballists at the Fair Grounds in 1885. The family lived at the corner of Brazos and Walker on a lot that would one day be taken by the city hall complex.[117]

Rielly and his younger brother, Armand, had both been working as Houston firefighters just a few years before. The younger Rielly stuck with the career, as the driver of a fire wagon for several more years.[118]

Joe Dowie, a New Orleanian whose career high point was a partial season

Canadian-born Jay Clarke would come to the Buffaloes in 1915, but as a teenager in 1902, he is said to have hit eight home runs in eight times at bat.

Private Collection

with the Baltimore Orioles in 1889, came in to play and manage. At age 37, he was a true baseball veteran. Also making his Houston debut was pitcher-outfielder Bob Edmondson who would stick around the Buffs for the next five years.

Unlike most previous teams, the Buffs roster contained several native Texans whose careers would largely revolve around their home-state league. They included leading hitter Sam Leslie, pitcher Bill Sorrells and Beaumont native Ivy Tevis, who would one day pitch and lose a no-hitter for Galveston.[119] Gerald Hayes would move from San Antonio to manage for Houston late in the year.[120]

Beaumont's Ivy Tevis enjoyed stellar seasons pitching in Houston before returning to his home town and a long career in public works and local law enforcement.

Tyrrell Historical Library, Beaumont, TX

The Buffaloes finished the 1903 season ranked third of the four teams, seven games below the break even mark. In the post season series, San Antonio defeated Galveston handily under the field guidance of Wade Moore with the highlight being a no-hitter thrown by Eddie Taylor in game six.[121]

The dysfunctional season of 1904 was filled with small crowds, mixed signals and major uncertainty about a home field for the Houston entry in the South Texas League. The Houston club had actually started the year well enough, winning the first half of the season in a squeaker over Galveston thanks to a favorable league ruling regarding player eligibility. Bill Sorrells was on his way to a 24-23 record and an eye-popping 332 strikeouts. In spite of that, attendance was lacking.

Wade Moore, San Antonio's manager and part owner, sold his interest in the Alamo City and came to Houston as a player in May. Shortly after he arrived, Moore attempted to jump to Beaumont for more money, but the league and the National Board both voted to make him stay and honor his contract with the Rielly. He took it well, serving as the team's catcher for the season and two more after that.[122]

The root of the team's problems was the sale of the six block parcel of land at Travis and McGowen that had been home to Houston professional baseball for decades. The new land owner, Otto Witte, agreed to let the team use the ball yard through the end of September, but by July 1st, the deal was off, and Rielly was readying new digs.[123]

The team prepared a field and grandstands at the Harrisburg Road Track, a horse racing facility that sat at what is today the northwest quadrant of Harrisburg and Milby.[124] With the midseason change of venue, however, crowds dropped from intimate to miserable, bringing in only 52 dollars in gate receipts at the first game there.[125] The primary issue was that the streetcars stopped well short, either several blocks west or northwest of the horse track. The baseball team briefly tried to fill the gap by having patrons transfer to smaller horse drawn carts, but in a city that was reliant on public transportation, it was a death knell.[126]

As owner/manager Rielly continued to pay rent for the horse track, his rhetoric in the press became unpredictable at best. One day he was praising the ambrosial ease of transportation to the park, then vowing that Houston would go without baseball the next. In spite of his sporadically cheery pronouncements, it was abundantly clear that a new park would be needed in 1905.

The situation got so dire in the last half of the season, that the *Post* quit referring to the team as Houston at all, listing them instead as "Rielly's Team"[127] alongside Galveston, Beaumont and San Antonio.

By the start of August, that newspaper's scribes were calling the squad that had been known as the Lambs for the first two months of 1904 by names like Ramblers, Travelers or Wanderers.[128] In spite of what some Texas League histories might infer, none of these nicknames were ever remotely official. Rielly twice threatened in the press to play the remainder of the season on the road. Perhaps it was symbolic when a swarm of bees passed across the field during a game causing the Houston team to lie down until the danger was over.[129]

As for the South Texas League season of 1904 as a whole, interest was so low by late August that the four clubs kept moving the announced end of the season closer to the start of September. Finally the consensus was to simply cancel the last few games on the schedule with a mere three days notice to the state's press. In Galveston's case, their manager, Marsene Johnson, hosted his players and those of visiting San Antonio at his beach house for swimming, fishing, an oyster roast and a fish fry in lieu of playing the final game.[130]

A post season series to win medals donated by Mistrot's Department Stores was held between Houston and Galveston, but even that didn't go well. With one squad being largely homeless, the usual home and home series was out of the question, so all the games were played in Galveston. Defying the odds in those days before lighted ball parks, three of the first five contests ended in a tie. The official scorer even quit after the Sand Crabs manager jumped on him for not allowing a run to score on a double play which retired the side.[131]

With Galveston leading the championship 4 games to 3, but with the teams "playing to empty benches" at the park, Claud Rielly forfeited the final two contests to end the 1904 postseason with a whimper.[132]

Tail firmly tucked between their legs, the team took a late train to Houston "where they will be paid off in the morning and scatter to their destinations." Four of the Buffaloes would travel together to enjoy the World's Fair at St. Louis.[133]

The new park would indeed arrive in 1905, and with it a new, more stable era for Houston baseball. Like most things related to the city's baseball team during that period, however, it didn't come easily.

1 O'Neal, Bill. The Southern League. (Eakin Press, 1994)
2 O'Neal, Bill. The Pacific Coast league (Eakin Press, 1990)
3 HP 5 June 1888
4 Wetterau, Bruce. The New York Public Library Book of Chronologies. (prentice Hall, 1990)
5 GDN 14 November 1887
6 HP 15 November 1887
7 Ft. Worth Daily Gazette 15 November 1887
8 Ft. Worth Daily Gazette 1 November 1887; Ft. Worth Daily Gazette 2 November 1887
9 http://www.baseball-reference.com
10 Ruggles, William B.. The History of the Texas League. (Texas Baseball League, 1951)
11 Ft. Worth Daily Gazette 16 November 1887
12 Ft. Worth Daily Gazette 16 November 1887; Ft. Worth Daily Gazette 18 November 1887
13 Ruggles, William B. The History of the Texas League. (Texas Baseball League, 1951)
14 HP 25 November 1887
15 Kirkland, Kate Sayen. Captain James A Baker of Houston, 1857-1941. (Texas A&M Press, 2012)
16 Maxwell, Robert S.. Whistle in the Piney Woods: Paul Bremond and the Houston East and West Texas Railway. (East Texas Historical Association , 1963); Kirkland, Kate Sayen. The Hogg Family and Houston: Philanthropy and the Civic Ideal. (University of Texas Press, 2009)
17 Young, Dr. Samuel O.. A Thumbnail History of the City of Houston, Texas: From its Founding in 1836 to the Year 1912. (Rein & Sons, 1912); Handbook of Texas Online.
18 HP 19 January 1888
19 HP 19 January 1888
20 United States Census, Harris County, Texas, 1880; Houston City Directories; Harris County Archives; Ruggles, William B.. The History of the Texas League of Professional Baseball Clubs 1888-1951. (Texas Baseball League, 1951)
21 HP 14 August 1899
22 Ruggles, William B.. The History of the Texas League of Professional Baseball Clubs 1888-1951. (Texas Baseball League, 1951)
23 HP 19 January 1888
24 Railroad Commission of Texas. Rail Division Reports. Reports Sent to the Comptroller. Texas State Archives and Library.
25 http://www.baseball-reference.com
26 United States Census, Montgomery County, Alabama, 1910
27 http://www.baseball-reference.com; Grand Catalogue of Phi Kappa Psi Fraternity, Gamma Chapter of Ohio, 1910; Grand Catalogue of Phi Kappa Psi Fraternity, Gamma Chapter of Ohio, 1922; St. Paul, Minnesota City Directory, 1886; Arkansas Baseball Encyclopedia http://www.arkbaseball.com; United States Census, Marshall County, Virginia, 1860; United States Census, Wayne County, Ohio, 1880;
28 Ruggles, William B.. The History of the Texas League of Professional Baseball Clubs 1888-1951. (Texas Baseball League, 1951); Encyclopedia of Minor League Baseball. Third Edition. (Baseball America, 2007); http://www.baseball-reference.com; HP 10 July 1904
29 HP 10 July 1904
30 HP 17 May 1888
31 HP 7 March 1888
32 GDN 11 April 1942
33 HP 24 February 1896
34 http://www.baseball-reference.com
35 GDN 2 April 1888
36 http://www.baseball-reference.com
37 HP 10 July 1904
38 Ruggles, William B.. The History of the Texas League of Professional Baseball Clubs 1888-1951. (Texas Baseball League, 1951)
39 Ruggles, William B.. The History of the Texas League of Professional Baseball Clubs 1888-1951. (Texas Baseball League, 1951)
40 Houston Architectural Survey. Southwest Center for Urban Research and the School of Architecture. (Rice University, 1980)
41 HP 10 July 1904
42 HP 10 July 1904; Encyclopedia of Minor League Baseball. Third Edition. (Baseball America, 2007)
43 http://www.baseball-reference.com; Sullivan, Ted. Humorous Stories From the Ball Field. (M.A. Donahue & Co., 1903)
44 HP 10 July 1904
45 Encyclopedia of Minor League Baseball. Third Edition. (Baseball America, 2007); Ruggles, William B.. The History of the Texas League of Professional Baseball Clubs 1888-1951. (Texas Baseball League, 1951)
46 Ruggles, William B.. The History of the Texas League of Professional Baseball Clubs 1888-1951. (Texas Baseball League, 1951)
47 Ruggles, William B.. The History of the Texas League of Professional Baseball Clubs 1888-1951. (Texas Baseball League, 1951)
48 http://www.baseball-reference.com
49 Ruggles, William B.. The History of the Texas League of Professional Baseball Clubs 1888-1951. (Texas Baseball League, 1951)
50 HP 14 May 1890
51 Encyclopedia of Minor League Baseball. Third Edition. (Baseball America, 2007)
52 Western League versus Western Association. SABR Minor League Newsletter. June 2002.
53 Somers, Dale A.. *The Rise of Sports in New Orleans.* (LSU Press, 1972)
54 HP 10 July 1904
55 HP 25 May 1891
56 HP 1 June 1891
57 GDN 8 April 1892
58 Sullivan, Ted. Humorous Stories from the Ball Field. (M.A. Donahue & Co., 1903)
59 HP 11 April 1892; Encyclopedia of Minor League Baseball. Third Edition. (Baseball America, 2007)
60 Ruggles, William B.. The History of the Texas League of Professional Baseball Clubs 1888-1951. (Texas Baseball League, 1951)
61 HP 22 April 1906
62 HP 12 April 1892;
63 Encyclopedia of Minor League Baseball. Third Edition. (Baseball America, 2007)
64 HP 7 July 1892
65 Ruggles, William B.. The History of the Texas League of Professional Baseball Clubs 1888-1951. (Texas Baseball League, 1951)

66 Encyclopedia of Minor League Baseball. Third Edition. (Baseball America, 2007)
67 Sporting Life, 21 April 1906; McComb, David. *Texas: A Modern History*. (University of Texas Press, 1989)
68 Official Records of the Texas League; Dallas Morning News 22 May 1892
69 http://www.baseball-reference.com
70 HP 19 July 1892
71 HP 23 July 1892
72 Ruggles, William B.. The History of the Texas League of Professional Baseball Clubs 1888-1951. (Texas Baseball League, 1951); Houston City Directories; GDN 11 June 1894
73 HP 12 June 1895; Encyclopedia of Minor League Baseball. Third Edition. (Baseball America, 2007)
74 HP 13 July 1895
75 HP 10 July 1895
76 HP 6 August 1895; HP 10 July 1904
77 Ruggles, William B.. The History of the Texas League of Professional Baseball Clubs 1888-1951. (Texas Baseball League, 1951)
78 HP 30 August 1895; HP 5 September 1895
79 Ruggles, William B.. The History of the Texas League of Professional Baseball Clubs 1888-1951. (Texas Baseball League, 1951)
80 Texas Secretary of State Corporate Filings
81 United States Census Harris Co, TX 1900; United States Census Harris Co, TX 1910; United States Census Harris Co, TX 1920; United States Census Harris Co, TX 1930; Texas Death Certificate; Dressman, Fran. Gus Wortham: Portrait of a Leader. (Texas A&M Press, 1994)
82 HP 10 July 1904
83 HP 10 July 1904
84 GDN 5 July 1896, GDN 24 July 1896; Sporting Life 15 August 1896
85 http://www.baseball-reference.com
86 Encyclopedia of Minor League Baseball. Third Edition. (Baseball America, 2007); http://www.baseball-reference.com
87 HP 22 Dec 1895
88 GDN 12 May 1896
89 GDN 22 June 1896
90 GDN 10 July 1896
91 GDN 5 May 1896
92 Sporting News 1 August 1896; Ruggles, William B.. The History of the Texas League of Professional Baseball Clubs 1888-1951. (Texas Baseball League, 1951); Sporting Life 15 August 1896
93 Ruggles, William B.. The History of the Texas League of Professional Baseball Clubs 1888-1951. (Texas Baseball League, 1951)
94 HP 17 May 1896; HP 24 May 1896; http://www.baseball-reference.com
95 HP 7 June 1897
96 Ruggles, William B.. The History of the Texas League of Professional Baseball Clubs 1888-1951. (Texas Baseball League, 1951)
97 Ruggles, William B.. The History of the Texas League of Professional Baseball Clubs 1888-1951. (Texas Baseball League, 1951); Encyclopedia of Minor League Baseball. Third Edition. (Baseball America, 2007)
98 Ruggles, William B.. The History of the Texas League of Professional Baseball Clubs 1888-1951. (Texas Baseball League, 1951); Encyclopedia of Minor League Baseball. Third Edition. (Baseball America, 2007): Texas Almanac (Texas State Historical Association, 2012)
99 HP 28 February 1898
100 HP 28 February 1898
101 http://www.baseball-reference.com
102 O'Neal, Bill. The Southern League. (Eakin press, 1994)
103 http://www.baseball-reference.com; Ruggles, William B.. The History of the Texas League of Professional Baseball Clubs 1888-1951. (Texas Baseball League, 1951); Encyclopedia of Minor League Baseball. Third Edition. (Baseball America, 2007)
104 http://www.baseball-reference.com
105 HP 18 May 1899
106 HP 14 August 1899
107 HP 16 August 1900
108 GDN 7 April 1900; San Antonio Light 22 April 1900
109 http://www.boxrec.com
110 San Antonio Light 22 April 1900
111 GDN 17 March 1901; United States Census 1900 Galveston County, TX; United States Census 1920 Galveston County, TX
112 Dallas Morning New 13 January 1901; GDN 19 March 1901
113 HP 30 June 1901
114 DDR 4 November 1901
115 San Antonio Light 5 February 1902
116 Encyclopedia of Minor League Baseball. Third Edition. (Baseball America, 2007); Ruggles, William B.. The History of the Texas League of Professional Baseball Clubs 1888-1951. (Texas Baseball League, 1951)
117 Gallegly, Joseph. Footlights on the Border: The Galveston and Houston Stage Before 1900. (Mouton & Co, 1962); Houston City Directory 1904
118 United States Census 1900 Harris County, TX; HP 26 April 1885; United States Census 1910 Harris County, TX
119 O'Neal, Bill. The Texas League: A Century of Baseball. (Eakin Press, 1987)
120 Encyclopedia of Minor League Baseball. Third Edition. (Baseball America, 2007)
121 Ruggles, William B.. The History of the Texas League of Professional Baseball Clubs 1888-1951. (Texas Baseball League, 1951)
122 HP 1 July 1904; http://www.baseball-reference.com; Ruggles, William B.. The History of the Texas League of Professional Baseball Clubs 1888-1951. (Texas Baseball League, 1951)
123 HP 1 July 1904; HP 1 August 1904
124 HP 3 July 1904
125 HP 1 August 1904
126 HP 1 August 1904
127 HP 5 August 1904
128 HP 13 August 1904; HP 22 August 1904; HP 29 August 1904
129 HP 20 July 1904; HP 21 July 1904; HP 4 August 1904; HP 21 August 1904
130 HP 2 September 1904
131 HP 9 September 1904
132 HP 12 September 1904
133 HP 12 September 1904

KEY

GDN – *Galveston Daily News*
HP – *Houston Post*
HC – *Houston Chronicle*
HI – *Houston Informer*
CD – *Chicago Defender*

TEXAS STATE HOTEL
HAVERTY

CHAPTER FIVE

WEST END PARK

BY MIKE VANCE

Coming off a 1904 season that easily ranks as the one of the barmiest in the city's history, all of Houston's baseball people understood that securing a new ball park took top priority. That urgency was certainly not evident on the pages of the city's press, however.

West End Park was no longer the home of the Buffaloes, but it was still the site of most high school football in Houston in this 1939 aerial photo.

Bob Bailey Collection, Dolph Briscoe Center for American History, University of Texas at Austin

Media was a far cry from the modern 24-hour news cycle, so progress reports on the search for a location were sparse at best. A brief article about upcoming winter meetings for the South Texas League, meetings that were postponed multiple times, mentioned that Claud Rielly had secured a new location for his park, but did not mention where.

On January 19, 1905, the *Houston Post* finally announced that the new Houston baseball park would "be located at the intersection of Heiner and Andrews streets.[1] The park will be 400 feet square and the San Felipe street car line will pass by the gates. The street car management has promised five minute service."[2]

Perhaps with a remembrance of the previous year's attendance troubles, the article pointed out that the park was six blocks closer to the center of downtown than the old park.

The property itself covered about four square blocks and was part of several acres belonging to the estate of farmer, and early Houston mayor, John

Day Andrews. Specifically, it was owned by Andrews' daughter, Mrs. Eugenia Flewellen of Waco. She and her husband would be the lease holders on the property for many years.[3]

The site was adjacent to a tract owned by the William Marsh Rice estate that was being considered for the new Rice Institute. The Rice land would quickly prove too small to hold the envisioned school. Most everything else around those parcels was established residential and commercial property in Fourth Ward on the southwestern edge of downtown.

The selection of the site might not have taken much imagination on Rielly's part, since baseball was not new to that spot. The year before, while the professionals were being dispossessed, the unpaved intersection of Andrews and Howe that would soon shade the left field corner was referred to as the Fourth Ward grounds, home to various amateur games.[4]

In late spring of 1904, the crack team representing Levy Brothers department store took on a club called the Owls and another known as the Gieske Brothers Stags, presumably sponsored by the large shoe store on Main. The *Post* noted the location of the field as being at the aforementioned corner "near Cash's Grocery on the San Felipe car line."

Like much associated with the South Texas League, construction of the new ball park appears to have been a bit improvised. The initial story in mid-January trumpeted that construction would begin in days, but it would be another month before work actually started.[5] It was cut short by a dispute over ownership of the ball club and a desire by the team's bankroller to seek another location. Construction halted in its infancy. The only work accomplished was lumber for the grandstand being cut into needed lengths.

A close up from the aerial photograph shows Antioch Baptist Church just past the left field fence of West End Park.

Bob Bailey Collection, Dolph Briscoe Center for American History, University of Texas at Austin

Luckily for Houston baseball aficionados, things worked themselves out.[6] Reports from mid-to-late February show that while Maurice Michael was the financial backer, Claud Rielly would continue as business manager and Wade Moore would be team captain, field manager and in charge of player personnel.[7]

When it was decided that Michael's alternate site choice was too small, the Andrews plot won out, and it fell to Rielly and Heights carpenter and construction man, Charles W. Raper, to whip a baseball park into shape.

Complicating matters was the fact that the St. Louis Cardinals had planned to hold their spring training in Houston, as they had the year prior, but as delays mounted, they began hedging their bets. An especially wet winter that included a notable four-and-a-half-inch rainfall in one day, turned the construction site into a mud hole.[8] The Cardinals decided to train in Marlin, Texas instead.[9] A preseason series between Houston and Waco was also cancelled.

Still, Houston's newspapers reported progress almost every day that was sunny enough to work.[10] Details about the black sandy loam that would be used to top the playing field and wrangling over benches versus chairs whetted the readers' appetites.[11][12] Scores of them visited the construction site daily, occasionally interfering with the workers.[13]

In February, a representative from the Spaulding Company came to town to sign a deal for the new uniforms that the local boys would be wearing during the inaugural season at their new park.[14] For the first time in club history, the Houston nine would boast different apparel at home than they wore on the road, just as the big leaguers had done for some time. The former would be white trimmed in blue, and the latter were gray trimmed in brown. To make things even more special, the leftover togs from 1904 would be used for practice.

As March 1905 wound to a close, so did ballpark construction. Choices had been made, and plans were becoming reality. The field was oriented with home plate in the northwest to catch the prevailing southerly breeze. Benches were used for most of the grandstand, save for the row of four-person boxes that lined the front and featured chairs. The grandstand was said to accommodate 3000 with another 1500 in the bleachers down the left field line. A segregated section for African-American fans was also available on the right field side. For a city whose total population had yet to reach 75,000, the park had ample seating.[15]

The streetcar company made improvements on the line to ensure that service was fast and regular. Rielly, Raper and crew built plank sidewalks from the car stops to the grounds and gravel walkways to the seats.

A commodious press box was placed into the angle of the grandstands behind the catcher.[16] As for the diamond itself, the right field fence was extended 50 feet to "give the right gardener ample territory to show his sprinting ability."

Game action finally came on April 2, when Baton Rouge of the Cotton States League arrived for a series. A good crowd braved threatening weather to attend the inaugural game, but the locals left disappointed, as the Cajuns prevailed by a score of 2 to 0. Moore's Marvels managed only one single against Baton Rouge's pitcher, Baker, and not until the eighth.[17]

The new ball park now needed a name, so the owners ran a contest to find one.[18] After two weeks and what they claimed were more than 1000 entries, the three-man committee unanimously agreed on West End Park. The award of a season ticket went to Mr. John T. Schulte, a teenager, and son of an immigrant merchant who lived on La Branch.[19]

Over the first few days of play, Houstonians settled in. Within two weeks the city's small boys had begun to cut holes in the fence.[20] In a nod to current events, the *Post* reported that "down

This World War I era photo at West End Park shows that clubhouse laundry service was not necessarily a daily perk for Texas Leaguers.

Houston Metropolitan Research Center, Houston Public Library

near center field it looks like a Russian battleship after an encounter with a Jap torpedo boat."

After exhibition series with teams such as Dallas[21] and Corsicana from North Texas, Houston opened the South Texas League season on the road, visiting all three other cities. In the team's absence the finishing touches were applied in anticipation of the official league opener, including a nice coat of green paint with white trim applied to the grandstand.[22]

Marvels won the home opener on May 8, besting the San Antonio Bronchos 2 to 0. Few empty seats were to be had, and the crowd was described as enthusiastic. For the record, game time was at 4:05, and Houston's mayor, Andrew L. Jackson cracked a few jokes as he welcomed the crowd before throwing out the first pitch.[23]

Praise for the new ball park was widespread.[24] Even San Antonio's manager, Bill Morrow, in a backhanded manner, joined the chorus. He allowed that when he first saw the location, it was the biggest mud hole in the city, but that team management deserved a great deal of credit for turning such a miserable place into a beautiful park, one of the nicest, neatest and most convenient in the South.

A telephone was installed at the yard right around opening day, an event notable enough to make the newspaper.[25] Another possible first for the park occurred when Jim Rielly had his watch stolen in the stands two weeks prior to the league opener. He later retrieved it from a pawn shop for the sum of two dollars.[26]

The first weekend of the season, management brought in Tony Castellane, a daredevil who had been performing

West End Park circa 1910, before a fire and a hurricane forced changes to the grandstands.

Story Sloane's Gallery

bicycle stunts at Highland Park, an amusement venue on White Oak Bayou. He was schedule to loop the loop at West End Park on Friday, Saturday and Sunday when crowds would top 3000 each day.[27] Though the stunts might have gone off without a hitch, on Thursday, Galveston's Mike Burns injured himself when he ran into the looping apparatus and had to leave the game.

As soon as the white South Texas League team left again for the road, the top African-American team in Houston moved into the park. Renting to the "colored team" was common practice for white team owners across the country at a time when inter-racial contests were hard to find anywhere in the 45 states. By mid-April, the Prairie View College team met a local black ball club at the new grounds.[28]

Though segregation in the former Confederate states was generally quite strict, and in practice the policy was separate but unequal, Houston baseball crowds did not consist of just a single race. When reporting on the number of patrons to witness the first official league game at West End Park, the sports page noted that "the colored bleachers were loaded to the guards."[29]

Likewise, when the Dillard Colts, billed as the champion black team of the city, hosted African-American teams from La Grange and Beaumont to start May 1905 at West End Park, nearly every article reminded readers that "a portion of the grandstand has been reserved for the white patrons."[30, 31] Such was the rule in Houston where fans often paid to see good baseball played by whatever team was in town.

In the early days of West End Park Houston ball cranks were not witnessing the long ball. Three full weeks after the first contest with Baton Rouge, city haberdashers were offering various items to the first player to make the horse hide leave the yard.

To say that the ample distance in right field made it tough to clear that fence in the heart of the dead ball era is quite the understatement. Houston's Fred "Newt" Hunter, not known as a slugger, did it first in the inaugural season. It would be four more years before the second ball left West End Park in right. Hobe Ferris of the St. Louis Browns accomplished the feat during spring training of 1909, and in July of the same year, Galveston's third sacker Bill Yohe pounded one out to right. A month later, Yohe made his big league debut with the Washington Senators.

From the early days, West End Park was a multi-sport venue. The YMCA hosted a statewide track and field meet there in 1909. There were events such as the wrestling match between Pat Brown and Cyclone Mitchell in 1915. High school football teams from both Houston and the Heights used the ballpark to host rivals from places like Bryan or Beaumont.

But some of the biggest events at West End were premier college football matchups. Often in conjunction with the giant fall festival No-Tsu-Oh (Houston spelled backwards), a signature gridiron match was scheduled for mid-November each year.

From 1908 through 1911, the Texas Longhorns played Texas A&M in an annual Monday game at West End Park, splitting the four evenly between them. The UT wins in 1908 and 1911 led to major trouble, though. In '08, when Texas students marched at halftime with brooms held as shouldered rifles, indicating that the Horns intended to sweep both contests scheduled against the Aggies that year, it drew an immediate angry response from the Corps, a small group of whom vaulted the ballpark fence and started a melee that culminated in an Aggie cadet stabbing a Texas student.[32]

When another near riot took place after a particularly rough 6-0 Longhorns win in 1911, one that included what Texas fans thought was the deliberate breaking of a Horns player's leg and gangs of Farmer students roaming downtown to attack anyone dressed in Longhorn colors, Texas cancelled the traditional nightshirt victory parade that was to have snaked through downtown Houston. Soon after, the university president terminated the football series with A&M altogether.[33]

Instead, over the next few years prior to WWI, No-Tsu-Oh party-goers and fans saw the Aggies play Oklahoma and Tulane and saw Texas play Oklahoma, Ole Miss and Sewanee[34]. In the earliest years of Rice football, the Owls often called West End Park home, including a big game against Notre Dame in 1915.[35]

The first decade for West End Park did have two disastrous interruptions. A pre-dawn fire in early December 1911

Andy Anderson

It is not every sportswriter who has both a park and an elementary school named after him, but then again, not every sportswriter is Ralph "Andy" Anderson. A native of Pittsburgh, Anderson entered the U.S. Army as a mounted engineer after two years at Carnegie Tech. It was the beginning of a lifetime of work to help handicapped veterans and others with disabilities. Anderson set up rehabilitation programs connected to outdoor activities, in hundreds of trips to VA Hospitals around America, with inventions that allowed those who had lost an arm to cast a rod and reel or swing a golf club; and he wrote of their individual plights in his columns.

Professionally, Andy Anderson started as sports editor of the *Houston Post* following the Armistice, staying with the paper until 1923. That was the year he was hired away by the rival *Houston Press,* where he would remain the rest of his career. Anderson enjoyed tremendous respect in sports circles. He served as best man for baseball star, Dizzy Dean. A believer in youth sports, Anderson also promoted sandlot baseball. He had a side-business building and operating small town golf courses, and in addition to his writing duties he hosted a radio show that focused on outdoor sports. An avid fisherman, he was elected to the Sportsman's Club Fishing Hall of Fame. Houston's Ralph A. "Andy" Anderson Elementary School opened in Westbury in 1961.

destroyed the grandstand and four small houses that were packed close by.[36] Team owner, Otto Sens, who was hunting in Cypress when he learned of the blaze, knew that he had only one year remaining on his lease, so investing the estimated $8,000 to rebuild the grandstands was no foregone conclusion.

The *Galveston Daily News* reported that plans for an improved "baseball plant" had been drawn months earlier and further speculated that a new lease would be in hand "before the first nail is driven." Talk of building a concrete stadium went nowhere, but the rebuilt grandstand did boast a few improvements. Seats were raised with concessions set underneath.[37]

One thing not offered at the concessions when West End Park first opened was beer.[38] Management announced a strict policy that, just as at the old park, no alcohol would be allowed. How strict the enforcement actually was, however, is open to debate. One memoir describes how an empty bucket lowered from the press box would find its way back up the rope with a load of cold beverages for the "thirsty scribes." One doubts they meant colas.

The second catastrophe for the park came on August 17, 1915, when what would today be a Category 4 hurricane hit the upper Texas coast. By the time the storm's center had traveled from Galveston to Houston, sustained winds were closer to 80 mph, but still strong enough to blow down outfield fences and rip the roof off the wooden grandstands, depositing the remnants some distance away.[39]

By the next day, the club's owners were estimating their loss in the range of $3000 and were already making plans to move the remainder of the Buffs' home games for the first time since 1904. By the end of the week however, "Herculean efforts (had) succeeded in putting the park in some sort of shape for play for the remainder of the season."

Baseball thrived at West End thanks to a new generation of fans that were nurtured by the team. By 1922, the ball club was operating a thriving "Knot Hole Gang," letting member youths come inside the park as opposed to watching through the holes that had been cut in the outfield fence even before the first official game.

The gang was hardly inclusive. It was open only to white boys between seven and sixteen. In return for 25 cents and "signing an agreement of clean sportsmanship and high ideals and morals," they received a membership card that allowed them admittance to all games except Sundays and holidays.[40]

There was one more major change in store for West End Park in the early 1920s. In April of 1922, team president John H. Crooker finally purchased the land on which the ball yard sat. The previous ownership duo of Sens and Roberts had been slowly chipping away at it for several years. Crooker and partners paid $40,000 for the privilege of becoming one of the few minor league clubs in America that completely owned its own grounds.[41]

West End Park was home to professional baseball in Houston for 23 seasons. During those years the Texas League finally came into its own, evolving into one of the stronger and more consistent circuits in the minors with the local Buffaloes as one of its most stalwart and successful members.

The Buffs won three league titles at West End and shared two others. It was here, in 1912 and 1913, that they snagged the first back-to-back pennants in team history, followed by a co-championship in 1914.[42, 43] The ball park in Fourth Ward was also the location of more major league spring training stays than any other in Houston history.

Some of the best players of the era came through West End. Two of the Buffs own Hall of Famers, Tris Speaker and "Sunny Jim" Bottomley, plied their trade there.

The roll call of visiting players who graced the West End dugout includes many all time greats such as "Home Run" Baker,[44] Chief Bender, Ty Cobb,[45] Eddie Collins, Sam Crawford, Hughie Jennings,[46] Walter Johnson,[47] Connie Mack, Christy Mathewson,[48] John McGraw,[49] Herb Pennock, Eddie Plank, Branch Rickey, George Sisler[50] and Rube Waddell[51] just to name a few.

In 1928, the Houston Buffs moved to fancy new digs southeast of downtown, but that didn't mean the immediate demise of West End Park. High school sports continued to prosper there as the Houston board of education purchased the park for an athletic field just three

Rice football's first big contests were played at West End Park including a ballyhooed game against Notre Dame in 1915. Woodson Research Center, Fondren Library, Rice University months after the Buffs left.[52]

Houston's other pro baseball team that year was the Black Buffs of the Texas-Oklahoma-Louisiana League, the regional version of the Negro Leagues.[53] After a few games renting the new Buff Stadium, Black Buffs owner, James B. Grigsby, realized that profits would be higher if the team continued to play in Fourth Ward with its large African-American population and West End Park's significantly lower rent. The team continued to call the park home for several more seasons and even hosted a "Negro world championship" series there against the Kansas City Monarchs.[54]

The location of West End Park is largely forgotten today. Its grandstand footprint sits mostly underneath the elevated portion of Interstate 45 as it curves its way around the western edge of downtown. The outfield fences would be found beneath a CenterPoint power station. Portions of Andrews, Heiner and Howe Streets still exist, but not the intersection that was the center of Houston's baseball universe for most of the early 1900s.

---

1 HP 19 January 1905
2 HP 19 February 1905
3 GDN 6 December 1911
4 HP 24 July 1904
5 HP 8 February 1905
6 HP 25 February 1905
7 HP 24 February 1905
8 HP 19 March 1905
9 HP 3 March 1905
10 HP 5 March 1905
11 HP 10 March 1905
12 HP 14 March 1905
13 HP 3 March 1905
14 HP 11 February 1905
15 Charter of Houston Base Ball Association filed with Secretary of State of Texas on 21 February 1920; Ankenman, Fred, Sr.. Four Score and More: The Autobiography of Fred N. Ankenman, Sr.. (Texas Gulf Coast Historical Association, 1980)
16 HP 26 February 1905
17 HP 2 April 1905
18 HP 1 April 1905
19 HP 16 April 1905
20 HP 18 April 1905
21 HP 7 April 1905
22 HP 6 May 1905
23 HP 9 May 1905
24 HP 2 April 1905
25 HP 10 April 1905
26 HP 20 April 1905
27 HP 10 May 1905
28 HP 20 April 1905
29 HP 10 April 1905
30 HP 3 May 1905
31 HP 5 May 1905
32 GDN 14 November 1909
33 GDN 15 November 1911
34 GDN 14 November 1912
35 GDN 25 November 1915
36 GDN 6 December 1911
37 HC 19 January 1912
38 HP 30 March 1905
39 San Antonio Light 22 August 1915
40 Ankenman, Fred, Sr.. Four Score and More: The Autobiography of Fred N. Ankenman, Sr.. (Texas Gulf Coast Historical Association, 1980)
41 HC 16 April 1922
42 O'Neal, Bill. *The Texas League.* (Eakin Press, 1987)
43 Official Records of the Texas League. http://www.milb.com/history/page.jsp?ymd=20100302&content_id=8648436&vkey=history_l109&fext=.jsp&sid=l109
44 GDN 25 March 1912
45 GDN 3 April 1916
46 GDN 23 March 1921
47 GDN 9 March 1909
48 HC 20 March 1910
49 GDN 23 March 1921
50 GDN 8 March 1917
51 HC 15 March 1910
52 Daily Court Review 10 July 1928
53 HI 16 March 1929
54 HI 21 September 1929

KEY

GDN – *Galveston Daily News*
HP – *Houston Post*
HC – *Houston Chronicle*
HI – *Houston Informer*
CD – *Chicago Defender*

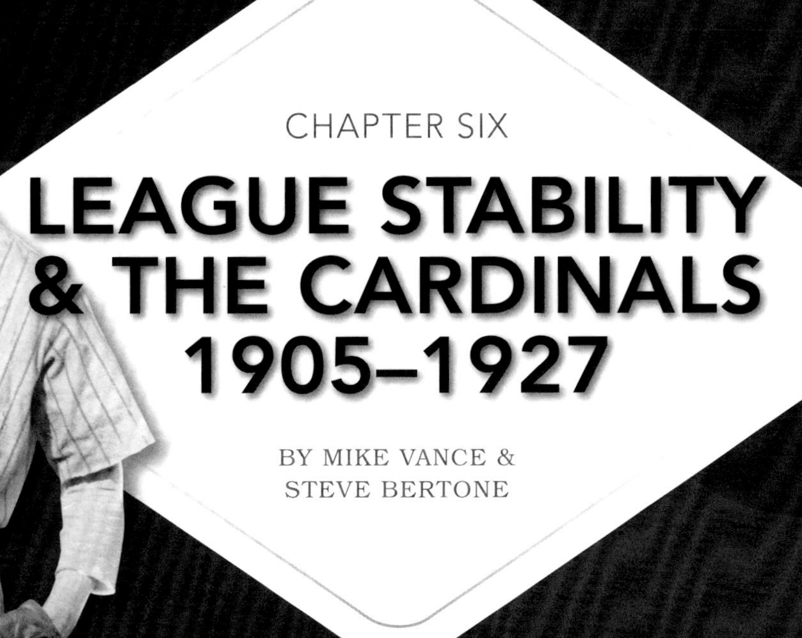

CHAPTER SIX

LEAGUE STABILITY & THE CARDINALS 1905–1927

BY MIKE VANCE & STEVE BERTONE

To say that the 19 years since the dawn of professional league baseball in Texas and Houston had been marked with instability would be rank understatement. The move to West End Park was the start of improved fortunes and profitability for the city's team, though. With the exception of three years during the height of World War II, Houston would never again be without a full season entry in a professional baseball league.

THE HOUSTON BUFFALOES — 1914 CHAMPIONS

Top row: Davis, of; Ware, p; Kitchens, c; Napier, p; Edmundson, p; Criss, p. Middle row: Dodd, utility; Allen, c; Sens, club president Newnam, 1b (manager); Roberts, bus. mgr.; Lucid, trainer; McDonald, 3b. Bottom row: Frierson, of; Mowry, of; Rose, p; (mascot) Seitz, 2b; Hille, 3b.

Big Pat Newnam sits in the center of this team shot of the 1914 Buffaloes flanked by the two team owners, Otto Sens and Doak Roberts.

Author's Collection

The West End Park era began with another turn in the South Texas League under manager Wade Moore. After publicly asking for suggestions for a new team name to replace the Lambs, local writers tagged the team Moore's Marvels and used that moniker throughout the year. They played in the same four-club league that had struggled to finish a year before, and Houston's Bliss Gorham was back as league president.[1]

Not quite so settled was the question of the Houston team's ownership. The first two months of the year brought reports of Claud Rielly selling the team to Houston theatre manager Maurice Michael. Days later, Sam Leslie, who had been signed as a player and field manager, showed up sporting papers that showed him as part owner. Though Michael publicly disputed the claim, Rielly paid him $450 to cede it. Eventually reports appeared that had both Michael and Rielly as co-owners of the ball club. Sam Leslie played out the season for the Temple Boll Weevils.[2]

If the ownership was ever in doubt, Houston's superiority over its three league rivals was not. Halfway through the schedule, the clubs decided to do a split season in the hopes of keeping interest high, but Houston won the second one, too. Three 22-year olds anchored the pitching staff. Southpaw Ed Karger, who would start a six-year run in the majors the following year, posted 24 wins, and "The Fifth Ward Peach," Clarence Nelson, won 23. Bill Sorrells added 19 victories for good measure.[3]

Not all clubs fared as well. Beaumont lost so much money that they were sold and moved to Brenham, though they played only four games there with the rest all coming on the road. As for Galveston, they went through a record eight different managers, and when the season closed, owner Marsene Johnson sold the team.[4]

In spite of those difficulties, the South Texas League still had one more year left in it, and this time they played it with a six-team circuit that included a Lake Charles squad which could manage only a 30-94 record.[5] That would influence the season's outcome because, in the second half, Austin had the good fortune of playing the Louisiana team 27 times.

Pitching seemed to outpace hitting in the South Texas League for 1906. Ivy Tevis, now pitching for Galveston, no-hit his former Houston club soon after the season opened. The only catch was that his mound opponent, hometown favorite Clarence Nelson, allowed only a single hit himself, and Houston won the game 1-0. Manager Con Harlow's Buffs enjoyed an 18-4 year from Nelson. Young Prince Gaskill posted 19 wins, the most in the league, all before being sold at the midway point along with shortstop Forrest Crawford.[6]

The Austin Senators, riding that cushy schedule quirk, eased past the Buffs in the second half. That set up one of the oddest post-season series in Texas history. When Houston took the field in game one, Austin manager Warren Gill protested the fact that the Buffs had added two players from the Dallas roster

Pitcher Ed Karger played with the Buffaloes and earned extra money throwing some semi-pro ball during his time in Southeast Texas.

Courtesy Library of Congress

Doak Roberts had major success as an owner in both Corsicana and Houston before heading the Texas League.
Courtesy Texas League

and one from Galveston, and he continued to protest every single game since Buffs brass refused to budge. On the field the eight games played were split 4 and 4, but with the league upholding Gill's complaints, all eight games were considered forfeited to Austin.[7] Thus ended the life of the South Texas League.

On April 18, 1907, the two Texas leagues began play merged into one. The new circuit was made up of eight clubs that covered much of the state. They enjoyed a balanced schedule with continuous play, meaning no split season. In fact, the newly consolidated league would not have a split season for another 13 years.

With the bigger league came some changes to Houston's club. Claud Rielly was still the owner, but he had formed a partnership with Doak Roberts, the successful, longtime owner of the ball team at Corsicana and most recently at Cleburne.[8]

Wade Moore returned as the Buffaloes player/manager, serving as both the team catcher and occasional pitcher. The top hurler on the squad was Ivy Tevis, a late signee who would lead the league with 24 wins. Tevis had played in Houston in 1903 and 1904 before switching to the Galveston club for a couple of years. His numbers in 1907 were the best of his professional career, which would end only one season later at the age of 35. He was also one-third of a trio who accomplished something special on the hill. Tevis, W. E. Hester and Tex Covington combined to shut out Houston opponents for 57 straight innings.[9]

That was only part of the story on Tevis, however. Late in the year, with Austin and San Antonio locked in a pennant race, the Bronchos faced Houston in a double header. Tevis pitched and won both ends, throwing two shutouts and allowing only four total hits over the 18 innings. Following the second contest, fans hoisted him onto their shoulders and allegedly carried him all the way to the Rice Hotel. Fans and sponsors gave Tevis a new Panama hat and suits of clothes totaling over $500. Max Stubenrauch of First National Bank and

Buffs owner Otto Sens was best known around Texas as a top target shooter.
Houston Metropolitan Research Center, Houston Public Library

hotelier/sportsman Otto Sens presented him with a horse and saddle.[10]

After the 1908 season, Tevis was offered a contract with Indianapolis in the American Association, but he balked at the money, saying he would "be damned if he'd go that far up country to pitch for $200 a month." He returned to Beaumont where he served as dog pound master, street commissioner, deputy sheriff and then constable. He was a regular in area old-timers games. When he died in 1942, all the newspaper accounts still trumpeted his doubleheader shutouts.[11]

The hitting stars of the 1907 Buffs would prove to be a pair of young outfielders who joined the team after playing for the Cleburne Railroaders the season before. Joining holdover Bob Edmondson were George Whiteman in left and 19-year-old Tris Speaker in right field.[12]

George Whiteman would not reach the same level of accomplishment as his teammate Speaker, but he did have three trips to the bigs. His last one was quite memorable. In 1918, he was the left fielder for the Boston Red Sox, sharing duties with part-time pitcher Babe Ruth. At the age of 35, he batted .266 over 71 games. In the World Series against the Chicago Cubs, he had five key hits and made several outstanding catches. It was the final major league appearance for George Whiteman, but he would continue in pro ball for another 11 years, several of them back in Houston.[13]

As for Speaker, in only his second season of professional baseball, he

George Whiteman played and managed in Houston then made the city his permanent home.

National Baseball Hall of Fame Library, Cooperstown, NY

The best big league career of any member of the Buffaloes belonged to Tris Speaker who played his second professional season in Houston.

National Baseball Hall of Fame Library, Cooperstown, NY

would win the Texas League batting title with a .314 average. It was the first of many baseball accomplishments over the next two decades for the man who is widely considered the greatest player to have ever worn a Houston uniform. On his way to being one of the earliest men enshrined at the Baseball Hall of Fame, Speaker would amass more doubles and more outfield assists than anyone in the history of the game. He would help win three world's championships including one as the player/manager for the Cleveland Indians. Speaker, a native of Hubbard, near Waco, was the first person elected to the Texas Sports Hall of Fame in 1951.

In 1907, however, he was not a young man who was easy to know. By the first week of May, Speaker had drawn a five game suspension for tangling with an umpire. It was the beginning of a rough patch for the team. The local newspapers called them "listless and indifferent" and opined that they "ran the bases like spavined mules."[14]

The situation boiled over in the newspaper a week later with Speaker and Edmondson having a "row on the field," and an anonymous player complaining to the reporter that Moore doled out playing time based not on ability, but on favoritism. Allegedly it was so bad that Speaker refused to play when Moore was in the lineup.[15]

For young Speaker, the troubles didn't end there. On July 3rd, he was fined five dollars for using obscene language. The following day, he had drawn yet another suspension.[16]

At the start of September, with Houston's season having ended with a middle of the pack finish, George Whiteman and Tris Speaker were sent to the Boston Red Sox. Their contracts had been owned by Doak Roberts who had the ball club in Cleburne that first signed Speaker as a professional. The price that Roberts got for Speaker was $800.[17]

The 1908 season saw the Texas League expand across the state line. Temple's Boll Weevils had finished the 1907 season playing all of its games on the road. The following year, the team was sold and moved to Shreveport. Having an out-of-state entry had been a bone of contention in earlier Texas League permutations, but this time there were seemingly no issues, perhaps because visiting ball clubs got a $75 guarantee instead of the customary $50.

Claud Rielly still owned the Buffaloes, but Doak Roberts was getting a cut for running the team's operations. Houston began the year without Speaker, of course, but George Whiteman had been sold by the Red Sox in February, and wound up back in Houston. Buffaloes pitching was led by Bill Jarvis with 20 wins. Outfielder Arthur Wallace led the Buffs with a .292 batting average.

One of the most interesting resumes on the Buffaloes in 1908 belonged to outfielder/manager Harry Blake. Blake had played for the Cleveland Spiders from 1884 to 1898. In one of the most shameful events in baseball history, Spiders owners Frank and Stanley Robinson sent Blake and 15 of his fellow Spiders, three of them future Hall of Famers, to the St. Louis Perfectos, also owned by the Robinson Brothers. The decimated Spiders would finish the 1899 season with a record of 20-134, the worst in major league history. His single year in St. Louis would be Harry Blake's last in the big leagues. By the end of 1908, he had only one year left in professional baseball. He closed his career with his hometown club of Portsmouth in the Ohio State League.[18]

Blake was not the only manager of the Buffaloes for the 1908 season. Ben Shelton and Charles McFarland would also take their turns at the helm. Shelton had been first baseman and manager of the legendary Cleburne Railroaders in 1906. His career-defining action was mentoring Tris Speaker on the art of playing outfield. Charles "Chappie" McFarland had pitched in the National League for three different teams prior to his stint in Houston. In addition to being skipper, he won 7 games for the Buffaloes in 1908.

Unique in the history of Houston baseball was the team's adoption of a small child. On a May train trip to Dallas, pitcher W.E. Hester was handed a 19-month old baby boy to hold while his mother took a bathroom break. The young Hillsboro girl, who was later found to have been deserted by her husband and left destitute, jumped off the train at the next stop. The Buffs eventually realized that the happy boy had been totally abandoned. They decided to keep him as a team, making a solemn pact to care for the child, give him a good home and retain him as a club mascot.

The child had a note pinned to him giving his name as Edmund Walters. Small fundraisers were held at each park on the road trip, raising over $2,000 in a matter of days by simply exhibiting the young one prior to the game and then passing the hat. After touring with the team for an early portion of the season, the child was said to have been adopted by third baseman Roy Akin.[19]

After overseeing the Buffs four years beyond their move to a new home, Claud Reilly resigned in October 1908, leaving the team in the capable hands of Otto Sens and Doak Roberts. The latter man continued to call Corsicana home.[20]

Sens, the son of German immigrants, had grown up in downtown Houston in the Tremont Hotel, a Market Square establishment which his family owned. Above all, Sens was a sportsman. He was a champion trap shooter whose name appeared in Winchester shotgun ads as a perennial winner of competitions, including 1908's Sunny South Handicap. He would prove a good and popular fit for both the city and the ball club. In August, Sens would host the entire team for an evening at his fancy bay house at Strang. His manager and star outfielder especially enjoyed the outing, missing the train home, and arriving for the next day's contest in the middle innings.[21]

For the second year in a row a Texas baseball franchise would relocate out of state when the Austin team moved to Oklahoma City. The 1909 battle for the

The big pillow mitt used by Bill Killefer protected a backstop's fingers, but still it required both hands to catch.
Courtesy Library of Congress

pennant was the closest the newly re-formed Texas League had seen yet. Six of the eight teams finished the season with an above .500 record. The Buffs wound up 86-57.

There were few low points, though Houston did get no-hit by Robert Holmes of Waco in August. Throughout the roster, the Buffaloes were a quality club. They sported eight players who would see Major League service in their careers. Houston was led by first baseman Pat Newnam and outfielder Joe Mowry.[22]

Also starring on the club was 21-year-old catcher "Reindeer Bill" Killefer in his third year of pro ball. A Michigan native, he had played with Austin the previous year and also played as a non-enrolled ringer for Coach Billy Disch at St. Edward's University there. Though he batted only .244 during his time with the Buffaloes, he developed a reputation for being a top notch defensive catcher and superb at calling pitches. Dubbed "Demon" by Houston fans, he also added 32 stolen bases to his season's resume.

His 13 years as a major league player began with the St. Louis Browns before the 1909 season ended thanks to scout Charley Barrett, a former Buff, and he would follow that with another nine years as a big league manager. His most enduring playing connection was as the battery mate whom Grover Cleveland "Pete" Alexander called the "greatest catcher... he ever saw any pitcher work with."[23]

The Houston pitching staff didn't have anyone the caliber of Pete Alexander, but they did have four pitchers, Harry Stewart, Chuck Rose, Cy Watson and Everett Hornsby, who put up double-digit win totals. Hornsby and Bill Killefer became good pals, with the catcher also befriending Hornsby's little brother, Rogers.

Jeff Tesreau was also with the Buffs briefly. He posted seven wins split between four different Texas League clubs in 1909. He would spend most of the following decade as a star pitcher for the New York Giants, with more wins in the 1910s than Christy Mathewson, Rube Marquard or any other hurler on the team.

Right-hander Chappie McFarland who had decided to make Houston his permanent home also appeared on the roster. He had just spent the off season as a manager at the Majestic Theatre downtown. The 1909 season was his last in baseball. He died in Houston in 1924.[24]

Managing the Buffaloes, and playing shortstop, was 30-year-old Austin native Hunter Hill. He had bounced around pro

Taken from the 1910 St. Louis Browns team photo, this view shows four of nine former or future Houston players on that squad (Truesdale, Abstein, Allen and Bailey) along with future Hall of Famers Bobby Wallace and Rube Waddell.

Courtesy Library of Congress

ball including stints with the St. Louis Browns and the Washington Nationals. He was used to the Buffs logo, most recently he had been with the Buffalo Bisons of the Eastern League. Under his direction the team would win their first championship in the combined Texas League, clinching the pennant in the final week of the season. Hill would continue to be player/manager until relieved of this position during the 1911 season.[25]

Coming off such a glorious championship year, the Buffaloes opened the 1910 campaign with great hope. Mowry and Newnam were back, along with top outfielder Hub Northen, destined for the bigs before the year was out. Pitchers Rose, Watson and Hornsby were returning, along with Roy Mitchell and Alex Malloy, each of whom would be good for 16 wins that year.[26]

On opening day the Houston Rooters, an organized group of fans, were fresh off a meeting and a rally and were ready to go. To the sound of cannon fire, brass band music and trumpets, a parade of more than 50 automobiles drove dignitaries and baseball fans from the Turnverein on Texas Avenue to the ballpark club where Mayor Horace Baldwin Rice flashed a smile and hurled the first pitch across the plate for a strike. Over six thousand fans roared as the pennant was finally raised[27]

As often happened, Houston would lose some players during the season, and

Jeff Tesreau pitched for the Buffaloes and three other Texas League clubs in 1909 before going off to find fame in New York. He was the winningest pitcher for the Giants in the decade of the 1910s, a time that included this 1912 World Series start against Smoky Joe Wood and the Red Sox.

Courtesy Library of Congress

as in all minor league cities, it was bittersweet. In June, popular first sacker Pat Newnam was traded to the St. Louis Browns who sent Frank Truesdale, Walter Salm and $2,000 in cash to the Buffaloes. Still, fans were sad to see him go. In the weeks after his departure, stories of his progress ran locally including more than one about how Newnam's spirit was being used to inspire the lowly Browns.[28]

In the end, the 1910 season proved to be extremely controversial. The pennant race among the top five teams in the league was tight all season. On the final day of their season, Dallas swept a doubleheader against Ft. Worth. Houston still had three games to be played against Galveston. A tripleheader was planned between the two teams with three five inning games. Houston lost the first game and won the second. Halfway through the third, the Sand Crabs became enraged over an umpire's call and walked off the field giving Houston a forfeit. It meant Dallas had won the league championship by one game, or so it seemed at the time.

Earlier in the 1910 season Houston had seven games thrown out, four of which were wins, because of an accusation made by San Antonio pitcher Harry Ables. He claimed that a Houston player had offered him money to "let up" in a game. Houston's protest to the Texas League and National Association went unheeded until the league ruled that the alleged bribe had been a misunderstood joke.

Arguments over who deserved the title persisted into the winter. It was even suggested that Dallas and Houston play a championship series to settle the dispute at the start of the 1911 season. Both owners refused. Finally the Texas League declared the two teams "co-champions," a travesty in the eyes of both teams that remains in the official record books to this day.[29]

On paper, the 1911 roster seemed to be a good mixture of players young and old, but the result did not produce one of the Buffaloes better teams. Thirty-year-old Pat Newnam was back at first base, though the Browns still owned his contract and would briefly call him up again during the year. That stint would be his last time in the big leagues, and the Hempstead-born Newnam would remain a Buffs fixture through the end of World War I. He rejoined pitchers Hornsby, Rose and Watson and everyday veterans

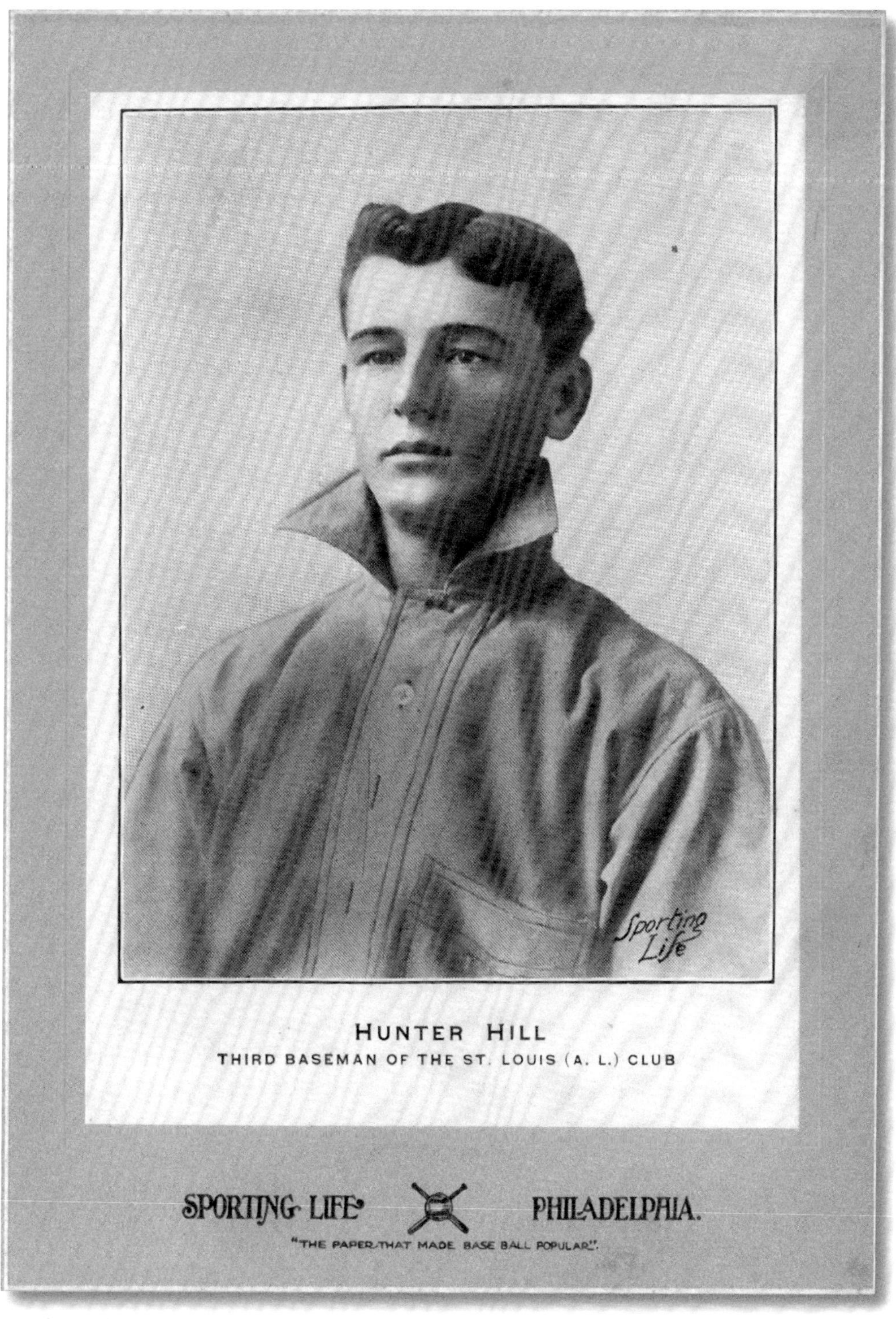

Austin native Hunter Hill was player/ manager in Houston for most of three seasons.

National Baseball Hall of Fame Library, Cooperstown, NY

Frank Truesdale's first four seasons of professional ball were played in Houston.
Courtesy Library of Congress

like Malloy and Whiteman.[30]

There were plenty of promising youngsters, too. Catcher Sled Allen was another player who had seen time at St. Louis the previous year. Only 24, he couldn't know that his big league cup of coffee would be his last. He, too, would stay around Houston for some time before ending his days, on field and off, in West Texas.[31]

One of the interesting rookies was 23-year-old George Foster, a pitcher better known as "Rube," who had grown up in Indian Territory and southeast Kansas working in the coal mines. The 1911 season was his first in professional baseball. He did not arrive in Houston until late July, having pitched in Savannah and Muskogee already. He would finish the year by giving the Buffs a 7-13 record, but there were better times in store.[32]

Sporting much of the same nucleus that had been so successful in the previous two season, the 1911 Buffs never gelled. They began just under the .500 mark and stayed there.[33] At the start of the final road trip, Sens and Roberts, who had never been out of contention in their short ownership tenure, fired Hunter Hill and replaced him with young Sled Allen. Six Houston regulars refused to make the trip, and the next game brought a catcher in centerfield and a few borrowed players in Buffs uniform. The team finished sixth.[34]

As is often the case with a roster considered loaded by the so-called experts, results vary from year to year. Again with many players from the previous season, and now under the field leadership of part-time second baseman John Fillman, the 1912 Buffaloes burst from the gate. San Antonio and Waco would hang around all season, but the Buffs secured the Texas League flag.

The heroes were numerous. The pitching staff still had Chuck Rose and Cy Watson, who no-hit the Ft. Worth Panthers in mid-June. They were joined by Rodger Edmondson and Farmer Ray, with all four of them posting double-digit wins. But the diminutive right-hander, Rube Foster, topped them all, posting a 24-7 mark to lead the Texas League in win percentage. The roster also included holdovers Pat Newnam, Sled Allen and George Whiteman along with newcomers Gil Britton and Chick Knaupp.[35]

Again, a late season pitching arrival would fail to bear fruit until the following season. Dode Criss had been a member of the 1906 Cleburne Railroaders, winning 19 games that season. In 1912, Mississippi native Criss was coming off four seasons with the St. Louis Browns, where he had stuck around thanks to his play as a backup first baseman and pinch hitter, rather than for his pitching prowess. After a brief stay with Louisville to start the year, Criss, now 27, joined the Buffs. He served solely as a position player for Houston in 1912, but he would spend the following five seasons as a pitcher, winning a total of 67 games.

After baseball, Sled Allen moved to Lubbock where he was a sports promoter and nightclub owner. Among the up and coming acts he booked were Ray Charles, Little Richard and Elvis Presley.

National Baseball Hall of Fame Library, Cooperstown, NY

Coming off this championship year, the 1913 Buffaloes looked a good deal like the 1912 version. In the infield were Pat Newnam, Chick Knaupp and Gil Britton; George Whiteman, Gerald Davis and Joe Mowry roamed the pasture, as scribes of the day liked to refer to the outfield. All six of these men carded over 148 games

Pitcher George "Rube" Foster had his winningest season in Houston before a strong three year peak with the Boston Red Sox.
National Baseball Hall of Fame Library, Cooperstown, NY

played and 500 plus at bats. It was a well established daily lineup.

The pitching staff showed a bit more change. The top pitcher from the previous season, Rube Foster, was gone, having been picked up by the Boston Red Sox. By 1915 he would be the ace of the Red Sox pitching staff. He finished that season with 19 wins and two big victories in the World Series. In June 1916, Foster would throw the first no-hitter at Fenway Park, blanking Bob Shawkey and the Yankees. It earned a $100 bonus from ownership.

It would be the high point for Foster. A sore arm and a request for a slight raise did not fly well with new Sox owner Harry Frazee. On April 1, 1918, Rube was traded to the Cincinnati Reds. When they wouldn't meet his price, Rube Foster elected to retire from baseball. He bounced between a furniture store job, some minor league stints, the Secret Service and farming. His brief major league numbers were impressive, though: a 58-33 pitching record and a 2.35 career earned run average.[36]

Back in Houston, Chuck Rose and Dode Criss picked up the slack, winning 26 and 16 respectively. They were joined by newcomer Andy Ware and Robert "Farmer" Ray. In his fifth season with the Buffs, Rose might be considered the ace of the staff. Over his seven seasons in Houston, he won 135 games and was part of five Texas League Titles.

Like his former teammate Rube Foster, he was son of English immigrants and left mining to play baseball. Rose got a much earlier jump on it, going to Fargo of the Northern League at age 16. His lone major league stint had come early, too. Chuck Rose made his debut in the bigs as the starting pitcher for the St. Louis Browns against Ty Cobb and the first place Detroit Tigers in September 1909. His stay lasted exactly three games, and save a short turn in Aurora, Illinois, he'd been in the Bayou City ever since.[37]

The 1913 race was a close one between Houston and Dallas, and postponements earlier in the year set up a six-game series in North Texas over the span of three days. With their catcher badly injured on the eve of the crucial matchup, the Buffs spent the unheard of sum of $1,200 to purchase Frank Kitchens from Ft. Worth. It paid off. Houston took four of the six contests, and the Buffs posed in white suits and straw boaters to commemorate their second straight pennant.[38]

Pat Newnam, long time first baseman for the Buffaloes, took over as manager for 1914. The club had repurchased his contract from the Browns in May of 1911, making this the midway point of an uninterrupted seven year stay. He would remain the Buffaloes manager until 1918 finishing his Houston managing tenure with a 359–333 record.

Newnam certainly seems to have had a penchant for running on the base paths. In July, John Frierson swiped six bags in one game, a Texas League record that is still on the books.[39]

For the Buffs dynasty, it was another year, another staff ace. This time it was Andy Ware who led the club with a 26-8 record after posting 20 wins a year prior. Ware had lost portions of his fingers earlier in life, giving him a vicious spin on his pitches. The baffling movement didn't last forever. The next year he posted only eight victories, and by World War I, he was out of baseball.[40]

No team in the Texas League had ever bested the century mark in wins, but in 1914, two did: the Houston Buffaloes and the Waco Navigators. Waco led the league much of the summer, then in August, the Buffaloes took a one game lead. On the final day of the season, Waco took a doubleheader from Dallas while Houston defeated Galveston in the first game of a twin bill, but had the second game called because of darkness before it became official. This gave the Buffaloes the league championship by a few percentage points. Waco protested not only the second Labor Day game in Houston but a 9-1 Buffs victory back in June. In the end, the league chose to give both teams' identical records of 102-50 and yet another shared title.[41]

After three years at the top, the Buffs returned to the second division in 1915.

Dode Criss played only in the field during his first year in Houston, but spent the next five seasons with the Buffs as a successful pitcher.

National Baseball Hall of Fame Library, Cooperstown, NY

The Texas League champion 1913 Buffaloes posed for their team picture at the train station instead of the ball park.

Houston Metropolitan Research Center, Houston Public Library

One place to look for reasons was a pitching-oriented team that had an amazing seven hurlers work more than 200 innings the previous season. In 1915, four of those same men each topped 230 frames. By comparison, the 2012 World Champion San Francisco Giants had only two starters go more than 200 innings, with none even reaching 220.

Catching these possibly overworked moundsmen in 1915 were Sled Allen and Jay "Nig" Clarke.

Jay Clarke was a member of the Wyandotte Indian tribe. Because of his dark complexion and the racial sensibilities of the time, Clarke spent most of his career known by his nickname of "Nig" which was applied by hecklers and teammates alike.[43] Jay Clarke broke into professional baseball playing for the Corsicana Oil Citys owned by Doak Roberts.

On June 15, 1902, in his rookie season, he made his mark in baseball. The Oilers were to play the Texarkana Casketmakers. Because of Corsicana's Blue Laws, baseball games could not be played on Sunday, so the game was moved to a smaller field in Ennis, just south of Dallas. On that day, Clarke was credited with hitting eight home runs in eight times at bat. It was a professional baseball record that has never been equaled. The final score was Corsicana 51, Texarkana 3.[44]

Clarke spent nine seasons in the majors with the Tigers, Naps, Browns, Phillies and Pirates, a legacy that included his being the battery mate for Addie Joss' perfect game in 1908. His partial season with the Class B Buffaloes was the lowest level of baseball he would reach until a final year at Salisbury, Maryland at age 42.[42]

Both the ballparks in Houston and Galveston were severely damaged by a category 4 hurricane in August 1915. Early reports suggested that the Buffaloes would have to play out the final games of their season on the road, but quick construction work salvaged a few final home series. The Galveston Pirates elected to call it a season with the approval of the Texas League.[45]

If Houston had been the Texas League team to beat in the first half of the decade, that honor now belonged to the Waco Navigators.

The Navs would win their second consecutive Texas League Championship in 1916, but from first to last it was the most balanced season the league had enjoyed in some time. A difference of 23 games separated the Navigators from last place Dallas. The Buffs finished the season one game over .500.

For a team that close to mediocrity, the Buff's pitching staff posted impressive numbers. Six pitchers on the staff would end the season with 10 or more wins. They were led by Roger Edmondson at 21-15, but Walt Dickson's 18-8 and Buddy Napier's 14-10 marks also deserve mention.

Dickson's numbers merit particular note. In what would be his final season in organized baseball, he put together a mark that still stands out today.

Dickson, a native of New Summerfield, Texas, had started playing pro baseball late in life, joining the Temple Boll Weevils in 1905. He reached the bigs four seasons later as a 31-year-old rookie with the New York Giants. After losing seasons with the Boston Braves and the Pittsburgh Rebels of the Federal League, Dickson found himself back in his home state, but he was due one last hurrah. At age 37, Walt Dickson pitched in 31 games while allowing only 26 earned runs for an ERA of 1.06. He did not have long to savor the accomplishment. Dickson, who had gone into the cotton buying business, died of tuberculosis just two years later in Ardmore, Oklahoma.[46]

The season of 1917 brought a hurdle not faced in the United States since the previous century: war. The American declaration came just days before the season opened, at a time when baseball already faced increased competition for the public entertainment dollar. In 1914 there had been 42 minor leagues in operation; by 1917 the Texas League was one of just 20.

Tough Walt Dickson came to Houston following two seasons with the Pittsburgh Rebels of the Federal League.

National Baseball Hall of Fame Library, Cooperstown, NY

By May, the last-place Galveston team folded. In order to keep the league balanced it was decided that Beaumont, which was also experiencing poor attendance, would cease operations as well. The Texas League became a six-team organization. For the first time, minor league baseball was losing its popularity. During the 1917 season, Sunday doubleheaders became the norm in the Texas League and would continue to be so for many years to come.

The Houston Buffs of 1917 were like most other Houston teams of this decade. The league was dominated by pitching. Ed Hemingway and Bill Stellbauer, a Baylor alum, led the team in hitting, batting .276 and .275 respectively. Both men had very short major league careers.

Compared to the Buffs staffs of previous years, the pitching was mediocre. Lindy Hiett, new to Houston, and Gene "Blue Goose" Moore, who had been traded from Galveston midway through the previous campaign, pitched the entire season for the Buffs and recorded 16 wins apiece; each had double-digit losses, as well. Moore would leave a legacy to baseball, though. He had a son, also named Gene Moore, who would have a successful 14-year major league career as an outfielder.[47]

The 1918 baseball season reflected an America at war even more than the previous season had. The severity of the situation had finally been realized. As contracted as the league had been at the outset of the war, now that mobilization was fully established, the number of functioning leagues was again cut in half. Only 10 minor leagues fielded a total of 66 teams with the Texas League composed of the same six clubs that had ended the 1917 season.[48]

In May, the Provost Marshall General, Enoch H. Crowder, issued the "Work or Fight" order which enumerated the occupations deemed essential to the war effort. Needless to say, ballplayer was not one of them. Come the start of July, everyone between 21 and 31 could be called up. Many ball players did not wait to be drafted but elected to enlist or find work in a priority industry.[49]

Gil Britton was one such player. He had already spent nine seasons in professional baseball including a three game big league stint with the Pittsburgh Pirates. Having played third base for the Buffs at the start of the decade, the club resigned him for 1917. Still only 25, Britton chose to enlist after the season. Following his service, he went back to his hometown of Parsons, Kansas and never returned to baseball.[50]

Since almost every one of the six Texas League cities were also home to Army training camps, already enlisted players were sometimes given passes to come play a Sunday doubleheader with their club. It was not uncommon around the state for "farewell games" to be held for baseball men being deployed.[51]

An initial effort had been made across the minor leagues to sign players either younger, or more often older than draftable age. At least six Buffs players were past the age, and two were still under 21. The majority of Houston players, though, were open to being called. Still the games went on.

The most productive pitcher on the Buffs staff was right-hander John Joseph "Oyster Joe" Martina who had joined the club late in the season before. A New Orleans native, he played parts of eight seasons in Beaumont both before and after his stop in the Bayou City. That was still only a fraction of his 21 years of minor league baseball, however. Remarkably, he would post double digit wins at age 20 and at 40, amassing a total of 349 victories in the minors before he was done, the second highest number on record.[52]

An incident of interest took place in late April. When a neighbor lost another calf to wolves, team owner Otto Sens called for the boys on the team to head down to his sports resort home by the bay to go on a wolf hunt. Manager Newnam led one group and Eddie Noyes the other. The fierce mother wolf escaped, taking three cubs from her den, but the ballplayers captured five other young wolf pups alive and took them to downtown Houston where they were shown off in front of C.L. and Theo Bering's Sporting Goods store. Attempts to adopt the animals were rebuffed.[53]

In July 1918, the "Work or Fight" rules took effect in earnest, further straining baseball. Though the game was never officially closed down, the effect was largely the same. Some national star players such as Ty Cobb, Christy Mathewson, George Sisler and Grover Alexander volunteered to be commissioned officers and were sent to Europe. Cobb, Mathewson and Branch Rickey joined chemical warfare divisions. Though training was supposed to be safe, an accidental inhalation of mustard gas damaged Mathewson's lungs, contributing to his early death from tuberculosis in 1925.[54]

As the season went on, meetings were held to consider a course of action for the Texas League. On June 12, the Southern Association announced it was stopping

Native New Orleanian "Oyster Joe" Martina pitched one inning in the big league post season. It came for Washington in Game 3 of the 1924 World Series, making him part of the only baseball championship in Senators/ Nationals history.

Courtesy Library of Congress

play. Several other minor leagues followed suit including the Texas League three weeks later. Before the month of July was over, all but the International League had ended their season. The big league teams held on until Labor Day.

On the patriotic scale, Houston had several players enter the service of their country, more than the other Texas League clubs. Among the Buffs signing on were Ed Duffy, Ray Neusel, Glenn Myatt, John Smithson, Oral Craig, Wray Query, Bill Stellbauer, Ed Holloway, Tony Citrano, Clyde McCarty, David Glenn and Roger Edmondson.[55]

In 1919, with the World War behind them, businessmen began to invest more in entertainment ventures. It didn't necessarily happen overnight, but the timing was fortuitous. Sens and Roberts had been concerned about making money on baseball the previous year. In early May of 1918, reports were floated that the club was losing $100 a game while at home. Fans were exhorted to come to the game, and a merchants committee was formed to boost season ticket sales lest the club leave the city. The end of the wartime economy must have been welcome news.[56]

On the field, the Buffs were taken over by Al Bridwell as a player/manager. Bridwell might be best remembered for the game-winning hit nullified by "Merkle's Boner" of a base running mistake that ultimately gave the Cubs the 1908 National League pennant. After a solid 11 years in the bigs, mostly with the Giants and Dodgers, this was the Bridwell's first shot at running a ball club.

Four Houston Buffs players from this team, all between 20-and 22-years-old, would go on to have various degrees of success as major league ballplayers. Six-foot-six inch Slim Harriss, who led the Buffs with 21 wins and a 1.57 ERA in 1919, would spend nine seasons in the majors as a pitcher for the Athletics and Red Sox. Catcher Glenn Myatt, a Sugar Land resident who was fresh back from the Navy, didn't complete the year in Houston. He was purchased by the Athletics from the Buffs before the season ended. Proving the value of a competent backstop, it would be his first of 16 seasons in the majors, 12 of which were with the Cleveland Indians.[57]

Art Reinhart was destined for five seasons as a Cardinals pitcher, including one unfortunate inning in 1926. The man who would see the most success in the show, however, was Beeville native Curt Walker, a Southwestern University boy, who would compile a .304 career batting average during 12 seasons in the big leagues.[58]

In mid-February 1920, Sens and Roberts sold the Buffs to a corporation registered as the Houston Base Ball Association. Both Sens and Roberts remained major shareholders, in effect taking on five new partners. Capitalization for the enterprise was $100,000, a big jump from the $11,000 that Sens and Roberts had paid Claud Rielly for the team just over 10 years prior. Of course, now they owned a portion of the dirt underneath the ball park, and that totaled 17 city lots.[59]

The charter specifically outlined an array of assets. In addition to an interest in the land, there were 25 player contracts, a club house, groundkeeper's house, a grand stand that held 3500, bleachers holding 1500 more, 2000 "circus seats" that were moved in for football and special events, 400 chairs, 1000 cushions, 32 base ball uniforms and a batting cage.

The new partners were John H. Crooker, Dan Japhet and John D. Clay who held the same ownership percentage as Sens and Roberts; H. L. Robertson and George Pruter with slightly less; and L.A. McDonald and Ben H. Johnston

(TOP)
Branch Rickey had come to know Houston during his time with the St. Louis Browns, but it was during his tenure running the Cardinals that he made a far bigger impact on the Buffs.
National Baseball Hall of Fame Library, Cooperstown, NY

(BOTTOM)
After 16 Major League seasons, Glenn Myatt spent his retirement years around Houston, a city he had grown to know in the minors.
Houston Metropolitan Research Center, Houston Public Library

rounding it out with just $5,000 each. Most of the new men were in the oil business.[60]

Crooker was a seventh-grade dropout who had studied the law and gained a license to practice in Texas in 1911. An ambitious man, he quickly became a justice of the peace and then was elected Harris County District Attorney only three years later. At the onset of the World War, Crooker resigned that office and joined the Army's Judge Advocate General Corps.[61]

In 1920, he was newly returned to Houston. His in-laws were both lawyers, as well, specifically a former Harris County Judge and the first woman licensed as an attorney in Texas. Crooker

(TOP)
Best known as a member of John McGraw's New York Giants, Al Bridwell managed in Houston.

(BOTTOM)
Slim Harriss (right) stands with Tom Zachary, the man famous for giving up Babe Ruth's record-setting 60th home run in 1927.

Both images courtesy Library of Congress

had also just started a new firm with Roscoe C. Fulbright that remains in business today as one of the largest in the nation.

Sens was persuaded to stay on as club president with Crooker as vice-president and Doak Roberts remaining as business manager. The big, and still somewhat unanswered question, is who was truly calling all of the shots. Almost from the moment of the sale, rumors circulated that the St. Louis Cardinals owned some of the stock through the names of local businessmen.

The Cards were most decidedly not one of the National League's elite clubs, and their new club president intended to change that in order to protect his substantial investment. He was a relocated New York City native named Sam Breadon, who had made his money selling high class Pierce-Arrow automobiles. Breadon still retained the street smarts of his lower Manhattan childhood, and he was not a man afraid of bending a rule or two.[62]

Curt Walker, who was born and died in Beeville, TX, had lackluster numbers during his year in Houston.

National Baseball Hall of Fame Library, Cooperstown, NY

The reason for any subterfuge was that the rules of baseball's National Agreement strictly prohibited a major league team to control a minor league one. The incoming commissioner of baseball, Kenesaw Mountain Landis, hated the concept of farm teams and would continue to oppose it for many years.[63]

Sam Breadon was not the only change in St. Louis management. Branch Rickey, not very successful as a player, had taken over the Cards as both field manager and general manager. In 1919, the club had come into a good deal of money when they sold their home grounds of Robison Field after signing a lease agreement to play at the St. Louis Browns-owned Sportsman's Park. Various sources reported that Rickey had used some of the proceeds to quietly buy a half-ownership in the Ft. Smith Twins of the Western Association and 18% of the newly sold Houston Buffaloes. He wanted safe places for his young players to hone their skills.[64] To the chagrin of the new ownership group, whoever they truly were, the 1920 season was one of

St. Louis Cardinals owner Sam Breadon helped build the Buffaloes organization as part of a minor league empire, but his parsimony eventually ran off Branch Rickey, the architect of that success.

National Baseball Hall of Fame Library, Cooperstown, NY

the least memorable for the hometown team or its Gulf Coast neighbor. Houston and Galveston finished with 101 and 100 losses respectively.[65]

The new third baseman and manager for the Buffaloes was Jewel Ens. He had been in the minor leagues since 1908, never playing above the AA level. Then in 1922, Jewel Ens made his big league debut as a 32-year-old reserve infielder for the Pittsburgh Pirates. He would later manage the Buccos for three years. He stayed in baseball as a coach and manager till he died prior to the season of 1950.

An analysis of the 1920 statistics indicates that it might not have been entirely the manager's fault. Two Buffs pitchers, David Glenn and Rube Kroh, managed to lose more than 20 games. One lone high point was when George Little no-hit the equally dismal Galveston club on July 5th. And of the regular hitters, only Fred McDonald and Bill Stellbauer, in his final year at Houston, managed to top .280. High mark for homers on the club was Roy Leslie's six.[66]

At the close of the 1920 season the Texas League challenged the Southern Association to a championship playoff. It would be the beginning of the annual event known as the Dixie Series. The Fort Worth Panthers won the series against the Little Rock Travelers, and the Texas League moved up to Class A for the 1921 season.[67]

Fortunes can turn quickly in the minor leagues, and so they did for the Buffaloes who were now getting a steady stream of talent through the St. Louis Cardinals organization.

There were more major changes in club management during the off season. Otto Sens, who had to be coaxed to remain as team president in 1920, had been replaced in that post by John H. Crooker. Doak Roberts had moved on to become president of the Texas League where he would serve for the next nine years.[68]

Named to take Roberts' place as business manager in December 1920 was Fred Ankenman. His name was already known in Houston baseball circles thanks to an extensive career playing for a spate of amateur and semi-pro teams in the city. Soon he was running the teams, and about 1912, he was one of the organizers of the Houston City League.

He was written up often for his baseball exploits and business savvy with teams such as the Adoue-Blaine, Barringer-Norton Men's Clothing, the Gas Company, the Hustlers, Lucey Manufacturing Co., Peden Iron & Steel, the Pete Dalies and Modern Plumbing. The frequent movement was indicative of the value Houston companies placed on a good baseball player.[69]

Ankenman and Crooker already knew each other. In 1919, Ankenman had left a job with Southern Pacific for a piece of the American Dream. He and two friends had started a company to sell small drilling tools. Among the men who agreed to serve on their board was Crooker.

Though the oil tool business soon failed, Ankenman made an impression as a man who knew how to run a baseball team. When the new ownership was faced with the loss of Roberts, their most knowledgeable man, they turned to Fred Ankenman to take his place. It was the beginning of a relationship that would last for over 20 years.[70]

The agreement between the minor and major leagues had expired a year before, so issues such as big league clubs being able to draft minor league players as opposed to signing them wholesale was back under scrutiny. One thing that would affect Houston more than any other was the ostensible end of a ban on farm teams.[71]

Buffaloes manager Jewel Ens was a late blooming player, making his debut at age 32.

National Baseball Hall of Fame Library, Cooperstown, NY

Prior to the 1921 agreement, the relationships between majors and minors was pure capitalism. Minor league player contracts were sold to the highest bidder. When a big league team wanted to send a man down to a lower level for seasoning, though, the arrangements operated on a series of gentleman's agreements. Players were sent down with a wink and a nod that they'd be sold back when the

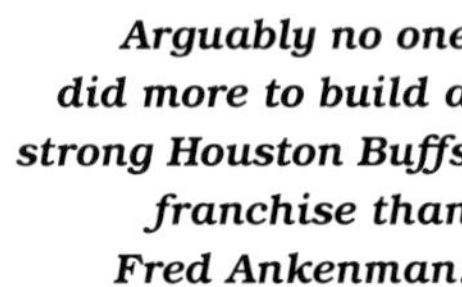

Arguably no one did more to build a strong Houston Buffs franchise than Fred Ankenman.

Courtesy Texas League

bigger club saw enough improvement or had a need. When another big league club happened along with a better offer, though, these agreements often went out the window.

Minor league teams often established informal pipelines for player sales with certain clubs. In the Buffs' case, a fair number of early 20th century players had gone back and forth to the St. Louis Browns at a time when that American League club occasionally trained in Houston. Two coincidences enter into play: Browns owner Robert Hedges was among the first to see the economic allure of ownership in minor league clubs, and it was his same Browns who offered the first opportunity as both big league player and manager to young Branch Rickey.[72]

The 1921 agreement didn't expressly allow for farm systems, but neither did it say no. It remains a mystery as to why Commissioner Landis allowed the loophole to remain open, but there is no doubt that Rickey's Cardinals jumped through it with both feet. There was one catch, however. The Texas League still forbade big league ownership.

As the new year got underway, newspapers reported that Branch Rickey was in town to pay a call on friends including Otto Sens and John H. Crooker. Rickey and Crooker had been in Lake Charles to meet with Connie Mack, who was there to set up spring training for his A's, for discussion about a series of exhibition games. Rickey had known Mack for some time, and relations had also been close between Mr. Mack and the Buffs. Several Houston players had first gone to the majors as members of the Philadelphia A's.[73]

Sens and Rickey were occasional hunting partners, an activity that the former enjoyed tremendously. One of Rickey's favorite tales was of a night time alligator hunt at Sens' home/lodge. All of the men would remain friends for years. Father Robert Crooker, the team owner's son, recalled that Mr. Rickey stayed at their home whenever he was in Houston. This type of close personal relationship lends more believability to the idea of a shadow ownership.[74]

In late March of 1921, local headlines read "Deals with Rickey Fix Houston Team." The Cardinals had sent three youngsters south who would make up three quarters of the Buffs starting infield. Irwin Weimer at third and Homer Ezell at short were touted as exciting upgrades. Neither would ever have an at bat for the Buffs after spring exhibitions.[75]

The third prospect was another story entirely. Twenty-one year old first baseman James Leroy Bottomley, who was only in his second season of professional baseball, was said to have "class that is pronounced." The scout who had discovered the youngster for the Cardinals two years earlier, was former Buffs player Charlie Barrett.[76]

With a cocked hat and big grin, Jim Bottomley earned the nickname "Sunny Jim." National Baseball Hall of Fame Library, Cooperstown, NY

Barrett was a St. Louis native who had played for six different Texas League clubs at the opening of the 20th century. His Houston stint came during the ill-fated season of 1904. It was that same season when he met, then a young Dallas Giants player, Branch Rickey. Described by most everyone as extremely good natured, Barrett had been a scout for the Browns when Rickey was there, and was the first to jump to the Cardinals after his pal became the boss. When Barrett died, 35 years after they'd first met, Rickey described him as "the closest friend I've had in baseball."

In spite of the promise the two Cardinals men saw, Bottomley was not an exceptional hitter for the Buffs. In 130 games, he batted .227 and showed only

Bruce Layer

Bruce Layer had come to the *Houston Post* from the *San Antonio Express*. A highlight for him there certainly came in 1923 when he was handed the tournament winning golf ball signed by Texas Open champion Walter Hagen after that links titan had won $6,000, the richest purse ever in golf. The *Post* media enterprises took full advantage of Layer over the years. In the 1920s and 1930s, he was writing a sports column, and often a golf column, for the newspaper and appearing on two different radio stations controlled by the paper. His wife, Della, was a PBX operator, running the telephone switchboard at the *Post*. Layer did play-by-play of the first game at Buff Stadium in 1928, and a year later was performing that duty on KTLC, a *Post* station that was soon to be absorbed by the local KXYZ. By the mid-1950s, Layer was still doing double duty on KPRC radio and television including some Buffs broadcasts with Dick Gottlieb. He was still a member of the working press for KPRC into the late 1960s. Bruce Layer died in Houston in 1981.

a smattering of power with 16 doubles, five triples, and four home runs. It was his worst year in baseball. His breakout would come the following season in Syracuse where he hit .348 with power. Before the season was over, he was in St. Louis, and when the 1923 season started, Sunny Jim, along with his angled cap and ever-present smile, was entrenched as the first baseman for the Cardinals. He would stay there for the next nine seasons, playing in four World Series.

In his 16 total seasons, he compiled a .310 career average, led the National League twice in doubles, twice in runs batted in, twice in total bases and once each in hits, triples and home runs. He was league M.V.P. in 1928, and his record of 12 ribbies in one game still stands today. Bottomley was elected to the Baseball Hall of Fame by the Veterans Committee in 1974.[77]

The winningest pitcher on the 1921 Buffs was Clyde Barfoot, who had already spent considerable time in both Galveston and San Antonio among other stops. He racked up 22 wins for the club, went up to the Cardinals for two seasons, then returned to Houston in 1924 when he posted 19 more W's. Barfoot was already 32 when he came through Houston for the second time, but he had a lot of innings left in him. His final season of professional ball came in Chattanooga in 1938 when he was 46 years old.

Blessed with the new players, the Buffs turnaround was remarkable. Manager George Whiteman led them to 92 wins, but the team still finished 15-and-a-half

Clyde Barfoot's two strong seasons in Houston bookended two quiet years with the St. Louis Cardinals.

National Baseball Hall of Fame Library, Cooperstown, NY

Buffs first baseman Del Gainer was just one object of disagreement between Houston and St. Louis management.
Courtesy Library of Congress

games behind the league-leading Ft. Worth Panthers who won both halves for an impressive total of 107 Texas League victories.[78]

A milestone was reached as the Buffs opened the 1922 season. On the 26th of April, the Houston Base Ball Association paid $40,000 and finally acquired the last portion of the land on which West End Park sat. Otto Sens and Doak Roberts had been buying it bit by bit for years, and John Crooker and company finished off the deal.[79]

It would be part of his legacy to the Buffs. By the time the year ended, Crooker had sold most of his stock in the team. In a move that had been planned from the outset of the group's purchase, he stepped down as club president, replaced by Ford dealer Herbert L. Robertson, know to his friends as "Robbie." Though Crooker had sold his stock directly to the Cardinals, the shares were held in Robertson's name. It would soon prove to be a less than perfect situation.[80]

Fred Ankenman would write later that this shuffle of stock was done to increase the holdings of the Cardinals, and allow them to have greater control over the development of their players in spite of any Texas League policy to the contrary. Others around the nation saw it that way, too. Though the local press clearly represented Robertson as the man in charge, the Sporting News and others had begun to flatly refer to Houston as a farm team of the Cards. It was hard to dispute when Robertson and Ankenman were going to St. Louis to pow wow with that "friend of Houston," Branch Rickey[81]

Houston was not alone in not-so-subtly flaunting the Texas League's no farm club policy. Two other teams were flirting with Major League affiliation by the early-1920s: Fort Worth with the Detroit Tigers and Wichita Falls with the Pittsburgh Pirates. It was paying dividends. The Wichita Falls Spudders would have a run of 25 straight victories in 1922, and the Cats were in the midst of six straight Texas League titles.[82]

Though the 1922 Houston Buffaloes would have a full dozen men on their roster who saw big league service at some point in their career, the sum total was clearly less than the individual parts. It was a team with little distinctive hitting or pitching.

Ray Blades was a member of that Houston Buffs team, a holdover from the previous season and one of the biggest bright spots in the lineup. He had signed with Branch Rickey as an amateur player at the old age of 23 after serving in the World War. Leading the Texas League with a .330 average, Blades was called up to the St. Louis Cardinals in August of 1922, and he would stay in the outfield there for 10 years. He would go on to manage in the Cardinals farm system after that, finally being named skipper of the big club in 1939.[83]

A favorite player on the 1922 Buffs was Gene Bailey, a hometown kid from the Fifth Ward and Houston High School. He would have five seasons in the majors, playing the outfield for the Robins, Red Sox, Braves and Athletics. After he retired from the game, Bailey returned to Houston, working as a machinist in the oil refineries.

Just as the Buffaloes had their time to rule the league 10 years earlier, the early 1920s belonged entirely to the Ft. Worth Panthers. The Texas League had adopted a split season in 1919, but the Cats' domination was so strong that the split did not matter. In 1922, they won both halves for the third straight year.[84]

In November 1922, Hunter Hill, who had worked most recently as an umpire, was announced as Houston's new manager. George Whiteman had held the job for two years before being replaced by Roy Thomas on an interim basis for the last of the 1922 season. Hill had a history in the city, not all of it pleasant. After winning pennants for two years straight, he had been abruptly fired as Buffs field boss during the 1911 season. This was new ownership, however, and more importantly, he was trusted by Branch Rickey in St. Louis.

Team president Robertson took the opportunity of Hill's hiring to "spike that wild eyed rumor" that Rickey and Sam Breadon of the Cardinals owned "as much as a half of one share" of the Houston ball club. With pride and ego

San Marcos' own Pete Compton topped the .300 mark in his two seasons at Houston.

Courtesy Library of Congress

flaring, Robertson wanted to make certain that the press understood that Hill was his hire. As to reports in the *Sporting News* that called any out-of-staters the owners of the Buffs, he "emphatically denied" them and said that he had been "treated unjustly."[85]

If Robbie was hoping to make a point with the writers, it didn't take. The *Sporting News* continued calling Houston "the Cardinals second team." They had a good point, too. The entire 1923 season would prove to be somewhat of a revolving door with players not entrenched in St. Louis being shuffled between the Mound City, Houston and the Cards highest affiliate in Syracuse. The "alien ownership of the club and the policy of the St. Louis Nationals of shuffling players in and out" would sink the season.[86]

The 1923 Buffaloes roster was made up of many ballplayers who would soon be in the major leagues. A total of 16 would have big league service on their resume, but still Houston was headed for another middle of the pack finish.

The team had gotten much younger than the previous season. With players such as Eddie Dyer, Les Bell, Ernie Vick and Heinie Mueller, all 23 or younger, the team should have been more competitive, but they didn't remain long enough to get into a rhythm. Only Bell and Ray Schmandt notched over 500 at bats for the Buffs all year.

One Les Bell mark from that year does remain in the record books to this day: 5 doubles in a game on May 28.[87]

Eddie Dyer was a local hero who had not only pitched at Rice University but made All-Southwest Conference in football, as well. The lefty threw a no-hitter at Rice two years earlier. His mound opponent for Baylor that day was future Hall of Famer Ted Lyons.[88]

Signed by the Cardinals, Dyer left school just short of graduation. His playing career was an inconsistent affair during which he would play outfield and pitch, making appearances with the Cardinals every year from 1922 to 1927 without ever sticking. While with Syracuse in 1927, Dyer injured his pitching arm, and with it, his big league aspirations. Branch Rickey saw his leadership and baseball smarts, though, and Eddie Dyer would make his mark in Cardinals baseball.[89]

For the Buffs in 1923, however, Dyer could muster no better than 3 and 5, splitting the season between Houston and Wichita Falls. The pitching stalwarts were a couple of veterans, Marv Goodwin, an Army Air Corps flyer who also had six years in the show under his belt, and Jack Knight, who had enjoyed a brief call up to St. Louis only a year before. Though they posted 19 and 21 wins respectively, their losses were in double digits, as well. Goodwin was notable as one of the 17 big league pitchers whose spitball was grandfathered in after the rules otherwise outlawed them.[90]

Under the heading of records no player wants to hold, Houston's Bill Bailey lost 16 consecutive games, a mark that still stands in the Texas League books.[91]

Despite the fact that the team failed to

reach .500, Hunter Hill was given another year as field boss. The St. Louis-based *Sporting News* credited Hill with developing Les Bell into a fine shortstop, and Bell's subsequent nine productive seasons in the National League bore that out. For Houston, though, the problem was that Bell was now with the Cardinals, creating a big need at shortstop with the Buffs.[92]

When Rickey asked for veteran outfielder Del Gainer during the off season, H.L. Robertson and Houston fans began to squawk. Once again the Buffs president scurried off for a meeting with Rickey. The Buffaloes management wanted an end to the one-sided shuffling of players and had specific names in mind for their roster.[93]

Two weeks later, complaints along the bayous had grown louder. Some Houston writers, believing Robertson's description of the ownership situation, were flatly calling for "abolishing the agreement" with the Cardinals. From the Houston viewpoint, one particular analysis of how the many player moves affected the Buffs was spot on: "A ball team is a machine. After putting in new parts it has to run awhile before it functions smoothly, and once it does work right it is the correct thing to let it alone."[94]

Tensions were running high between the baseball parties in Houston and St. Louis, but it was a player who had yet to get much notice who would ultimately prove to be the breaking point. Twenty-year old Charles Hafey, known to the world as Chick, had led the Fort Smith Twins in both triples and home runs in

(TOP)
Gus Mancuso went from Houston's sandlots all the way to the 1930 World Series where he posed with opposing catcher Mickey Cochrane.
National Baseball Hall of Fame Library, Cooperstown, NY

(BOTTOM)
Another Buffs backstop, Harry McCurdy, went on to be a Houston school principal.
Houston Metropolitan Research Center, Houston Public Library

Big Ed Konetchy is shown during his time with the Browns. In the Texas League, Konetchy was a Ft. Worth Panther and a slugging thorn in Houston's side.

Courtesy Library of Congress

1923. When the season was over, and at the direction of the St. Louis Cardinals who owned both Hafey's contract and the Ft. Smith ball club, Houston bought his services for the sum of $2,500.[95]

Hafey was far from alone as a talented player on the 1924 Buffs. Del Gainer, who had remained in Houston after all, hit .350 for the year. Also batting over .300 were Pete Compton, Bill Hollahan, Jack McCarty, Tex McDonald and John Monroe. Five of those men put up double digit totals in triples indicating that there was both speed and power on the team.

On the pitching side of things, five hurlers posted double digit wins led by Jack Knight with 21 and reliable Clyde Barfoot with 19. Knight's ERA of 2.34 was tops in the whole league.[96]

The Buffs started out hot in the spring, and finished the first half of the season second only to untouchable Ft. Worth. Cooling off as the summer heated up, Houston nonetheless finished with the second best overall record in the league. The downside being that still put them 30-and-a-half games back of the Cats. Late in the season, Hunter Hill was replaced as skipper by pitcher Marv Goodwin. It would be Hill's final stint as a manager.

On the plus side of the ledger, attendance at West End Park topped the 100,000 mark for the first time ever. Robertson had to be feeling his oats.[97]

As the Buffaloes season was winding down, the Cardinals called for outfielder Chick Hafey. It wasn't surprising since he was hitting .360 with 20 triples and 9 home runs at the time. What was a bit shocking to Rickey and Breadon in St. Louis were the terms proposed by H.L. Robertson.

Robbie had asked his business manager Fred Ankenman to set a fair price for Hafey and to consider the Cardinals "just as with any other foreign club." That was ignoring the not widely known fact that they owned the majority of Buffaloes stock. When Robertson sent the proposal to St. Louis, they hit the ceiling.

He was demanding "$20,000 and a satisfactory player" in exchange for Hafey.

Because the National League team's ownership stake was still surreptitious, they couldn't publicly point out that they already controlled Hafey's contract to begin with. In the end, and over loud protests from Breadon, they were forced to pay the asking price or lose Hafey to someone else. It was the final straw.[98]

At the fall meetings after the season ended, it was openly admitted to league officials that St. Louis had owned control of the Houston Buffs for at least two years, going back to the John Crooker buyout. The National League club was now seeking both a deal to buy out Robertson's 42% and approval from the Texas League brass.[99]

Thirty-eight games into the 1925 season, Branch Rickey was replaced as field manager of the Cardinals by their star player, Texan Rogers Hornsby, so his full attention was now focused on his duties as GM. Negotiations still would not be completed overnight.[100]

In spite of the drama at the top, there was still baseball to be played in 1925, and the Texas League was booming. Four clubs would top the magic mark of 100,000 fans for the season. Dallas would jump over 200,000. Financially, the times were good.

Marv Goodwin was back to start the season as manager, and he would rack up a lively 21-9 record on the mound. He was so successful that he would finish the year with the Cincinnati Reds where, at age 34, he would get another shot at Major League success. Pete Compton replaced him as field boss.

One addition to the team who was not impactful on the field at the time was a local amateur star. Gus Mancuso had worked at both the Texas Company and First National Bank as a teenager largely so he could play on their baseball teams. The son of Sicilian immigrants, he bounced between four teams around Texas during his first year as a full time professional. Mancuso would remain a fixture in Houston baseball for many more decades.[101]

For the second year in a row, Del Gainer put up nice numbers for the Buffs, hitting .328 with 15 dingers. Two youngsters topped the old man, though. Harry McCurdy, the catcher who had been the "satisfactory player" sent to Houston in the Chick Hafey deal, batted .361 with 16 round trippers and 22-year-old Homer Peel led the team with 19 home runs and 16 triples, batting .355 to boot. The dead ball era was indeed over in the Texas League. Ft. Worth's Ed Konetchy led the entire circuit in homers with 41.[102]

It would be the last of the six straight pennants for the Panthers, but they did dominate the league. Houston again finished second, this time only 17 games back.[103]

With the Texas League season over, Branch Rickey returned to Houston determined to finally close a deal. He met with a variety of attorneys including his friend John H. Crooker who was still lead counsel for the Houston Base Ball Association. Media interests did not know exactly what to think about the

Houston car dealer H.L. Robertson was the public face of the Buffs ownership in the early 1920s, often to the distaste of the St. Louis Cardinals.

Courtesy Arabia Shrine Temple, Houston

ownership controversy. The *Chronicle* noted that "ever since the St. Louis Nationals had an openly active interest in the Houston club there has been a persistent rumor that more of the local stock was owned in St. Louis than the average fan believed."[104]

Robertson seemed to be playing hard to get. He had "not yet set his asking price" one day, and his office "claimed" that he was out of town on business the next. If every man had his price, though, Robbie's was believed to be north of $200,000.[105]

On October 18, the Houston baseball community got a sobering reminder about the nature of games versus life. Marv Goodwin, who had been sold to the Reds only a few weeks prior, had returned home to Houston and resumed his Air Corps reserve duties as a flight trainer at Ellington Field south of town. He and a mechanic were up in a Curtiss Jenny with a 150-horse-power Hispano motor when the plane suddenly went into a tailspin at only 200 feet.

Goodwin managed to roll the aircraft so that it hit wing first. The mechanic walked away with minor bruises, but Lieutenant Goodwin badly fractured both legs. He was brought into Baptist Hospital downtown, and the following day, it was thought that he was improving. X-rays showed no skull fractures.

Two days later, however, Goodwin's recovery took a disastrous turn. Serious head injuries had been missed. His two brothers in Houston and his family in Virginia were notified to prepare for the worst. Marv Goodwin, who had made local baseball fans so proud of him just weeks earlier, died on October 22, 1925.[106]

The management struggle continued. Finally at the start of December, the Buffs ownership battle came to an end. The *Houston Chronicle* reported the details of the sale saying Breadon and Rickey had laid out $170,000 to obtain the remaining rights to the Buffaloes from H.L. Robertson, R.C. Fulbright and "a minor stockholder or two." Joining the

Cardinals ownership group as well was W.A Parrish of Baker Botts Parker and Garwood, perhaps as a reward for legal advice. Fred Ankenman was named team president and received 5% of the stock.

Ankenman reported later that he almost didn't get the job in spite of the fact that he had done yeoman's work for the franchise. Mr. Rickey eventually told him that Cards owner Sam Breadon was strongly opposed to giving Ankenman the position because he blamed him in part for the high price attached to Chick Hafey[107]

In the landscape of the mid-1920s, only St. Louis, and Detroit on a smaller scale, had bought into the idea of establishing a baseball farm system. The newness of the concept might have still been causing some denial in Houston. The *Chronicle* opined that the sale "does not necessarily mean that the Buffs of the future will be a farm for the St. Louis Cardinals, though real help will be expected from that National League source."[108]

As to placating the Texas League, the Cardinals promised that in return for the other league owners not interfering with their open and above-board control of the Buffs, they will "provide Houston with one of the finest baseball stadiums in the United States." The league said yes with a caveat. St. Louis agreed to sell its Houston holdings at a fixed price if a local buyer could be found within the next several months. It never happened.[109]

The Texas League president at the time was Doak Roberts who had owned a share of the team when the Crooker group bought the club in early 1920. If anyone should know that there had been Cardinals influence in Houston for years, it would have been him.

Just as the 1926 season was getting underway, the Buffs were faced with another untimely death. H.L. Robertson, less than five months removed from being team president and owner of a substantial amount of the club stock, died suddenly at his home. He was but 40 years old.

In addition to his baseball connections, Robbie had, until recently, been partners in Robertson-Pearson Ford dealership. He owned the Logan Candy Company and Empire Electric. He was a past potentate of the Arabia Temple Shrine in Houston, and his Masonic lodge brothers turned out in droves for the funeral.

The most touching aspect of the day was the presence of members of the Buffs Knothole Gang at his funeral. Robertson had helped found the organization, and the many boys who benefitted were undoubtedly grateful. There was a special service just for the Knothole Gang members, and an honor guard of the boy baseball fans joined the uniformed Shriners to accompany the casket from Trinity Episcopal Church to the train depot from which Robbie's remains headed to interment in San Antonio.[110]

On the field, the 1926 campaign brought the Buffaloes back toward the bottom of the standings. New manager Joe Mathes could do nothing with a pitching staff that was pedestrian all year.

An ugly dispute over the contract of Chick Hafey was the catalyst that brought St. Louis ownership of the Buffs into the open.

National Baseball Hall of Fame Library, Cooperstown, NY

Del Gainer, now 39, started well at the plate but was quickly promoted to Syracuse, the top farm team in the growing Cardinals system. Ray Powell and Homer Peel were the top hitters who stuck around the Buffs. Both were comfortably over .300, numbers to warrant a promotion of their own, but there was a logjam in the outfield at St. Louis. Over the next few years, the Cards strong organization would mean Houston's gain.

Meanwhile in St. Louis, 1926 brought the ultimate rejoicing. For the first time ever, the National League franchise won a World Series title. That also meant happiness in Houston where not only were the city's baseball fans beginning to build a strong allegiance to the Cardinals as their big league club of choice, but also several of the championship players were formerly Bayou City favorites.

St. Louis regular season starters Jim Bottomley, Les Bell and Ray Blades were all former Buffs. So, too, was Chick Hafey who along with Bottomley and Bell played in every Series game. Blades had established himself as one of the top leadoff hitters in baseball before shredding his knee in late August while trying to climb the left field wall in pursuit of a hard line drive. He spent October wearing a plaster cast. Former Buffs pitcher Art Reinhart also saw action, taking the loss in Game 5.[111]

With the option period for a Houston buyer expired, the Cardinals organization got on with building a grand new home for the Buffs in 1927. The club made improvements in the player personnel, as well, and it showed in the standings. The team was back over the .500 mark, finishing third behind Wichita Falls and Waco.[112]

Twenty-three year old Fred Frankhouse put up 21 wins for the Buffs. His late season call up to St. Louis would mark the start of 13 seasons in the National League. Ken Penner almost matched him for victories, tallying 19 of his own and leading the Texas league with a 2.52 ERA.[113]

Ernie Orsatti's .330 average also

earned him a trip to the Cardinals, and he would stick around there for most of the next nine years. Though he was now 38, Ray Powell continued to hit Texas League pitching, posting a .323 clip for the year, and Ed Hock was another Major League veteran who was helping the Buffs at the plate. He led the team in at bats on his way to a .314 average. Two youngsters also busted over .300 for the Buffaloes: Wally Roettger and Pepper Martin, both of whom had bright futures in the National League.[114]

The feeling of good things to come was prevalent. Everything about the 1927 season in Houston pointed toward auspicious days ahead for the Buffs. Attendance had topped 141,000, their highest ever. They were poised to move into their new state-of-the-art ballpark the next spring and bring local baseball into the modern era.[115]

---

1 HP 27 February 1905; Ruggles, William B.. The History of the Texas League of Professional Baseball Clubs 1888-1951. (Texas Baseball League, 1951)

2 HP 19 February 1905; HP 22 February 1905; HP 25 February 1905; HP 11 March 1905; http://www.baseball-reference.com; Spalding's Official Baseball Guide for 1905; Houston City Directory 1905-06

3 HP 14 May 1905; http://www.baseball-reference.com

4 Encyclopedia of Minor League Baseball. Third Edition. (Baseball America, 2007); Ruggles, William B.. The History of the Texas League of Professional Baseball Clubs 1888-1951. (Texas Baseball League, 1951)

5 Ruggles, William B.. The History of the Texas League of Professional Baseball Clubs 1888-1951. (Texas Baseball League, 1951)

6 Encyclopedia of Minor League Baseball. Third Edition. (Baseball America, 2007); Ruggles, William B.. The History of the Texas League of Professional Baseball Clubs 1888-1951. (Texas Baseball League, 1951); Beaumont Enterprise 13 May 1942; Houston Press 13 May 1942

7 Ruggles, William B.. The History of the Texas League of Professional Baseball Clubs 1888-1951. (Texas Baseball League, 1951)

8 HP 11 April 1907; HP 12 April 1907; Gay, Timothy M. *Tris Speaker: The Rough and Tumble Life of a Baseball Legend.* (Lyons Press, 2007)

9 http://www.baseball-reference.com; Ruggles, William B.. The History of the Texas League of Professional Baseball Clubs 1888-1951. (Texas Baseball League, 1951)

10 Iva Tevis Collection, Tyrrell Research Library, Beaumont Public Library; Houston City Directory 1905-06; Beaumont Enterprise 1 January 1935; HC 12 May 1942; Beaumont Enterprise 13 May 1942

11 Beaumont Enterprise 1 January 1935; HC 12 May 1942; Beaumont Enterprise 13 May 1942

12 Encyclopedia of Minor League Baseball. Third Edition. (Baseball America, 2007); http://www.baseball-reference.com; Ruggles, William B.. The History of the Texas League of Professional Baseball Clubs 1888-1951. (Texas Baseball League, 1951)

13 http://www.sabr.org/bioproj/person/42a33ee6

14 HP 17 June 1907; HP 27 May 1907

15 HP 25 June 1907

16 HP 3 July 1907; HP 4 July 1907

17 Gay, Timothy M. *Tris Speaker: The Rough and Tumble Life of a Baseball Legend.* (Lyons Press, 2007)

18 Encyclopedia of Minor League Baseball. Third Edition. (Baseball America, 2007); http://www.baseball-reference.com; Ruggles, William B.. The History of the Texas League of Professional Baseball Clubs 1888-1951. (Texas Baseball League, 1951)

19 Ruggles, William B.. The History of the Texas League of Professional Baseball Clubs 1888-1951. (Texas Baseball League, 1951); HP 17 May 1908; HP 21 May 1908; Sporting Life 30 May 1908

20 Sporting Life 10 October 1908; HP 20 November 1908; Ruggles, William B.. The History of the Texas League of Professional Baseball Clubs 1888-1951. (Texas Baseball League, 1951)

21 United States Census 1900 Harris County, TX.; Houston City Directory 1877-78; A Newspaper Reference Work. (Houston Press Club, 1913); Sporting Life 15 February 1908; GDN 13 August 1909

22 *Reach Official American League Guide 1910-11*; http://www.baseball-reference.com

23 http://sabr.org/bioproj/person/5ae1b077

24 Sporting Life 28 March 1908; http://www.baseball-reference.com;

25 Encyclopedia of Minor League Baseball. Third Edition. (Baseball America, 2007); http://www.baseball-reference.com; Ruggles, William B.. The History of the Texas League of Professional Baseball Clubs 1888-1951. (Texas Baseball League, 1951)

26 http://www.baseball-reference.com; GDN 10 April 1910

27 HP 10 April 1908; HP 13 April 1908; HP 17 April 1908

28 HP 23 May 1910; http://www.baseball-reference.com; HP 5 June 1910

29 GDN 26 November 1910; Ruggles, William B.. The History of the Texas League of Professional Baseball Clubs 1888-1951. (Texas Baseball League, 1951); Encyclopedia of Minor League Baseball. Third Edition. (Baseball America, 2007)

30 http://www.baseball-reference.com

31 http://www.baseball-reference.com

32 http://sabr.org/bioproj/person/1b44e1da

33 HP 15 May 1911; Encyclopedia of Minor League Baseball. Third Edition. (Baseball America, 2007)

34 Ruggles, William B.. The History of the Texas League of Professional Baseball Clubs 1888-1951. (Texas Baseball League, 1951)

35 http://www.baseball-reference.com; Encyclopedia of Minor League Baseball. Third Edition. (Baseball America, 2007)

36 http://sabr.org/bioproj/person/1b44e1da

37 http://www.baseball-reference.com; Encyclopedia of Minor League Baseball. Third Edition. (Baseball America, 2007)

38 Ruggles, William B.. The History of the Texas League of Professional Baseball Clubs 1888-1951. (Texas Baseball League, 1951); O'Neal, Bill. The Texas League. (Eakin Press, 1987)

39 http://www.milb.com/content/page.jsp?sid=l109&ymd=20100316&content_id=8811502&vkey=history

40 http://www.baseball-reference.com; O'Neal, Bill. The Texas League. (Eakin Press, 1987)

41 Ruggles, William B.. The History of the Texas League of Professional Baseball Clubs 1888-1951. (Texas Baseball League, 1951); O'Neal, Bill. The Texas League. (Eakin Press, 1987)

42 http://www.baseball-reference.com

43 Powers-Beck, Jeffrey P.. The American Indian Integration of Baseball. (University of Nebraska Press, 2004)

44 Ruggles, William B.. The History of the Texas League of Professional Baseball Clubs 1888-1951. (Texas Baseball League, 1951); O'Neal, Bill. The Texas League. (Eakin Press, 1987)

45 Corsicana Daily Sun, 18 August 1915; San Antonio Light 22 August 1915

46 http://www.baseball-reference.com; Daily Ardmoreite 10 December 1918; Daily Ardmoreite 11 December 1918; World War I Draft Registration for Walter Raleigh Dickson

47 http://www.baseball-reference.com

48 Encyclopedia of Minor League Baseball. Third Edition. (Baseball America, 2007)

49 HP 24 May 1918; New York Times 6 October 1918;

50 http://www.baseball-reference.com

51 Ruggles, William B.. The History of the Texas League of Professional Baseball Clubs 1888-1951. (Texas Baseball League, 1951); HP 28 May 1918

52 http://www.baseball-reference.com; http://www.baseball-reference.com/bullpen/George_Payne

53 HP 26 April 1918

54 Alexander, Charles C.. Ty Cobb. (Oxford University Press, 1984)

55 Baseball Magazine, May 1919.

56 HP 5 May 1918; HP 6 May 1918

57 http://www.baseball-reference.com; HP 23 April 1918

58 http://www.baseball-reference.com

59 HC 15 February 1920; Charter of Houston Base Ball Association filed with Secretary of State of Texas on 21 February 1920; HC 26 April 1922

60 Charter of Houston Base Ball Association filed with Secretary of State of Texas on 21 February 1920; HC 15 February 1920; HP 15 February 1920

61 http://www.grandlodgeoftexas.org/node/466; Handbook of Texas Online, John H. Crooker; Texas Bar Journal, January 1976; Handbook of Texas Online, Hortense Ward

62 Lowenfish, Lee. *Branch Rickey: Baseball's Ferocious Gentleman.* (University of Nebraska Press, 2007)

63 Alexander, Charles C.. Breaking the Slump: Baseball in the Depression Era. (Columbia University Press, 2002); Powers, Albert T.. The Business of Baseball. (McFarland, 2003)

64 Brian Finch, St. Louis Cardinals Museum; Guinn, Jeff and Bragan, Bobby. When Panthers Roared: The Fort Worth Cats and Minor League Baseball. (TCU Press, 1999); Encyclopedia of Minor League Baseball. Third Edition. (Baseball America, 2007); Lowry, Philip J.. Green Cathedrals. (Addision-Wesley Publishing, 1992); http://sabr.org/bioproj/park/88929e79

65 Encyclopedia of Minor League Baseball. Third Edition. (Baseball America, 2007); Ruggles, William B.. The History of the Texas League of Professional Baseball Clubs 1888-1951. (Texas Baseball League, 1951)

66 http://www.baseball-reference.com; Encyclopedia of Minor League Baseball. Third Edition. (Baseball America, 2007)

67 Encyclopedia of Minor League Baseball. Third Edition. (Baseball America, 2007)

68 Sporting News 6 January 1921; Ruggles, William B.. The History of the Texas League of Professional Baseball Clubs 1888-1951. (Texas Baseball League, 1951)

69 Ankenman, Fred, Sr.. Four Score and More: The Autobiography of Fred N. Ankenman, Sr.. (Texas Gulf Coast Historical Association, 1980)

[70] Ankenman, Fred, Sr.. Four Score and More: The Autobiography of Fred N. Ankenman, Sr.. (Texas Gulf Coast Historical Association, 1980)

[71] HC 9 February 1920; HC 18 January 1921; Burk, Robert F.. Much More Than a Game: Players, Owners and American Baseball Since 1921. (University of North Carolina Press, 2001)

[72] Wiggins, Robert, The Federal League of Baseball Clubs: The History of an Outlaw Major League. (McFarland, 2008); Burk, Robert F.. Much More Than a Game: Players, Owners and American Baseball Since 1921. (University of North Carolina Press, 2001)

[73] HC 7 January 1921; GDN 9 January 1921; GDN 16 January 1921

[74] HC 7 January 1921; Author Interview with Father Robert W. Crooker, 17 January 2013; Ankenman, Fred, Sr.. Four Score and More: The Autobiography of Fred N. Ankenman, Sr.. (Texas Gulf Coast Historical Association, 1980)

[75] http://www.baseball-reference.com; http://sabr.org/bioproj/person/a861245f; HP 2 April 1921

[76] Sporting News 21 March 1921; http://sabr.org/bioproj/person/ea08fc60; Lowenfish, Lee. *Branch Rickey: Baseball's Ferocious Gentleman.* (University of Nebraska Press, 2007)

[77] http://sabr.org/bioproj/person/ea08fc60; http://www.baseball-reference.com

[78] Encyclopedia of Minor League Baseball. Third Edition. (Baseball America, 2007)

[79] HC 26 April 1922

[80] Sporting News 2 November 1922; Ankenman, Fred, Sr.. Four Score and More: The Autobiography of Fred N. Ankenman, Sr.. (Texas Gulf Coast Historical Association, 1980)

[81] Sporting News 24 August 1922; Sporting News 23 November 1922; Ankenman, Fred, Sr.. Four Score and More: The Autobiography of Fred N. Ankenman, Sr.. (Texas Gulf Coast Historical Association, 1980)

[82] Encyclopedia of Minor League Baseball. Third Edition. (Baseball America, 2007); Ruggles, William B.. The History of the Texas League of Professional Baseball Clubs 1888-1951. (Texas Baseball League, 1951)

[83] http://sabr.org/bioproj/person/92a8ae6f

[84] Encyclopedia of Minor League Baseball. Third Edition. (Baseball America, 2007); Ruggles, William B.. The History of the Texas League of Professional Baseball Clubs 1888-1951. (Texas Baseball League, 1951)

[85] GDN 5 November 1922; Sporting News 23 November 1922; Sporting News 1 February 1923

[86] Sporting News 21 June 1923; Sporting News 19 July 1923; Sporting News 27 September 1923

[87] http://www.baseball-reference.com; Texas League Record Book

[88] HP 16 April 1921

[89] http://sabr.org/bioproj/person/b3e94581; http://www.baseball-reference.com

[90] http://www.baseball-reference.com; http://sabr.org/bioproj/person/13be7ab3

[91] http://www.milb.com/content/page.jsp?sid=l109&ymd=20100316&content_id=8811502&vkey=history

[92] Sporting News 28 November 1923; Sporting News 14 February 1924

[93] Sporting News 14 February 1924

[94] Sporting News 28 February 1924

[95] http://sabr.org/bioproj/person/96ae4951; http://www.baseball-reference.com; Encyclopedia of Minor League Baseball. Third Edition. (Baseball America, 2007)

[96] http://www.baseball-reference.com

[97] Encyclopedia of Minor League Baseball. Third Edition. (Baseball America, 2007)

[98] Ankenman, Fred, Sr.. Four Score and More: The Autobiography of Fred N. Ankenman, Sr.. (Texas Gulf Coast Historical Association, 1980); Sporting News 14 August 1924; Sporting News 28 August 1924

[99] Sporting News 5 November 1924

[100] http://www.baseball-reference.com

[101] http://sabr.org/bioproj/person/32dfe3a5; http://www.baseball-reference.com

[102] http://www.baseball-reference.com

[103] Encyclopedia of Minor League Baseball. Third Edition. (Baseball America, 2007); Ruggles, William B.. The History of the Texas League of Professional Baseball Clubs 1888-1951. (Texas Baseball League, 1951)

[104] HC 9 September 1925

[105] HC 13 September 1925

[106] HP 19 October 1925; HP 20 October 1925; HP 21 October 1925; HP 23 October 1925; http://sabr.org/bioproj/person/13be7ab3

[107] Ankenman, Fred, Sr.. Four Score and More: The Autobiography of Fred N. Ankenman, Sr.. (Texas Gulf Coast Historical Association, 1980)

[108] HC 6 December 1925; Sporting News 17 December 1925

[109] Ankenman, Fred, Sr.. Four Score and More: The Autobiography of Fred N. Ankenman, Sr.. (Texas Gulf Coast Historical Association, 1980); Ruggles, William B.. The History of the Texas League of Professional Baseball Clubs 1888-1951. (Texas Baseball League, 1951)

[110] HC 30 April 1926

[111] http://sabr.org/bioproj/person/92a8ae6f; http://www.baseball-reference.com; Devaney, John and Goldblatt, Burt. The World Series, A Complete Pictorial History. (Rand McNally & Co, 1981)

[112] Ruggles, William B.. The History of the Texas League of Professional Baseball Clubs 1888-1951. (Texas Baseball League, 1951)

[113] Encyclopedia of Minor League Baseball. Third Edition. (Baseball America, 2007); http://www.baseball-reference.com

[114] Encyclopedia of Minor League Baseball. Third Edition. (Baseball America, 2007); http://www.baseball-reference.com

[115] Encyclopedia of Minor League Baseball. Third Edition. (Baseball America, 2007)

KEY

GDN – *Galveston Daily News*
HP – *Houston Post*
HC – *Houston Chronicle*
HI – *Houston Informer*
CD – *Chicago Defender*

HOUSTON
1954
DIXIE
Series
PRESIDENT-TEXAS BASEBALL LEAGUE
HO
BA
ASS
BU
ST
4
BOX
4
SEAT
BOX SEA
Est. Price 3.18
Fed. Tax .... .32

CHAPTER SEVEN

THE DIXIE SERIES

BY BILL McCURDY

With a post-World War I boom lifting the state, the Texas League had finally found stability, and the hunger for other hills to climb on the field and at the turnstiles was bound to grow. At the same time, the Southern Association, eight clubs that played in cities stretching from New Orleans to Atlanta, was reaching for a similar increase in competition, income and recognition.

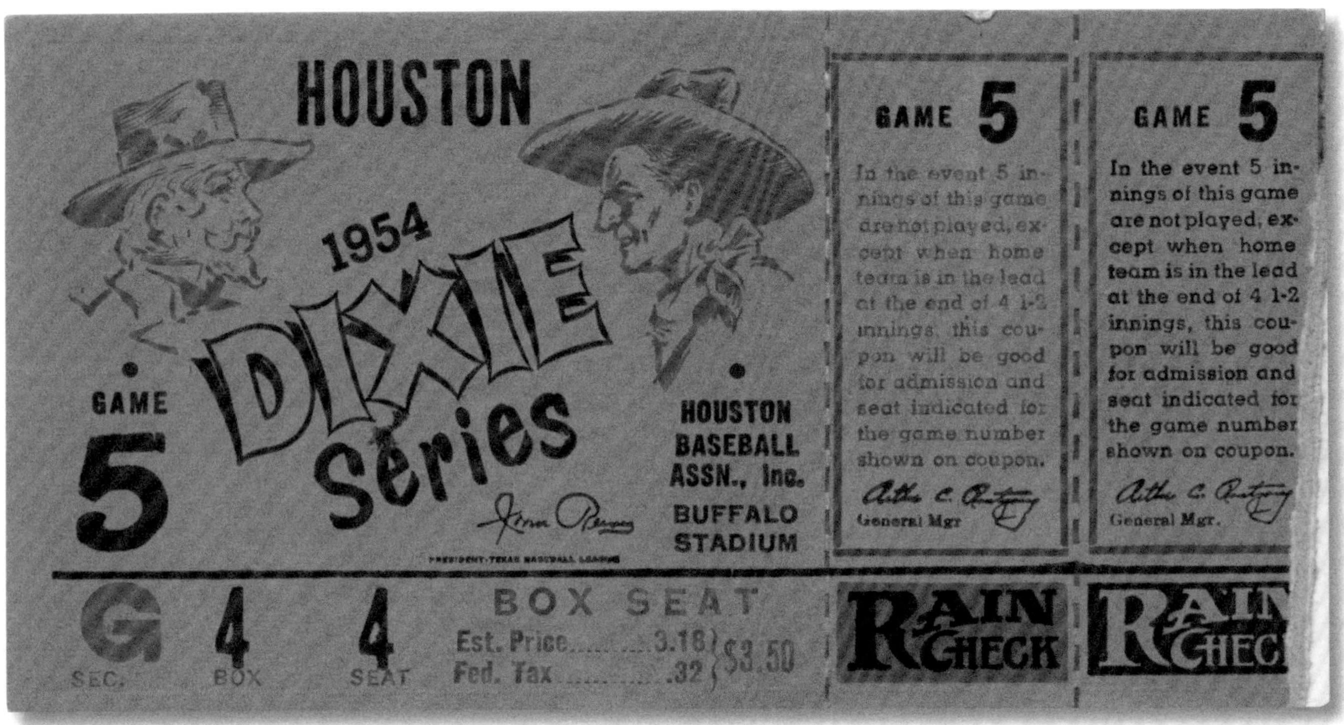

The 1954 Dixie Series tickets featured caricature-like drawings of a John Wayne-like cowboy versus a Southern Colonel.
Courtesy Tom Kennedy

Prior to the 1920 season, ownership groups from the two leagues came together to plan a post-season playoff series between the champions of the Texas League and the Southern Association. It would be modeled after the Major League World Series with the championship decided in a best-of-seven, home and home based competition.

They picked a name that fit the mindset of those early 20th century times: The Dixie Series would annually pit the southeast and southwest sections of the country against each other over an area that covered the territory of the old Civil War Confederacy.

The Dixie Series thrived continuously from 1920 through 1958, only missing three seasons (1943-1945) due to World War II, when there was no play in either league.

1928: HOUSTON BUFFS DEFEAT THE BIRMINGHAM BARONS, 4 TO 2

Winning the Dixie Series seemed to be the pre-ordained finish to the year, which began with Commissioner Landis coming to Houston to watch the club open the new jewel of a ballpark they called Buff Stadium. And so it happened. Led by the hitting of Carey Selph and the pitching of "Wild Bill" Hallahan, the Buffs took the Barons in six games.

It didn't start well, though. In Game 1 at Birmingham, Ed Wells bested Bill Hallahan on a 2-0 shutout, blanking the Buffs on 5 hits. Buffs first baseman

Speed Walker had 2 doubles, and Ed Hock also punched out two singles.[1]

The next day, The Buffs were coasting behind a 3-0 lead in the seventh when the Barons rallied with 2 outs to tie the game at 3 and chase starter Ken Penner. Manager Pancho Snyder put first game starter Hallahan in the game to relieve, but the Barons' Jimmy Johnson stole third and home to give the Barons a lead they would not surrender. The Barons added a run in the bottom of the eighth to make the final score 5-3 and send the Series back to Houston with the Barons holding a commanding lead.[2]

Home agreed with the Buffs. In Game 3, they launched a 17-hit barrage in support of Jim Lindsey to edge Birmingham 6-4 and grab their first win in the Series.[3]

A day later, "Wild Bill" Hallahan atoned for his opening game loss, tossing a two-hit shutout to tie the Series at 2. The score was 6-0, and a standing room crowd of 17,352 watched the action. Homer Peel had three hits and Carey Selph and Heinie Schuble added two each to lead the 11-hit Buffs attack.[4]

Hallahan wasn't through yet. In Game 5, he came on late in relief of Penner to preserve a 5-4 win over the Barons that gave the Buffaloes a 3-2 lead in the Series, going back to Birmingham.[5]

On the road in Game 6, on Wednesday, October 4, 1928, the Buffs finished off the Barons by a score of 5-1 to gain their first ever Dixie Series title. Carey Selph led Houston with a home run included in his 4 for 5 day at the plate. On the mound, Frank Barnes took over early for Jim Lindsey to earn the win.

Overall, it was bunched hitting and Houston's four 20 game winners that came through for them, putting the quietus on a Birmingham club that batted .331 as a team in 1928. Total receipts for the Series were $110,091.00. The players split $39,486.00.[6]

Start of Houston Radio Baseball

Amateur radio had been in Houston for years when the *Post-Dispatch* launched KPRC on the evening of May 9, 1925, but the event marked the start of highly promoted commercial radio in the city. It was not long before baseball became part of the radio lineup. That fall's World Series between the Pirates and Senators marked the first time the sport was heard on Houston airwaves.

Within three weeks, KPRC was running an evening baseball recap talk show every night following *Uncle Judd's Kiddie Hour* and just prior to a nightly music program that varied from opera luminaries to Blanchard's Dance orchestra to Frank Tilton, blind pianist. One of the most popular programs that first month featured Miss Gene Dennis, psychic reader, who was deluged with thousands of queries from listeners asking for advice on oil leases or land purchases, where lost jewelry was located, if their daughter had musical talent or who stole their son's tires.

By 1927, on the second anniversary of KPRC radio, Houston Buffs games were regularly broadcast on the radio. The station presented road games from far away places such as Wichita Falls and Fort Worth "just as soon as it comes over the wire." The man doing the re-creation of the contests was Stanley G. Davis. When the new Buff Stadium opened in April 1928, *Post* sports editor, Bruce Layer was at the microphone for KPRC in a "specially constructed booth" at the ballpark. The station broadcast every game in 1928 with another early pioneer Houston play-by-play man, I.S. Roberts, handling every game after Opening Day.

1931: BIRMINGHAM BARONS DEFEAT THE HOUSTON BUFFS, 4 TO 3

The excitement generated by "Dizzy" Dean is hard to overstate. On the first

It was young Dizzy Dean for Houston versus old Ray Caldwell for Birmingham in the 1931 Dixie Series.

Houston Metropolitan Research Center, Houston Public Library

day of the series, *Birmingham News* sports editor Zipp Newman called him "the greatest showman of his day," adding that "people will watch Dizzy Dean today who have never seen a baseball game and they won't care about the outcome." He was half right. A record Dixie Series crowd of 20,074 fans came out to Rickwood Field, but they rooted rabidly for the Barons.[7]

Going for Birmingham was Ray Caldwell, a 43-year-old grandfather who had married his third wife only a couple of weeks prior. He had pitched his first professional game in 1906, four years before Dizzy Dean was born. Such lights as Grantland Rice had said that Caldwell had as much talent as Walter Johnson, but that he chose to drink and party it away. He showed many flashes of brilliance during 11 years in the majors, but after another decade in the minors, he was getting by on control, junk and guile.[8]

In the end, Caldwell bested Dean 1 to 0, giving up 7 hits to Dean's 5, but benefitting in the eighth when the Barons pushed across the only run of the game on three bunched hits. Dizzy had pitched well, facing the minimum through six. It was, however, the first time in Dean's career that he had gone nine innings without striking anyone out. For decades, baseball fans in Alabama called it the greatest game ever played.[9]

Without the Great Dean on the hill, attendance for the second game dropped to less than half. Perhaps the home town fans sensed the outcome: a 3-0 shutout by Dick McCabe who had been signed off the Fort Worth roster to replace the injured "Tex" Carleton. Three of the four Barons hits were by McCabe mound foe, Jimmy Walkup.

Back in Houston for Game 3, it was another pitcher's duel with slow-balling George Payne allowing a single hit and winning 1-0 thanks to well-timed hits from Joe Medwick and Homer Peel.[10]

Dizzy Dean was almost as good the next night, scattering three hits and winning 2-0. The Buffs runs came on back-to-back ground rule doubles to left by Selph and Peel and an Ed Hock sac fly. The Buffs were only a win away.[11]

It was not to be as easy as all that, though. In Game 5, Clay Touchstone stopped the Buffs by a score of 3-1. Game 6 certainly broke the mold of what had been until now a pitchers' series. The Barons pounded five Buff pitchers for 23 hits in 14-10 victory that tied the Series at 3 games each. Houston had 18 hits of their own with Guy Sturdy pounding out two homers, but it was not enough. The teams now faced a Game 7.[12]

In one of the great comebacks in Dixie Series history, the Barons defeated Dizzy Dean, 6-3, to take the Series from the Buffs. Even the mightiest may fall, if they are hit in the right places at the right time. So it was with the great 1931 Houston Buffs.[13]

1940: NASHVILLE VOLS DEFEAT THE HOUSTON BUFFS, 4 TO 1

The story of this Dixie Series appears to be rather simple. The Vols brought their killer instinct, and the Buffs did not. As

Clark Nealon

Clark Nealon came to work as the "fourth man on a four man sports staff" for the *Houston Post* in 1936, recruited by fellow San Antonian Bruce Layer who was sports editor there at the time. After a stint in the Army, Nealon went to the rival *Press*, finally returning to the *Post* as sports editor in 1951 to stay. Nealon was known as a straight shooter, helping young writers as he had been helped himself. Among his protégés was Mickey Herskowitz. He was also a booster of the Houston sports scene to other cities, recalling in his later years the many Houstonians who went on to greatness from Bayou City football and baseball sandlots and from the city's golf courses, as well. With the disclaimer that he was not being a "good old days type," Nealon spoke of the "civic enthusiasm" that Houstonians had for their Buffs, rating the city as one of the five best minor league towns (along with San Francisco, Minneapolis, Los Angeles and Atlanta) in America when he moved to Houston. Clark Nealon died in his longtime hometown of Houston in 1992.

(Left: Joe Page, NY Yankee relief pitcher; right: Clark Nealon).

a result, one of the highest rated clubs in minor league history flopped. The newspaper accounts give the impression that the Series was not even as close as some of the final scores suggest.

The Vols jumped on Sam Nahem early for a big lead in Game 1, and in spite of second baseman Danny Murtaugh's three for four effort and Tom Winsett's three-run blast in the eighth, it was too late. "Ace" Adams shut the door on the Buffs in frosty football weather, hanging on for a 7-5 victory and the series lead.[14]

The second game was more promising. Teddy Wilks took over from Howie Pollet in the fifth with Houston trailing, and then held on as the Buffs rallied for a 6-4 win. Unfortunately, moving back to Houston wasn't much of a tonic.

In the first game at home, both clubs got good pitching. Starters Howie Krist of Houston and "Boots" Poffenberger of the Vols were both strong, and they went to extra innings knotted at one apiece.[15]

Jittery defense by the Buffs let the Vols take the lead in the top of the tenth. The Buffs tried to rally in the bottom of the frame and had Danny Murtaugh at third and Red Davis at first. With two outs, a long fly ball to deep center by Johnny Wyrostek was not quite enough, and Nashville carded a 2-1 win in Game 3.[16]

Game 4, a repeat pitching matchup from the first game, lacked all drama. Before a crowd of 8,400 fans, Ace Adams again stopped the Buffs, this time striking out six and shutting them out 6-0. Houston's back was against the wall.[17]

Teddy Wilks started Game 5 for the

Buffs and looked solid, but he left in the seventh for a pinch hitter. The Vols again took advantage of a faltering Buffs defense in the tenth for two runs. The 5-3 win decided the Series. The Vols were the champions in five games.[18]

1947: HOUSTON BUFFS DEFEAT THE MOBILE BEARS, 4 TO 2

The 1947 Houston ball club was filled with aggressive players like Solly Hemus, Hal Epps, Eddie Knoblauch, Johnny Hernandez, and Billy Costa, and mentored by the always testing manager Johnny Keane. Though other Buffs teams were rated higher, many long time fans choose this club as their favorite of all time.

Game 1 proved to be a sterling start to the series in Houston. Stan Benjamin had four RBIs and Gerry Burmeister had three as the Buff crushed the Bears 8-2 behind the dancing knuckler deliveries of right-hander Al Papai. The only extra base hit of the game for the Bears was a dinger from Chuck Connors, the future star of "The Rifleman" TV series.

Houston's advantage didn't last long. The Bears tied the series at one behind the dominant pitching of ace Frank Laga and his 6-0, five-hit shutout of the Buffs. Things didn't improve for Houston when the Series moved to Mobile, either.[19]

The Bears jumped on Buffs starter Clarence Beers for two in the first and four in the sixth, while Pat McGlothin held the Buffs largely in check. Growing stronger as the game aged, the Bears hurler added seven K's over the last four innings on the way to a 7-2 Bears win in Game 3.[20]

In the fourth game, the pattern of one-sided wins continued. This time Papai was the beneficiary of a 15-hit Buffaloes offensive stampede led by Hal Epps. The Associated Press game report waxed poetically: "Houston and a harvest moon rode high over Mobile tonight as the Texas League Buffs slammed back into the Dixie Series with a 13-2 victory over the Southern Association Bears."[21]

In Game 5, it was Jack Creel's turn. He shutout Mobile 7-0 on five hits. The run support came from across the board. Eddie Knoblauch rapped five hits, and Solly Hemus and Hal Epps added three apiece to pace the Houston Buffs to a big win over John Hall and a 3-2 Series lead. The Buffs headed home needing only one win in two tries, if needed.[22]

The matchup was a good one for Houston. Their top pitcher, Clarence Beers, was on the mound. The 25-game winner needed everything he had, because, for the first time in the series, the game was not a rout. Instead it came down to a great pitchers' duel with 2 outs in the bottom of a scoreless ninth.

After Hemus led off the inning with a pop out to third, starter Frank Laga of the Bears walked Costa and Knoblauch to earn the hook from his manager, Al Todd. Reliever Paul Minner then fanned the Buffs' Stan Benjamin, but hopes were quickly dashed by a Hal Epps single up the middle that scored Billy Costa from second with the Dixie Series winning run.

In the end, superior hitting and pitching won the six-game Dixie Series for the 1947 Buffs. In taking the last three games in a row, the Buffs outscored the Bears, 21-2, allowing no runs in the last two games.[23]

1951: THE BIRMINGHAM BARONS DEFEAT THE HOUSTON BUFFS, 4 TO 2

The 1951 Buffs looked primed to take the Series behind the slugging of Jerry Witte and Larry Miggins, with their combined 65 regular season home runs, and the pitching of Wilmer "Vinegar Bend" Mizell and Al Papai. Luck dictated otherwise.

To get the Dixie Series started in what he felt was the proper spirit, Buffs President Allen Russell had a band on the field play "Dixie" in honor of the Barons and "The Eyes of Texas" in honor of the Buffs. The ones seemingly stirred were Illinois-born pitcher Mickey Haefner, just back in the minors after eight big league seasons, and New Englander Jimmy Piersall, a 21-year-old who had put up a .346 average for Birmingham that season.[24]

Led by Piersall's 4 for 4 day, the Barons cracked out 12 hits, four for extra bases, to rough up four Buff pitchers. Starter Al Papai was gone after 5 and 1/3 innings, and the Birmingham bunch romped to a 7-3 first game win over the Buffs.

The Buffs star youngster, Wilmer Mizell, got the start in Game 2, and all the offense happened in the bottom of the first. Ben Steiner singled, moved to second, then came home on a single up the middle by center fielder Roy Broome. The 1-0 Buffs lead held up as the final score as Mizell won the pitchers' duel with Ralph Brickner, striking out 14 Barons hitters along the way.[25]

The first bad news happened after the ballgame when the Buffs' top reliever, Jack Crimian, flew home to Delaware after learning that his wife had given birth to a child who soon died. Obviously, his return to the series was uncertain.[26]

A crowd of 16,681 Barons fans turned out at legendary Rickwood Field to welcome their boys home for Game 3, but they were disappointed at the outcome. Buffs hurler Fred Martin subjected the Barons to a second straight shutout loss. With 2 outs in the top of the sixth in a scoreless tie, Roy Broome tripled and Eddie Kazak walked for the Buffs. Larry Miggins then crushed a Bobo Newsom pitch for a 360-foot home run over the left field wall and provided the final margin in a 3-0 Buffs win.[27]

Al Papai, who had led Houston with 23 wins during the regular season, again took the ball for Game 4. His outing was decent, but a sixth-inning homer by George Wilson put the Barons on top to stay. The 3-2 win left the series tied at two.[28]

Game 5 proved to be another tight one. The Buffs took the lead in the top of the fourth when Larry Miggins smashed his second homer of the Series. Jerry Witte doubled off the scoreboard to score Roy Broome.

Trouble came in the bottom of the sixth. The masterful Mizell walked two men and then retired to the clubhouse where a mysterious illness that had sidelined him in recent days apparently returned.[29]

It was the turning point in the series. With Jack Crimian back from his wife's bedside and in the game, the Barons quickly bunched walks and singles into a four-run splurge that gave them both the lead and enough runs to win the game. The Series now headed back to Houston with the Barons holding a 3-2 lead and a chance to end it all in six.[30]

In Game 6, Mike Clark of the Buffs gave up four runs and the first seven hits by the Barons before he was replaced in the third inning. That was it for the Barons, but it would prove to be more than enough. Birmingham's veteran, Mickey Haefner, was perfect through seven innings, retiring all 21 Buffs whom he faced. Houston pushed across two runs in the bottom of the eighth, but it was too little, too late. The Barons had taken the 1951 Dixie Series, 4 games to 2, on a somber night in Houston baseball.[31]

1954: THE ATLANTA CRACKERS DEFEAT THE HOUSTON BUFFS, 4 TO 3

Two old Brooklyn Dodger buddies, managers Whitlow Wyatt of Atlanta and Dixie Walker of Houston, squared off against each other in the 1954 Dixie Series. The powerful Buffs took a 3 games to 1 lead behind the bats of Ken Boyer, Bob Boyd and Willard Brown, but they apparently lacked the killer's heart that could put away an Atlanta team that fought relentlessly when cornered. The Crackers battled back in three straight "do or die" games to take the series.

A full house of Crackers fans showed up to watch Game 1 of the series. Glenn Thompson suffered from wildness early, and he was gone before the end of the second inning. None of the four relievers who followed Thompson could halt the Buffs from building on their early lead. A three-run homer by Fred McAlister in the sixth iced the game for Houston on their march to a 10-4 victory.[32]

Luis Arroyo went the distance for the Buffs, holding the Crackers to four runs on seven hits. Atlanta fans booed Dixie Walker loudly for leaving their team as manager after the 1952 season, but the show of disapproval had no effect on the final score as the home team lost.[33]

Houston's good fortune continued in Game 2 as Willard Schmidt limited the Crackers to two hits, and none beyond the second inning, while striking out 11 and pitching the Buffs to a 7-2 win. With two road victories, the Buffaloes were heading home in total command of the series.[34]

The Atlanta Crackers, however, had other thoughts. Persistence was the Crackers theme as they battled back four times to ultimately win their first game, 7-4, at Buff Stadium. After relentless effort, Dick Donovan emerged the winner at the expense of Buffs reliever Jim Atchley. With 12 hits to the Crackers' 13, the Buffs still could not stop the boys from Atlanta.[35]

Atlanta used a couple of singles, a hit-and-run, an error and a wild pitch to break on top of Game 4, but that would be it for the Crackers. The Buffs got a homer from Bob Boyd and doubles by

Ken Boyer and Russell Rac to take it with a final tally of 5-2. Houston was only one win away from taking it all.[36]

They came close on Saturday night in Game 5. It was a tough pitcher's duel between Atlanta's Glenn Thompson and Houston's Luis Arroyo. Thompson got the better of it. He pitched a masterful game for the Crackers, limiting the Buffs to three hits, two by Bob Boyd and one by Russell Rac, and gave up no runs. Atlanta scored in the top of the first, and that was all Thompson needed. With the Buffaloes failing to close things out at home, the clubs traveled back to Atlanta on Sunday to resume the series.[37]

Houston drew first blood in Game 6. The Crackers followed in the bottom half of the fourth by bombing Buffs starter Willard Schmidt for five runs. It included a Pete Whisenant triple that bounced over right fielder Willard Brown's head and scored runners Frank Torre and Bob Montag. The Buffs never got up from that knockdown and took the loss that squared the series.[38]

Whether it was a hangover from the previous night or the 1-0 heartbreaker back at Buff Stadium, the deciding Game 7 was never even close. The Crackers dominated as their starter Glenn Thompson again shut down the Buffs. After Houston scored in the top of the first on a Blasingame triple and a sacrifice fly, the Crackers jolted Hugh Sooter for three in the bottom of the fourth before finishing him off one frame later.

In the fifth, the Crackers put men at second and third with one out, causing Buffs manager Walker to pull Sooter in favor of lefty Luis Arroyo. Arroyo then walked Chuck Tanner to set up the double play with the left handed Bob Montag coming to the plate. Then, in spite of his 39 long balls on the season and good hitting in the Series, Crackers manager Whitlow Wyatt pulled Montag and brought in the right handed Jim Solt to pinch-hit against the lefty Arroyo. Solt made Wyatt look like a genius by knocking a grand slam to left that made it 7-1 and put the Crackers victory in the bag. Before 13,293 screaming fans, the Atlanta Crackers had come back from a three-games-to-one hole to take the 1954 Dixie Series over the Houston Buffs.[39]

1956: THE HOUSTON BUFFS DEFEAT THE ATLANTA CRACKERS, 4 TO 2

Two years after coughing up a three-to-one series lead, the Buffs had a shot at revenge against the Atlanta Crackers. Benny Valenzuela, Pidge Browne, Bob Smith and Harry Walker provided much of the stick work while Billy Muffet, Ted Wieand and Bob Mabe provided the major pitching answers that allowed the Buffs to overcome the southerners in six games. Weather problems may have affected the play of the Crackers, too. After a two-day rain delay in Houston, with the series tied through four games, the Georgians suffered through two straight losses and surrendered the 1956 Dixie Series title to Houston.

It had started well for the Crackers. Pitcher Charles Bicknell dominated the Buffs, 7-2, in Game 1 to give Atlanta a

Houston's Buffaloes did indeed feast on Atlanta Crackers in 1956. Courtesy Tom Kennedy

Choices for Your Listening Pleasure

Broadcasting rights for the Houston Buffaloes have not always been exclusive. There was a time in the early 1950s when fans could find the team on multiple radio stations at once, each brought to them by a different sponsor. With the Buffs reigning as the undisputed king of Houston sports and the only professional outfit in town, competition was fierce from year to year. A perusal of score card covers through the latter part of that decade shows Loel Passe (pictured left) and KTHT featured in 1954 and 1955, Guy Savage and Gus Mancuso of KXYZ the following two seasons and Dan Rather, Art McGee and Len Lowry of KTRH rounding out the decade.

1-0 lead in the Series. A small crowd of 5,319 showed up to watch as Bob Mabe, the only 20-game winner on the Buffs staff, took it on the chin.[40]

Turnout was no better for the second game, but the Buffaloes hitters were. Houston's Benny Valenzuela homered in the first, but starters Billy Muffet of the Buffs and Dick Grabowski of the Crackers battled each other even at 2-2 through six innings. In the seventh, pitcher Muffet broke the tie with a sacrifice fly that scored the go-ahead run and drove Grabowski from the game. Player/manager Harry Walker later blasted a three-run homer to right and the Buffs added four more to make the final score 10-2.[41]

A trip back to Houston did nothing to cool the bats of the Buffs. The Crackers got their only run on the second pitch of the game when leadoff man "Sour Mash" Jack Daniels hammered a 330-foot HR to right field. The Buffs countered with a big five run third. Pidge Browne knocked in four runs on 2 doubles and a single while Bob Smith kicked in with a two run homer and a double, and Ted Wieand dunked the Crackers at the plate for an 8-1 Houston win in Game 3.[42]

As so often happens in baseball, the following game saw the tables turned. Atlanta used four long balls to pound the Buffs back into a series tie with an 8-3 Game 4 clubbing. Jack Daniels shot a pair of two run homers, and Sammy Meeks and Bob Montag each added homers to seal the deal.[43]

Just when momentum might be turning toward the Crackers, Mother Nature intervened. Heavy afternoon rains and 55 mph winds that blew down a 40-foot long section of the left center field fence and scattered stadium roof shingles all over the playing field wiped out baseball in Houston for the next two days.[44]

By Friday, the standing water had lessened enough to play Game 5, and by then, the Crackers bats were cold. Bob Mabe shut out Atlanta with a 12-strike-out, four-hit night. The Buffs blew open a tight game with four runs in the eighth to seal a 5-0 victory and take a series lead back to Georgia.[45]

Using some late inning help from reliever Phil Clark in Game 6, Buffs starter Billy Muffet turned back the Crackers for a 4-2 win that clinched the 1956 Dixie Series for the Buffs. The Crackers come-back character from two seasons prior was nowhere to be found as they left 10 men on base after falling behind by two runs. Only a miserable 2,840 fans turned out to watch the locals lose to Houston in six games.[46]

1957: THE HOUSTON BUFFS DEFEAT THE ATLANTA CRACKERS, 4 TO 2

For the second year in a row, the Houston Buffs played and defeated the Atlanta Crackers in a six-game Dixie Series. It was the third time in four years that the two clubs had met in the series. It was also the first time in 32 years that a Texas League club had won two in a row.

Ruben Amaro, Ray Dabek, Benny Valenzuela and Harry Walker provided some key hitting for Houston in the series and Lady Luck also seemed to be sitting in the Buffs dugout on several key umpiring calls.

The 1957 Dixie Series did not get off to a flying start for the Buffaloes. Atlanta came into the series riding a streak of seven straight wins in the Southern Association playoffs, and they did not show signs of cooling off yet. Starting with an Ev Joyner two-run homer in the first inning of Game 1, the Crackers rolled over three Buffs pitchers for 11 runs and 14 hits for an 11-1 playoff win. Pitcher Ken Mackenzie, a Yale-educated Canadian, dominated; and the Crackers were off to a one-game lead.[47]

Don Nottebart would later achieve recognition as a pitcher for the Houston Colt .45s and Astros, but in 1957, he was still trying to work his way to the big leagues as a member of the Atlanta Crackers. On the night of Game 2, it did not go well.

Tied 1-1 in the bottom of the ninth, Nottebart gave up singles to Buffs Pidge Browne and Harry Walker before intentionally walking catcher Ray Dabek to set up a double play. Walker then put in Tony Stathos as a pinch runner for Browne at third and sent up Nels Burbrink as a pinch hitter. Nottebart promptly walked Burbrink to force in Stathos with the game-winning run for a 2-1 Buffs victory. The Buffs triumph sent the Series back to Atlanta tied at a game apiece.[48]

In Game 3, the Crackers parlayed timely hitting, clutch pitching and solid defense to defeat the Buffs 5-1 on only eight hits. Starter Corky Valentine did yeoman's work for Atlanta. They also pulled off a triple play when left fielder Ev Joyner snared a sinking liner and then got the ball back in time to double up two Buffs who had been off and running.[49]

Game 4 started under threatening skies on a chilly 55-degree night. Atlanta fans responded accordingly. Only 611 of them paid to watch the post season playoff contest. It was one that the Buffaloes would win with small ball. Houston posted single tallies in the first, second, third and seventh that proved more than enough for a 4-1 win over the Crackers and a 2-2 tie in series. Nelson Chittum and Phil Clark held the Crackers to one run and seven hits, and the Buffs were paced by catcher Nels Burbrink's four hits in five tries.[50]

The excitement in Game 5 came late. Trailing 3-2 in the top of the seventh, the Buffs loaded the bases on a single, a double by Ruben Amaro and an error. A rhubarb then delayed the game when Buffs manager Harry Walker tried to sub Tony Stathos for the runner at first, but then immediately asked for a change that would allow him to place Stathos on third as the runner for Fred McAllister. The Crackers manager protested the change, but to no avail. When play resumed, Atlanta shortstop Joe Morgan (not "Little Joe" of Astros and Reds fame) flubbed an easy grounder off the bat of Herbie Adams that allowed the tying and lead runs for the Buffs. Benny Valenzuela then slashed an RBI single for an insurance run that nailed the final score at 5-3, Buffs.

Only 1,305 fans even saw the fifth game in Atlanta.[51] The Buffs' Tommy Hughes and the Crackers' Don Nottebart both held their foes to four hits in Game 6. It was the close calls that made the difference at Buff Stadium.

The Buffs scored first when Wally Shannon reached first on a throwing error by Frank DiPrima that pulled first-baseman Buck Riddle's foot off the base. The Crackers tied things at one in the fourth when Sammy Taylor homered.

Then in the seventh, with Harry Keister on base, Ruben Amaro bashed a line-hugging homer to left. The Crackers protested that it was foul. Their complaint fell on deaf ears. The 3-1 margin stood up to give the 1957 Dixie Series crown to the Houston Buffs over the disgruntled Atlanta Crackers.

It was not only the first back-to-back Texas League win in over three decades, it was also the last of eight Dixie Series appearances for the Houston Buffs. They finished with an even record of four wins and four losses.[52]

After the 1958 season, the Dixie Series ceased to exist. The end coincided with the Houston's last season as a member of the Texas League. In 1959, the Buffaloes would move up to face AAA competition in the American Association under independent ownership by Marty Marion and his group of investors.

1 Lubbock Morning Avalanche, Thursday, September 27, 1928, p. 4
2 Corsicana Daly Sun, Friday, September 28, 1928, p. 1
3 Port Arthur News, Sunday, September 30, 1928, p. 9.
4 Gulfport and Biloxi Daily Herald, Monday, October 1, 1928, p. 3
5 Galveston Daily News, Tuesday, October 2, 1928, p. 6
6 Gulfport and Biloxi Daily Herald, Thursday, October 4, 1928; http://www.baseball-reference.com
7 Brownsville Herald, Thursday, September 17, 1931, p. 7
8 Gregory, Robert. *Diz: The Story of Dizzy Dean and Baseball During the Great Depression.* (Penguin, 1992); http://sabr.org/bioproj/person/8311d756
9 Gregory, Robert. *Diz: The Story of Dizzy Dean and Baseball During the Great Depression.* (Penguin, 1992)
10 San Antonio Light, Sunday September 20, 1931, p. 41
11 San Antonio Express, Monday, September 21, 1931, p. 8
12 San Antonio Light 22 September 1931; GDN 24 September 1931
13 Brownsville Herald, Sunday, September 27, 1931, p. 8
14 Galveston Daily News, Thursday, September 26, 1940, p. 9
15 Big Spring Daily Herald, Friday, September 27, 1940, p. 3
16 Galveston Daily News, Sunday, September 29, 1940, p. 19
17 Galveston Daily News, Monday, September 30, 1940, p. 9
18 Galveston Daily News, Tuesday, October 1, 1940, p. 6
19 Corpus Christi Times, Sunday, September 28, 1947, p. 36
20 Corpus Christi Times, Tuesday, September 30, 1947, p. 15
21 Galveston Daily News, Wednesday, October 1, 1947, p. 11
22 Galveston Daily News, Thursday October 2, 1947, p. 8
23 Lubbock Morning Avalanche, Saturday, October 4, 1947, p. 8
24 Witte, Jerry and McCurdy, Bill. A Kid From St. Louis. (Pecan Park Eagle Press, 2000); http://www.baseball-reference.com
25 A Kid From St. Louis, Ibid, p. 288
26 A Kid From St. Louis, Ibid, p. 287
27 Galveston Daily News, Monday, October 1, 1951, p. 7
28 Galveston Daily News, Tuesday, October 2, 1951, p. 11
29 A Kid From St. Louis, Ibid, p. 291
30 Galveston Daly News, Wednesday, October 3, 1951. p 11
31 Galveston Daily News, Friday, October 5, 1951. p 23
32 Corpus Christi Times 22 September 1954
33 Corpus Christi Times 22 September 1954
34 Baytown Sun, Thursday, September 23, 1954, p. 25
35 Corpus Christi Times, Friday, September 24, 1954, p. 31
36 Galveston Daily News, Saturday, September 25, 1954, p. 14
37 Galveston Daily News, Sunday, September 26, 1954, p. 8
38 Galveston Daily News, Tuesday, September 28, 1954, p. 10
39 Baytown Sun, Wednesday, September 29, 1954, p. 8
40 Galveston Daily News, Sunday, September 30, 1956, p. 13
41 Galveston Daily News, Monday, October 1, 1956, p.9
42 Corpus Christi Times, Tuesday, October 2, 1956; Abilene Reporter News, Tuesday, October 2, 1956
43 Hattiesburg American, Wednesday, October 3, 1956, p. 10
44 Danville Bee, Thursday, October 4, 1956; San Antonio Express, Friday, October 5, 1956
45 Corsicana Daily Sun, Saturday, October 6, 1956, p. 8
46 Galveston Daily News, Sunday, October 7, 1956; San Antonio Express, Sunday, October 7, 1956
47 Corpus Christi Times, Tuesday, October 1, 1957, p. 19
48 Corpus Christi Times, Wednesday, October 2, 1957, p. 22
49 Galveston Daily News, Friday, October 4, 1957, p. 21
50 San Antonio Light, Saturday, October 5, 1957, p. 4
51 San Antonio Light, Sunday, October 6, 1951, p. 46
52 Galveston Daily News, Monday, October 7, 1957, p. 9

KEY

GDN – *Galveston Daily News*
HI – *Houston Informer*
HP – *Houston Post*
CD – *Chicago Defender*
HC – *Houston Chronicle*

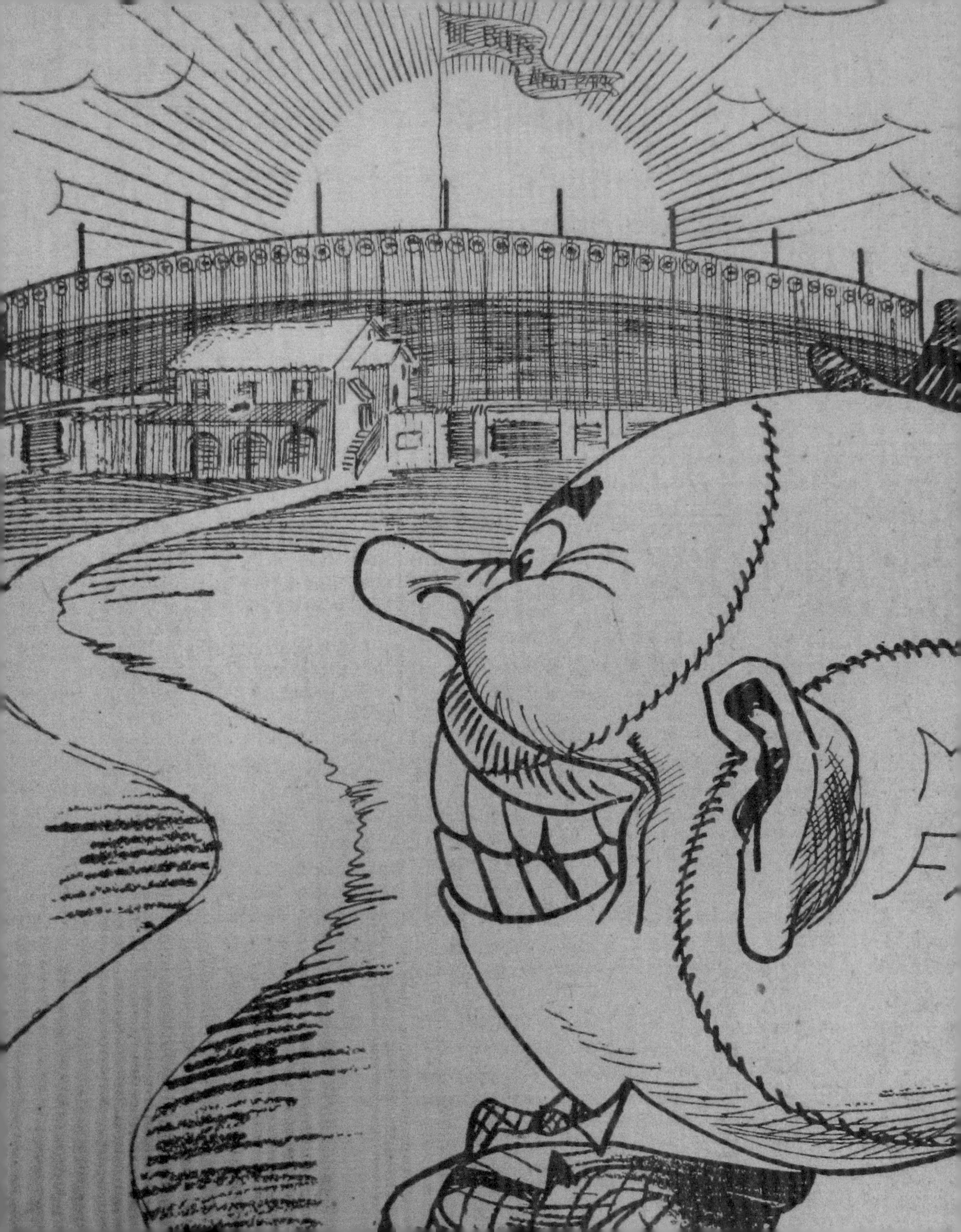
THE BUFFS

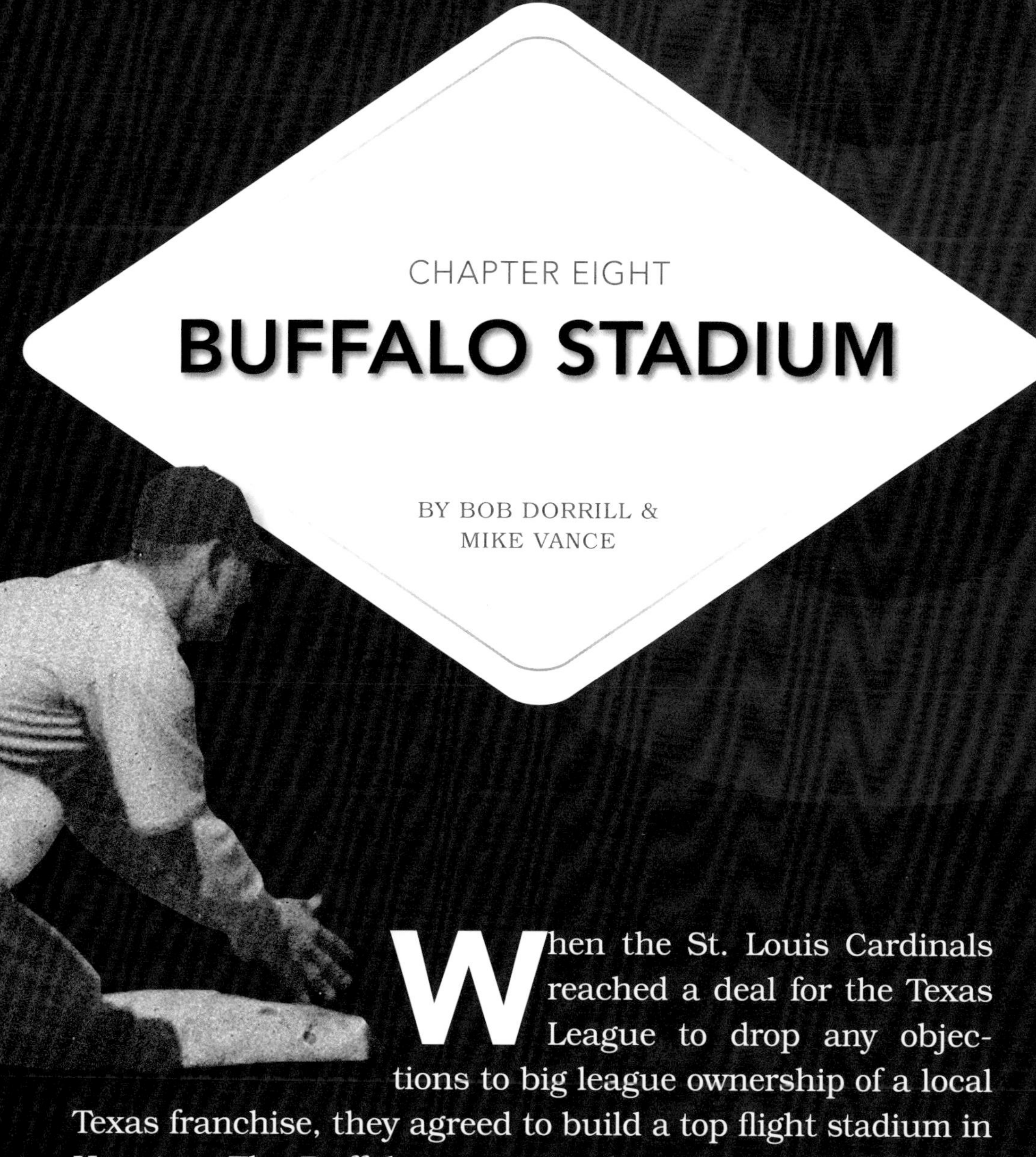

CHAPTER EIGHT

BUFFALO STADIUM

BY BOB DORRILL &
MIKE VANCE

When the St. Louis Cardinals reached a deal for the Texas League to drop any objections to big league ownership of a local Texas franchise, they agreed to build a top flight stadium in Houston. The Buffaloes previous home was only 23 years old, just 13 if one was counting from the major renovation following the 1915 hurricane, but it was built mostly of wood. Stadium technology had bypassed Houston.

Houston Post ***cartoonist Bert Blessington depicted a happy local fandom when spectacular new Buffalo Stadium opened in 1928.***
Courtesy Harris County Archives

The job of finding a new location for this ball park fell squarely to club president Fred Ankenman. Ankenman settled on a tract of about eight acres that fronted St. Bernard Street southeast of downtown. It was a narrow two-lane artery that would later be renamed Cullen Boulevard. The St. Louis organization paid $75,000 for the land.[1]

More worrisome than potential traffic jams, however, was the fact that the city had just signed off on a street plan to develop the land for housing. Ankenman immediately began lobbying City Council to set aside the adoption of the new street grid. One councilman objected, asking that the ball club pay the city for its trouble even though all the work had been done by the developer's office. In the end, the obstacle was overcome, and the Buffs got the variance on their new stadium site.[2]

The club acquired an additional four acres south of the first tract that would be used for parking, which would be free of charge to those who chose to drive. Others would be arriving via the interurban tracks running along the edge of the property. This line, which ran a short distance west of the home plate side of the ball park, provided service between Houston and Galveston. To the northwest it led directly to Union Station which is now part of Minute Maid Park, the current home of the Houston Astros.

Construction on Buffalo Stadium was started in 1927, designed and supervised by G. W. Thompson, a firm out of Syracuse, New York, another Cardinals farm city. Assisting with design and engineering work was the Houston firm of Henry F. Jonas & Tabor. Construction superintendant was Harrison Dann, a Floridian whose most notable previous work had been the Jacksonville stadium that would one day be known as the Gator Bowl. In 1928, the capacity for Buff Stadium was the larger of the two. Thompson and Dann would team up once more the following year for a new baseball park in Rochester, NY, again built at the expense of the parent St. Louis Cardinals.[3]

The ball park was situated with the batter facing east and with St. Bernard Street running behind the right field fence. In the summertime, the steady breeze from the Gulf of Mexico meant the wind would generally be blowing in to the park. This helped cement Buffalo Stadium's reputation as a pitcher's park. The fences were deep: 344 feet in left, 434 in center and 323 feet in right. Covered in advertising, they stood 12-feet with a 24-foot scoreboard in left center. A huge flag pole sat in center field some five feet in front of the outfield wall. The overall effect on the batter was just as the *Post* reported when the place opened: "to get a home run in Buffalo stadium, the batter will have to slam out quite a hefty knock."[4]

Between the size and wind, the setup discouraged home run sluggers and inspired exceptional pitching performances. Two of the most famously dominant seasons came from Dizzy Dean, who went 26-10 for the Buffs with a 1.53 era in 1931, and Howie Pollett, who posted a record of 20-3 with 1.16 era in 1941.[5]

Buffalo Stadium wasn't just big on the inside, either. It was a giant step forward all around. The previous Buffs home held about 4,000 when configured for baseball. According to Opening Day press, the new stadium was designed to hold as many as 13,697, though most estimates put capacity at around twelve thousand. The cost for building such a grand ball park was $400,000, making it a true palace for the fans.[6]

A signature feature of the ballpark was a set of 80 metal buffalo medallions, three feet in diameter, that ringed the top of the exterior walls. Several of these medallions exist in private collections. In 1963, the company that demolished the ball park would sell them for $4 each.

While the stadium itself was concrete and steel, the ticket office was a white stucco building with a Spanish-style tiled roof. It made for an impressive entryway steeped in Texas flavor.

Like most ball parks of the day, the dugouts and locker rooms were spartan. Concrete block walls, hard wooden benches and a prayer for the slightest of breezes was all the comfort players got.

The playing surface was Bermuda grass, 250 loads of sod to be exact. It was supplemented by 1000 pounds of grass seed and three train carloads of fertilizer. Buffalo Stadium opened on April 11, 1928. In spite of heavy rains on the two days prior, the field was judged to have been in "perfect condition."[7]

The Houston Buffaloes, led by veteran right handed pitcher Ken Penner, won 7-5 over the Waco Cubs, and a record crowd, including overflow viewers from outside the park, was said to number as many as fifteen thousand. The park was dubbed a "baseball paradise;" the crowd size was helped by the fact that the Houston Independent School District released students 50 minutes early so they could attend the game. Many businesses were said to have taken a full half-day off in order to join the afternoon festivities.[8]

The celebration kicked off with a grand parade that left City Auditorium 90 minutes before game time and headed down Polk Avenue. The lead car was occupied by Governor Dan Moody, Mayor Oscar Holcombe and Jesse Jones. The trio was slated to combine on the ceremonial first pitch with Moody tossing to Holcombe and Jones donning the umpire's gear.[9]

Attendance at the new Buff Stadium set records for the team.

Courtesy Mary Bavouset

Jones was the hero of the hour in Houston in 1928. He had used a mix of national contacts and cold cash to secure the Democratic National Convention for the city that summer. The American media and political spotlight would be on the Bayou City like never before, and a glorious opening day parade fit right into the city's mood for celebration.[10]

Behind the lead car came autos bearing members of both teams, some bands and other organizations. The city was segregated, however, so this parade was not all. Shorty Lubbock was the organizer of a separate parade for African-American baseball fans, complete with three more bands and 150 cars. Lubbock, was a white man, a popular insurance broker noted for his support of athletics in the city. He was a fixture at Rice football games. Given his support of black fans, there is some irony that it was Lubbock,

Lights were added to Buff Stadium in its third season. Iconic, sloping light towers would come in the 1950s.

Courtesy Texas League

as local Democratic Party chair in 1930, who was named as the defendant in a lawsuit seeking to open the all-white primary.[11]

Baseball Commissioner Kennesaw Mountain Landis along with St. Louis Cardinals General Manager Branch Rickey travelled by train from St. Louis to attend the dedication ceremonies, and Landis described the facility as the "finest minor league plant" in the United States. For club president Fred Ankenman, it was a most gratifying day including the gift of a gold wrist watch from the sports editors of Houston's three daily papers.[12]

KPRC radio's sports director, Bruce Layer, reported each play of the opening game over AM radio airwaves from the new broadcast booth. Newspapers from around the area clamored for press passes.

Houston Press sports editor Andy Anderson reported that there were about 3,000 ladies in the park that day. The fact was newsworthy to him because he was taking patrons to task for engaging in a game of cushion tossing, and he expressed concern for the safety of the ladies. From the eighth inning on, more than a few seat pads were hurled through the air, and at least one woman had her hat knocked askew, vowing never to return.

Most fans, however, were not deterred by flying seat cushions. In their first season at the new ballpark the Buffaloes drew 186,459 fans and finished in first place.

Even Bayou City mosquitoes were not a problem. Vendors not only trod Buff Stadium stairs with peanuts, popcorn and cold bottled drinks, they also offered insect repellent. Three squirts of Flit cost a nickel.[13]

At West End Park, the Knothole gang had been restricted to white boys between ages 7 and 16. With the move to Buffalo Stadium, a "Colored Knot Hole Gang" was added. The African-American youngsters had seats in the left field bleachers and the white ones down the right field line. In later years, the respective sides of the field for the two races would be switched. The Kiwanis Club sponsored the white youths, and a local school teacher "had general control" of the black children.[14]

Though promotional night games under electric lights had been tried as early as 1880, including a celebrated night-time contest in Houston in 1892, it was during the late 1920's that lights had started to become a factor in minor league baseball. Portable lighting systems began appearing as early as 1909, but it was the 1920s before usage became regular. The barnstorming Kansas City Monarchs, alternately an independent outfit or members of the Negro National League, had cashed in on the trend by carrying light standards and generators with them.[15]

Though it took decades, some baseball bosses eventually realized that night games could be more than a novelty. Without the lights, crowds were limited to patrons who could get off work in time for a 3 or 4 p.m. start on weekdays. Many laboring people could not do that. Lights could mean money.

In 1930, minor league owners around the country decided to pursue lighting in earnest. Independence, Kansas was home to the first official night game, a Class C affair on April 28, 1930. Des Moines followed within the week. By June, the first Texas League night game had been played at Waco's Katy Park when the hometown Navigators hosted the Ft. Worth Cats. The Buffs, next on Waco's schedule, got to experience it for themselves.[16]

Buff's management had been eager for lighting. They approved a $30,000 allocation for the immediate installation of stadium lights in the third season of the ballpark. They were buying a fixed light system with six towers and "over 150 huge reflectors diffusing mellow light." With Dallas in town on July 22, 1930, the Buffs had entered the era of night baseball. Over 14,000 enthusiastic fans showed up to witness this historical event, many from outside the ballpark.[17]

Just two weeks later, the Houston Black Buffs entertained the New Orleans Black Pelicans under the stadium's lights. The Black Buffs had been playing their games at West End Park, but the modernity of night baseball warranted higher rents for the management.[18]

The only complaint over night baseball came from owners of nearby chicken coops. It seemed the birds confused the floodlights with daylight, and hens would lay and roosters crow well off schedule, though the noise was much more bothersome than the extra eggs. Lloyd Gregory speculated that Fred Ankenman would soon be hitting up the poultry owners for some of the egg money.[19]

By the following season, close to half the league games were played under the lights, a welcome development during the Texas summers. That included the first ever Opening Night in Texas League history when Houston hosted Beaumont on April 17, 1931.[20]

In the 1940s and 1950s, Miss Lou Mahan played a ballpark organ that provided the soundtrack for Buffs baseball. From the standard ascending and descending chords that followed a foul ball up and down the screen to particular songs aimed at a given player, everything Miss Lou played either fit the moment in the game or the mood of the Buff fans at the time.

In 1950, slugger Jerry Witte was mired in a devil of a home run drought. As Witte stepped into the batter's box with men on base, Miss Lou's organ belted out the melody to the pop standard *It's Been a Long, Long Time*. The baseball patrons, mentally singing along, rewarded her with appreciative laughter, applause, and rousing cheers for Jerry Witte.[21]

Another constant in the Buffs postwar baseball experience was announcer Morris Frank. Frank had been a writer and columnist first in Lufkin and then for the *Houston Post* when he hooked up with Allen Russell in 1943 and became his public address announcer for the semi-pro league that played in Buff Stadium. When the Texas League resumed play following the War, Frank was

With a large ball park, Houston became an even more popular stop on the exhibition circuit.

Houston Metropolitan Research Center, Houston Public Library

the easy choice as the PA voice of the Buffs because of his wonderful humor, warmth and natural brightness.

Frank, who later moved his column to the *Chronicle*, presided as master of ceremonies for the early Houston Baseball dinners from 1947 forward and also filled that role at innumerable banquets for other Texas charities. He was a passionate supporter of programs that advanced reading and education. After his death in 1975, the City of Houston built and dedicated a new library location in his name and honorable memory.[22]

The sound of Morris Frank's twangy, piney woods accent flew into the Houston air. It will forever play loudly, clearly, and fondly in the minds of those who were there to hear him:

> "Leading off for the Houston Buffaloes…the 2nd baseman… Hemus…Solly Hemus…2nd base…."

Buff Stadium didn't just offer the sights and sounds of baseball, there was a distinctive smell, too. Fair Maid Bakery sat some two blocks north of the ballpark, marked by a large illuminated sign that stood above the left centerfield wall. At night, the wonderful aroma of baking bread tempted Buffs fans who could salivate and see the "Fair Maid Moon" in the distance.

In the late 1940's the league initiated a contest to select "The Texas League Golden Girl." Each club had the opportunity to pick their own nominee. One evening a number of lovely young women came to the ballpark dressed in swimsuits, and individual players were asked to walk each contestant to home plate where they would be introduced to the crowd.

One Buff, local hero and father of 12, Larry Miggins, was asked to escort Miss Kathy Grandstaff to home plate. He took one look at the young lady and politely declined, saying "Why she's practically naked." So a teammate, Al Papai volunteered to take his place. Miss Grandstaff won the Buff contest, and, as the winner, traveled on to Los Angeles to represent the team for the league title. It turns out that Grandstaff became a very big winner; first she won the "Texas League Golden Girl" title and decided to stay in California and become a model. Then she changed her name to Kathy Grant, met and married singer Bing Crosby and became a movie star in her own right. As Al Papai liked to tell his teammates, "Remember guys, I made her what she is today."

Allen H. Russell, who took over as president of the Buffs in 1946, received a modest salary of $250 a month but also earned a bonus of 5% of the profits. A master promoter already, the extra financial incentive drove him even more. Under Russell, the Buffs enjoyed their most successful attendance years of all time. From 1946 through 1953 the Buffaloes outdrew the major league St. Louis Browns on three separate occasions.

The new club president tried any promotion that showed a shred of promise, and that included wringing all extraneous talents out of his ball players. Larry Miggins sang in uniform on more than one occasion. Danny Gardella, perhaps best known for his challenge of the reserve clause, entertained fans with *The Donkey Serenade*. It was difficult to go to Buff Stadium without being aware of Allen Russell.[23]

Russell was noted for his dedicated resistance to rainouts. He would personally dump gasoline on a wet Buff Stadium infield, set it ablaze and then run like crazy to get away from the eruption that would dry the infield to get in a game that otherwise would have had to be cancelled.

Russell also understood the value of keeping female baseball fans happy. To make summer ball games more comfortable, he added air-conditioning to the ladies restrooms soon after he took over. His belief was that while the women would be impressed, the men didn't much care about such things. It was the first appearance of this cool amenity in any baseball park in America.[24]

August Busch bought the St. Louis Cardinals in 1952, and officially changed the name of the Houston park to Busch Stadium. Longtime fans stubbornly persisted on using the Buff Stadium label. At the same time the fences were moved in 20 feet, the hope being to make the contest between the pitcher and hitter a little more even and "provide a more interesting type of baseball for Houston fans."

Just as in most of America, segregation was also evident at Buffalo Stadium.

Bob Boyd and Willard Brown brought racial integration to the Buffs lineup in 1954. One year later, the separate seating policy ended in the stands. Prior to that time black fans had to sit in the "colored section" down the right field line.

During the same years, Houston mayor Roy Hofheinz had overseen desegregation of most city facilities, including municipal golf courses, libraries, City Hall restrooms and airport waiting areas. As was true of the other public facilities, integration in Houston happened relatively quietly as opposed to many places in the Deep South.

Still, many racial barriers remained around Houston. Most private businesses were not integrated, and black Texans were not allowed to share restrooms or drinking fountains at those places, if they were even allowed in.

At Buff Stadium, co-mingling of races seemed to face somewhat of a lag time. No white fans were rushing to sit farther out in right field, and many of the African-American patrons seemed to prefer sticking with the traditional placement until they were sure there would not be trouble.[25]

"After all, they came to watch a ballgame, not to be hassled," said Bill McCurdy, a diehard Buffs fan in the mid-1950s. "When you take the lock off the jail cell door, it still takes a minute for people to trust that they can walk through."

Though the Buffaloes were the primary occupant of the stadium, they were far from the only one. It hosted many high

When the circus came to town, the big top set up in the stadium parking lot next to the brand new Gulf Freeway.

Houston Metropolitan Research Center, Houston Public Library

The Fair Maid Bakery neon bread loaf is visible in this night shot at Buff Stadium.
Houston Metropolitan Research Center, Houston Public Library

school games and tournaments plus a variety of semi-pro baseball contests over the years including one sponsored by the *Houston Post.* Allen Russell, in his first baseball work there, had organized City League contests during WWII.

The University of Houston Cougars officially started baseball as a sanctioned sport in 1947 with Buff Stadium as their home. They would continue to utilize the park through the 1950s.

Buff Stadium also served as the home of the Negro American League Houston Eagles in 1949 and 1950. The stage for that had been partially set earlier in the 1940s. With the Texas League shut down during wartime, the City of Houston was leasing the ball park from the Cardinals. In 1944, several Negro American League games were on tap.[26]

Football was no stranger to the ball park either. Jack Yates and Wheatley high schools played an annual Thanksgiving night game that was the biggest yearly social event in African-American Houston. Prairie View A&M faced Wiley College in another annual gridiron tilt.[27]

When Houston finally got professional football via the American Football League, Buff Stadium became the first practice field for the city's new Oilers. During preseason, in the heat of the summer, many players claimed that the best indicator of which players were making the new team was how many cans of insect repellant the equipment manager gave them.[28]

Many non-sports fans came to Buff Stadium at least once a year when the circus hit town. Pulling in with its long train, the Ringling Brothers, Barnum & Bailey Circus stopped on a siding near the park. The famous elephant parade wound through the East End. The big top was set up adjacent to the first base line on the parking lot that bordered first the interurban tracks and later the brand new Gulf Freeway.

Buff Stadium was home to many triumphs. Eight Texas League Championship teams played there. Houston fans were also blessed with eight future Baseball Hall of Famers who called the Buff Stadium facilities their own. They were Dizzy Dean 1930-31; Joe Medwick 1931-32, 1948; Walter Alston 1937; Earl Weaver 1951-52; Willard Brown 1954-55; Billy Williams 1960; Enos Slaughter 1960 and Ron Santo 1960. The end of the ball park's run, however, was in sight.

By 1958, baseball forces in Houston were focused on preparation to secure a major league franchise. All but the wildest optimists knew that Buff Stadium's days were numbered. Four years later, the Houston Colt .45s entered the National League at Colt Stadium, a temporary location, until the nearby Astrodome—The "Eighth Wonder of the World"—could be completed.

There had been a push to expand Buff Stadium to a capacity of closer to 30,000, but bad blood that developed between what could be described as the winning and losing baseball groups was the final nail for the park and the team name. In July 1961, an old timers game dubbed the Last Roundup of Buffaloes was held, bringing a true who's who of former players. In mid-September that same year, Hurricane Carla knocked down a good deal of outfield fence, forcing the relocation of a few home games. Just over a week later, the ball club played their final minor league home game, an 11-4 playoff loss to the Louisville Colonels in front of a tiny crowd. The last hurrah was a Major League All-Star exhibition that October. After that, there was nothing left for it but deterioration.[29]

The Buff Stadium property was sold in 1963 to Sammy Finger for one million dollars, and the stadium itself brought in $19,750 at auction. It was disassembled and the pieces moved to the site of another area landmark. The Hitchcock Naval Air Station had housed anti-submarine blimps which patrolled above the Gulf of Mexico during WWII. Purchased in 1950 by wildcat oilman John Mecom, it became home to tracks for expensive horses and more expensive race cars.[30]

In April 1963, the deconstructed ball park was moved farther down the Gulf Freeway and piled on the enormous old blimp pad in stacks of concrete blocks and structural steel. There were "no plans for the broken down stadium structure... but the steel might possibly be used for other construction."[31]

With the ball park structure gone, the stadium site southeast of downtown was soon covered by the vast Finger Furniture Center. For many decades, the location of home plate at Buff Stadium was memorialized in its original position in the Houston Sports Museum inside the furniture complex. The small baseball showcases experienced a period of neglect following the death of Sammy Finger and then underwent a renaissance when his grandson Rodney became head of Finger Furniture.

Eventually the changing landscape of the furniture business ended the Houston Baseball Museum. The gigantic store itself ceased to be. With much difficulty, the home plate marker was removed from its concrete resting place and preserved to await a home elsewhere. It is doubtful that the reinvented Buff Stadium site will contain even a nod to Houston's former baseball palace.

1 Ankenman, Fred, Sr.. Four Score and More: The Autobiography of Fred N. Ankenman, Sr.. (Texas Gulf Coast Historical Association, 1980); SN 2 June 1927

2 Ankenman, Fred, Sr.. Four Score and More: The Autobiography of Fred N. Ankenman, Sr.. (Texas Gulf Coast Historical Association, 1980)

3 HP 11 April 1928; Mandelero, Jim and Pitoniak, Scott. *Silver Wings: The Story of the Rochester Red Wings.* (Syracuse University Press, 1996)

4 HP 11 April 1928; HP 3 July 1930

5 http://www.baseball-reference.com

6 HP 11 April 1928

7 HP 11 April 1928; HP 12 April 1928

8 HP 11 April 1928

9 HP 10 April 1928; HP 11 April 1928

10 Fenberg, Stephen. Unprecedented Power: Jesse Jones, Capitalism and the Common Good. (Texas A&M Press, 2011)

11 HP 11 April 1928; The Thresher 29 October 1920; The Thresher 9 December 1921; Zelden, Charles L.. *Voting Rights on Trial.* (ABC-CLIO, 2002); United States Census Harris County, TX 1910; United States Census Harris County, TX 1920; United States Census Harris County, TX 1940; Abilene Reporter News 15 July 1948

12 HP 12 April 1928; Ankenman, Fred, Sr.. Four Score and More: The Autobiography of Fred N. Ankenman, Sr.. (Texas Gulf Coast Historical Association, 1980)

13 Gregory, Robert. Diz: The Story of Dizzy Dean and Baseball During the Great Depression. (Penguin, 1992)

14 Ankenman, Fred, Sr.. Four Score and More: The Autobiography of Fred N. Ankenman, Sr.. (Texas Gulf Coast Historical Association, 1980)

15 Boston Daily Globe 3 September 1880; http://research.sabr.org/journals/under-the-lights

16 http://research.sabr.org/journals/under-the-lights ; Guinn, Jeff and Bragan, Bobby. When Panthers Roared: The Fort Worth Cats and Minor League Baseball. (TCU Press, 1999); HP 5 July 1930

17 HP 4 July 1930; San Antonio Express 22 July 1930; HP 22 July 1930; HP 23 July 1930

18 HI 2 August 1930

19 Gregory, Robert. *Diz: The Story of Dizzy Dean and Baseball During the Great Depression.* (Penguin, 1992); HP 6 August 1930

20 GDN 28 March 1931

21 McCurdy, Bill. *A Kid from St. Louis.*

22 http://www.texasescapes.com/AllThingsHistorical/Morris-Frank-BB705.htm

23 Yonkers Journal News 9 March 2005; New York Times 13 March 2005

24 Russell, Allen. *Touching All Bases* (Gulf Publishing, 1990)

25 Beeth, Howard and Wintz, Cary. *Black Dixie: Afro-Texan History and Culture in Houston.* (Texas A&M Press, 1992)

26 Russell, Allen. *Touching All Bases* (Gulf Publishing, 1990)

27 Russell, Allen. *Touching All Bases* (Gulf Publishing, 1990)

28 Nash, Bruce and Zullo, Allan. Football Hall of Shame. (Simon and Schuster, 1991)

29 HP 1 August 1961; HP 29 August 1961; HP 13 September 1961; Baytown Sun 22 September 1961; HP 16 October 1961

30 http://www.airfields-freeman.com/TX/Airfields_TX_Houston_SE.htm

31 GDN 11 April 1963

KEY

GDN – *Galveston Daily News*
HI – *Houston Informer*
HP – *Houston Post*
CD – *Chicago Defender*
HC – *Houston Chronicle*

CHAPTER NINE

DIZZY DEAN & THE PRE-WAR YEARS 1928–1942

BY MIKE VANCE & BILL McCURDY

The grand opening of Buff Stadium on April 11, 1928, was a shining example of Branch Rickey's cardinal red brilliance in overseeing the growing St. Louis empire. It was also a milestone for the Buffaloes themselves, validating Houston as a top-notch baseball town.

Ultimately, though, those without a financial stake measure success by the product on the field, and the Bayou City stood tall there in 1928, too. For the first half of the season, the Buffs found magic almost everywhere they turned, and it was easy to see that they owed their thanks to a St. Louis roster that was already filled to the brim with good players.

Young Dizzy Dean towered over the city of Houston during his playing days with the Buffs. Houston Metropolitan Research Center, Houston Public Library

For the second time in three years, the Cardinals were headed to the World Series. This time, the early outcome was a disappointing four-game sweep loss to the New York Yankees, but the far more lasting impression was the baseball world's growing view of the Cardinals as winners. In the nine years that passed from their first successful trip to the World Series, 1926-1934, the Cardinals made it to the top of the National League five times, winning it all three times.[1]

It's possible that Branch Rickey threw Houston a bone or two as he placed his top minor league talent around the farm system given that the season marked the opening of their new showplace stadium. Either way, the pieces fell together for the Buffaloes.

Outfielder Red Worthington, destined for the Boston Braves, led the league with 211 hits, and his batting average of .352 was high among the leaders. There wasn't much power on the 1928 club, but four other starters topped the .300 mark. Two of the four were youngsters: George "Watty" Watkins, who added a remarkable 21 triples, and second baseman Carey Selph each had big league time ahead of them. The other two had careers heading the other direction.

Ray Powell was coming off nine seasons in the majors. Already 39, this

A hometown boy who grew up to be a World Series star, Watty Watkins was ever popular in Houston. Courtesy John Watkins

was the last of four straight seasons in Houston. Powell would hang around the lower minors for several more years.

The other was manager/catcher Frank "Pancho" Snyder, who at .329 had the second best average on the squad. He was only 34, but was coming back to the minor leagues for what was almost the first time in his career. At only 18, the San Antonio native had spent a handful of games at Flint, Michigan, before moving straight to the St. Louis Cardinals. He would remain in the National League for the next 16 seasons. His baseball high points included two World Series homers for the New York Giants where he was the

Kern Tips

Native Houstonian Kern Tips started as a sports reporter for the *Houston Chronicle* in 1924 while he was still a student at Rice Institute. Two years later, the paper hired him full-time, and he remained there as columnist and sports editor for the next eight years when he left to become general manager of KPRC Radio. At a time when the separation between ballplayers and the people who covered them was not very great, Tips and his colleagues at the other two Houston papers served as witnesses for Dizzy Dean's last minute wedding. He was best known for his 32 years as the voice of Southwest Conference football, including being beamed around the globe on the Armed Forces Network. His recognizable voice and homespun phrasings of "booming kick," "prodigious punt" and describing a botched handoff as a "malfunction at the junction" were often imitated, but he was most revered for a descriptive poetry that let radio listeners feel the cool fall air and see the band marching on the field. Kern Tips is in numerous broadcasting Halls of Fame and was once voted sportscaster of the year five consecutive times.

After five seasons with the Buffaloes, Carey Selph moved on to oversee amateur ball in Houston.
National Baseball Hall of Fame Library, Cooperstown, NY

star backstop in the early 1920s.

Houston was his first full season gig as a manager, a job that Snyder wanted and the Cardinals wanted him to have. Rickey had first spotted Snyder when he was a teenager at Flint and Rickey was coaching baseball at University of Michigan. After a couple of seasons as both catcher and skipper in Houston and Ft. Worth, Snyder had two final years of playing with St. Paul of the American Association before going back to the New York Giants as a coach. Frank Snyder eventually returned to his hometown of San Antonio where he worked in public relations at the Lone Star Brewery and coached youth baseball.[2]

The biggest strength of the 1928 Buffs was in the pitching. The club boasted four 20-game winners who led them to their Promised Land: Jim Lindsey finished with a stellar record of 25-10, followed by Bill Hallahan at 23-12, Ken Penner at 20-8, and Frank Barnes at 20-9. Lindsey led the league in wins, and Hallahan posted the lowest ERA at 2.25 and the most strikeouts with 244.[3]

Pitcher Hallahan had honestly earned his nickname of Wild Bill for his lack of control on the mound. Twice after he left Houston, he would lead the National League in both strikeouts and walks. By the time he came to the Buffs, Hallahan had already been up with the big club, even making a brief appearance in the 1926 World Series. Rickey felt that the young man needed more seasoning, perhaps in warm weather, and Fred Ankenman made a successful trip to Binghamton, New York, to get the player's consent.[4]

The new ball park and a winning campaign kept the turnstiles turning, as did the sheer growth of the city. Between 1910 and 1930, the city's population came close to quadrupling, and some of those newcomers were baseball fans. Home attendance for Houston in their first season at Buffalo Stadium was 186,469.[5]

When the 1928 regular schedule ended, both Houston and Wichita Falls had won a stellar 104 games and half a season. They met in the playoffs starting at the Spudders' field up north. Wild Bill Hallahan posted a victory in game one, again in Houston in game three and posted a save in the clinching game four. He would repeat almost the same feat for the Cardinals in the 1931 World Series.

The Buffs went on from there to defeat the Birmingham Barons in a six-game contest for the club's first Dixie Series crown in their first try.[6]

The 1929 Texas League season was another instructional year for fans of the Houston Buffs. They learned, one more time, that it was easy to go straight from "the penthouse to the outhouse" in a single year when the talent supply was in the hands of a big league club that pulls all the strings. The team fell all the way from first place to sixth in the final standings. A look at the roster explained why.

Jim Lindsey was the only returning ace from 1928's quartet of 20-game winners. Lindsey again did his job, finishing the 1929 season at 21-10, 2.87, but it wasn't enough. Joe Brown and Paul Wachtel posted double digit wins, but each had even more losses.

At the plate, no player on the 1929 Buffs had enough at bats to qualify as a legitimate .300 hitter, but utility man and future Gashouse Gang member Pepper Martin came close at .298. Martin was one of the few bright spots.

Local favorite Gus Mancuso returned to the Buffs in a limited number of games, and another native Texan, infielder Ray Cunningham, was on his way to a short career with the parent Cardinals despite hitting only .216 in 1929. Cunningham

Ray Powell spent four seasons in Houston late in his career.

Courtesy Library of Congress

San Antonio native Frank "Pancho" Snyder was half-Mexican-American, earning him a following among Houston's Hispanic community.

Courtesy Library of Congress

"Wild Bill" Hallahan did indeed have trouble with bases on balls.

National Baseball Hall of Fame Library, Cooperstown, NY

would much later distinguish himself by living past his 100th birthday as the world's oldest surviving major leaguer.[7]

Manager/catcher Pancho Snyder was batting at a .319 clip when he left to manage at Ft. Worth late in the season. He and third baseman Ed Hock were the only two everyday starters leftover from 1928. Snyder was replaced as field boss by Gene Bailey.[8]

Many in Houston's baseball community were saddened with news over Thanksgiving week that Texas League president and former Houston management figure Doak Roberts had died of heart trouble at age 59. The Buffs had known some of their most successful times under the leadership of Roberts and Otto Sens.[9]

The Great Depression technically began with the Stock Market Crash at the end of October 1929, but that did not mean everyone in the nation was suddenly poor overnight. In fact, Houston's economy held up fairly well in 1930, all things considered. The Buffs even experienced a gain of over 55,000 in attendance.

There was also a new manager in town. Joe Schultz had over a decade of good Major League time under his belt. Playing all the infield and outfield positions, Schultz had also compiled a respectable .285 career average in the show. The Pittsburgh native had two cousins who also played in the bigs, as did his son, Joe, Jr.[10]

In what was becoming the norm at their pitcher-friendly stadium, even mediocre pitchers sometimes put up showy numbers. Allyn Stout, who was headed for six years at the back of National League rosters, went 18-8 and led the Texas League with 166 strikeouts, and Ralph Judd, fresh off his own big league cup of coffee, managed a record of only 9-11 yet still posted the league's lowest ERA at 2.62. George Payne and Floyd Rose also won in double digits for the Buffaloes.[11]

The year 1930 was known as the year of the hitter in the Major Leagues and boasts the highest cumulative batting

Ken Penner earned the first victory in Buff Stadium history.

Houston Metropolitan Research Center, Houston Public Library

Former Buffaloes star Pepper Martin (left) and former Houston sandlot player Lon Warneke (right) flank Mickey Owen in the 1939 Cardinals dugout.

Houston Metropolitan Research Center, Houston Public Library

average to date. Multiple teams posted combined batting averages over .300. The spitball was mostly gone. The ball was lively. Life was good.

All of that coupled with big gaps in the Buff Stadium outfield meant a gaggle of high average men in Houston, too. Top of the list was Eddie Brown at .358. Carey Selph, Joel Hunt, Adolph Schinkle and Boyce Morrow also topped the magical .300 mark. Homer Peel hit .384, but with only 58 game appearances as a Buff, he didn't qualify for the official honor.[12]

The 1930 season was most memorable for two events that took place in mid-summer. Following a suddenly growing trend to increase attendance, Fred Ankenman oversaw the purchase of lights for the ball park. By July 22nd, the Buffs were playing their first night game at the now even more gleaming Buff Stadium.

The other development was in the personnel department. Don Curtis, a part time scout and part time railroad man, had signed a young pitcher he saw in San Antonio in the fall of 1929. Jay Hanna Dean had just bought his way out of the U.S. Army at Fort Sam Houston and was pitching for semi-pro teams across South Texas.

Though the Buffs owned his contract, the decision was made to send him to St. Joseph, Missouri, another Cardinals farm team managed by Houston favorite Gene Bailey. Young Dean, better known by the nickname of "Dizzy," etched a 17-8 record for the Saints before moving up to

Two Houston Buffaloes with the St. Louis Browns, Don Gutteridge and Bayou City native, Frank Mancuso.
Courtesy Frank Mancuso, Jr.

Houston and going 8-2.[13]

Right from the start, the Houston press knew Dean was good for a story. They referred to him as a "brilliant hurler" and "sensational," but also tagged him as "cocky," "colorful," "eccentric" and "nuts." If they ran out of superlatives to describe his pitching talents, Dean was more than ready to supply some of his own. All indications are that the writers meant every word about the big country kid fondly. Team president Ankenman, who Dean consistently called Ackerman, said of Diz that he "never knew a better hearted guy" in his life.[14]

Late in 1930, Dean even reached St. Louis in time to make his big league debut with the Cardinals, coming out of it with a 3-1, three-hit win over Pittsburgh. The single Cardinals win gave Dizzy Dean a grand total of 26 wins in 1930, with the last one coming as a big league victory. It was the start of big things to come, just not immediately in St. Louis.[15]

When Dean reported to Bradenton, Florida for 1931 spring training, he almost instantly fell out of favor with Gabby Street, the Cardinals manager. His never-ending braggadocio and unrelenting desire for advances on his salary didn't sit well with Branch Rickey, either.[16]

By the time the Cardinals broke camp, Dizzy Dean had endeared himself with the press but over-talked his way to the far end of the bench. His situation didn't hurt the ball club, though. St. Louis went on to win another World Series that year with six different pitchers posting double-digit wins. Among them were former Buffs Wild Bill Hallahan and Flint Rhem. Not among them was Dizzy Dean.[17]

At the start of May, Fred Ankenman and Joe Schultz were thrilled to learn that the self-styled "Great Dean" would be returning to the Buffaloes. He might be a handful, but he could throw. Dean was happy, too. When he was told of the demotion, he sent a collect telegram to Schultz saying he'd be back in Texas in time to pitch the next night.

True to his word, he got off a train at Union Station at 2 in the afternoon, checked into the Ben Milam Hotel across the street, went to Buff Stadium and started the ball game at 3:30. He pitched a three-hit shutout. The most entertaining season in Buffs baseball history had begun.[18]

Dizzy was fond of what he considered practical jokes. One of his favorites was feigning serious injury to get a rise out of the team bosses. He also went AWOL a couple of times, simply because it suited him, or he thought it would be fun. Once ordered by manager Schultz to take the 11 a.m. run of the hourly Interurban to join the team in Galveston by noon, Dean showed up 24 hours late, explaining that he missed the 11 o'clock train the day before, so caught it the next day.[19]

In Fort Worth one day, Dean was pulled from a game in which his hitting had outshone his pitching thanks to a home run in the first frame. Instead of heading for the dugout, Dean went to the outfield scoreboard where he removed the appropriate numeral one saying, "If I'm leavin', my run's going with me."[20]

He blew through money so fast that at one point Branch Rickey told Dean he was already getting advances on next year's salary. He missed curfew, had a prolonged fist fight on the mound and generally behaved like a fun-loving, somewhat out of control kid. In mid-June, it all came to a screeching halt. Dizzy Dean got married.

His bride was Pat Nash. Older than

Future Buffs skipper Joe Schultz as a young Brooklyn player pictured with his cousin, the veteran infielder Hans Lobert.

Courtesy Library of Congress

The famous 1931 Buffs featured two future Hall of Famers, Dizzy Dean, seated third from left, and Joe "Ducky" Medwick, standing far right.

Houston Metropolitan Research Center, Houston Public Library

Outfielder Homer Peel was a hitting star on two Texas League champion Buffs teams.

Houston Metropolitan Research Center, Houston Public Library

Dean, she was a hosiery clerk at Paul's Shoe Store on Main. People described her as a party girl who had already dated at least two of his teammates, Carey Selph and Eddie Hock. Both Rickey and Ankenman tried their best to talk the pitcher out of it, but on June 15th, Dizzy and Pat were married by Rev. Harry Knowles of First Christian Church. Sports writer Andy Anderson was Dean's best man.[21]

Those who were worried that Dean had made a bad decision were wrong. His spendthrift habits came to an abrupt end. Pat took care of Dizzy, describing herself as his "banker, bookkeeper, manager and girlfriend." She could have also added fun and close companion. When he died in 1974, the two had been married for 43 years.[22]

Pat was not the only Dean family

member who was known in Houston. Losing his mother at age eight, Dizzy had grown up as an itinerant cotton picker with his father and two brothers. Youngest brother, Paul, also a pitcher in the Cardinals organization by 1931, joined Dizzy on the Buffs for a cameo appearance.

Their father was also in town along with older brother Elmer, a mentally retarded man who had just rejoined the family after having been "lost" for nearly four years. The Buffs gave Elmer a job selling peanuts at the stadium, and he excelled at it. In fact he proved to be such a popular vendor that the Buffs signed him to a contract, and he kept his job even after his star brother had moved on to Major League fame.

On the diamond for the Buffs, Dizzy Dean was everything he advertised, going 26-10 with a 1.53 ERA for the 1931 Texas League champion Buffs. In addition to the most victories, Dean also set a new league strikeout mark with 303. In Fort Worth in June, he pitched and won both halves of a doubleheader then threw eight innings of relief the next day to pick up another win.[23]

Forty-one year old pitcher George Payne backed Dean with a 23-13 mark, and Tex Carleton rounded out the 20-game winner trio with a record of 20-7 and an ERA of 1.90 in spite of missing the last five weeks of play due to a broken finger. Side-arming righty Carleton, only a youngster himself, was enjoying his third season in Houston. He went to the majors a few months later and stayed for eight years, including appearances in three World Series.[24]

Injuries during his Major League career robbed Dizzy Dean of the pure heat he possessed in Houston. By the time he reached the Cubs, he didn't have much left in his arm.

National Baseball Hall of Fame Library, Cooperstown, NY

The Buffs had plenty of hitting to support their talented pitching staff, too. Joe Medwick was the Texas League leader with 19 home runs and 126 RBIs while also averaging .305. Outfielder Homer Peel paced the Buffs with a .326 mark and second baseman Carey Selph followed closely at .322. Houston finished in first place with a 1931 Texas League record of 108-51, just one game shy of the Fort Worth Panthers' all-time league

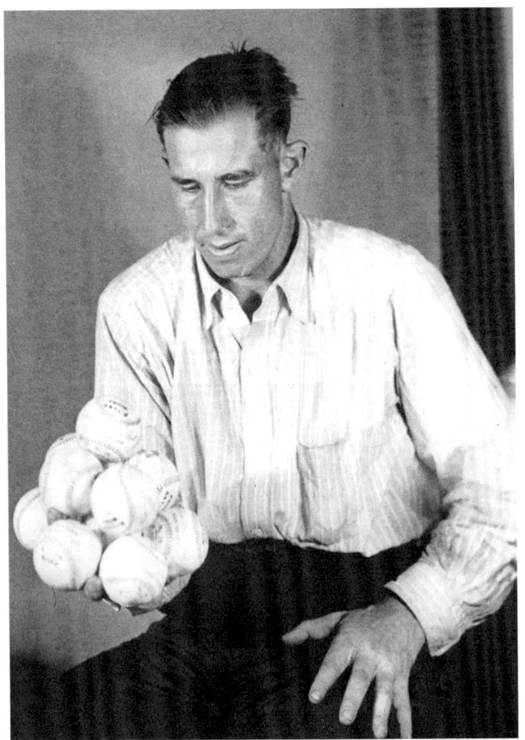

Dean brother, Elmer, sold peanuts at Buff Stadium and was a popular fixture.
University of Kansas Libraries

record. That was good enough for a 14-game edge over second place Beaumont. Belying the fact that the nation was in a worsening economic depression, home attendance climbed to 229,540. The average game drew about 3,000 fans, but when Dean pitched it meant at least 5,000 more.[25]

On July 24th, a female Buffs fan wrote to sports columnist Lloyd Gregory of the *Houston Post-Dispatch* to let him know that she had decided to call Joe Medwick "Ducky" because, as she stated, "he walks like a duck." Gregory concurred with the woman's observations and started referring to Medwick as "Ducky" in his daily column, "Looking 'Em Over." Use of the nickname spread from there and included the sale of candy called Duckie Wuckie Bars that proved quite popular at the ball park. In spite of how much he detested the moniker, by the time the young ballplayer left Houston for St. Louis, he was stuck with the fact that he was now "Ducky" Medwick for life.[26]

When a 2006 study ranked the best minor league teams of all time, the 1931 Houston Buffaloes of Dizzy Dean and Ducky Medwick checked into the lineup at number 42. The season was not perfect for Houston, however. In spite of boasting two Hall of Famers-to-be, they could not find success in the Dixie Series. The Buffs fell in 7 games to the Birmingham Barons.[27]

By the time the season started in 1932, there was no more ignoring the great financial crisis that gripped the United States. It was a full blown depression. The loss of jobs and the fear of the unknown among those breadwinners who still held employment brought little but anxiety. These were hard times. People still needed a night at the movies or the ballpark to help them escape reality for a few hours each week, but the incredible slowdown had put a serious kink in how much escape people could afford.

Buffs President Fred Ankenman made an effort to help. As a gesture of goodwill in 1932, the Buffs held a special game day for the unemployed in which those who were out of work got in free. Overall, the numbers at the gate fell to 112,341. The Texas League saw two teams forced to switch cities on account of low attendance, the first such occurrence since 1904.[28]

In Houston, Dizzy Dean had gone to his big league calling with the St.

Louis Cardinals in 1932, but young Joe Medwick returned to the Buffs for one more season under the third year of Joe Schultz as manager. He had plenty of good players with him, but "Ducky's" numbers stood out.

Medwick pounded out 198 hits and 26 homers to go with a .354 average. Homer Peel, the man who had been overwhelmingly voted Buffs fan favorite the year before, had one more hit than Medwick to capture the league lead in that department. Both men made the Texas League All Star team.[29]

Ralph Judd, who had brief success with the New York Giants, and 43-year old George Payne each had 18 victories to lead the way among 1932 Buffs pitchers, with veteran Elmer Hanson checking in with 17. Former big leaguer Mike Cvengros and Ed Heusser were also double-digit winners in 1932. For Cvengros, this was the first of six straight seasons in Houston that would close out his career.

The Buffs were still a talent laden team, but the magic of the previous season was gone. They slipped to third place with a record of 88-66. Winning it all was a top notch Beaumont team that included pitcher "Schoolboy" Rowe and Texas League MVP Hank Greenberg. They would both be part of the Tigers in the 1934 World Series that is still considered one of the best as they went up against the Cardinals with Dizzy Dean and a slew of ex-Buffaloes.[30]

By the time the 1933 baseball season got under way, America was at the nadir of its economic troubles, bringing the rest of the developed world with it. Since the stock market crash in October 1929, U.S. industrial production had fallen 46% and about one in four Americans were out of work. Voters overwhelmingly opted for change.

In his first inaugural address as the President of the United States, Franklin Delano Roosevelt delivered the

Pitcher Tex Carleton put up great numbers for the 1931 Buffaloes but missed the final five weeks of the season with a broken finger.
Houston Metropolitan Research Center, Houston Public Library

Mike Cvengros was a consistent winner for five of the six seasons he pitched for the Buffs. He retired after his only losing year in Houston.
Houston Metropolitan Research Center, Houston Public Library

philosophical lesson that America needed to hear. He said, "The only thing we have to fear is fear itself." America could not eat it, but they sure could try to live it. It still didn't bring enough confidence to get the Buff Stadium turnstiles whirring, however. Home attendance dropped again, this time descending under the 100,000 mark.[31]

Though not of international importance, the Buffaloes underwent a leadership change of their own. Thirty-one year old second baseman Carey Selph took over as player/manager for the 1933 Buffs. Selph collected 184 hits and batted a team-topping .310 while also leading the Buffs to a first place finish with a record of 94-57.[32]

Ed Greer at 22-10 and Mike Cvengros at 21-11 paced the 1933 Buffs on the mound, and the now 44-year old George Payne at 19-11 fell one win short of making it another Buffs 20 game winner trio. All three posted an ERA of 2.75 or better.[33]

In spite of their strong regular season finish, the Buffs lost to eventual league champion San Antonio in the first round of the playoffs.

In 1934, Carey Selph returned for his second season as player/manager and, for the second year in a row, Selph's .323 batting average was the only plus .300 mark among Buffs hitters. Selph added "pugilist" to his resume, though not successfully, after he got his nose smashed during a fist fight with Beaumont second baseman Al Vincent. The injury cost Selph a week of healing.[34]

Minor league baseball is filled with

stories of good players who were given little to no shot at the bigs. Twenty-year old Mays Copeland posted a 16-10 mark for the 1934 Buffs in only his second year of pro ball. He would later get two-thirds of an inning with the 1935 Cardinals in one no-decision game, giving up a run and two hits, but he would never see the big leagues again for the rest of his career.

Another major league mark that was almost as inconspicuous belonged to George Washington Payne who was spending his fifth and final season on the Houston roster. At age 45, it had been 14 years since Payne notched his 12 relief appearances for the Chicago White Sox. It had been more than 20 years since the Kentuckian had made his professional debut for the Charleston Sea Gulls, recruited from nearby Fort Moultrie where he was in the Army.[35]

For the 1934 Buffs, he posted a winning record of 13-12, and he wasn't done yet. George Payne collected his final minor league victory for the Cardinals of Worthington, Minnesota at age 51. It brought his minor league wins total to 348, the third highest mark in the history of minor league baseball.[36]

There were several position players of note on the roster, but none put up impactful numbers for the ball club that year. Don Gutteridge, a future big leaguer with World Series connections to the Cardinals, Red Sox and Browns, played third base for the 1934 Buffs and hit .272 with eight triples and seven home runs. It was enough to move him along to the Cards' top farm club at Columbus, Ohio, the following year and eventually on to a dozen years in the show.

When his playing days were over, Gutteridge remained in baseball as a coach and manager, including a stint at the helm of the Chicago White Sox. After that, it was scouting until he finally retired to his hometown of Pittsburg, Kansas in 1992. Longevity was part of his makeup. When he died at the age of 96, he had been married to his wife, Helen, for an amazing 74 years.[37]

Fred Ankenman's son, a Fred, Jr. who went by the name of Pat Ankenman, spent some time with the Buffaloes in 1934. Just 21 years old, he was a five-foot-four middle infielder, an All-American out of the University of Texas and a great source of pride for his father who was put in the position of having to sign him. He would play one solitary game with St. Louis

Lloyd Gregory's Talk Show

As the dean of local sports writers of his day, *Houston Post* editor Lloyd Gregory was involved in multiple radio and television shows with the KPRC stations. In the years just after World War II, he hosted The Houston Sports Panel that featured fellow journalists Morris Frank, Dick Freeman and Andy Anderson. The listeners were encouraged to submit questions for the guests, though Texas law at the time prohibited them from receiving any prize worth more than 25 cents for doing so. Those whose questions were chosen got a publicity photo of the four writers.

Famed Notre Dame football coach, Frank Leahy, was in Houston to speak to a group of high school coaches when he made an appearance. Afterwards Leahy said, "I received $1,000 last week for appearing on a TV show in California. I didn't get a nickel from you guys, but worked a lot harder on your show."

and log only slightly more time with the WWII-era Dodgers.[38]

Catcher Harry McCurdy returned to the Buffs in '34 on his descent from a major league career in which he batted a respectable .282. It was a return stop for McCurdy who had played with the Buffs in 1924 and 1925. He would remain in pro ball for only two more seasons.

Heading the other direction from McCurdy was a 22-year-old named Johnny Keane. He would be back with the Buffs a dozen years later as the manager of the 1947 Dixie Series champions, but on this trip he hit only a buck 38 in 19 games.

Both McCurdy and Keane would make their permanent homes in Houston. Harry McCurdy, in particular, left a mark on hundreds of Houstonians, spending many years as a teacher and principal at Hogg Junior High School in the Heights.

In spite of their many big league connections, the Buffaloes were decidedly minor league on the diamond. They sank to sixth place with a mediocre record of 76-78. The cash-strapped baseball public responded accordingly, and home attendance dropped all the way down to 61,180, or about 795 fans per game.[39]

Following the season, Carey Selph, who had finished eighth in the voting for Texas League MVP, walked away from professional baseball. He sent a letter to Fred Ankenman asking that he be placed on the voluntarily retired list. Ankenman first met the prospect with disbelief, saying to the press that Selph had talked about retiring before, but that "he will be back next year, I'm sure."[40]

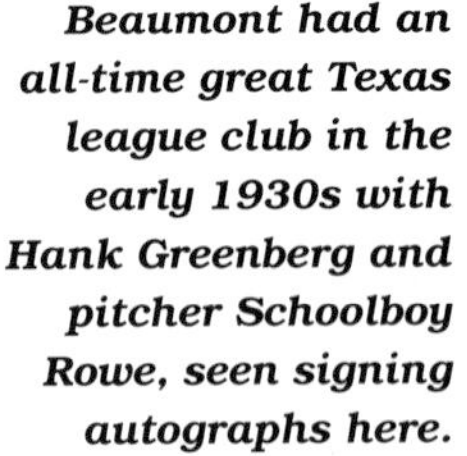

Beaumont had an all-time great Texas league club in the early 1930s with Hank Greenberg and pitcher Schoolboy Rowe, seen signing autographs here.

Tyrrell Library, Beaumont Public Libraries

Carey Selph, kneeling third from left, was player/manager and the only man who hit over .300. Unfortunately the club did not have much other offense on which to hang their hats.

Houston Metropolitan Research Center, Houston Public Library

The resignation stuck, though. Selph concentrated on his insurance business and also became head of the Houston Amateur Baseball Federation. He also played some semi-pro ball for teams like the Barber's Hill Gushers. In later years, Carey Selph and former Buff teammate Pat Ankenman ran the Ozark Boys Camp in his native Arkansas, keeping a healthy interest in the game all the way up until his death in 1976.[41]

The 1935 Buffs rose from sixth place to fifth, but the crowds continued to be dismal with only Galveston drawing fewer fans. The new field manager was 29-year-old Ira Smith who had spent some time with the 1929 Buffs as a shortstop. He returned this time not only as field boss but as a pitcher. He would amass a record of 5-4, mostly in relief, over the course of the season.[42]

The rest of the 1935 Buffs pitching staff roster hardly read like the Hall of Fame, but there were high points. Veteran

Johnny Watwood, an Auburn University ex, saw big league time with Sox of both the White and Red variety.

National Baseball Hall of Fame Library, Cooperstown, NY

Mike Cvengros and 25- year old Fiddler Bill McGee each managed 15 wins and sub-3.00 ERAs. For McGee, it was worth a late call up that was the start of eight seasons in the bigs.[43]

Among the position players, Lynn King also earned himself a late season trip to St. Louis after compiling 192 hits, enough to lead the Texas League. Jimmy Sanders, a career minor-leaguer in his early 30s, finished at .307 as the only other Buff to crack .300.

Native Houstonian Johnny Rizzo, a 23-year old who had come to the Buffs at the end of the previous season, led the team in hitting with an average of .312 and nine home runs. Rizzo, who employed a quirky batting stance similar to "Bucket Foot" Al Simmons, was on his way to five seasons as an outfielder with four different National League clubs. His rookie year in the Majors could hardly have gone better. Breaking in with the Pirates, he hit .301 with 23 homers and 111 RBIs to finish sixth in National League MVP voting. Though he would never come close to duplicating that output, Rizzo's nine ribbies in a single game remains a Pittsburgh record to this day.[44]

Ira Smith was back in 1936 along with several of the starters from the year before. Local favorite Rizzo hit .307 and matched his nine round trippers again. Johnny Keane was again a fixture at shortstop, contributing a steady .272 average at the plate.

Big Alabama-born first baseman Johnny Watwood had joined the Buffs after five years in the American League. He led the team with a .339 mark that reflected no power. He failed to homer in 425 official times at bat.

Future big league player and manager Herman Franks hit .260 as a catcher for the Buffs. Also making his Houston debut was outfielder Hal Epps, a good hitting Georgia boy who was only 22. Epps batted a solid .285 in 95 games.[45]

On the mound, player/manager Ira Smith found himself among the club leaders. He posted a 13-6 mark and a hot

2.32 earned run average, even though he still threw mostly in relief. Smith also hit .313 in 80 times up, leaving the impression that he also may have been one of his own favorite pinch hitters or late inning substitutes.

Steady Mike Cvengros again led the team with 15 victories followed by John Stevenson with 14 and Jim Lyons who posted a shiny 11-3 record and a 2.17 ERA.

Overall progress continued. The 1936 Buffs ascended from fifth place to second with a record of 83-69. As would be the case so often with the four-team Shaughnessy playoff format, however, they lost in the first round, this time to Tulsa. At the very least, they headed toward the next year with a hopeful outlook for better baseball and an improved financial situation.[46]

One big factor affecting 1937 was the call up during the season of manager Ira Smith as a pitching move to help the Cardinals' farm club in Rochester. Two of the more senior Buffaloes, Johnny Watwood and Mike Cvengros, each took a turn as manager. In fact, Cvengros took over after Watwood, too, was sent up to Rochester. The unsettled situation couldn't have helped a lineup that didn't have much in the way of star power.

One of the most glaring differences came from Cvengros himself. After posting a total of 75 victories over the previous five seasons in Houston, the reliable pitcher saw his record drop to a abysmal 4-16. It would be the final year on the mound for Mike Cvengros who retired at age 36.

Johnny Rizzo garnered attention from Houston baseball fans even as a teenager playing on local sandlots. He continued his meteoric rise with a fabulous rookie year in the National League.
Private Collection

Some observers around the the 1937 Buffs believed they had a genuine "phenom" in the making. Twenty-year old fireballer Johnny Grodzicki went 18-11 with a 2.88 ERA while pitching for a losing club. It would prove to be one of the ups in an up-and-down career that suffered from control issues and years lost to World War II.

The speedy and athletic Hal Epps was

Several well-known big league managers spent some time as players for the Buffs including Herman Franks who would later lead the San Francisco Giants.

Houston Metropolitan Research Center, Houston Public Library

the top Buffs hitter at .305. His defensive prowess was earning him a reputation with the Houston fans that would bring him the nickname of "The Mayor of Center Field."

A couple of marginal contributors from 1937 are also worthy of mention. Future Hall of Fame Dodger manager Walter Alston hit .212 in 65 games as the Buffs first baseman, and native Houstonian Red Munger broke in as a pitcher with no record for 11 innings, but he did post a 2.45 ERA. The final result on the field was that Houston dropped all the way to a disappointing seventh place finish.[47]

Cardinals farm club presidents maintained a degree of freedom to make deals during the 1930s. They often had their own bird dogs, and Cardinals General Manager Branch Rickey would regularly instruct Fred Ankenman to make a deal with a prospect.

In 1937 the Houston club managed to ink a deal for a $1,000 signing bonus with a 16-year old American Legion pitcher in New Orleans. It would take two more years before the young Howie Pollet would begin his professional career, but he would pay solid dividends for the Cardinals organization.[48]

Branch Rickey was serious about business, but he was also a playful trickster. His enjoyment of the practical joke sometimes even trespassed into the territory of minor cruelty. For example, in the 1930s Houston club president Fred Ankenman traveled to the Cardinals' annual winter meetings with a request for a hotel roommate that did not snore. He had a serious problem sleeping with any distraction. Rickey assigned him to share a room with the worst known snorer in the farm system.

That night, Ankenman tried everything to block the sound, including toilet paper stuffed in his ears, but nothing helped. He finally put on his robe, went down to the front desk and was given a private room across the hall from the one that he had been painfully sharing. The next morning, his roommate awakened to the sight of no Ankenman. His clothes, however, were still on a chair near an open window. The roommate quickly concluded that Fred must have sleepwalked out the open window during the night.

The snorer panicked. He was horrified over the repercussions that might come with losing a fellow executive right up until he called the front desk and learned that the Houston club president was now sleeping safely across the hall. Ankenman failed to mention if the parsimonious Rickey later sent him a bill for the private room.[49]

The 1938 season was not a banner year, but it was a step up. With Ira Smith back from Rochester for a fourth season as the pitching field manager of the Houston Buffaloes, they managed a middle of the pack fifth-place finish.[50]

With 17 wins, Jim Winford led all Buffs pitchers, and future great Cardinals pitchers Harry Brecheen and Mort Cooper offered support with 13 victories each. Cooper also posted a 2.32 ERA and led the entire Texas League with 201 strikeouts. The previous season's hot prospect, Johnny Grodzicki slipped to 12-21 while allowing more than four earned runs a game. Two other future St. Louis hurlers, Red Munger and Ted Wilks, still cutting their professional teeth, were mostly non-factors. So, too, was Paul "Daffy" Dean who was trying to regain his old form after an arm injury from which he would never recover.

Walter Alston struggled as a Buffaloes first baseman but turned into a Hall of Famer as manager of the Dodgers.

National Baseball Hall of Fame Library, Cooperstown, NY

Hal Epps led all Buffs hitters in 1938 with a second straight .305 mark, and also for the second year in a row, Epps was the only .300 plus hitter on the entire club. Power hitting was a pure embarrassment. The entire Houston ball team combined to hit only 30 home runs on the season.[51]

In 1939, Eddie Dyer returned home to Houston to manage the Buffaloes. He brought with him much better results on the diamond. Over the next three years, Dyer led the Buffs to three consecutive

The Buffs got two twenty-win seasons from Howie Pollet who then returned to the city and became a successful businessman after baseball.
Houston Metropolitan Research Center, Houston Public Library

first-place finishes and one league playoff championship.

The biggest part of the improved equation was the addition of new pitching and the maturing of what they already had. Twenty-two year old Murry Dickson paced the Buffs pitching staff with a record of 22-15, tying for the league lead in wins. He was the first 20-game winner for Houston since the first place club of 1933. Dickson would go on to win 15 as a key figure in the success of the 1946 Cardinals; he would later become a 20-game winner for the 1951 Pittsburgh Pirates, a tough task on a team that only won 64 all year.

In 1939, Dickson was far from alone as a good pitcher on the Buffs staff. Harry "The Cat" Brecheen tied for the best win percentage in the Texas League with a record of 18-7. Ernie White won 15 and Frank Barrett had 13. For good measure, both White and Barrett tossed no-hitters within a month of each other.[52]

Ted Wilks split time as a starter and reliever, posting a mark of 14-15. White, Breechen and Wilks all posted ERAs at 2.62 or lower. The 1939 season also marked debut of 18 year-old rookie Howie Pollet who was called up from New Iberia in the Evangeline League in time to go 1-1 for the Buffs.[53]

Two hitters finally made it over the .300 mark for the Buffs. Hal Epps hit a very respectable .287 himself. First baseman Johnny Hopp hit .312, but mustered little power with only three dingers. Eddie Lake added a league leading 129 runs scored.

The big Buff banger in 1939, though, was a 38-year-old outfielder with one of the most unfortunate nicknames in baseball history. Nick "Tomato Face" Cullop, approaching his 20th year in pro ball, led the club with a batting average of .318. His 25 homers led the entire league. It earned him MVP honors for the circuit.[54]

The 1939 campaign finished with a terrific Buffs win spurt as they pulled away to finish with a mark of 97-63. It was cause for celebration. Making ownership just as happy was a home attendance on the year of 125,364, their first time in seven years they reached six-digits in attendance. On the down side, the Buffs were eliminated from pennant contention in a first round playoff loss to eventual champion Fort Worth.[55]

At least part of the increased attendance could be traced to a Houston economy that was being improved by local industries ramping up for war. Isolationist factions in Congress had passed a series of strict neutrality acts in the latter half of the 1930s, but a 1937 act allowed "cash and carry" sales of materials to belligerent nations in Europe. Locally that meant growth for industries related to shipping and petroleum. Houston's population had increased by about a third during the 1930s. Many of those new residents had decent jobs and liked baseball.[56]

No matter what turbulence roiled international events, on the ball field the 1940 Buffs only got better. Twenty-four year old Howie Krist went 22-9 with a sparkling 1.71 earned run average. It wasn't even the best E.R.A on the team. "Subway Sam" Nahem scored a 1.64 to lead the league. Krist would later post the best winning percentage in the National League when he went 13-3 for the 1943 Cardinals.

Also coming into his own was 19-year-old lefty Howie Pollet. The New Orleanian went 20-7 with an excellent 2.88 ERA himself. Pollet would win 131 games over 14 big league seasons, including a pair of 20 win efforts for the Cardinals.[57]

Four other Buffaloes also had double digit wins and allowed fewer than three runs a game on average. Hank Nowak, Steve Warchol, Ted Wilks and Edward Wissman all managed the feat. Of those, only Wilks was destined to see the show.

On the offensive side, 20-year-old outfielder Johnny Wyrostek came to life in his second year as a Buff to lead all hitters at .305. Outfielder Tom Winsett also reached .300, just a point above second baseman Danny Murtaugh at .299. Murtaugh, destined to be a World Series-winning manager of the Pittsburgh Pirates, rapped 186 hits for the highest total in the Texas League. "Tomato Face" Cullop again led the club with 25 homers followed by Winsett's 18.[58]

It all added up to a stellar 105-56

The 1946 World Champion St. Louis Cardinals had several former Buffs as starting pitchers. One was Harry "The Cat" Brecheen who posted three wins over the Red Sox in the Fall Classic.

National Baseball Hall of Fame Library, Cooperstown, NY

The Dean Brothers, popularly known as Daffy and Dizzy, both pitched in Houston, both starred for the Cardinals and both saw their careers shortened by arm trouble partially brought on by extensive off-season barnstorming tours.

National Baseball Hall of Fame Library, Cooperstown, NY

record behind second year manager Eddie Dyer. The Buffs finished 16 games above second place San Antonio before taking the two playoff series matches they had with Oklahoma City and Beaumont for the Texas League pennant. To the shock of many, the Buffs then fell in 5 games to the Nashville Vols in the Dixie Series.[59]

The 1940 baseball season concluded with an uneasy quiet. With bloody war continuing to rage in all other parts of the globe, Americans were concerned. In Europe, only Britain remained free of Hitler's clutches. In spite of the passing of a fourth Neutrality Act the year before, an increasing majority of people felt that it was only a matter of time before the United States would enter the conflict.

Almost coinciding with the close of the 1940 campaign was the passing of the Selective Training and Service Act. The military draft would have a profound effect on baseball and on the nation as a whole.

The 1941 Houston Buffs were the third and widely considered the greatest of the clubs managed in the Bayou City by Eddie Dyer. All three Dyer clubs finished first in the Texas League, even though the 1940 Buffs were the only one of the trio that conquered the playoffs and won the official Texas League championship.

In what was becoming a tradition in Houston of mediocre hitting and great pitching, much of the 1941 Buffs greatness was wrapped up in the talent of the club's three 20-game winners. Fred Martin led the Texas League in wins with 23 and posted a 1.44 ERA to boot.

He was likely not even the best pitcher on the team. Howie Pollet, who turned 20 in late June, put up a record of 20-3, a miniscule 1.16 ERA and 151 K's. The latter two numbers led the Texas League.

The third 20-game winner was Ted Wilks who used his big season to show that he, too, was now ready for the Cardinals. In fact, Martin, Pollet, and Wilks were all headed for the big leagues, though for Martin, it would have to wait until after the coming war.[60]

The hitting didn't reach the level of the mound work. Danny Murtaugh was the club's leading hitter through 69 games until Branch Rickey dealt him to the Philadelphia Phillies in early July.

Walter Sessi, a youngster headed for a late season call up of his own, finished the season with an average of .301 to lead Buffs hitters. Hal Epps scored 106 runs to top the league, and outfielder Bill Norman picked up 107 RBIs on the season to lead the Texas League in that department.

Houston won 103 games, heading second place Tulsa by 16 and a half. Still, the first place Buffs fell in the first round of the playoffs to fourth place Dallas, the eventual 1941 Texas League champions.[61]

In spite of the fact that they won two fewer games than their 1940 counterpart and failed to reach the Dixie Series, some baseball historians chose the 1941 Buffs as one of two Houston clubs on their list of the 100 greatest minor league teams

Few Buffs were as beloved in Houston for as long as Eddie Dyer who starred at Rice, played and managed for the Buffaloes and then built a strong business presence in his home town.
National Baseball Hall of Fame Library, Cooperstown, NY

of all time.

Under the foreboding shadow of war, the 1941 baseball season brought two iconic major league hitting achievements. Ted Williams of the Boston Red Sox finished the year with an average of .406, making him the last man to top the magical .400 mark. And Joe DiMaggio of the New York Yankees set another still standing record by hitting safely in 56 consecutive games. It fired the imagination of every baseball fan in the country.[62]

Then, on Sunday, December 7, 1941, the noontime radio brought sobering news. The Japanese Navy had led a surprise attack on Pearl Harbor. America's entry into World War II had begun with "a day of infamy."[63]

After much debate and discussion, a decision was made. The Texas League would be among the majority of minor leagues that would attempt to play a 1942 season. Ten of the 41 leagues that finished the previous year elected to shutdown until further notice.[64]

Eddie Dyer started off the season with a promotion. He would enter the wartime years as the director of the Cardinals farm system. In 1946, he was called back to St. Louis to manage the Cardinals. He led them to a World Series title in his first try followed by three consecutive second place finishes.

Fired after ending up in fifth place in 1950, Dyer returned to Houston and business interests that included insurance, real estate and oil. Partnering with him in this enterprise was his old protege Howie Pollet who also kept his hand in baseball as a coach, including mentoring pitchers for the Astros during their first season in the Astrodome.[65]

For the 1942 Buffaloes, a new manager was needed. They turned to a career minor leaguer, outfielder/first baseman Clay Hopper of Porterville, Mississippi. He already had 13 seasons of managing under his belt, but this was the first time his role would not include playing. Unbeknownst to him at the time, Hopper was on his way to a date with destiny.[66]

At the end of the 1942 season, he would accept a job from Branch Rickey, by then the new general manager of the Brooklyn Dodgers. Four seasons later he was promoted from Mobile to manage their AAA International League farm club, the 1946 Montreal Royals. Hopper's promotion to manager was no casual appointment. Rickey was confident that this particular son of the Deep South was just the man he needed to help Jackie Robinson first break the color line. The baseball traditions of bigotry and invisible barriers took their first blow at Montreal, not a year later at Brooklyn.[67]

As it turned out, Rickey's judgment of character and ability proved right again. Montreal would finish 1946 in first place as a 100-game winner and the subsequent league playoff champion. Jackie Robinson would hit a hot .349 as the International League batting champion, and Clay Hopper would be selected as Minor League Manager of the Year.[68]

The 1942 Texas League season was far less magical for Clay Hopper. With America now at war, baseball players were being swept up in the military service draft as swiftly as other young American men. It did not take long for minor league leaders in most places to see the attrition of both players and fans. In Houston, the year's attendance dropped by over 60%. By early summer 1942, five of the leagues that previously had decided to continue playing had now cut their losses by shutting down.[69]

Paul "Daffy" Dean was back for a third season in Houston. He put up a very solid 19-8 mark and a sterling 2.05 ERA The younger Dean's success landed him a year with the St. Louis Browns and two seasons with minor league Little Rock in 1944 and 1946, but he was not very good. A history of arm injury, likely exacerbated by overuse in lucrative barnstorming appearances with his brother, had ended a second Dean's future, but without the attribution of greatness that fell upon Dizzy.[70]

Sharing the pitching limelight in Houston was 20-year-old George Kleine

Danny Murtaugh spent a year and a half as a good hitting middle infielder for the Buffs before getting his shot in the big leagues. He later managed Pittsburgh to two World Series titles.

Houston Metropolitan Research Center, Houston Public Library

Morris Frank

Morris Frank left the Lufkin paper at the start of 1937 to take a job with the *Houston Post*. The likeable writer with the lightning-fast wit quickly became a fixture in the Bayou City. When the South Coast League started in 1943, Allen Russell hired Frank to be the public address announcer at Buff Stadium. With the resumption of Texas League play in 1946, Frank became the PA voice of Buffs, and his piney woods accent remained a staple of Houston ballgames.

Frank presided as emcee for the early Houston baseball dinners from 1947 forward and also filled that role at banquets for hundreds of causes and charities, consuming countless mediocre meals along the way. Once chided for eating pork in spite of his Jewish upbringing, Frank replied, "My daddy told me it was a worse sin to pass up a free meal than it was to eat ham." He was known for ribbing well-known audience members, and his friend Lloyd Gregory wrote that "A Texan really hasn't arrived until ole Morris gives him the 'treatment.'"

Evidently wisecrackery ran in the family. A woman once said to Frank's wife, Nell, "I bet you've heard your husband make two thousand speeches." Nell Frank replied, "No. I've heard him make the same speech two thousand times."

Morris Frank was a passionate supporter of programs that advanced reading and education. After his death in July 1975, the City of Houston dedicated a new branch library in his name and honorable memory.

who also garnered 19 wins and an earned run average almost as good as Dean's. Kleine apparently was done in by the military service that kept him out of baseball from 1943 to 1945, though. He tried a brief comeback with Columbus in 1946, but walks sank him. The war would end the lives or careers of many players from 1942 teams, as it would affect the lives of all Americans from that greatest generation.[71]

The 1942 Buffs had a few good position players, too. Outfielders Eddie Knoblauch, Emil Verban and Hal Epps ended up around the .300 mark as did shortstop Jeff Cross. The roster was also young in spite of the steady march of the draft. Only Jim Bucher, a utility man with five National League seasons under his belt, was over 30 years of age.[72]

The 1942 Texas League season played out with the understanding that it would be the last run for Houston Buffs baseball for the foreseeable future. The course and duration of the war were too uncertain and inescapable in the minds of fans to let baseball work its distractive magic.

President Roosevelt had given baseball the green light to continue during the war, but even the big leagues were in trouble due to the shrinking number of available qualified players. The talent drain was even greater at the minor league level. Unless leagues cared to make a travesty of the sport by using 4-F amateur players and then charging fans money for watching, the only choice was to shut down until further notice.

The 1942 Buffs finished in fifth

place, a full 10 games behind first place Beaumont, though they did manage a winning record of 81-70.[73]

On the business side, they closed out the schedule with an operational loss of $41,926.30, similar to deficits across professional baseball in a country consumed by war. By the time these figures were available to Cardinals owner Sam Breadon, long-time general manager Branch Rickey had been forced out by the cost cutting boss. It left no buffer between owner Breadon and the long-time "Rickey men" who were still in place throughout the Cardinal farm system.[74]

Citing the financial loss in Houston, Breadon sent a scathing letter to Ankenman, expressing his belief that Houston and the Texas League were no better than a Class B operation and that they would be treated as such in all plans for 1943. He ordered Ankenman to save money by taking over direct control of all operations that had to do with advertising, concessions, and most everything else. Further, Breadon informed Ankenman that his salary as Buffs President had been dropped to $250.00 per month.[75]

Fred Ankenman was deeply hurt by Sam Breadon's new austerity and by his heedlessness of all the things that the Houston club had done well during Ankenman's 22 years of work for the Cardinals organization.

He did not react immediately; instead, he waited until after the first of the year. On February 6, 1943, Ankenman both wired and mailed a gracious letter of resignation to the Cardinals owner, thanking him for the opportunity to have served the interests of the St. Louis and Houston baseball clubs all those many years. He made it clear that he could no longer serve as the Buffs president under the conditions put forth by Breadon.[76]

A sea of written support from fans, Houston newspapers, the Texas League, and the National Association of Minor Leagues swiftly engulfed Fred Ankenman. Soon enough, he found himself in a new career with the City of Houston tax office, but he remained a Houston Buff at heart for life. Branch Rickey was one of his strongest friends in the year of his departure from the Buffs, and the two men remained close until Rickey's death in 1965.[77]

There was no immediate rush for Cardinals owner Sam Breadon to find a replacement for Fred Ankenman as president of the Houston Buffs. There would be no Texas League season in 1943. The league had agreed to suspend all competitive operations for the duration of World War II.

It would be 1946 before the Texas League again resumed play. Service to country limited the careers of more baseball men than ever the keenest minds shall ever be able to count. In addition to the devastating loss of the lives of so many players, fans and other Americans, three Texas League seasons were lost forever.

1 http://mlb.mlb.com/mlb/history/postseason/mlb_ws.jsp?feature=recaps_index

2 Lowenfish, Lee. *Branch Rickey: Baseball's Ferocious Gentleman.* (University of Nebraska Press, 2007); San Antonio Express 21 December 1960; San Antonio Express 6 January 1962

3 http://www.baseball-reference.com

4 Ankenman, Fred, Sr.. Four Score and More: The Autobiography of Fred N. Ankenman, Sr. (Texas Gulf Coast Historical Association, 1980)

5 Encyclopedia of Minor League Baseball. Third Edition. (Baseball America, 2007); Population of 100 Largest U.S. Cities 1790 to 2000. Campbell Gibson, Population Division, *U.S. Census Bureau.* Published June 1998

6 Encyclopedia of Minor League Baseball. Third Edition. (Baseball America, 2007)

7 Baseball Reference.Com, Ibid.

8 Encyclopedia of Minor League Baseball. Third Edition. (Baseball America, 2007)

9 Texas Bureau of Vital Statistics, Death Certificate, J. Doak Roberts

10 http://www.baseball-reference.com

11 http://www.baseball-reference.com

12 http://www.baseball-reference.com

13 Ankenman, Fred, Sr.. *Four Score and More: The Autobiography of Fred N. Ankenman, Sr.*. (Texas Gulf Coast Historical Association, 1980); http://www.baseball-reference.com/minors/team.cgi?id=4f8069bc; Gregory, Robert. *Diz: The Story of Dizzy Dean and Baseball During the Great Depression.* (Penguin, 1992)

14 Gregory, Robert. *Diz: The Story of Dizzy Dean and Baseball During the Great Depression.* (Penguin, 1992); Ankenman, Fred, Sr.. *Four Score and More: The Autobiography of Fred N. Ankenman, Sr.*. (Texas Gulf Coast Historical Association, 1980)

15 Weiss, Bill and Wright, Marshall Wright. *The 100 Greatest Minor League Baseball Teams of the 20th Century* (Outskirts Press, 2006); Gregory, Robert. *Diz: The Story of Dizzy Dean and Baseball During the Great Depression.* (Penguin, 1992)

16 Gregory, Robert. *Diz: The Story of Dizzy Dean and Baseball During the Great Depression.* (Penguin, 1992); Ankenman, Fred, Sr.. *Four Score and More: The Autobiography of Fred N. Ankenman, Sr.*. (Texas Gulf Coast Historical Association, 1980)

17 http://www.baseball-reference.com

18 Gregory, Robert. *Diz: The Story of Dizzy Dean and Baseball During the Great Depression.* (Penguin, 1992)

19 Ankenman, Fred, Sr.. *Four Score and More: The Autobiography of Fred N. Ankenman, Sr.*. (Texas Gulf Coast Historical Association, 1980)

20 Gregory, Robert. *Diz: The Story of Dizzy Dean and Baseball During the Great Depression.* (Penguin, 1992)

21 Gregory, Robert. *Diz: The Story of Dizzy Dean and Baseball During the Great Depression.* (Penguin, 1992); Ankenman, Fred, Sr.. *Four Score and More: The Autobiography of Fred N. Ankenman, Sr.*. (Texas Gulf Coast Historical Association, 1980)

22 Gregory, Robert. *Diz: The Story of Dizzy Dean and Baseball During the Great Depression.* (Penguin, 1992); http://www.tshaonline.org/handbook/online/articles/fdeac

23 Weiss, Bill and Wright, Marshall Wright. The 100 Greatest Minor League Baseball Teams of the 20th Century (Outskirts Press, 2006); http://www.baseball-reference.com; Encyclopedia of Minor League Baseball. Third Edition. (Baseball America, 2007); Gregory, Robert. *Diz: The Story of Dizzy Dean and Baseball During the Great Depression.* (Penguin, 1992); http://www.tshaonline.org/handbook/online/articles/fdeac

24 http://www.baseball-reference.com; http://sabr.org/bioproj/person/80d4f848

25 Encyclopedia of Minor League Baseball. Third Edition. (Baseball America, 2007); Gregory, Robert. *Diz: The Story of Dizzy Dean and Baseball During the Great Depression.* (Penguin, 1992)

26 HP 24 July 1931; Lowenfish, Lee. *Branch Rickey: Baseball's Ferocious Gentleman.* (University of Nebraska Press, 2007); Sporting News 7 July 1932

27 Weiss, Bill and Wright, Marshall Wright. The 100 Greatest Minor League Baseball Teams of the 20th Century (Outskirts Press, 2006; http://en.wikipedia.org/wiki/Dixie_Series

28 Encyclopedia of Minor League Baseball. Third Edition. (Baseball America, 2007); Ruggles, William B.. The History of the Texas League of Professional Baseball Clubs 1888-1951. (Texas Baseball League, 1951)

29 http://www.baseball-reference.com/minors/team.cgi?id=4471cd65; Gregory, Robert. *Diz: The Story of Dizzy Dean and Baseball During the Great Depression.* (Penguin, 1992)

30 Encyclopedia of Minor League Baseball. Third Edition. (Baseball America, 2007); Ruggles, William B.. The History of the Texas League of Professional Baseball Clubs 1888-1951. (Texas Baseball League, 1951)

31 Franklin D. Roosevelt, Inaugural Address, March 4, 1933, as published in Samuel Rosenman, ed., *The Public Papers of Franklin D. Roosevelt, Volume Two: The Year of Crisis, 1933* (Random House, 1938); Encyclopedia of Minor League Baseball. Third Edition. (Baseball America, 2007)

32 Encyclopedia of Minor League Baseball. Third Edition. (Baseball America, 2007)

33 http://www.baseball-reference.com/minors/team.cgi?id=3a526980

34 http://www.baseba;;-reference.com; Port Arthur News 13 July 1934; Corsicana Daily Sun 14 July 1934

35 http://www.baseball-reference.com; http://kykinfolk.com/rockcastle/family/payne/

36 http://www.baseball-reference.com/minors/team.cgi?id=ee065e2e; http://www.baseball-reference.com/bullpen/George_Payne

37 http://www.baseball-reference.com/minors/team.cgi?id=ee065e2e; http://sabr.org/bioproj/person/83015aa9

38 Ankenman, Fred, Sr.. Four Score and More: The Autobiography of Fred N. Ankenman, Sr.. (Texas Gulf Coast Historical Association, 1980); http://www.baseball-reference.com

39 Encyclopedia of Minor League Baseball. Third Edition. (Baseball America, 2007)
40 GDN 14 October 1934;GDN 13 September 1934
41 San Antonio Express 18 November 1934; Daily Court Review 9 February 1935; Port Arthur news 27 March 1935; GDN 18 June 1935
42 Encyclopedia of Minor League Baseball. Third Edition. (Baseball America, 2007)
43 http://www.baseball-reference.com/minors/team.cgi?id=0809b393; Finoli, David and Ranier, Bill. Pittsburgh Pirates Encyclopedia. (Sports Publishing, LLC, 2003)
44 http://www.baseball-reference.com/minors/team.cgi?id=0809b393; GDN 9 September 1934
45 http://www.baseball-reference.com
46 http://www.baseball-reference.com
47 http://www.baseball-reference.com/minors/team.cgi?id=25193e3b; Encyclopedia of Minor League Baseball. Third Edition. (Baseball America, 2007)
48 Ankenman, Fred, Sr.. Four Score and More: The Autobiography of Fred N. Ankenman, Sr.. (Texas Gulf Coast Historical Association, 1980); http://www.baseball-reference.com
49 Ankenman, Fred, Sr.. Four Score and More: The Autobiography of Fred N. Ankenman, Sr.. (Texas Gulf Coast Historical Association, 1980)
50 http://www.baseball-reference.com/minors/team.cgi?id=5156ee97; Encyclopedia of Minor League Baseball. Third Edition. (Baseball America, 2007)
51 http://www.baseball-reference.com/minors/team.cgi?id=5156ee97
52 Encyclopedia of Minor League Baseball. Third Edition. (Baseball America, 2007)
53 http://www.baseball-reference.com/minors/team.cgi?id=3b087097
54 http://www.baseball-reference.com; Ruggles, William B.. The History of the Texas League of Professional Baseball Clubs 1888-1951. (Texas Baseball League, 1951)
55 Encyclopedia of Minor League Baseball. Third Edition. (Baseball America, 2007)
56 http://history.state.gov/milestones/1921-1936/Neutrality_acts; Population of the 100 Largest Cities and Other Urban Places in the United States: 1790 to 1990. Campbell Gibson, Population Division, *U.S. Census Bureau.* Published June 1998
57 http://www.baseball-reference.com/minors/team.cgi?id=6ea772e1
58 http://www.baseball-reference.com; Encyclopedia of Minor League Baseball. Third Edition. (Baseball America, 2007)
59 Encyclopedia of Minor League Baseball. Third Edition. (Baseball America, 2007); http://en.wikipedia.org/wiki/Dixie_Series
60 http://www.baseball-reference.com
61 Encyclopedia of Minor League Baseball. Third Edition. (Baseball America, 2007)
62 http://www.baseball-reference.com/players/w/willite01.shtml; http://www.baseball-almanac.com/feats/feats3.shtml
63 Miller, Francis T. History of World War II. (Universal Book and Bible House, 1945); Goodwin, Doris Kearns. No Ordinary Time. (Simon and Schuster, 1995)
64 Encyclopedia of Minor League Baseball. Third Edition. (Baseball America, 2007)
65 Nowlin, Bill and Stahl, John Harry. Drama and Pride in the Gateway City; The 1964 St. Louis Cardinals. (University of Nebraska Press, 2013)
66 http://www.baseball-reference.com
67 http://www.baseball-reference.com; http://en.wikipedia.org/wiki/Clay_Hopper; Lowenfish, Lee. *Branch Rickey: Baseball's Ferocious Gentleman.* (University of Nebraska Press, 2007)
68 http://www.baseball-reference.com/minors/player.cgi?id=hopper001rob
69 Encyclopedia of Minor League Baseball. Third Edition. (Baseball America, 2007)
70 Gregory, Robert. *Diz: The Story of Dizzy Dean and Baseball During the Great Depression.* (Penguin, 1992); http://www.baseball-reference.com
71 http://www.baseball-reference.com/minors/team.cgi?id=4e9f37d2
72 Baseball Reference.Com, Ibid
73 Encyclopedia of Minor League Baseball. Third Edition. (Baseball America, 2007)
74 Lowenfish, Lee. *Branch Rickey: Baseball's Ferocious Gentleman.* (University of Nebraska Press, 2007); Ankenman, Fred, Sr.. Four Score and More: The Autobiography of Fred N. Ankenman, Sr.. (Texas Gulf Coast Historical Association, 1980)
75 Ankenman, Fred, Sr.. Four Score and More: The Autobiography of Fred N. Ankenman, Sr.. (Texas Gulf Coast Historical Association, 1980)
76 Ankenman, Fred, Sr.. Four Score and More: The Autobiography of Fred N. Ankenman, Sr.. (Texas Gulf Coast Historical Association, 1980)
77 http://en.wikipedia.org/wiki/Branch_Rickey

KEY

GDN – *Galveston Daily News*
HP – *Houston Post*
HC – *Houston Chronicle*
HI – *Houston Informer*
CD – *Chicago Defender*

Caribbean
Air
Command

CHAPTER TEN

THE MINORS TO MAJORS TRANSITION 1946–1961

BY BILL McCURDY & MIKE VANCE

The story of the post-war Houston Buffaloes begins with Allen Russell, the man who would next take over for the St. Louis Cardinals as president of the ball club. He was born in a sawmill camp on Friday, October 13, 1911, near the Piney Woods town of Jefferson. From East Texas to Alabama to Tennessee to Colorado to Oklahoma and, finally, back to Jefferson, the family went wherever they needed to go to find work.[1]

The Buffs traveled to the Canal Zone in Panama for Spring Training courtesy of the U.S. Air Force.
United States Air Force Photo.

(PHOTO PAGE 215: ***Solly Hemus***)

As an adult, Russell had a varied work history of his own, from sharecropping to picking cotton, polishing marble, working wild horses into shape for domestic use and running a mobile pants-pressing service for oil field workers. His first job in professional baseball was as a parking lot attendant at Buff Stadium in the 1930s, along with another man, who happened to be his boss at their daytime WPA job.

When the Buffs decided that they needed one less new worker, Allen Russell saved his night job by making a deal with his daytime boss. Russell agreed to cancel an unpaid $12.00 poker debt in exchange for the man letting him keep the Buff Stadium parking lot job.[2]

In 1937, Russell began a string of jobs in various planning capacities for oil, livestock and home expositions at the Sam Houston Coliseum and other local venues. By late 1941, he was promoting a National Defense Exposition, when World War II and rationing came along and tore the bottom out of the trade show business. Russell found work as a clerk in the timekeeping department of the Todd Houston Shipyard, one of multiple Ship Channel operations that were manufacturing Liberty ships for the war effort. He worked the graveyard shift so that he would have time to seek other employment during the daylight hours, two jobs being a necessity to support his family.

Meanwhile, by 1943, the wartime shutdown of the Texas League left the St. Louis Cardinals owning an empty Buff Stadium in Houston, with nothing but maintenance and security bills staring them in the face. The Cardinals cut a deal to turn the venue over to the City of Houston who hired Allen Russell away from the shipyard to run the operation. Soon he was placed in charge of all income-producing properties operated by the City's Parks & Recreation Department, including the Houston Zoo.

In 1945, with the war winding down, Russell received a job offer from the St.

Club President Allen Russell was the driving marketing force behind a very successful Buffaloes operation in the years immediately following World War II. Houston Metropolitan Research Center, Houston Public Library

Johnny Keane piloted the Buffs to start the post-War era and even notched a handful of at bats. Houston Metropolitan Research Center, Houston Public Library

One of the many players returning from military service was the popular Eddie Knoblauch. Houston Metropolitan Research Center, Houston Public Library

Louis Cardinals, helped along by the ringing endorsement of his friend, Eddie Dyer. He took it in spite of the fact that his city employee status protected him from the draft. When professional baseball returned to Houston in 1946, Allen Russell was the new president and general manager of the operation.

Just as before the war, double-A Houston was still involved in a Cardinals system roulette with their two top farm clubs at Columbus and Rochester. While the system had plenty of prospects, the best players were not always distributed to the Buffs in a way that made a championship team likely.

Future Cardinals and Yankees manager Johnny Keane was in his first year at the helm of the Buffs, but he didn't have much talent on hand. There were high points. Outfielder Eddie Knoblauch returned from military service to lead the 1946 Buffs with a .306 average, almost exactly what he had posted in 1942. Knoblauch would never rise above double-A ball, but he would still amass a 16-year career that included over 2,500 hits, 426 of them doubles, and a lifetime average of .313. His brother Ray, a minor league pitcher, gained local Houston fame as the longtime coach at Bellaire High School. Eddie's nephew Chuck was the family member who finally reached the Majors.[3]

Roman Brunswick was the top pitcher with a 16-12, 2.69 mark. Four other Buffs hurlers, Lester Studener, Clarence Beers, Earl Dothager and Arthur Nelson also posted double digit wins. It translated to a sixth place finish, 36.5 games

back of the first place Fort Worth Cats.[4]

Still, local fans were thrilled to get their team back. Energized by the disappearance of wartime restrictions, and with the vast majority of soldiers and sailors getting back to a normal civilian life, the 1946 Buffs drew 161,421 fans, more than three times the number who showed up to watch the sixth place Buffs of 1942. League wide attendance also broke a record.[5]

The fans were fiercely faithful to the Buffs, too. Patrick Lopez, who attended games regularly both with his parents and as a Knot Hole Gang member felt that the nation "seemed to turn its attention away from the hardships of war and embrace" baseball. In Houston that meant that "everyone knew the batting order, hitting averages, who was pitching that day. The city was loyal to the team."[6]

During the 1946 season, Allen Russell became famous for an act he would repeat time and time again after a hard rain at Buff Stadium on game night. He had the grounds crew liberally douse any wet ground in the infield and shallow outfield with gasoline. Then he raced toward it with a box of large kitchen matches, throwing lit matches at the connecting bodies of gas and quickly dodging as he did.

"It beat the heck out of issuing rain checks," Allen Russell would proudly claim.

(TOP LEFT)
Clarence Beers spent parts of four seasons in Houston including posting 25 wins and Texas League Pitcher of the Year honors in 1947.
Houston Metropolitan Research Center, Houston Public Library

(TOP RIGHT)
Tall right-hander Al Papai was a Buffaloes mainstay in the years following World War II.
Houston Metropolitan Research Center, Houston Public Library

Houston centerfielder Hal Epps was much revered by the knot hole gang kids at Buff Stadium in the post-War years.
Houston Metropolitan Research Center, Houston Public Library

Postwar Buffs player Jim Basso (second from left) regretted never reaching the Major Leagues, but his career highlights did include being invited for drinks at Ernest Hemingway's home while playing winter ball in Cuba.
Private Collection

When manager Johnny Keane returned to the Buffs' helm for his second season in 1947, he led a charmed life. Many of the World War II replacement players were gone from the professional ranks, and almost every man on the Buffaloes roster had a record of recent military service.

It helped greatly that the club was blessed with a pair of mound aces. Clarence Beers at 25-8, 2.40 and Al Papai at 21-10, 2.45 could both be counted on as starters. Their big years would earn each a chance with the Cardinals the following season, though neither were able to capitalize on it. Beers' unfortunate big league career lasted only two-thirds of an inning.[7]

At the plate for Houston, first baseman Johnny Hernandez with a .301 average and 17 homers, plus center fielder Hal Epps at .302 were the leading hitters. Defense was solid. Second baseman Solly Hemus and shortstop Billy Costa shored up the middle infield, and catcher Gerry Burmeister had a knack for handling pitchers and would-be base stealers.

The defensive star of the '47 Buffaloes was Hal Epps in center. Known as a clutch hitter who compiled a lifetime .300 average in the minors, his range in the outfield was where he shone even brighter. "His speed enabled him to make graceful and even dazzling catches," wrote Mickey Herskowitz. In a day before padded fences and warning tracks, Epps was also known for crashing into the walls in pursuit of the long fly.[8]

The Buffs took over the league lead on May 9 and were never headed, though it remained close. They nipped the Fort Worth Cats on the last day of the season behind the pitching of Clarence Beers and a game winning single by Epps in the last of the ninth to win the league crown by a mere half game. Then the Buffs took out Tulsa in four and Dallas in six to win the full Texas League championship. Finally, they climbed the highest mountain available to them, defeating the Mobile Bears of the Southern Association to win the 1947 Dixie Series.[9]

After the season, Allen Russell staged an off-season banquet to celebrate the triumph of the Buffs. It became the model for Houston's annual winter baseball dinner, a special gathering of local fans that has occurred most years since that time.

Another triumph of 1947 was the attendance. During the championship season, Buff Stadium attendance rose to an amazing 382,975, surpassing the 320,474 fans who spent their money to go see the last place St. Louis Browns of the American League that same season.[10]

Not everything was a positive development, however.

In 1947 failing health of Cardinals owner Sam Breadon led him to sell the Cardinals and all its minor league properties to Robert Hannegan and Fred Saigh for $3 million dollars. Breadon died of prostate cancer 18 months later at the age of 72.

Allen Russell called the sale of the Cardinals by Breadon the one thing that negatively changed "my pleasant relationship with the parent Cardinals." Russell could no longer count on getting the players and favors he needed with a phone call to St. Louis. To the new ownership, Russell was not the golden boy that he had been to the late Breadon.

The 1948 season brought the Buffaloes back toward Earth. Much of the personnel was back on the field, but

"The Mad Russian," Lou Novikoff, was another Houston fan favorite in days when minor league players were very approachable.

National Baseball Hall of Fame Library, Cooperstown, NY

A testimonial dinner for Solly Hemus in 1958 brought out some of the big guns in Buffs and Cardinals baseball. L to R – Hemus, Eddie Stanky, Eddie Dyer, Harry Walker and Marty Marion.

Houston Metropolitan Research Center, Houston Public Library

Early Television and Baseball

The early telecasts used a camera on the first base side to show the mostly right-handed batters from a facial side shot. We also got to see the numbers on the backs of left-handed batters. In Houston, at least, there was no corresponding angle camera on the third base side to cover lefties. A second camera was usually positioned behind home plate, and behind the screen, to show the ball coming in to the batter and, when hit, going out to the fielders. On those early ten-inch-diameter screens, the view also compared favorably to watching baseball as it might be played out on an ant farm. You saw this fuzzy little round object move in, move out, and then disappear into the far dominions of a poorly lighted minor league field.

You had to develop a capacity for reading the body language of the tiny fielders to know if the ball had been handled or not. Some people bought magnifying glass accessories that gave you a larger, even furrier picture of what was going on in the more distant regions of the outfield.

In spite of these descriptions, however, keep in mind that we didn't know any better back then. Getting any kind of moving picture at home seemed miraculous to us at the time. We didn't know HD from VD. How good could things get? Our expectations were low. We just cared that it moved. It took us a while to free ourselves from the amazement that standing in front of the screen did not block out the picture as it would at the movies. We also weren't too bright back in the day.

– Bill McCurdy

gone were their top two starting pitchers. Cloyd Boyer at 16-10 and Pete Mazar at 15-10 were the biggest winners, and James Bryant, Jack Creel and Bud Byerly also won in double digits. Right handed fireballer Boyer, a Buff favorite, led the league with 188 strikeouts and earned himself Texas League All-Star honors. One of 11 children from rural southern Missouri, he was the older brother of two future big league third basemen, Ken and Clete Boyer.[11]

There were solid years from several players at the plate, but nobody stood out. Eddie Knoblauch, .295; Sam DiBlasi, .290; Solly Hemus, .288; and Hal Epps, .282 were the four leading hitters for average. As was the norm in Houston, there was a dearth of power. Don Bollweg with 13, and Johnny Hernandez with 11, paced the Buffs in home runs. It would be the next to last year for Hernandez who had developed a serious vision problem. Though he never reached the show, his son, Keith, did, winning a batting title and two World Series rings.[12]

Johnny Keane's three-year tenure as manager of the Buffs ended in 1948. The Buffs fell to third place with a record of 82-71, finishing 10 games back of Fort Worth. They were eliminated in the first round of the playoffs by Tulsa.[13]

Keane may have finished his third season as Buffs skipper on a down note, but 401,383 fans still showed up to watch the games at Buff Stadium. For the second straight season, the club surpassed the home attendance for the big league St. Louis Browns. Their club-

(TOP)

The short pants experiment in the summer of 1950 was mercifully short-lived. It was hard on the players' knees and pride.

Houston Metropolitan Research Center, Houston Public Library

(BOTTOM)

Short pants didn't bother the local team at Albrook Air Force Base in the Panama Canal Zone when the Buffs visited in 1951.

United States Air Force Photo

Five Buffs players enjoy a night on the town. Standing from left: Solly Hemus, Wayne McLeland and Billy Costa. Seated from left are Jerry Witte and Larry Miggins.

record gate totals meant a profit in excess of $300,000.[14]

The year 1949 brought the Houston debut of a phenomenon that would someday far outpace gate receipts as the main source of income in baseball, though the clubs certainly didn't grasp that at the time. The television era came to Houston on January 1, 1949, in the form of station KLEE-TV, located at channel 2 on the local dials. The immediate trouble was that there just were not many local dials. During its first few weeks on the air, KLEE, which would become KPRC, went into only about 2,000 Houston homes.

In the spring, Buffs games became part of the broadcasting rotation. Some pundits blamed TV for lower attendance, but most critics faulted the lousy play of the team and the growing number of leisure time choices facing Houstonians. It also was no longer possible to blame low attendance on people working. With only Sunday games a sure thing for the daytime, night baseball had all but eliminated work conflicts as the reason real fans stayed away.[15]

The new manager of the Buffaloes in 1949 was catcher Del Wilber. Looking down the bench, Wilber could take solace in the fact that Houston did have some hitters. Second baseman Solly Hemus batted .328, left fielder Eddie Knoblauch finished at .313 and Del Wilber himself posted a mark of .305. The power man in the group was young Larry Miggins, whose 21 round trippers on top of a .268 average paced all Buffs.

Miggins was a native New Yorker who had attended Fordham Prep in the Bronx, the high school that also put out Frankie Frisch, Snuffy Stirnweiss and Miggins' classmate Vin Scully. He had been signed by his neighborhood club, the New York Giants, and was on third base for Jersey City in 1946 when Jackie Robinson of the Montreal Royals played in his first game in previously all-white professional ball. Robinson safely laid down two bunts in front of Miggins in that game.[16]

The biggest deficit on the Houston Buffs roster in 1949 was pitching. Former ace Clarence Beers was back, but he posted a losing record. Hard-throwing Jack Creel was tops on the Buffs staff with a mark of 16-10, 3.39. No other Buff pitchers finished with a winning balance.

It all added up to a seventh place finish with a record of 60-91. That put Houston a full 38.5 games back of the first place Fort Worth Cats.

The following season did not bring improvement. The 1950 Buffs posted an almost identical record to 1949, slipping to 61-93 for a complete drop into eighth place in the Texas League. It ended a remarkable record run. Since the inception of the league in 1888, a Houston team had never finished in last place.[17]

Kemp Wicker, a journeyman pitcher who had spent time with the pre-war Yankees, started the 1950 season as the Buffs manager, but he was soon replaced by Benny Borgmann, a notably round little man. After 14 seasons as a minor league player and a few more as manager, The cards thought Borgmann was the man to lead the Buffs.

In terms of personnel, 1950 saw a future Major League star make a quick stop in Houston on his way to success. Twenty-year old Wally Moon, fresh off a good college ball career at Texas A&M, garnered one career Buffs single in four at bats before he was off to Omaha and a brighter baseball life.

Minor league slugging legend Jerry Witte also became a Buff in early June 1950 by reassignment from the parent Cardinals. At 34 years old, Witte had played only 19 games among a crowd of younger first base candidates at Triple-A Rochester.

Witte petitioned for his reassignment to Double-A Houston. Seeking out Johnny Keane, who was then the manager at Rochester, Witte laid his case plainly on the line.

"Johnny," Witte argued hard, "I'm no prospect, anymore. I'm a suspect. You've got two guys who can handle first base just fine, and I ain't no third baseman. Help me go somewhere warm, somewhere I can play at first base."[18]

Witte hit only .249 for the 1950 Buffs in 99 games, but his 30 home runs placed him among the league leaders in power production, while also providing fans an ongoing display of Ruthian art.[19]

Jerry Witte played for his hometown St. Louis Browns before ending his career with three seasons in Houston.
Private Collection

Suicide at Buff Stadium

On June 11, 1950, Dick Gottlieb, the baseball play-by-play man who was bringing Buffs games to Houston through the new medium of television, was broadcasting from an open area of Buff Stadium. With the large cameras and heavy cables unable to fit into the press box, Gottlieb and his audio engineer were in metal chairs behind a table in the stands. As the camera swung around to see Gottlieb deliver a live commercial for a sponsor such as Henke & Pillot Grocery or Hamm's Beer, a drunk man seated himself next to the announcer and started demanding attention by tugging on the TV man's arm. Twice Gottlieb tried to shoo the man away and then turned his attention back to the field. Suddenly there was what Gottlieb later described as "a huge explosion," adding that he "thought the world had come to an end." The man had shot himself in the head. Gottlieb, his sound engineer and all of their score cards were covered in blood. The announcer's first reaction was to assure his pregnant wife over the air that he was fine. He then told the audience that a man had just shot himself and tried to throw the broadcast back to the studio, but no one at the station was paying attention. Instead, the director in the control truck said, "Let's see it," and the slumped, bloodied body appeared on TV screens across Houston. Though the grisly visage remained for only about eight seconds, it was long enough for a justice of the peace who was watching the game to call a verdict of suicide in from home.

The 1952 Buffaloes scorecard featured an ad for Philco TV sets at a time when the technology was brand new to most Houstonians.

Courtesy Tom Kennedy

There were few other high notes. Little Joe Presko, at 16-16, was the only pitcher with double digit wins. Presko also led the Texas League in strikeouts with 165.

Offensively, Chuck Kress at .297 and Vann Harrington at .296 were the best full-season hitters for average, while, aside from Witte, only Kress and Jack Hussey hit double-digit homers with 12 and 13 respectively.[20]

Still riding the crest of post-war enthusiasm, the turnout was good. The 1950 Buffs again outdrew the big league Browns by more than 8,000 fans, for the third time in five years. This time, it was pulled off by a last place minor league club over a supposed major league team.[21]

Progressive Allen Russell did one more thing to boost the gate late in the season. He put the Buffs in short pants, ostensibly to save them from the killer heat. His real thought, however, was that by showing some bare, muscular legs, he would lure more women to the ballpark.

The players reluctantly went along with the ruse. Their shorts were little more than regular baseball pants that had been cut off about the knees and hemmed. It made the players who were standing still appear as though they were each wearing blousy little skirts, and the shorter, wider and older you were, the worse you looked. Portly manager Benny Borgmann drew laughs whenever he had to walk to the mound and deal with a pitcher.

Finally, about two weeks into the adventure, the player complaints about strawberry burns from sliding and mosquito bites simply piled too high. By this time, of course, Allen Russell had seen enough to know that the shorts were not helping the gate, anyway. So, the boys went back to wearing their regular long uniform pants. The 1950 Buffs got to finish the season looking like a real baseball team, even if they couldn't play like one.

Rocketed by the kind of instantaneous progress that was possible when a talented farm system feeds a minor league club, Houston reaped the benefits of being the only Class Double-A team of the St. Louis Cardinals. The team that finished dead last in 1950 was a runaway winner in 1951. Houston topped the league by 13.5 games with a 99-61 record, and they closed the regular season with a head of steam. The Buffs defeated Beaumont and then swept second place San Antonio in four games for the Texas League pennant.[22]

They won the crown with pitching and power. Knuckleballer Al Papai (23-9, 2.51) led the league in wins. Octavio Rubert (19-5. 2.28) was tops in win percentage. Vinegar Bend Mizell (16-14, 1.97) had the highest strikeout total on the circuit with 257. Hurlers Fred Martin (15-11, 2.54), Dick Bokelmann (10-2 0.74), and Mike Clark (10-7, 2.78) also sported stats that spoke loudly for the Buffs pitching depth.[23]

Jerry Witte with a league leading 38 homers and Larry Miggins with 27 dingers supplied new manager Al Hollingsworth with the power. The top batting average on the team belonged to Eddie Kazak at .304. No other regular player was within 40 points of him.[24]

Manager Al Hollingsworth led the Buffaloes to the Texas League title in 1951, his first year at the helm of the club.

Houston Metropolitan Research Center, Houston Public Library

Kazak was one of many war veterans on Texas League rosters, but his story was remarkable. In Normandy, soon after D-Day, Kazak suffered a bayonet wound to his left arm and had his right elbow blown apart by shrapnel. After 18 months of Army hospitals and surgery, including one that replaced his elbow with a "plastic patch," Kazak returned to pro ball, against doctors' advice. He suffered a shooting pain every time he threw, but by 1949, he told *The Sporting News* that, "The arm began to come back with exercise, and it has been getting better ever since." Eddie

One of Allen Russell's greatest promotions for the Buffs was when he brought Wilmer Mizell's entire hometown of Vinegar Bend, AL to a Houston ball game on a bus. Mizell played up the country boy image for the press.

Houston Metropolitan Research Center, Houston Public Library

Kazak continued to play pro ball past his 40th birthday in 1960.[25]

Two noteworthy events took place during the 1951 season. On July 12, Buff Stadium hosted the annual Texas League All Star Game. The North prevailed 7-3, their first win since 1940. Joe Nuxhall of Tulsa was the winning pitcher, and Bob Turley of San Antonio gave up a five spot in the seventh to take the loss. Houston's Wilmer Mizell worked three and a third innings without giving up a hit. The South All Star lineup was loaded with Buffs: Ben Steiner at second, Eddie Kazak at third, Jerry Witte at first, Larry Miggins in left and Les Fusselman at catcher.

On September 7, 1951, Allen Russell pulled the greatest promotional stunt of his seven-seasons at the Buffs' helm. It was "Vinegar Bend Night," and Russell had bussed all 80 residents of "Vinegar Bend," Alabama to Houston so that they could watch their favorite son, Wilmer Vinegar Bend Mizell, pitch his best against the Shreveport Sports. Mizell struck out 15 Sports batters as his hometown folks whooped it up in the big city. The single flaw in the script: Shreveport won the game 3-1.[26]

Left-handed Mizell was a popular player in Houston, as would be most pitchers who kept their ERA under two. His country-boy charm was also something that sportswriters loved. By the 1952 season, he was with the big league Cardinals, winning 10 games but with more than a touch of wildness that earned him the league lead in walks. Mizell spent nine seasons in the bigs, eventually facing rib and arm troubles. He quit pitching by age 31, moving to a career as a conservative three-term North Carolina Congressman and political appointee in three Republican administrations.[27]

The minor league roller coaster was again evident in Houston in 1952. The Buffs descended from the pennant to the Texas League cellar. The ball club went 66-95 under second-year manager Al Hollingsworth, bad enough to finish 26 games behind the first place Dallas Eagles.

Talent-wise, the 1952 Buffs were a walking definition of threadbare. Perennial Buffs pitching star Al Papai was their big winner at 14-13, with Mike Clark, Bob Clear and Octavio Rubert next in victories with nine each. As evidenced by the earned run averages of

The Buffaloes' Jerry Witte is greeted by teammates after hitting a walk-off home run against Bob Turley of the San Antonio Missions.
Private Collection

Floyd Wooldridge at 2.34 and Clark at 1.90, the problems hardly rested entirely upon the pitchers. Even with that good E.R.A, Wooldridge went 7-18.[28]

A lack of offense and poor defense made strong contributions to the loss column in 1952. Among the regulars, Lou Farotto led the herd in batting at .279. He was followed by Ed Mierkowicz, Strick Shofner and Mel McGaha, the only other players above .250.[29]

Aging first baseman Jerry Witte hit 19 long balls in his last season of professional ball, but his batting average dropped all the way to .202. It was time to retire, and Jerry Witte knew it.[30]

For the second year in a row, future Hall of Fame manager Earl Weaver was present in the early part of the 1952 season, trying to make the team as a young second baseman. Batting only .219 in 57 games, Weaver proved that he wasn't

Third baseman Ken Boyer played his final year of minor league baseball in Houston before moving to the Cardinals and a career that would include a National League MVP Award in 1964. Houston Metropolitan Research Center, Houston Public Library

ready for AA ball and was sent down to Omaha, never returning to Houston again as a player.

The most important story of the 1952 season had social ramifications. A milestone was reached in the Texas League. The Dallas Eagles, long an independent organization, had become a farm team of the Cleveland Indians under the new ownership of flamboyant oilman Dick Burnett. Knowing that the Indians had more African-American talent in their system than any other club, it was viewed around the league as inevitable that the color barrier would be broken in Texas.

Dave Hoskins, a 26-year-old Mississippi native, was carefully selected to be the first black ballplayer in the circuit's history, having been personally recommended by Indians exec Hank Greenberg. Right-hander Hoskins succeeded in a big way. His outstanding pitching record of 22-10, and a 2.12 ERA paced the Texas League in wins and set him up for a big league shot with the Cleveland Indians in 1953. Additionally, Hoskins, who had previously played outfield, hit .328 on the season.[31]

For the most part, integration went smoothly. Hoskins said that his Dallas teammates had been "swell" as were most fans around the league. The biggest trouble came in Shreveport in early June. Hoskins received three letters the morning of his appearance that threatened him with a sniper's bullet if he took the mound. He kept his mouth shut and pitched, understanding that revealing the peril might cause the manager to skip his turn. His early nervousness dissipated, and he won the game 3-2.[32]

Louisiana officials were so upset with Dave Hoskins' integration of the league that they reacted with proposed legislation outlawing interracial sporting events. Local officials in Shreveport and Baton Rouge passed similar laws causing a situation which would come to a head a few years later.[33]

Hoskins quickly proved to be the biggest draw at the gate that the league had known for some time. When Houston hosted Dallas on April 27 with Hoskins on the mound, the game drew over 11,000 fans, over half of whom were black. He bested the Buffaloes 9-2. The other two games in that series, when Hoskins was not pitching, averaged 2,935 fans.[34]

Dave Hoskins was joined in the league by a second African-American

Former White Sox first sacker Bob Boyd was the first African-American to play for the Houston Buffaloes, breaking the color barrier in 1954.

Houston Metropolitan Research Center, Houston Public Library

player later that year when Oklahoma City signed pitcher Bill Greason. The two met as mound opponents in another league first on August 3.[35]

With the season's end came another change. Allen Russell was tired of the uphill struggle in Houston. The cutback in bonus checks from the Cardinals, and the frequent first-to-last-place drops in the standings continually tore down what he was trying to build. Also, the latest news was that current Cardinals owner, Fred Saigh, would be headed to jail soon for income tax evasion.[36]

Russell made it known that he was resigning his post as president and general manager of the Houston Buffs. Over a span of 15 years, Russell had played roles from parking lot attendant to politics and marketing, moving Houston baseball closer to the modern era.

The off-season also brought the first serious flirtation with bringing the Major Leagues to Houston. After outdrawing the Browns four times, there were those who believed the city could support a team. George Kirksey, a public relations man with a love for the game, put together an offer to buy the St. Louis Cardinals from cash-strapped Fred Saigh and bring them south. When word leaked that such talks were underway, a firestorm arose among the Redbirds' supporters. Saigh went with a local buyer lest he be run out of town.[37]

The year 1953 came with a new team owner in Houston, too. After August Busch of beer-brewing fame stepped in and bought the Cardinals in March, he changed the names of both Sportsman's

Park in St. Louis and Buffalo Stadium in Houston to Busch Stadium.

Art Routzong took over as General Manager of the ball club. Routzong was not the promoter that Allen Russell had been, but he had more training running a business on a balanced budget. He would remain in Houston for five seasons before he was called to St. Louis in 1958 to serve as Business Manager of the Cardinals.[38]

The team that Busch and Routzong inherited in Houston was not a good one. Floyd Wooldridge at 15-13 was the Buffs' leading pitcher in 1953. His 2.20 ERA was enough to lead the league, but he was the lone bright spot on the mound. The only other Buffs pitcher to gather double digit wins was Al Papai, now 36 years old, and he had a losing record at 11-16.[39]

There were three hitters who topped .300: Harry Elliott, Eddie Phillips and Larry Ciaffone. Fred Marolewski and his 23 homers proved to be the only Buff with any decent pop.

The 1953 Houston Buffs finished the Texas League season in sixth place with a record of 72-82. Al Hollingsworth, who had begun the season as manager, was replaced by former Brooklyn Dodger Dixie Walker.

After three and a half years of having Houston's television airwaves to themselves, KPRC Channel 2 gained competition in 1953 in the form of KHOU-TV. There was also an increase in live network programming into the Houston area. Dizzy Dean, now a broadcaster, reached local viewers every Saturday with his TV "Game of the Week" telecasts of major league baseball.

With Art Routzong now ensconced in his second year as the Buffs General Manager, and "the People's Cherce," Dixie Walker, back in the saddle as the returning field boss, Houston welcomed a greater infusion of talent from the parent St. Louis Cardinals.

Willard Schmidt at 18-5 and Mike Clark at 13-0 paced the 1954 Houston Buffs' starting rotation. A less frequent starter, and future MLB relief star, was Luis Arroyo whose ERA of 2.35 easily led the ball club. His record of 8-3 included a no-hitter against Dallas in August.[40]

The Houston infield held the team's best offensive assets. They had .300 hitters around the horn with Ken Boyer (.319, 21 HR) at third base, Don Blasingame (.315) at shortstop, Howie Phillips (.306) at second base and Bob Boyd (.321) at first base.

The Texas League had continued to integrate. A year after Dave Hoskins and Bill Greason had broken the Lone Star color line, Tulsa and San Antonio had added African-American players. In 1954, Houston finally followed suit. Former Chicago White Sox prospect Bob Boyd connected with the club as the first black player in the 66-year history of the team.

After acquiring Boyd, the Buffs announced that he would be starting at first base in his first game on the roster on the evening of Thursday, May 27, at Buff Stadium.[41]

There was no outcry against Bob Boyd. Even the more unenlightened of Houston ball fans had accepted the inevitability of an integrated ball club. What transpired turned into somewhat of a celebration by many in attendance that a certain hurdle had been overcome.

The segregated grandstand section for black fans still existed down the far right field line near the foul pole. Even before Boyd and most of the Buffs took the field, the black fans of Houston filed in joyously, filling the relatively small, limited area in right field assigned to them. Of the announced attendance that night of approximately 5,000, just under half of the crowd was African-American.[42]

When Bob Boyd appeared at first base for infield practice, a roar erupted from the black grandstands. It was followed by a visceral vibration that all attending fans would remember. The cadent foot-stomping from the designated Boyd fan section began to radiate into the whites-only sections of the park. When lefty Boyd came to bat in the second with a man on base, the roar from the right side was decibel bending. The *Houston Post* called it "wild acclaim."

Early in the pitch count, Boyd lashed what would become a trademark rope that barely seemed to clear the shortstop's head before rising sharply to take a crazy carom high off the left field wall. It worked for a triple as Boyd delivered an RBI in his first official time at bat with the Buffs.

Suddenly, there was no more largely silent white ocean in the Buff Stadium stands as Houston fans rose together to cheer and applaud the beautiful three base hit.

By the time he got to Houston in 1954, Willard Brown had already been a Negro League star with the Kansas City Monarchs and compiled a record that would lead to the Baseball Hall of Fame. Here he wears the jersey of Santurce in Puerto Rico.

National Baseball Hall of Fame Library, Cooperstown, NY

When Boyd again came up in the fourth and lined another rope, this time off the right field wall for an RBI-double, the roar of the crowd was deafening. The sparkling performance was heralded by the press as an "impressive debut."[43]

"All that black players like Bob Boyd could do in 1954," said Bill McCurdy, who attended the game as a teenager, "was to show the world by their levels of play that blacks belong in baseball with whites as very capable human beings in their own rights."

Boyd was well-liked among local fans, always graciously acknowledging the applause. As the season progressed, there was no let up in attendance among black fans.

"His every move and play at first base," recalls Buffs fan Patrick Lopez. "Brought forth 'oohs and aahs' from the right field stands."[44]

The admiration that Buffs fans showered on Boyd did not transfer to the many other aspects of social segregation that existed in Texas. For the black fans who were euphoric at the chance to cheer one of their own, it was unclear when those barriers would fall. Though the Buffs clubhouse might be open, the stadium grandstands and restrooms still were not.

Former Kansas City Monarchs slugger Willard Brown came to Houston later in the season to become a second African-American player on the club. He had been with Dallas the previous year and a half, so was familiar with the racial snubs that came with life in the Texas League.

With Boyd and Brown as major parts of their offense, the Buffs went on to win the 1954 Texas League pennant with a five-game victory over Oklahoma City and another five-game win in the finals over Fort Worth. The Buffs then lost a hotly contested seven-game series with the Atlanta Crackers to again fall painfully short of the top of the heap.

Interestingly, manager Dixie Walker was the same man who had been tagged as the ringleader of the Brooklyn Dodgers' anti-Jackie Robinson faction in 1947. He was involved with an initial effort to keep Robinson off the team, and Ben Chapman, Robinson's most vicious heckler, was a good friend of Walker.

Walker shared a batting tip with Robinson early that year, and the two treated each other as cordial teammates on the 1947 Dodgers, though, if Walker homered with Robinson on base, there was no handshake at home plate. Walker repeatedly said later that much of his opposition was to protect his hardware and sporting goods business in Birmingham from loss of business if he played with a black man.[45]

Seven years of inevitable changes in baseball came to pass between Brooklyn and Houston. In the case of Dixie Walker's relationship to Bob Boyd or Willard Brown, there seem to be no reported incidents. Walker spoke of Jackie Robinson decades later: "I've gotten along with a lot of blacks since then- I managed 'em in the minor leagues and there's many I came to respect and like."[46]

The 1954 season also marked the end of the baseball road for one of the most popular Buffaloes, Larry Miggins. At the age of 28, and with a growing family that would eventually include 12 children,

The Buffs entertain a packed house as Harry Walker and a teammate kneel near the on-deck circle.

Houston Metropolitan Research Center, Houston Public Library

Miggins chose to go after his college degree. He eventually got his Masters degree and enjoyed a long career in the federal probation and parole office in Houston.

Long-time Cardinals and Red Sox player and coach Mike Ryba came aboard as manager of the Buffs for the 1955 season. He was coming off four years as a coach for the big club. In addition to a solid ten-year career playing in the majors, Ryba was also a veteran of the interracial barnstorming tours of the late 1930s that featured Dizzy Dean, Satchel Paige and Bob Feller. He was particularly close to the Dean brothers and several of the black ball stars.[47]

Austin-born Kansas City Monarchs star Newt Allen recalled of Ryba, "every time we ran across him it was like meeting up with a brother or something."[48]

The team that Ryba acquired had not suffered the dramatic falloff in talent experienced in previous years. The pitching staff was braced by the steady arms of Bill Greason with 17 wins, Bob Mabe with 16 and Harry Hoitsma who went 13-3 with an impressive 2.64 ERA.[49]

They had expertise at the plate, too. Three holdovers from the previous year paced the team in hitting. Russell Rac hit .312 with 21 home runs, Willard Brown posted .301, 19 HR and Bob Boyd batted .319 with 15 homers. Boyd's 197 hits led the league.[50]

The Buffaloes finished 86-75, and the ball club squeezed into the playoffs from a fourth place tie with Tulsa by taking a one-game playoff for a spot in the regular rounds. They then used the four-team

Houston finished first in the league in 1956, and advertisers jumped on board to support the winning ball club.

Courtesy Tom Kennedy

Shaughnessy playoff system to their advantage. Houston started by surprising first place Dallas in six games before falling to third place Shreveport in seven games for the Texas League pennant. They had come close to two pennants in a row.[51]

Around the Texas League, desegregation continued. Maury Wills and Eddie Moore were with the Ft. Worth Cats, Willie Tasby and Lenny Green played in San Antonio, Bill White and Jim Tugerson in Dallas, Frank Barnes at Oklahoma City and Marshall Bridges in Beaumont. The league was as integrated as any in America, with one exception: Shreveport.[52]

Dixie Walker's little brother Harry Walker took over as the new manager of the Houston Buffs in 1956 after a less than successful term at the helm of the

Ruben Amaro experienced much of the same racial discrimination that African-Americans endured on ball clubs in southern leagues. Houston Metropolitan Research Center, Houston Public Library

Houston native and former Buff Red Munger did finish his career in the Texas League, but playing for San Antonio before retiring to his home town. Houston Metropolitan Research Center, Houston Public Library

big league Cardinals. He proved more talented with Houston, and with a mark of 96-58, the club shot up to a first place finish. The team then took out the Tulsa Oilers in the first round and the Dallas Eagles in the finals to capture the 1956 Texas League pennant.[53]

Moving on to the Dixie Series, the Buffs were still unstoppable. They beat the Atlanta Crackers of the Southern Association in a hard-fought six game competition.

The team enjoyed good all-around talent. Bob Mabe (21-10, 2.83) and Tom Hughes (18-6, 2.70) paced the 1956 Buffs pitching staff. Mabe led the league in wins and strikeouts, and Hughes had the highest winning percentage on the circuit.

The hitters were numerous. Herb Adams topped all Buffs at .333, five points higher than Pidge Browne and manager Harry Walker. Browne also knocked 29 homers. Combined with Bobby Smith's 21 and Benny Valenzuela's 18, the Buffs had enough power to make opposing pitchers think twice.

Attendance remained flat, relative to the best Russell years following WWII, but the Buffs' total of 232,696 was still much better than any of the seven other Texas League clubs in 1956. Minor league baseball in general had seen a decline in revenue since the start of the decade. It was all the more reason for Houston baseball powers to be looking for a bigger draw.

By the start of the 1957 season, the racial situation in Shreveport had become a league wide problem because of a new law passed by the Louisiana legislature barring interracial competition. They had tried four years earlier, but in late 1956, the elected segregationists succeeded. When other teams traveled to play the Sports, they had to leave black players behind. Those players included the Buffs' Ruben Amaro and other notables like Willie McCovey who was playing for Dallas.[54]

For their part, the Texas League, which had enjoyed the economic benefits of black players for five years, questioned only the blow this caused to competitive balance, never going to bat for the rights of their African-American players.

The situation led to a league wide boycott by black fans that was joined by sympathetic whites and other white fans who feared possible violence. Boycotts against teams that practiced segregation had started earlier in other parts of the South. The New Orleans Pelicans of the Southern Association had refused to take black players sent to them by their parent Pittsburgh Pirates in 1955. Their African-American attendance dropped from over 40,000 in one year to only 3,400 the next.[55]

The fear that some whites had of protests escalating into trouble was not totally unfounded. A backdrop of civil rights violence in other parts of the South included bus boycotts that turned into police brutality and the murder of Emmett Till in Mississippi[56]

Shreveport lost so much money that the franchise was put up for sale before the end of the season. Dropped from the league in 1958, they moved to the Southern Association which would continue to be an all-white organization until 1961.

The fact that they could freely play ball in Houston and other Texas cities didn't mean that black players led a rosy life. In Texas cities in the mid-1950s, they were still forced to stay in separate hotels or at the Negro branch of the YMCA. Lodging in private homes was preferred, but was somewhat rare. Frank Robinson recounted accommodations where he had to sleep "four to a room and no shower, and we had to line up to get into the tub." Many black players had to do their bathing at the ball parks. Meanwhile the white players were in air-conditioned hotels.[57]

Though the praise was relative, when Joe Durham, who was with San Antonio in 1954, evaluated the situations in each Texas League city, he said that, "the best place was Houston. We stayed at the White Crystal Hotel on Lyons. They had a restaurant that seated about 250 people, and you didn't have to worry about the food. The rooms were nice, with

Dan Rather

Long before he hosted the CBS Evening News, Dan Rather counted Houston sportswriter and Southwest Conference football announcer Kern Tips among his influences. He conceded in 2001 that he once thought of sports broadcasting as a permanent career option. He called University of Houston football for a few years, but the highest level he reached on that path was broadcasting Triple-A Houston Buffs games on KTRH in 1959. Rather readily admits that it is not nearly as easy as it might sound. His first attempt at a home run call, "Bye-bye baseball," was poo-pooed by a sponsor, so he settled on a simple "Going, going, gone." He recounts that one of his most humiliating moments came while he was doing a re-creation broadcast of a Buffs road game. Sitting in the studio, Rather set out to describe a close play at the plate. He recalls that he was in a phase of trying to incorporate baseball slang such as "wheels" instead of "legs." When centerfielder Jim Delsing pegged a throw to home that particular game, Rather said, "The runner breaks. Delsing takes two steps. He makes a perfect throw, and he's out at the plate." After a pause, he added, "What a hose on that Delsing." Color man Art McGee "fell off his stool laughing." Dan Rather was so mortified that he was temporarily unable to continue.

radios, and a few had telephones. Dallas and Oklahoma City were nothing to write home about."[58]

Houston's Latino ballplayers experienced discrimination according to their skin tone. Benny Valenzuela had no problems at all, but infielder Ruben Amaro, who had a black Cuban father, was prevented from doing most activities with his teammates. They could, however, ride together on the train, the place were much bonding took place. At a movie theatre in Fort Worth, Amaro, who spoke some English, could buy a ticket based on his word that he was Mexican. Other dark-skinned players could not.[59]

The American black players and their dark-skinned Hispanic teammates couldn't eat at the same restaurants as their white peers, use the water fountains or ride in the same taxicabs. In Amaro's case, teammates Howie Nunn and Fred McAlister often tried to sneak him into restaurants on the road, hiding him among the crowd of players that filed in. Sometimes it worked, and sometimes it didn't. More than once, many of the Buffs refused to eat at a given place in solidarity with their teammates. As Amaro recalled, "It was rough." It would not be until Houston began flirting with the Major Leagues that the separate and unequal policy ended for black ballplayers in the Bayou City.[60]

On the field in Houston, Harry Walker returned in 1957 for a second year as manager of the Buffs. This time he played in more games himself, and the results were positive.

Phil Clark put up a record of 16-6 with a stellar 1.83 earned run average, most of his work coming in relief. Howie Nunn was almost as good with numbers of 16-7, 2.97, and Nelson Chittum also had 16 victories. Tom Hughes went 14-4 and again led the league in winning percentage. Billy Muffett added 14 more wins, and the team ERA was a nice 2.68. It was a pitching deep 1957 Buffs staff.[61]

The hitting, on the other hand, was not as powerful as it had been the year before. Nelson Burbrink, at .308, was the only player to average over .300, but he had no homers. Edwin Little paced the club in homers with 30, but batted only .243. Benny Valenzuela was the club's leading RBI man with 90.[62]

It was enough of a combination to lead the Buffs to a 97-57 record and a second place Texas League finish, five games back of the Dallas Eagles. From there the team defeated the third place San Antonio Missions in round one and then conquered first place Dallas in a full seven game series to take the pennant for their second year in a row.

The streak of consecutive championships continued as the 1957 Buffs again defeated the Atlanta Crackers of the Southern Association in six games, and Houston captured the Dixie Series title for the second season in a row.

The following season would be a restless one for Houston and the Texas League with Beaumont, Oklahoma City, and Shreveport no longer in the circuit. Beaumont had moved two years earlier, becoming the Austin Senators. In 1958, the Corpus Christi Giants and the Victoria Rosebuds had joined the League.

Stan McIlvaine was now on board as General Manager of the Houston Buffs after Art Routzong was called to St. Louis to serve as Business Manager of the Cards. The only stability at the top came with Harry Walker's return for his third season as manager.[63]

Walker was well recognized as the younger brother of Dixie Walker, but lesser known is the fact that their father, also called Dixie Walker in spite of the fact that he was actually born in Pennsylvania, pitched for four years with the Washington Senators. Harry and Dixie, Jr.'s Uncle Ernie was an outfielder for the St. Louis Browns.[64]

The younger pair of Walker brothers were both tall and lean. Harry stood 6'2" during his 11 years in the majors. During that time the left-handed hitter compiled a lifetime batting average of just under .300. In 1947, Harry Walker's combined .363 for the Cards and Phillies won him the NL batting title, something his brother had accomplished three years prior. Power was not his strong suit, however. He had only 10 career home runs. His nickname of "Harry the Hat" stemmed from his habit of adjusting his ball cap between pitches.[65]

Harry Walker continued coaching for another decade and a half after he left the Buffs. His final stop as a manager brought him back to Houston as skipper of the Astros for the better part of five seasons between 1968 and 1972. He finished his tenure with the Bayou City's big league club with a record that left him two games above .500.

Pitching was not spectacular for the 1958 Buffs. Glen Crable and Billy Bowman, two hurlers in their late 20s who would never make the show, tied for the most wins on the club with 12 each. Howie Nunn and Bob Miller were the other two main starters.

The club did have some players who could hit for average. Center fielder Herb Adams at .318 posted the highest mark, with infielder Russell Rac and left fielder Alberto Baro also topping .300. The top power numbers came from right fielder Ellis Burton with 22 homers and outfielder Charlie James with 19.

The 1958 Buffs finished the season only 5 games above .500, but that was good enough for second place. Harry "The Hat" was unable to pull out any surprise rabbits in his third time around the Texas League block, though. Houston lost in the first round of the post-season playoffs to third place Corpus Christi, who in turn defeated fourth place Austin to take the pennant in their first season in the loop.[66]

Attendance at Buff games in 1958 dropped to 121,234, an atrocious gate, but still better than anyone else in the Texas League, which was seeing its numbers diminish everywhere.[67]

It was also the end of a relationship that had started almost 40 seasons earlier. In conjunction with the close of the 1958 Texas League year, the St. Louis Cardinals sold the Houston Buffs and Buff/Busch Stadium.

The upside among fans was the anticipation that Houston was moving up the ladder to the Triple-A American Association in 1959 under new independent ownership. This change also furthered musings as to when Houston would make the next jump and convert Triple-A success into a spot in the major leagues.

Houston publicist George Kirksey had never wavered in his desire to bring big league ball to Houston. The top hurdle had been geography. Even with long-entrenched teams like the Browns and Braves showing a willingness to relocate, the closest Major League city was more than 1,000 miles from Southeast Texas. In 1957, though, California had come into the mix. Hope soared in Texas that it would be next.

Kirksey had enlisted the help of William Kirkland, chairman of First City National Bank, and through him had developed a bond with Craig Cullinan, an heir to a fortune made in the founding of Texaco. By the off-season of 1958, a shareholders group was formed called the Houston Sports Association (HSA). They also gained the support of Harris County Judge Bob Casey and laid the groundwork to follow a precedent set when Milwaukee put public money into financing a stadium.[68]

Before he had departed for St. Louis, Art Routzong had blamed all the public campaigning for a Major League franchise for seriously hurting interest in the previously untouchable minor league club. At the end of 1958, the Busch family had offered to sell the Buffs to the HSA for $100,000, but Craig Cullinan had declined to invest the money.[69]

The new world of Triple-A brought wholesale changes in personnel for 1959. Former great Cardinals shortstop Marty Marion was the new president/treasurer of the Houston Buffs and leader of the group that had purchased the club and Busch Stadium from the St. Louis Cardinals.[70]

Columbus, Georgia, native Spec Richardson was the new general manager of the team. Richardson would remain in that position for all three of Houston's final seasons as a minor league baseball town. The city's sports fans would see him again as GM of the Astros from 1967 through 1975. Many consider Richardson the worst GM in the first 50 years of major league ball in Houston. He traded away a 24-year-old Rusty Staub, 31-year-old Mike Cuellar and, most memorably, 27-year-old future Hall of Famer Joe Morgan.[71]

The Buffaloes in 1959 were functioning as a completely independent club, and holding no current player assignment agreements with any major league team. It made their ascent from Double-A to Triple-A baseball into a very steep climb.

Rube Walker began the season as manager of the 1959 Buffs, but the club finished the year under manager Del Wilber, their field leader in the Texas League back in 1949.

One big difference at the Triple-A level was the roster presence of far more big leaguers on their way out of the game. They were with the Buffs to either fight their way back to the majors, or in most cases, to draw another paycheck before either retiring or dropping further down the minor league ladder.

Young Bill Bethel at 13-11, veteran Dave Jolly at 11-10 and Mel Wright, who had a big league cup of coffee both behind him and ahead of him, with a 10-8 mark were the biggest winners on the losing club's pitching staff. The Buffs also

Former Cardinals star Enos Slaughter went to work for the rival Cubs organization as Houston manager.
Houston Metropolitan Research Center, Houston Public Library

Billy Williams excelled at the plate in 1960 and was very talented with the bat even before he got tips from legendary hitter Rogers Hornsby.

Houston Metropolitan Research Center, Houston Public Library

Buffs infielder Ron Santo did not hit like the future Hall of Famer he would become.

Houston Metropolitan Research Center, Houston Public Library

welcomed an old nemesis from Dallas. Dave Hoskins was on the way down as a moundsman in 1959, putting up only a 7-9 mark with an earned run average well north of four. Hoskins had not lost much at the plate, however, posting a .338 batting average as an often-used pinch hitter.[72]

Among the everyday players, veteran outfielder Jim Fridley, with a .282 average and 26 homers, and veteran catcher Ray Noble with a .294, 15 HR ledger, led the 1959 Buffs offense. Pidge Browne was back in Houston after a year at Omaha. Two other name players on the Buffs were 33-year-old vet Roy Smalley who had just completed 11 seasons in the National League, and young "Hot Rod" Kanehl who would become famous as a key member of the hapless expansion New York Mets, holders of the worst full-season mark in modern baseball history.[73]

The Minneapolis Millers took the American Association crown in 1959 with a seven-game series victory over the Fort Worth Cats, another Texas League alumnus which, along with Houston and Dallas, had made the move up to Triple-A. The Buffs were 58-104 with the worst total record in the entire ten-team circuit. Houston was the only club in the league to lose over 100 games. No other club in the American Association finished with a loss column that even reached the 90s.[74]

As the club's effort on the field foundered, the Houston Sports Association's efforts to bring the big leagues to Houston continued to heat up. In August of 1959, the HSA and representatives from cities such as Toronto, Denver, Minneapolis and New York, which had just lost both the Giants and Dodgers, formally announced their plans to start the Continental League, a third big league circuit that would be headed by Branch Rickey.[75]

Another major step was taken later in the off-season when the powers at HSA managed to pique the interest of former Houston Mayor and Harris County Judge Roy Hofheinz and his close friend, R.E. "Bob" Smith, an oil and real estate man worth nearly a billion dollars. Their involvement provided more money, more savvy and the final piece of the big league puzzle.[76]

Houston had finished their first season at the higher level with at least one certainty. Marty Marion was going to have to find a working agreement for 1960 with a big league team that was capable of supplying the Buffs with some Triple-A ready ballplayers. Garden fresh rookies and boiled over veterans would not make a winning ball club.

They found the answer in a working deal with the Chicago Cubs, the arch rivals of the Buffs' long time parent St. Louis Cardinals. It meant that Houston would be getting a core group of quality players for the 1960 campaign, and it brought a marked improvement.

The new manager of the Buffs was Enos "Country" Slaughter. The future Hall of Famer had ended his 19-year Major League playing career with an even .300 average and a signature moment in the 1946 World Series known as "the Mad Dash." Slaughter's first manager as a Cardinals minor leaguer had been Houstonian Eddie Dyer, who had instilled in his young charge the virtue of always running. The lesson stuck and assured one thing: the Buffs hustled. With Slaughter at the helm, they would have no choice.[77]

Big first baseman and career minor-leaguer Joe Macko led the 1960 Buffs with 27 home runs and 91 RBIs. Macko had already had one turn managing the Tulsa Oilers, and at age 32, he still had several years of ball in the Cubs organization ahead of him. He would make one brief final comeback with Dallas-Ft. Worth in 1970, the penultimate season of minor league ball for the Metroplex.[78]

Among the young pitchers, Jim Brewer, Dick Ellsworth and Moe Drabowsky contributed, and each would go on to a decent Major League career. The top winners for the 1960 Buffs, though, were two veterans who had already been to the show. Al Lary with a record of 12-8 and Ed Donnelly at 11-6 paced the team in victories.[79]

By far, the two players of lasting note among the first Cubs assignments were 22-year-old left fielder Billy Williams and 20-year-old third baseman Ron Santo. In

Pitcher Dave Giusti was one of the few ballplayers to see time with both the Buffs and the Colt .45s/Astros.

Houston Metropolitan Research Center, Houston Public Library

his second year of pro ball, Santo had impressed at double-A San Antonio the season prior. He regressed a little in 1960, hitting only .268 with seven long balls.[80]

Williams' time in Houston turned out to be his final ticket to the bigs, however. In his fifth minor league season, he got more at bats than ever before and used them to put up a stats line of .323, 26 HR and 80 RBIs. By all accounts, he was a natural. He had started filling in with the semi-pro Mobile Black Bears when he was only 13. Fellow Cubs Hall of Famer Ernie Banks said famously of him, "Billy Williams can hit." That talent was never in question.[81]

His troubles were two fold, first his fielding was suspect. His long time teammate Santo would later flatly say that Williams was "not a good fielder" and that as a first baseman, he "couldn't even catch popups." The organization moved him to the outfield, and it was widely assumed that he was only remained in the minors because he needed a full season to adjust to the new position defensively.[82]

The second issue was racism, which had festered to an ugly boil. Though he had grown up in a rigidly segregated environment in South Alabama, Williams had not had to face Jim Crow as an adult on his own. In 1959, as a 20-year-old with the San Antonio Missions, he reached a breaking point, quit the team and went home.

"I couldn't take the bigotry, discrimination and overt racism," Williams said.

Cubs scout and former Negro League star Buck O'Neil went to Alabama and talked him back into pro baseball. Houston in 1960 wasn't easy for Williams, but he had the solace of a new bride. A sterling season earned him a September call up to Chicago, and he never again returned to the minors.[83]

The Buffs finished in third place but were quickly eliminated from championship possibilities in a five-game first round loss to the Denver Bears. The exciting young prospects and the new Cubs-like garb did not spin the turnstiles at the ballpark, even for a winning team. Their

1960 home gate was even worse than the independent Buffs drew in 1959.[84]

The post-season produced news that went far beyond the field outcomes of the Houston Triple-A ball club. On October 17, 1960, the National League, pushed to the limit by the threat of the Continental League and a legislative assault on their anti-trust exemption, awarded two new franchises to Miss Joan Payson of New York City and another to Judge Roy Hofheinz and the Houston Sports Association. Beginning in 1962, Houston, Texas would join the National League as a full member of Major League Baseball.[85]

Marty Marion and his group now had only a short period of one year to wrap up the minor league business of the Houston Buffs. Any hopes the Marion group may have harbored that they would be awarded the Houston franchise based on their work with the Buffs and ownership of a stadium that was potentially upgradable to big league capacity were completely dashed by the promises of the HSA.

The Hofheinz group had obtained Harris County's approval to build the world's first air-conditioned, fully enclosed multi-purpose stadium on the plains south of the Medical Center, a site they would share with the Houston Livestock Show and Rodeo.[86]

Hofheinz and his HSA partners would have to work out a price for the purchase of the Marion group's minor league territorial rights to the Houston area in order for the HSA master plan to move forward. The big league franchise owners would learn that bitter, rejected suitors make for tough negotiators.

Only one year in the minor leagues remained between Houston and the baseball big time. Even though the Buffs ended up playing for the league championship, there had never been a year in which Houston fans had seemed less interested in what was happening on the field. Only 120,104 fans came to watch the Buffs play at home in 1961.[87]

Even the club itself seemed unfocused. The 1961 Buffs went through managers like so many bags of sunflower seeds, parading Grady Hatton, Fred Martin, Lou Klein and Harry Craft to the helm before the season ended.

They had some decent hitters. Bud Zipfel, Pidge Browne, Jim McAnany and Sammy Drake all topped .300 among the regulars. Zipfel with 21 dingers and Jim McKnight with 24 round trippers and 102 RBIs led the club in power. For young Zipfel it would mean a trade and a turn with the Washington Senators before the year was out. McKnight, who was born and would die in Bee Branch, Arkansas, had enjoyed a three game stint with the Cubs the year before. His big year in '61 got him a final, and longer, shot in 1962.

Among the pitchers on the roster, only Al Lary and Dave Gerard managed double digit wins. Dave Giusti, 21-years-old, came to the Buffs in the summer and went 2-0 in three appearances in his first year of pro ball.

Giusti, a native of Seneca Falls, New York, had just completed a run to the College World Series with Syracuse. The new Houston Major League team was

The 1961 season brought a quiet end to minor league baseball in Houston as fans waited for the National League.
Courtesy Tom Kennedy

already signing young talent, and Giusti was the club's first bonus baby, getting a check for $35,000. After more time in the minors than majors, Giusti became a part of the Astros rotation from 1965 through 1968. He is best known as the lights out closer for the 1971 World Champion Pittsburgh Pirates.[88]

The Buffs played at a mediocre pace, finishing 73-77, but their record was good enough to reach fourth place in a depleted six team American Association. They responded with a first round five-game series win over the Indianapolis Indians before losing the flag in a six-game series with the Louisville Colonels. The last game was an 11-4 drubbing. The hometown Buffaloes committed seven errors, including five by the normally solid shortstop J.C. Hartman. A two-run homer by Jack Waters in the home ninth prevented the beating from being even more one-sided.[89]

The fans faced the end with mixed feelings. The close of the 1961 season was a double-edged sword for long time Buff supporters. Houston had now played its final minor league game with the Louisville series. It was saddening to know that the city had now played its last game as the Buffs.

Any possibility that the Houston Sports Association would retain the Buffs name as the club moved to the big leagues evaporated with the acrimony of Marty Marion-Roy Hofheinz negotiations on the territorial rights sale price.

According to Hofheinz, there was no interest anyway. He wanted a new identity for his big league ball club, something which he could market. The visionary Judge understood how branding could make him money.

Houston's rich minor league baseball history had reached its end. It was time for the Major League Colt .45's. There was no question that the move to the majors meant something big on the field, as Houstonians who had travelled to see big league ball already knew.

"The difference was apparent," said

longtime fan Patrick Lopez who had spent a summer with friends in Cincinnati and become a regular at Crosley Field. "Major League players seemed to throw the ball harder, were faster on the bases, the ball seemed to explode off their bats. The home runs were more dramatic, real shots over the fence."

Buffs fan Larry Wimberly was 14 when the minor leagues ceased to exist in Houston. For him the city's step up brought mixed emotions.

"Looking back, getting a major league team actually created more of a separation of the team from the people. Players weren't as accessible. It was much more expensive, but you could go see the other major league stars you had heard about all your life. The cost limited the number of games you could go see, but by golly, I got to see Stan Musial play, and that was a big deal to me. If you're looking for a single statement, in the minor leagues we were a part of it, in the majors, you were looking through a fishbowl."

A Mad Russian Memoir

For some of us, the highlight of the 1949 season happened on a night that Lou "The Mad Russian" Novikoff was playing left field at Buff Stadium for the home team. Late in the game, during a time out for a critical Buffs pitching change, Lou decided to also take the break as a time to run inside the nearby clubhouse and use the facilities. Those of us in the Knothole Gang that night got to see it well. Left field was in front of us. The Buffs clubhouse was behind us.

It might have worked out okay, too, except for a couple of hitches. Play resumed without anyone noticing that Lou was missing from his position in left field, and Lou was still trying to cram his Buffs jersey back into his unbuttoned pants as he staggered hurriedly out of the clubhouse door on his way back to the field.

'RUN, LOU, RUN!' was the charge of all Knothole Gangers, but our exhortations were not enough to save the day. Before Lou could make it back, as I remember, an ordinary single to left became something like a game-changing triple thanks to his absence and, of course, it figured in the eventual demise of the Buffs' chances for winning the game that night. The exact details are now lost to me, but the vision of Lou Novikoff struggling to get back to the field remains fresh. And always will.

We Knothole Gangers all learned something from Lou Novikoff that night, and the lesson still stands today: When you gotta go, you gotta go!

– Bill McCurdy

1 Russell, Allen. *Touching All Bases* (Gulf Publishing, 1990)
2 Russell, Allen. *Touching All Bases* (Gulf Publishing, 1990)
3 http://www.baseball-reference.com; Encyclopedia of Minor League Baseball. Third Edition. (Baseball America, 2007); http://www.baseball-reference.com/bullpen/Eddie_Knoblauch; Coppedge, Clay. *Texas Baseball: A Lone Star Diamond History from Town Teams to the Big Leagues.* (The History Press, 2012)
4 http://www.baseball-reference.com/; Encyclopedia of Minor League Baseball. Third Edition. (Baseball America, 2007)
5 Encyclopedia of Minor League Baseball. Third Edition. (Baseball America, 2007); Ruggles, William B. *The History of the Texas League of Professional Baseball Clubs 1888-1951.* (Texas Baseball League, 1951)
6 Patrick Lopez, Houston Buffs Questionnaire. 15 May 2013.
7 http://www.baseball-reference.com
8 HC 26 August 2004. Herskowitz, Mickey. "Epps Basked in Love Affair With Baseball."
9 Ruggles, William B. *The History of the Texas League of Professional Baseball Clubs 1888-1951.* (Texas Baseball League, 1951)
10 Encyclopedia of Minor League Baseball. Third Edition. (Baseball America, 2007)
11 http://www.baseball-reference.com; Encyclopedia of Minor League Baseball. Third Edition. (Baseball America, 2007)
12 http://www.baseball-reference.com
13 Encyclopedia of Minor League Baseball. Third Edition. (Baseball America, 2007)
14 Ruggles, William B.. *The History of the Texas League of Professional Baseball Clubs 1888-1951.* (Texas Baseball League, 1951); Encyclopedia of Minor League Baseball. Third Edition. (Baseball America, 2007)
15 HP 2 January 1949; Harris, Jack, Huhndorff, Paul and McGrew, Jack. *The Fault Does Not Lie With Your Set: The First Forty years of Houston Television.* (Eakin Press, 1989)
16 http://www.baseball-reference.com; Newark Star-Ledger 19 April 1946
17 Ruggles, William B. *The History of the Texas League of Professional Baseball Clubs 1888-1951.* (Texas Baseball League, 1951)
18 Witte, Jerry and McCurdy, Bill. *A Kid From St. Louis* (Pecan Park Eagle Press, 2003)
19 http://www.baseball-reference.com
20 http://www.baseball-reference.com
21 Encyclopedia of Minor League Baseball. Third Edition. (Baseball America, 2007)
22 Encyclopedia of Minor League Baseball. Third Edition. (Baseball America, 2007)
23 http://www.baseball-reference.com; Encyclopedia of Minor League Baseball. Third Edition. (Baseball America, 2007)
24 http://www.baseball-reference.com
25 http://www.baseballinwartime.com/player_biographies/kazak_eddie.htm; Sporting News 25 May 1949
26 HP 8 September 1951
27 http://www.baseball-reference.com; Eisenbath, Mike. The Cardinals Encyclopedia. (Temple University press, 1999); http://bioguide.congress.gov/scripts/biodisplay.pl?index=M000833
28 http://www.baseball-reference.com
29 http://www.baseball-reference.com
30 Witte, Jerry and McCurdy, Bill. *A Kid From St. Louis* (Pecan Park Eagle Press, 2003); http://www.baseball-reference.com
31 Tygiel, Jules. *Baseball's Great Experiment: Jackie Robinson and His Legacy.* (Vintage Books, 1984); http://www.baseball-reference.com
32 http://www.tshaonline.org/handbook/online/articles/fhoci; Sporting News 14 May 1952; Tygiel, Jules. *Baseball's Great Experiment: Jackie Robinson and His Legacy.* (Vintage Books, 1984)
33 Tygiel, Jules. *Baseball's Great Experiment: Jackie Robinson and His Legacy.* (Vintage Books, 1984)
34 http://www.tshaonline.org/handbook/online/articles/fhoci; Lubbock Evening Journal 28 April 1952; Adelson, Bruce. *Brushing Back Jim Crow: The Integration of Minor-League Baseball in the American South.* (University of Virginia Press, 1999)
35 http://www.tshaonline.org/handbook/online/articles/fhoci
36 Russell, Allen. *Touching All Bases* (Gulf Publishing, 1990)
37 Titchener, Campbell B. *The George Kirksey Story: Bringing Major League Baseball to Houston.* (Eakin Press, 1989); Reed, Robert. *Colt .45s: A Six-Gun Salute* (Gulf Publishing, 1999)
38 The Minor League Blue Book, 1926-2012, as reported by our request from Mr. Steve Densa, Executive Director, Communications, Minor League Baseball.
39 http://www.baseball-reference.com
40 Encyclopedia of Minor League Baseball. Third Edition. (Baseball America, 2007)
41 HP 28 May 1954
42 HP 28 May 1954
43 HP 28 May 1954
44 Patrick Lopez, Houston Buffs Questionnaire. 15 May 2013
45 Kahn, Roger. The Era. 1947-1957: When the Yankees, the Giants and the Dodgers Ruled the World. (Bison Books, 2002); Daytona Beach Morning Journal, 18 December 1981;
46 http://sabr.org/bioproj/person/74909ba3; Daytona Beach Morning Journal, 18 December 1981; http://www.theatlantic.com/entertainment/archive/2013/04/what-really-happened-to-ben-chapman-the-racist-baseball-player-in-i-42-i/274995/; Parrott, Harold. "The Betrayal of Robinson" 1976. from *The Jackie Robinson Reader* (Dutton, 1997)
47 http://www.baseball-reference.com; Gay, Timothy. *Satch, Dizzy and Rapid Robert: The Wild Saga of Interracial Baseball Before Jackie Robinson.* (Simon and Schuster, 2010)
48 Gay, Timothy. *Satch, Dizzy and Rapid Robert: The Wild Saga of Interracial Baseball Before Jackie Robinson.* (Simon and Schuster, 2010)
49 http://www.baseball-reference.com
50 http://www.baseball-reference.com; Encyclopedia of Minor League Baseball. Third Edition. (Baseball America, 2007)
51 Encyclopedia of Minor League Baseball. Third Edition. (Baseball America, 2007)

52 Tygiel, Jules. *Baseball's Great Experiment: Jackie Robinson and His Legacy.* (Vintage Books, 1984); http://www.baseball-refernce.com

53 http://www.baseball-reference.com

54 Tygiel, Jules. *Baseball's Great Experiment: Jackie Robinson and His Legacy.* (Vintage Books, 1984); http://www.baseball-refernce.com; Adelson, Bruce. *Brushing Back Jim Crow: The Integration of Minor-League Baseball in the American South.* (University of Virginia Press, 1999)

55 Tygiel, Jules. *Baseball's Great Experiment: Jackie Robinson and His Legacy.* (Vintage Books, 1984)

56 Tygiel, Jules. *Baseball's Great Experiment: Jackie Robinson and His Legacy.* (Vintage Books, 1984); Houston Public Library Digital Archives. HMRC Collection. George T. Nelson recorded interview 22 August 1974

57 Adelson, Bruce. *Brushing Back Jim Crow: The Integration of Minor-League Baseball in the American South.* (University of Virginia Press, 1999); Tygiel, Jules. *Baseball's Great Experiment: Jackie Robinson and His Legacy.* (Vintage Books, 1984)

58 Adelson, Bruce. *Brushing Back Jim Crow: The Integration of Minor-League Baseball in the American South.* (University of Virginia Press, 1999)

59 Adelson, Bruce. *Brushing Back Jim Crow: The Integration of Minor-League Baseball in the American South.* (University of Virginia Press, 1999)

60 Adelson, Bruce. *Brushing Back Jim Crow: The Integration of Minor-League Baseball in the American South.* (University of Virginia Press, 1999)

61 http://www.baseball-reference.com; Encyclopedia of Minor League Baseball. Third Edition. (Baseball America, 2007)

62 http://www.baseball-reference.com

63 "The Minor League Blue Book," p. 27

64 http://sabr.org/bioproj/person/74909ba3

65 http://www.baseball-reference.com; Los Angeles Times 9 August 1999

66 Encyclopedia of Minor League Baseball. Third Edition. (Baseball America, 2007)

67 Encyclopedia of Minor League Baseball. Third Edition. (Baseball America, 2007)

68 Titchener, Campbell B.. *The George Kirksey Story: Bringing Major League Baseball to Houston.* (Eakin Press, 1989); Reed, Robert. *Colt .45s: A Six-Gun Salute* (Gulf Publishing, 1999)

69 Titchener, Campbell B.. *The George Kirksey Story: Bringing Major League Baseball to Houston.* (Eakin Press, 1989); Reed, Robert. *Colt .45s: A Six-Gun Salute* (Gulf Publishing, 1999)

70 "The Minor League Blue Book," p. 22-23.

71 "The Minor League Blue Book,;" Reichler, Joseph L.. *The Baseball Trade Register.* (Collier Macmillan, 1984)

72 http://www.baseball-reference.com

73 http://www.baseball-reference.com; Breslin, Jimmy. *Can't Anybody Here Play This Game?* (Viking Press, 1963)

74 Encyclopedia of Minor League Baseball. Third Edition. (Baseball America, 2007)

75 Lowenfish, Lee. *Branch Rickey: Baseball's Ferocious Gentleman.* (University of Nebraska Press, 2007)

76 Titchener, Campbell B.. *The George Kirksey Story: Bringing Major League Baseball to Houston.* (Eakin Press, 1989); Reed, Robert. *Colt .45s: A Six-Gun Salute* (Gulf Publishing, 1999); Ray, Edgar W.. *The Grand Huckster: Houston's Judge Roy Hofheinz, Genius of the Astrodome.* (Memphis State University Press, 1980)

77 http://sabr.org/bioproj/person/fd6550d9; http://www.baseball-reference.com

78 *http://www.baseball-reference.com*

79 http://www.baseball-reference.com

80 http://www.baseball-reference.com

81 http://www.baseball-reference.com; http://sabr.org/bioproj/person/ce0e08ff

82 http://sabr.org/bioproj/person/ce0e08ff

83 http://sabr.org/bioproj/person/ce0e08ff

84 Encyclopedia of Minor League Baseball. Third Edition. (Baseball America, 2007)

85 HP 18 October 1960; Titchener, Campbell B.. *The George Kirksey Story: Bringing Major League Baseball to Houston.* (Eakin Press, 1989); Reed, Robert. *Colt .45s: A Six-Gun Salute* (Gulf Publishing, 1999); Ray, Edgar W.. *The Grand Huckster: Houston's Judge Roy Hofheinz, Genius of the Astrodome.* (Memphis State University Press, 1980)

86 Ray, Edgar W.. *The Grand Huckster: Houston's Judge Roy Hofheinz, Genius of the Astrodome.* (Memphis State University Press, 1980)

87 Encyclopedia of Minor League Baseball. Third Edition. (Baseball America, 2007)

88 http://sabr.org/bioproj/person/a832a4d3

89 Encyclopedia of Minor League Baseball. Third Edition. (Baseball America, 2007); Baytown Sun 22 September 1961

KEY

GDN – *Galveston Daily News*
HI – *Houston Informer*
HP – *Houston Post*
CD – *Chicago Defender*
HC – *Houston Chronicle*

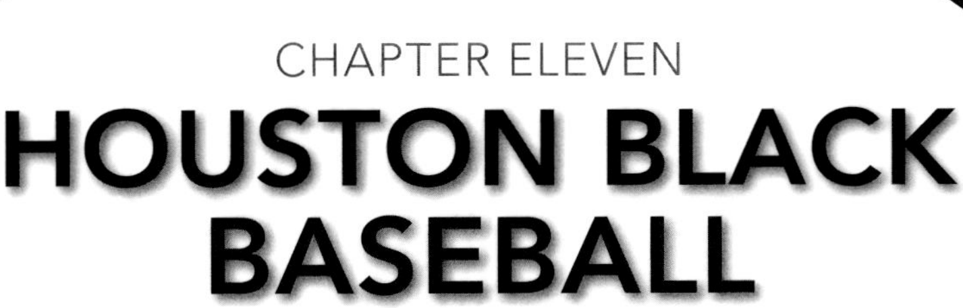

CHAPTER ELEVEN

HOUSTON BLACK BASEBALL

BY MIKE VANCE

Though they were generally segregated, the historic arc of African-American baseball closely follows that of white teams. Both leagues evolved together. The Slave Narratives, interviews done by the WPA Federal Writer's Project in the 1930s, contain memories of men then held in bondage playing a version of baseball. Just as the first famous white teams emerged in New York, Philadelphia and Washington, D.C. in the years immediately before the Civil War and in the decade following, so, too, did top black teams. Though not as well chronicled, the same developments occurred on the Texas Gulf Coast.[1]

Drawn from a grainy newspaper photograph taken in a cramped studio, the Houston Black Buffs adopted this pose in 1929.

Original artwork courtesy of Patrick Lopez.

Within a year of the prominent return of the game to Houston and Galveston after the Civil War, the local press was reporting on a team of newly freed slaves under the heading "Black Ballers." Houston's leading paper wrote that "There is a Base Ball Club in this city, composed of colored boys, bearing the aggressive title of 'Six Shooter Jims'. They wish us to state that they will play a match game with any other colored club in the state." There were many of these clubs, and they became a part of the sports and entertainment landscape. Mention of local black ball teams can often be found in descriptions of a town's Juneteenth celebrations.[2]

From the beginning, games between black teams brought out many white spectators. For more than 70 years, advertising and stories about upcoming African-American ballgames noted that ample seating would be provided for white patrons. Fans of all colors were welcome if they paid the ticket price.

From the latter half of the 19th century well into the 20th, the amount of press given black teams in white newspapers varied according to the newspaper and the editor. The *Galveston Daily News* often filled its sports columns with updates and challenges from the local black teams. The *Post*, Houston's top paper, gave frequent mention of the games, but rarely printed the entire lineups for each team. The lack of coverage does not mean that the baseball scene was any different in other Texas locales, only that the records still in existence today are more scant.

In the 1860s, Houston, Galveston and New Orleans picked up right where they had left off before the war as the leading baseball hotbeds along the Gulf Coast. All three had multiple teams of African-American players. In New Orleans, by far the largest city in the South, black teams often faced their white counterparts during the two decades after the Civil War. Though there are fewer records of inter-racial games in Texas, they did happen. One very notable game took place in Galveston.[3]

Demonstrating a camaraderie between Island ballplayers that crossed the lines of segregation, and coming on the heels of a well-publicized inter-racial game two weeks prior, the "colored champion" Flyaways faced a picked nine of white players in a contest for the "benefit of the professional ball tossers to assist them in getting to their respective homes" at the end of the first official Texas League season. Several of the white players, including James O'Neil, Harry Smith and Albert Ike, had just completed the campaign with the Galveston Giants which ended in the financial collapse of the circuit. The league's failure had left them stranded, and the drawing power of the black Flyaways bailed them out.[4]

After realizing many new freedoms and incremental real-life gains in the immediate aftermath of the Civil War, thanks largely to a combination of the Freedmen's Bureau occupation and the temporary disenfranchisement of ex-Confederates, by the early 1890s Southern blacks faced a severe erosion of their small progress. The rigid segregation laws that came to be known as Jim Crow brought an end to things such as the sharing of public transportation. It also marked the end of the sporadic inter-racial baseball contests.[5]

The black athletes of Houston fielded several teams in the 1880s and 90s. In 1893, the Houston Littlerocks garnered the most mention. A year later, the Houston Rosebuds were the top black team in the city with a few of the same starters who had been Littlerocks a year prior. When the Rosebuds met the Flyaways at Galveston's Beach Park for a season-ending match, enthusiasm was so high that a second contest was added. It is interesting to note that Nobles, the leading pitcher for Galveston in 1893, jumped to Houston one season later.[6]

Though the top team names changed frequently in the Bayou City, the Flyaways identity remained a constant on the island for about three decades in the late 19th and early 20th centuries. The Flyaways name originally belonged to a white Galveston team that represented the city in the first half of the 1870s. By the late 1880s, it was attached to the black squad that would build a reputation as one of the best in Texas. It was after 1911 before the Flyaways name gave way to the more conventional Galveston Black Sandcrabs who followed the model of using the white league team name, a model seen across both the Texas League and Southern Association. The Flyaways name continued to pop up again as late as 1915.[7]

There was never an absence of black baseball in the Bayou City. From the earliest days of the ballpark at Travis and McGowen, African-American clubs often filled dates when the white team was on the road. A heavily promoted contest between the Galveston Flyaways and the Houston Sunflowers, billed as "the Champion Colored Clubs of the State," took place just days after the opening of the first officially recognized Texas League season.[8]

A few weeks later, it wasn't a road trip, but a rain out that made the field available. The *Post* reported that the nascent Houston Babies and their foe had to forego the scheduled game because of wet grounds, but "Two local colored clubs occupied the Houston ball park Sunday and put up a splendid game, the score standing 2 to 1."[9]

The league fever caused by the re-emergence of the all-white Texas League in 1888, was shared by African-American ball clubs, too. The same month as the white circuit opened, mentions appeared in the white press referring to the "colored league." In April, the Galveston Flyaways and Houston Sunflowers were named as being part of "the state league of colored base-ball players," and in July, a series on the Island between the same two teams left the Flyaways in first place in spite of dropping the opener to the Sunflowers. Other clubs included in the loop were the Waco Reds, Dallas Browns, Fort Worth Light Weights and Austin Capitals. Presumably the Fort Worth team chose their own nickname, as opposed to it being assigned by unhappy fans.[10]

One of the higher profile leagues for African-American players was organized in January 1897. W.L. Jones of Galveston ran the circuit after Island businessman J. McNeal surrendered his post as league president. It was called the Lone Star Colored Baseball League, and the popularity of the game among Texas blacks was evident in the response it received. The League had interested teams not only on the island but in Fort Worth, Dallas, Beaumont, Shreveport, Palestine, Austin, La Grange, Cameron, Brenham, San Antonio, Waco and Houston.[11]

The big name attached to the league was John "Bud" Fowler, a New Yorker who had learned to play ball in Cooperstown. As early as 1878, Fowler became the first professional African-American baseball player, often being the only dark face on an otherwise white team. His career was filled with teammates and opponents

Calvert, Texas native Rube Foster went on to found the Negro National League in 1920. In subsequent years he brought his team, the Chicago American Giants to play in Houston.

National Baseball Hall of Fame Library, Cooperstown, NY

who objected vociferously enough to make him move on to another town, but his talent at the plate meant that another squad was usually there to take a chance on him.[12]

In the years that followed his professional debut, Fowler became the top promoter and organizer of black baseball in America. His teams were the first African-American clubs to barnstorm through major swaths of the country. This record of entrepreneurial success brought "Bud" Fowler to Galveston to be both field and general manager of the Flyaways in 1897. For his part, he was soon assuring the press of the impending success of the Colored League.[13]

Fowler's charges came close to winning it all but didn't quite reach the top. In mid-July, they faced the powerful Waco

East End Park in Fifth Ward was the scene of a packed house for the championship game of a black semi-pro league in 1926.

Houston Metropolitan Research Center, Houston Public Library/Sue Liuzza

Yellow Jackets for the "colored championship of Texas." Waco, boasting a talented teenaged pitcher from nearby Calvert named Andrew "Rube" Foster, defeated Galveston in a pair of hard fought contests. The early end to the season allowed Fowler to return to the North. By August, he was playing in Findlay, Ohio.[14]

The popularity of black baseball didn't mean that the players were accepted as pillars of society. Much like their white counterparts, a majority of the public viewed them as low contributors to the common good. One reason was violence among the players, both black and white. A particularly brutal instance took place in August 1895 in Caldwell, Texas, when black baller Will O. Myers killed another player with a bat. He was arrested three months later in San Antonio.[15]

Most of the players, though, were stand up members of the work force when they were not playing ball. The meager pay for games, often coming from money put up by each side to be split among the winning players, was not enough to provide a living for these men. The majority of them held day jobs as porters at

cotton presses, pressmen in print shops, longshoremen or common day laborers, generally the only types of employment open to them.

Among the stories of the early black ball players are some of particular interest. George Upps was the starting second baseman for the Galveston Flyaways. One of the older players on the club, he also served as team secretary. His chief source of income came from his job as one of the four African-Americans on the Galveston police force. He was also active in Republican politics in the Island City's Eighth Ward, ruffling more than a few feathers along the way.

In 1896, Upps was charged with attempted murder in his assault of a white man who "attempted to arrest a small colored boy." Any punishment meted out must have seen minor, since Upps was back with the ball club within five months. Upps continued his work as a police officer until his death of "acute indigestion" at the age of 41.[16]

The promise of a regional league for paid African-American players in Texas didn't die away with the demise of "Bud"

The Monarchs, a semi-pro team operated by the Liuzza Brothers, posed for a team photo in conjunction with a 1926 game on their home field.

Houston Metropolitan Research Center, Houston Public Library/ Sue Liuzza

Southern Pacific, the largest employer in Houston, organized separate athletic teams for their black and white employees.

Houston Metropolitan Research Center, Houston Public Library/ Sue Liuzza

Fowler and the Lone Star Colored League. The owners of black ball teams were just as determined to make a profit off their enterprise as their white counterparts.

Though the printed record of these black leagues is spottier than what remains in existence for white ball clubs, clear evidence shows that there were all-black baseball circuits in Texas, more often than not starting between 1900 and 1906 and continuing for decades.[17]

The economic problems that faced white Texas leagues also bedeviled the black leagues. High on the list was the cost of travel around the spacious Lone Star State. The clubs moved on the railroads, and negotiated special rates by the mile. Filings of travel schedules with the Texas Railroad Commission show that black clubs received the same deals as their white fellows, though the travel was in segregated cars.[18]

The Texas Colored Baseball League that formed in 1910 is typical of the period. The clubs were located in Houston, Dallas, Fort Worth, Oklahoma City, Waco and Gainesville. The schedule called for league games from the start of May through the first week of September, but the league appears to have broken up in July with many of the teams playing out the year in more of a barnstorming fashion.[19]

One of the prime movers in black baseball in Texas during the 1910s was Hiram McGar, owner of the Fort Worth Black Panthers. In 1916, he laid out a league plan that included an ambitious 142-game schedule. The teams included most of the major cities in Texas plus the Yellow Jackets of tiny Cleburne. After a league lull during World War I, McGar was back, this time with the Texas Negro League that operated throughout most of the 1920s. Houston's entrant was the Black Buffaloes, a team name that had been in use at least since 1909.[20]

The most common way to name a team in the 1920s was to add the word "black" before the name of the local white team. That tradition led to regular clubs that included the Dallas Black Giants, Fort Worth Black Panthers, Beaumont Black Exporters, Austin Black Senators and Shreveport Black Sports. When the name of the white ball club changed, so too did the name of the black team. The Waco Black Navigators of the late 1910s had become the Waco Black Oilers by 1924.

Among the early stars of the Negro National League, the first major black ball circuit which had been started by Texan Rube Foster, was Houstonian Leroy Grant. In 1910, Grant was only 22 years old and living with his father on Saulnier in Freedmen's Town. He listed his occupation in the census as a professional ballplayer. One year later, Grant would be playing with Rube Foster for the Chicago American Giants before moving to New York then back to Chicago for the bulk of his career.[21]

With big size, good power and an acceptable batting average, first sacker Grant became a favorite of fellow Texan Foster. He accompanied Foster to Fe in the Cuban National League following his debut season where other team members included Dolf Luque and Hall of Famer Louis Santop, another fellow Texan. By 1920, Grant was living in an extra room with Rube Foster's family in their house on Vernon Avenue in Chicago's South Side.[22]

Though today he is largely forgotten, several black baseball insiders of the late 1920s and into the 1930s, including the Hall of Fame player John Henry Lloyd, listed Grant as the best black first baseman of all time. He was the anchor for three straight Negro National League pennants with the Chicago American Giants. When that team spent a few days in Houston in March 1924, Leroy Grant was hailed and feted as a famous home town hero.[23]

The Houston Black Buffs fielded some strong teams in the 1920s, but as would be the case in the following decade, when good players got some recognition, they headed north for bigger paychecks. Infielder Saul Davis, who had come to the ball club in 1918, stayed for five seasons before heading north for a career that took him to Cleveland, Detroit, Memphis, Birmingham and Chicago. He also spent time with barnstorming teams such as the Black House of David and an All-Star team that toured under the name of former heavyweight boxing champion and Galveston native Jack Johnson.[24]

Four Black Buffs from the 1921 team, Thomas Calloway, William Hines, Lawson Perry and Bill Jackman, left for a brief while for the semi-pro St. Louis Tigers in 1922, though they soon returned to Houston. Third baseman Lunie Danage of the Black Buffaloes had already spent some time in St. Louis in 1920.[25]

Bill "Cannonball" Jackman was a dark-skinned, six-foot-three, right-handed pitcher who was in his mid-20s at the time. The native of Carta, Texas, was with Houston for parts of three seasons, during which he threw no-hitters against the San Antonio Black Aces and the Dallas Black Giants. By 1925, he was in the East Coast limelight with the Philadelphia Giants. Jackman played most of his career with independent barnstorming teams, and in his prime received $175 a game plus a 10 dollar bonus for every strikeout.

The Ks were numerous. Jackman's fastball was described as speedier than Bob Feller's or Satchel Paige's, the latter pitcher losing two celebrated matchups to Jackman. At his height, he earned notice in big league baseball circles, as well. New York Giants manager John McGraw "is reported to have made the facetious remark that he would pay $50,000 to the man who could make Jackman white."[26]

Though the Black Buffs primarily rented the home of their white namesakes, they did have a field of their own for a few years in the mid-1920s. Rube Foster brought his fabled American Giants there for spring training in 1924. Scott Street Park sat just east of the thoroughfare from which it drew its name, behind a row of houses and businesses and a few dozen yards south of Rosalie Street. It had a small grandstand behind home plate, hugging the northwest corner of the diamond. The field might have been a bit odiferous at times, too. The city's Scott Street Water Works and Sewer Pumping Station was located across the road.[27]

By the time that the Houston Black Buffaloes reached their glory years, they were playing full time at West End Park. They did make a brief move for the first half of the 1928 season. Team owner James B. Grigsby rented the new Buffalo Stadium southeast of downtown when the Texas League club was on the road. He quickly figured that with lower rent and greater proximity to the African-American commercial district along West Dallas Street in Freedmen's Town, West End Park offered the better economic option.

The years from 1929-1931 marked the prime of all-black baseball in the Lone Star State in the form of the Texas-Oklahoma-Louisiana (T-O-L) League. Though not recognized today as the equal of the Negro National League or the Eastern Colored League, the Northern press of the day had generally glowing things to say about the circuit at the time. In fact, the league sought a working agreement with those two other organizations.

Many of the Black Buffs games warranted large headlines in the Houston white press, and several of the players went on to extended, successful careers on the Negro Leagues teams back East. Their time in Houston is largely ignored, though, and a number of those players' biographies fail to even mention that they got their start in Southeast Texas.[28]

In addition to the Black Buffs, the T-O-L League opened in 1929 with clubs in San Antonio, Dallas, Fort Worth, Wichita Falls, Oklahoma City, Tulsa and Shreveport. The national black press reported that the circuit boasted the best uniforms in the country with teams wearing white at home and grey or blue on the road. Gone, too, were the days of train travel. "The clubs own some of the best busses made and they are able to make the entire circuit by motor." Most importantly, crowds were good. On Juneteenth, a contest between first place Houston and the second place San Antonio Black Indians drew around ten thousand fans.[29]

James B. Grigsby, the owner of the Black Buffaloes, was a local insurance man. His son, Ernest, served as the club's secretary. Grigsby was recognized as one of the top African-American businessmen in town. He had been president of the American Mutual Benefit Association for more than 20 years and was a benefactor of Wiley College. He lived in a comfortable home on Hadley Street in Third Ward.[30]

Leading things on the field was Roy Parnell. Most often reported to be a Houston native, some evidence suggests he might have been born in Louisiana. Either way, his hometown credentials cannot be denied. Parnell carried the nickname of "Harrisburg Red," and he was a local favorite. He was a right-handed hitting outfielder with a consistently high average. By 1929, he was in his mid-20s and had a couple of seasons with the Birmingham Black Barons already under his belt.[31]

Roy "Red" Parnell made his home in Houston, but his greatest achievements in baseball came with the Philadelphia Stars.

Blockson Collection, Temple University Libraries

Parnell lived in First Ward, a couple of blocks off Houston Avenue, and earned his off season living as a longshoreman, a popular occupation among Gulf Coast ballplayers. The job paid decently, and many positions were unionized, though white and black longshoremen maintained separate locals for decades.[32]

The lineup that Parnell oversaw included a former Birmingham teammate, Chuffy Alexander, who played a variety of positions. Alexander was tiny, barely five feet tall by many descriptions, and weighing in at as little as 125 pounds, but his speed was an asset. Saul Davis was back in town on the Opening Day roster, but didn't subsequently appear in box scores.[33]

Also on the ball club was middle infielder Dewitt Owens who would later shift more to the outfield with Birmingham and Indianapolis in the later 1930s. Owens would soon become a manager and mentor to Giddings, Texas-native Hall of Famer Hilton Smith. Bertram Johnson and Willie O'Bryan also played in the outfield for the Black Buffs in 1929. Both would later go on to teams up North.

Hustling middle infielder Chester Williams joined the team in July. Soon after his Houston stop, Williams became one of the first players signed by Gus Greenlee when he bought the Pittsburgh Crawfords, and Williams remained part of the very core of that team which is widely accepted as one of the greatest Negro League team ever. Williams made the East-West All-Star Game four times and batted over .300 for most of his time in the Steel City. After baseball, and a year in the U.S. Army, Williams returned to Lake Charles, Louisiana, where he opened a night spot called the Cotton Club. He was shot to death in a brawl there on Christmas Day in 1952.[34]

Catching duties for the 1929 Black

Buffs were primarily held down by Eppie Hampton, though Nelson "Rough House" Jones and George Danage made some early season appearances. Hampton had already spent several seasons with the Birmingham Black Barons and the Memphis Red Sox, and he would put in almost another decade of time with other Negro Leagues teams.[35]

A pair of Texas-born brothers, Green and Charles Beverly, were top stars for the Black Buffs in 1929. Green Beverly was named after his father who had gotten his colorful first name from his mother's family. He was a "rifle-armed" third baseman who often wore three layers of socks and would sometimes let a hard-hit ball be knocked down by his body before gunning the runner out at first.

Pitcher Charles Beverly, who went by the nickname of "Hooks" or "Lefty," was another player with a background as a Houston longshoreman, having played on a team for the Morgan Line. Lefty had pitched at Cleveland, Birmingham and Nashville before coming home for a couple of years in Houston. He left for the Kansas City Monarchs and also made stops with the Newark Eagles and the great Pittsburgh Crawfords. Like most of the Texas-born players, Hooks Beverly returned home after baseball. He died in Brookshire, Texas.[36]

Other pitchers on the club included "Black Tank" Steward, Lloyd Evans and Murray Gillespie, another lefty who would see time with some of the top black baseball teams across the South. The staff ace was Houston native Henry McHenry who was known as "Cream" because of his light complexion. Like Red Parnell, McHenry would later appear in two of the Negro Leagues East-West All-Star games, starting and winning the contest in 1940. He was known to have "a good curve and good control and also threw a fastball, screwball and knuckler." He also developed a reputation for being cocky and a bit high strung.[37]

McHenry went to the Monarchs of Kansas City and at least four different teams in greater New York City, including the Black Yankees. Most of his career came with the Philadelphia Stars from the late 1930s almost all the way through the 1940s. One of his teammates there was Roy "Red" Parnell. Cream McHenry finished his baseball career barnstorming with the Indianapolis Clowns.

There was another Houstonian All-Star on the Philadelphia Stars in the late 1930s and 40s. Andrew "Pat" Patterson, who coached at Yates High School during the off-season, would play in six East-West games during his time in the Negro Leagues. After starring in baseball and football at Wiley College, Patterson played big time black ball with the Homestead Grays, Pittsburgh Crawfords, Kansas City Monarchs, Mexico City Red Devils and Newark Eagles in addition to his two stints in Philly. He would be best known in his home town, though, for his long, successful tenure within the Houston Independent School District.[38]

The high points for the Houston Black Buffaloes were appearances in two series that were billed as the Negro World

KANSAS CITY MONARCHS—Perennial kingpin of mid-west teams and another pioneer outfit—perhaps best administrated of all Negro franchises. Jackie Robinson seen kneeling, second from left.

Jackie Robinson joined the Kansas City Monarchs at their Spring Training site in Houston in 1945 to start his professional baseball career.

National Baseball Hall of Fame Library, Cooperstown, NY

Championships, though the Northern press was quick to point out that, in their opinion, the series did not merit this title. In the post season of 1929, the Black Buffs faced the Kansas City Monarchs, winners of the Negro National League with a record-breaking 62 and 17 ledger. The Baltimore Black Sox had won the East coast-based American Negro League, but the Monarchs, who had struggled to make money in spite of their torrid victory pace, opted instead to head south and play the Texas-Oklahoma-Louisiana League champion Houston Black Buffs.

If money and recognition was the goal, Kansas City owner J.L. Wilkinson made the right choice. Game 1 was a 12-10 slugfest that was attended by over 11,000 people, some of whom had to stand in roped off sections of the outfield. So many people came from out of town to see the blackball stars, that "black citizens of Houston formed a housing committee" to see that everyone had a place to stay.[39]

The "World Series" was a big deal in Houston, too. Dozens of African-American owned businesses ran advertisements in a special edition of the *Informer* welcoming the Monarchs and other out-of-towners to the Bayou City. The opening contest was preceded by a parade from the Pilgrim's Building in the western edge of downtown to West End Park.

The *Chicago Defender* marveled at the huge crowds, numbers it noted never showed up for a Negro World Series game "in these parts." They paid Houston's fans the highest compliment, writing that "When it comes to being a sport, our

Southern brother has got it all over us."[40]

The two run margin in Game 1 was as close as the Black Buffs would come on the field, however. They dropped four straight to the Monarchs and their stars such as Bullet Rogan, Newt Allen, Chet Brewer and Andy Cooper.

In 1930, despite a few key player defections, the Black Buffs were again atop the T-O-L League. Their national reputation was that of a "very good and highly publicized team." In late September, Houston once more played for what was billed as the championship of Negro baseball. This time the opponents were the Chicago American Giants, and the series was played home and home. The teams split four games in Chicago in mid-September, resuming the series in Houston just over a week later.[41]

With their ace, McHenry, gone, the Black Buffs had added Robert "Lefty" Pipkin to take over as their top hurler for 1930. Pipkin had spent the previous season with the Birmingham Black Barons where his catcher at the start of the year had been Eppie Hampton, until that backstop moved along to Houston. Their Bayou City reunion went well. The Chicago press was calling Pipkin "one of the best twirlers in the South West."[42]

Chicago's new manager Willie Foster, a half-brother of the team's previous leader, Rube Foster, had been busy upgrading the ball club. He had lured Chester Williams away from Houston, and prior to the series against the Black Buffs, he made another addition. Heading into the Houston series that would be their biggest draw of the year, Foster rented a former Birmingham teammate of Lefty Pipkin, a practice not unknown in the Negro leagues.

The borrowed Black Barons pitcher was young Satchel Paige. He and Pipkin hooked up in a duel in the Windy City on September 12 which Paige won by the score of 4 to 3, racking up nine strikeouts along the way. On the 29th in Houston, Paige was less fortunate, being pulled from a contest that was won by

Houston native Henry McHenry, nicknamed "Cream," starred for Negro League teams in Philadelphia, New York and Kansas City after he left his home town.

Blockson Collection, Temple University Libraries

Pat Patterson excelled as an infielder in the Negro Leagues, making the All-Star Game four times. During the off season he was a multi-sport coach in Houston.

Courtesy Adrian "Pat" Patterson

the Black Buffaloes in 19 innings by a count of 3-2.[43]

The American Giants and Black Buffs won four games each in the Series. The following week, back in their home park in Chicago, Willie Foster's team, bolstered by the addition of the great Oscar Charleston, took three out of four against a white All-Star team that included Lefty O'Doul, Harry Heilman, Art Shires and Charley Gehringer.[44]

It was a type of matchup that became popular in the 1930s. The top black ball stars not only played league games but toured in the off season against barnstorming white teams that generally featured a name star or two and a roster rounded out by marginal big leaguers or local semi-pros. Houston's Charles "Hooks" Beverly was a veteran of a few of these inter-racial tours in California against a white team led by young Bob Feller.

The Black Buffaloes remained the class of the T-O-L for three years, but the exodus of their top players to better known teams and bigger paychecks started to take its toll in 1931. A season later, with the Depression taking a deeper and deeper hold, owner Grigsby cut his financial losses. He sold the ball club to J. M. Mitchell, another local businessman. Mitchell's promises to deliver a team "that will be worthy of their patronage" lasted only two months.[45]

Red Parnell and Chuffy Alexander, cornerstones of the Black Buffaloes, were sold to the Monroe Monarchs. The club from North Louisiana was an upstart operation owned by a white, transplanted Dallas native who had made his money in the oil business. Chester Williams, signed back with the Black Buffs in February, was playing with the Homestead Grays by late spring. Within weeks, Mitchell would get rid of the storied ball club entirely.[46]

It was certainly not surprising that the Great Depression brought the "lowest ebb" of Negro League baseball in America, just as it did to other leagues of the professional game. The Major Leagues were better equipped to deal

The amazing lineup of the Homestead Grays came through Houston in spring of 1930. Josh Gibson joined the team later that season.

National Baseball Hall of Fame Library, Cooperstown, NY

with such deep economic adversity, but the white minors and the Negro leagues suffered many team closures.[47]

Houston baseball fans and promoters were not willing to let the idea die, however. Into the breach stepped two Italian-American brothers, Jim and John Liuzza. They secured the rights to the Black Buffaloes name and set up a new Texas corporation in July 1932. Thc Liuzzas, whose family owned a popular grocery store in Fifth Ward, had been running a semi-pro African-American team called the Monarchs for several years, as well as a Mexican-American club called the Lions. The brothers had their own ballpark, called Monarch Field. They viewed the availability of the Black Buffs brand as a chance at an upgrade.[48]

Monarch Field was a 1500 seat wooden stadium on Gillespie Street near the Southern Pacific tracks. Some of the construction materials for both grandstands and the eight foot fence that surrounded the venue had come directly from the nearby rail yard facilities. Tickets to watch thc gamcs ranged from five to 15 cents. Occasionally the brothers had to threaten freeloaders out of nearby trees which they had climbed in an attempt to avoid the tariff.

The park sported small locker rooms and a concession stand run by the Liuzza Brothers' wives, Rose and Annie.

Seguin's "Smokey" Joe Williams, one of the greatest pitchers that Texas ever produced, faced Houston teams regularly when he started his career in San Antonio.
National Baseball Hall of Fame Library, Cooperstown, NY

They sold not only hot dogs and roasted peanuts for a nickel a bag, but often featured homemade Italian favorites such as sausage and spaghetti. Those same delicacies were also staples of Sunday postgame meals that the Liuzza women furnished for all the players in the backyard of their house and grocery on Cline Street.[49]

The brothers were veterans of semi-pro baseball themselves and no doubt loved the game. Jim Liuzza had been a crack player a decade earlier managing the Admiration Coffee team to a city championship series and later serving as skipper of the Houston Lighting and Power squad. They viewed the Black Buffaloes and Monarch Field not only as a way to stay in the game but as a supplement to their income. During the Depression, that was easier said than done.

One potential revenue stream was renting their ballpark. Other semi-pro and amateur teams used Monarch Field in the late 1920s and through the 30s. Even out of town match ups came to the park to take advantage of the large Houston market. One such pairing between the Austin Black Senators and an African-American team representing Newgulf Sulfur and their company town down the coast may have been a record setter. At least one source claims that the 27-inning game in August of 1934 was the longest Negro minor league contest ever played.[50]

In addition to playing a schedule around Texas and Louisiana, the Liuzza-owned Black Buffaloes barnstormed at great length. In July 1933, the team started on an ambitious tour of Mexico. Using Laredo as a jumping off point, they played a close game with the locals. The contest was well-hyped and drew a decent crowd in spite of the fact that it was scheduled only one day prior. Records show that such last minute arrangements were far from unique in what could be considered the Negro minor leagues.[51]

Unlike the United States where the players stayed in inferior hotels and ate from the back doors of restaurants, the Black Buffs were treated well in Mexico and other Latin American countries. They stayed with and played against white players with no repercussions.[52]

After crossing the border, the Houston team was booked to play in Mexico for the better part of a month, facing top teams in cities such as Monterrey, Tampico, Mexico City and Saltillo. They were promoted with posters and news items promising that the Black Buffaloes of Houston were a fast-fielding, hard-hitting ball club, but on the business side, it did not go well. By early August, the team was back playing games at Laredo and Nuevo Laredo with at least one of them promoted as a benefit in which all proceeds went to paying the team's way back to Houston.[53]

Though the Liuzzas owned the ball club and closely oversaw the operations, they also had African-American management working with the team, as well. Longtime Houston sportsman George Nelson, who spent several years active in local Civil Rights organizations, was with the team for a while in the 1930s. Another ex-player named L.S.N. Cobb acted as field manager for the Black Buffs later in the decade.

A trip to central Canada in 1936 went about as well as the earlier journey to Mexico. The club travelled to the Great North and back in two cars loaned by Houston Ford dealer Pat Davis. Jim and

John and Jim Liuzza posed at their new Monarch Park, just around the corner from their previous venue, East End Park. The Liuzzas later took over ownership of the Houston Black Buffaloes.
Courtesy Jim Liuzza

Annie Liuzza went with the ball club and sent updates back to John and Rose who were running the store. There were struggles at the gate as the team played white competition at small stops through Nebraska and the Dakotas. One game provided a payday of only two dollars. Jim Liuzza also complained about a lack of barbeque and hot sauce and having to eat spaghetti sauce that tasted like catsup.

Once in Saskatchewan and Alberta, there were long distances between games, flat tires and cold summer weather that was quite foreign to the Houstonians. The saving grace of the summer was a fifth place finish at the prestigious semi-pro tournament in Wichita, Kansas.

The Liuzza brothers stuck with the Black Buffs for several years in the 1930s. They marketed Monarch Field as a Spring Training home to the leading black ball clubs from the north. The Kansas City Monarchs and Chicago American Giants, both clubs with previous Houston relationships, came through the small park in Fifth Ward. So too did the New York Black Yankees. In the years approaching World War II, the Black Buffaloes slipped into oblivion. One last post-war attempt at revival by the Liuzzas went nowhere.

Houston did have one final chapter of segregated black baseball left, however. It came during the death throes of one of the best known franchises in the Negro Leagues. The Newark Eagles of the Negro American League had been the home of such players as Monte Irvin, Leon Day, Larry Doby, Ray Dandridge and Willie Wells.

Their owner was the famous Effa Manley. By 1948, two years after Jackie Robinson and other young black baseball stars began playing in the Major Leagues, Ms. Manley could see the writing on the wall. Crowds at Newark's Hinchcliffe Field had dropped to a level just above negligible. The team was sold to W.H. Young, a Memphis dentist.

The Houston Eagles started play in 1949. After opening on the road against the Birmingham Black Barons, they returned home to Buff Stadium where they were charging one dollar for general admission seats. Box seats could be had for 50 cents more.[54]

The first two teams into Houston were the Memphis Red Sox and the storied Kansas City Monarchs, and there was early interest. Memphis had been the adopted "home team" of local fans of Negro League ball. They had played games at Buff Stadium as the home club during the war years when the Texas League was shut down. Adding to an initial wave of excitement was the Memphis player-manager, Austin native Willie Wells, known as "El Diablo." Destined for the Hall of Fame, Wells was playing sparingly at age 43, but fans still turned out to see him.[55]

Promoters of the Eagles games put forth solid hitting outfielders Bob Harvey and Johnny Davis as their star players, and manager Reuben Jones announced that Curley Williams, a slightly built but good hitting shortstop, was "the next Jackie Robinson." The front office was not stingy with such hyperbole. They crowed that Houston is "likely to become

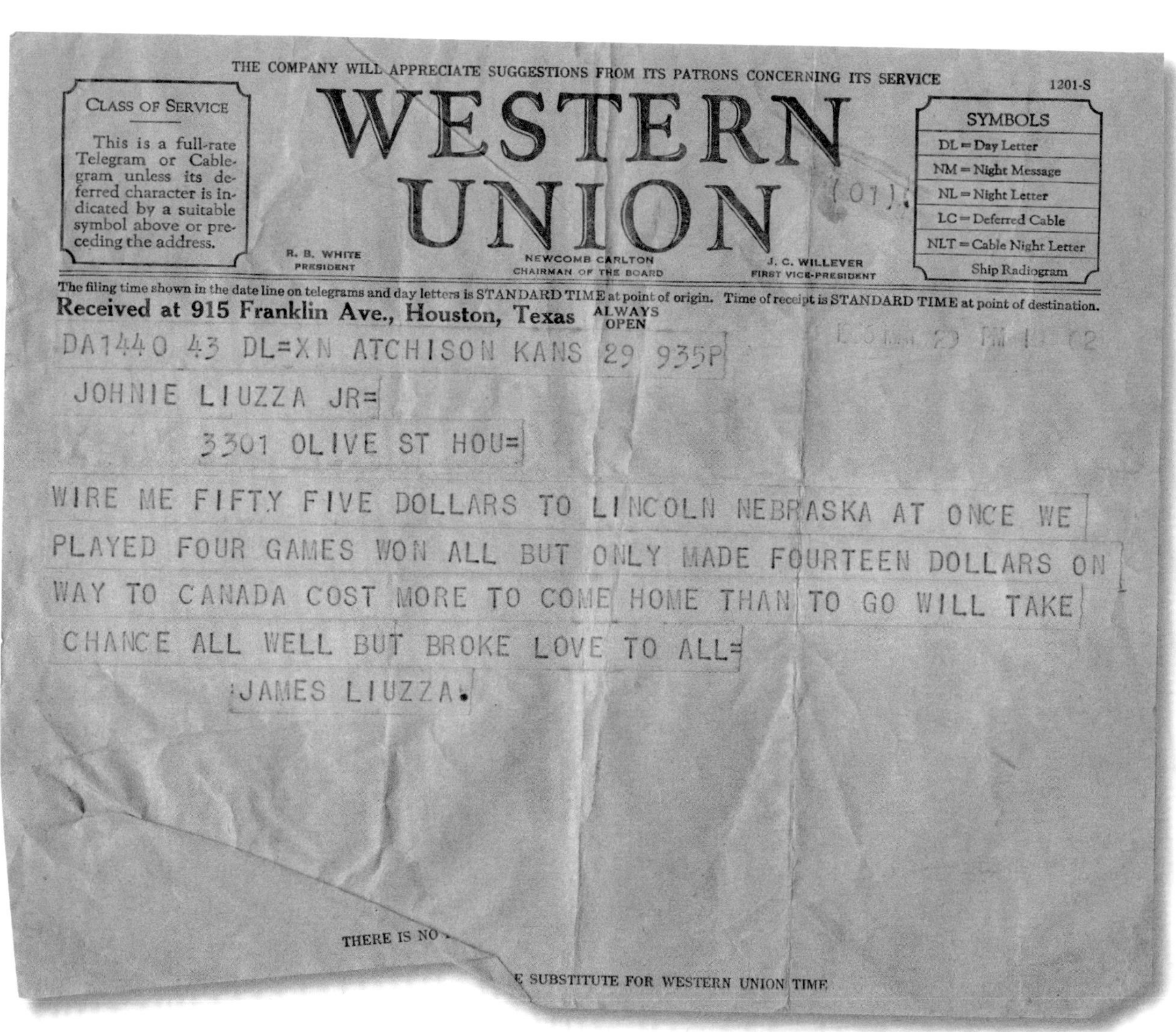

THE COMPANY WILL APPRECIATE SUGGESTIONS FROM ITS PATRONS CONCERNING ITS SERVICE 1201-S

CLASS OF SERVICE

This is a full-rate Telegram or Cablegram unless its deferred character is indicated by a suitable symbol above or preceding the address.

WESTERN UNION

R. B. WHITE, PRESIDENT — NEWCOMB CARLTON, CHAIRMAN OF THE BOARD — J. C. WILLEVER, FIRST VICE-PRESIDENT

SYMBOLS
DL = Day Letter
NM = Night Message
NL = Night Letter
LC = Deferred Cable
NLT = Cable Night Letter
Ship Radiogram

The filing time shown in the date line on telegrams and day letters is STANDARD TIME at point of origin. Time of receipt is STANDARD TIME at point of destination.

Received at 915 Franklin Ave., Houston, Texas ALWAYS OPEN

DA1440 43 DL=XN ATCHISON KANS 29 935P

JOHNIE LIUZZA JR=

3301 OLIVE ST HOU=

WIRE ME FIFTY FIVE DOLLARS TO LINCOLN NEBRASKA AT ONCE WE PLAYED FOUR GAMES WON ALL BUT ONLY MADE FOURTEEN DOLLARS ON WAY TO CANADA COST MORE TO COME HOME THAN TO GO WILL TAKE CHANCE ALL WELL BUT BROKE LOVE TO ALL=

JAMES LIUZZA.

THERE IS NO ... SUBSTITUTE FOR WESTERN UNION TIME

Jim Liuzza wired his brother for money as the Black Buffs tour proved less lucrative than expected.

Courtesy Jim Liuzza

one of the greatest Negro League baseball towns in the country." One month later they announced that "Luke Easter is the greatest attraction since Babe Ruth." None of it seemed to help. After the first spurt of fans, attendance leveled off at numbers in the hundreds.[56]

On the field, the club was less than mediocre. In spite of the success shown by a couple of youngsters, the franchise's two best players, future Hall of Famers Ray Dandridge and Leon Day, had refused to move to Houston, forcing the team to sell their contracts. Rueben Jones, whose black ball career dated to the first World War, retired as the Eagles manager halfway through the year. He was ultimately replaced by the team's catcher, Leon Ruffin. The Eagles finished the year dead last.[57]

Opening the following season as skipper of the Eagles was a favorite son returned home. Roy "Red" Parnell was back in Houston. He had been given a brief stint as manager after Reuben Jones quit the year before, but now he was promoted as being back at home. His family had never left, of course.

Harrisburg Red had not played with the home team since the start of the 1932 season. Since then, his playing career had taken him to New Orleans, Nashville, New York and Santo Domingo, but his longest stay had been with the Philadelphia Stars. He had maintained mostly high batting averages, made a couple of Negro League All-Star appearances and forged a reputation as a "smart ballplayer" despite battling a lifelong problem with excessive drinking.[58]

The 1950 club also boasted another home town hero. William Beverly, the son of Green Beverly who had starred with the Black Buffs in the early 1930s, joined the team as a 20-year-old pitcher. Known for his heater, he earned the nickname of "Fireball Bill." He bounced around the Negro Leagues and a minor league in Canada before retiring to Houston and a career in the oil industry.[59]

Parnell's charges started the 1950 season relatively well. Playing only on weekend evenings in an attempt to maximize attendance, the team won a big series from the Cleveland Buckeyes. It would prove to be something of a high water mark. Ultimately, the ball club slipped below .500. Worse yet, they did not draw fans.[60]

Houston hometown draws like Red Parnell and "Fireball Bill" Beverly were not enough to perform magic. By May, the *Informer* was writing that "Ladies Day and a brass band fail to attract people" to the ball games. The paper also warned that Negro League baseball, still needed as a proving ground for future big leaguers, was in danger of extinction if the public would not attend games. Their words proved prescient as the Eagles limped to the finish line of a second season in front of thousands of empty Buff Stadium seats. Roy Parnell's return to Houston baseball was anything but triumphant. Sadly, his days beyond baseball were numbered, too. Parnell died back in Philadelphia, at the young age of 48.[61]

With the best black players in the

The Black Buffaloes great northern tour at a stop for water. L.S.N. Cobb is thought to be the man at far left.

Courtesy Jim Liuzza

recently integrated majors, fans began to follow their heroes on teams like the Dodgers and Giants instead of the Monarchs and Clowns. The Negro Leagues had lost their relevance. At season's end, it was announced that the Houston Eagles were moving to New Orleans. After a single season there, the franchise ceased to exist altogether.[62]

It was the end of segregated baseball in Houston. It had been brought about by the very thing that the players had wanted for almost a century: a chance to compete equally with white players. From the 1950s forward, the best local African-American players would get that shot. From Houston-born Curt Flood to later Bayou City stars such as Michael Bourn, James Loney and Carl Crawford, local black ball players are now reaching the big leagues.

The breaking of the color barrier came too late for Red Parnell, Henry McHenry and the Beverlys. Former Black Buffaloes like Bill Jackman, Saul Davis, Chester Williams and Eppie Hampton did not get a whiff of a chance. Leroy Grant, perhaps the most lauded of Houstonians to play in the Negro Leagues never came close to getting consideration. The sad fact of human history that opportunities are never distributed equally does not diminish the sparkling play that these men put forth on the ball diamonds of Houston and the Negro Leagues.

1 Hogan, Lawrence. *Shades of Glory: The Negro Leagues and the Story of African-American Baseball.* (National Geographic, 2006)

2 Houston Daily Telegraph 14 July 1868; Brenham Weekly Banner 20 June 1879

3 Aiello, Thomas. *Kings of Casino Park: Black Baseball in the Lost Season of 1932* (University of Alabama Press, 2011); Hogan, Lawrence. *Shades of Glory: The Negro Leagues and the Story of African-American Baseball.* (National Geographic, 2006); Somers, Dale A.. *The Rise of Sports in New Orleans, 1850-1900.* (Louisiana State University Press, 1972); GDN 17 September 1888

4 GDN 30 September 1888; http://www.baseball-reference.com

5 Hogan, Lawrence. *Shades of Glory: The Negro Leagues and the Story of African-American Baseball.* (National Geographic, 2006);

6 GDN 3 September 1893; GDN 7 October 1894

7 Daily Houston Telegraph 20 September 1871; GDN 17 November 1874; GDN 3 August 1875; HP 4 May 1888; GDN 1June 1890; GDN 3 July 1910; HP 16 May 1915

8 HP 4 May 1888

9 HP 26 June 1888

10 GDN 29 April 1888; GDN 30 July 1888

11 GDN 6 January 1897; GDN 14 January 1897; HP 15 January 1897; GDN 25 January 1897

12 Dixon, Phil S.. *A Harvest of Freedom's Fields: Andrew 'Rube" Foster* (Xlibris, 2010); http://sabr.org/bioproj/person/200e2bbd

13 http://sabr.org/bioproj/person/200e2bbd; GDN 6 January 1897

14 GDN 16 July 1897; Dixon, Phil S.. *A Harvest of Freedom's Fields: Andrew 'Rube" Foster* (Xlibris, 2010); http://sabr.org/bioproj/person/200e2bbd

15 Dixon, Phil S.. *A Harvest of Freedom's Fields: Andrew 'Rube" Foster* (Xlibris, 2010)

16 GDN 19 July 1896; GDN 24 July 1897; GDN 6 January 1897; GDN 1 November 1901; GDN 31 May 1907; GDN 22 November 1907; GDN 31 July 1908; Texas Death Certificate, George Upps, 13 July 1908; United States Census Galveston County, Texas 1900

17 Lanctot, Neal. *Fair Dealing and Clean Playing: The Hilldale Club and the Development of Black Professional Baseball.* (Syracuse University press, 2007); HP 3 May 1915

18 Texas State Library and Archives. Texas Railroad Commission Records.; Dallas Morning News 25 April 1910

19 Dallas Morning News 25 April 1910

20 Presswood, Mark. *Texas Almanac.* (Texas State Historical Association, 2012); GDN 9 April 1909; GDN 1 August 1909; HP 13 April 1915; HP 3 May 1915

21 http://www.baseball-reference.com; Riley, James A.. *The Biographical Encyclopedia of the negro Baseball Leagues.* (Carroll Graff, 1994); United States Census Harris County, Texas 1910;

22 Riley, James A.. *The Biographical Encyclopedia of the negro Baseball Leagues.* (Carroll Graff, 1994); United States Census Cook County, Illinois 1920;

23 Chicago Defender 15 March 1924; Chicago Defender 22 March 1924; Chicago Defender 29 March 1924

24 Riley, James A.. *The Biographical Encyclopedia of the Negro Baseball Leagues.* (Carroll Graff, 1994)

25 Fort Worth Star 6 June 1921; St. Louis Argus 14 April 1922;

26 Thompson, Dick. Bay State Banner 20 March 2008; Riley, James A.. *The Biographical Encyclopedia of the Negro Baseball Leagues.* (Carroll Graff, 1994)

27 HP 18 April 1925; Sanborn Maps. Houston Texas Series 1924; HI 15 March 1924

28 HI 2 February 1929; HC 8 September 1929; HP 25 April 1932

29 Chicago Defender 13 July 1929; Chicago Defender 29 June 1929

30 HI 1 February 1930; HI 6 December 1930; Houston City Directory 1932

31 Holway, John. Voices from the Great Black Baseball Leagues. Revised Edition. (Dover, 2010); Riley, James A.. *The Biographical Encyclopedia of the Negro Baseball Leagues.* (Carroll Graff, 1994)

32 United States Census 1930 Harris County, TX; Houston City Directory 1931-32;

33 HI 27 April 1929; Riley, James A.. *The Biographical Encyclopedia of the Negro Baseball Leagues.* (Carroll Graff, 1994)

34 Riley, James A.. *The Biographical Encyclopedia of the Negro Baseball Leagues.* (Carroll Graff, 1994); HI 20 July 1929; HI 27 April 1929; http://www.baseball-reference.com; http://www.seamheads.com;

35 HI 27 April 1929; Riley, James A.. *The Biographical Encyclopedia of the Negro Baseball Leagues.* (Carroll Graff, 1994); HI 5 October 1929

36 Riley, James A.. *The Biographical Encyclopedia of the Negro Baseball Leagues.* (Carroll Graff, 1994); HI 5 October 1929

37 Riley, James A.. *The Biographical Encyclopedia of the Negro Baseball Leagues.* (Carroll Graff, 1994);

38 http://www.baseball-reference.com; Riley, James A.. *The Biographical Encyclopedia of the Negro Baseball Leagues.* (Carroll Graff, 1994); Finoli, David. *For the Good of the Country: World War II Baseball in the Major and Minor Leagues.* (McFarland, 2002)

39 Bruce, Janet. The Kansas City Monarchs: Chapions of Black Baseball. (University press of Kansas, 1985); Chicago Defender 28 September 1929

40 Chicago Defender 28 September 1929

41 Ribowsky, Mark. *Don't Look Back* (Da Capo Press, 1994); Chicago Defender 13 September 1930; HI 27 September 1930

42 Chicago Defender 13 September 1930; Riley, James A.. *The Biographical Encyclopedia of the Negro Baseball Leagues.* (Carroll Graff, 1994)

43 Ribowsky, Mark. *Don't Look Back* (Da Capo Press, 1994); Chicago Defender 4 October 1930

44 Chicago Defender 11 October 1930

45 HI 23 January 1932; Chicago Defender 30 January 1932

46 Aiello, Thomas. *The Kings of Casino Park: Black Baseball in the Lost Season of 1932.* (University of Alabama Press, 2011); HI 13 February 1932

[47] Lanctot, Neal. *Negro League Baseball: The Rise and Ruin of a Black Institution.* (University of Pennsylvania Press, 2008)
[48] Texas Secretary of State. Corporate Division Filings; HP 8 September 1929
[49] Houston Arts and Media Collection. Mike Vance, Interview with Jim Liuzza 12 August 2012
[50] http://www.baseballfever.com
[51] Laredo Times 11 July 1033; Laredo Times 12 July 1933
[52] HC 18 July 1982 comments from Pat Patterson and George Nelson
[53] Laredo Times 9 August 1933; Laredo Times 10 August 1933; HC 18 July 1982
[54] HI 23 April 1949
[55] Fink, Rob. *Playing in Shadows: Texas and Negro league Baseball.* (Texas Tech University Press, 2010)
[56] HI 7 May 1949
[57] HI 7 May 1949; HI 20 August 1949; Riley, James A.. *The Biographical Encyclopedia of the Negro Baseball Leagues.* (Carroll Graff, 1994); Fink, Rob. *Playing in Shadows: Texas and Negro league Baseball.* (Texas Tech University Press, 2010)
[58] HI 18 March 1950; HI 13 May 1950; Houston City Directory 1944; Riley, James A.. *The Biographical Encyclopedia of the Negro Baseball Leagues.* (Carroll Graff, 1994)
[59] Riley, James A.. *The Biographical Encyclopedia of the Negro Baseball Leagues.* (Carroll Graff, 1994); http://www.baseball-reference.com
[60] Fink, Rob. *Playing in Shadows: Texas and Negro league Baseball.* (Texas Tech University Press, 2010)
[61] HI 16 September 1950
[62] HI 13 May 1950

KEY

GDN – *Galveston Daily News*
HI – *Houston Informer*
HP – *Houston Post*
CD – *Chicago Defender*
HC – *Houston Chronicle*

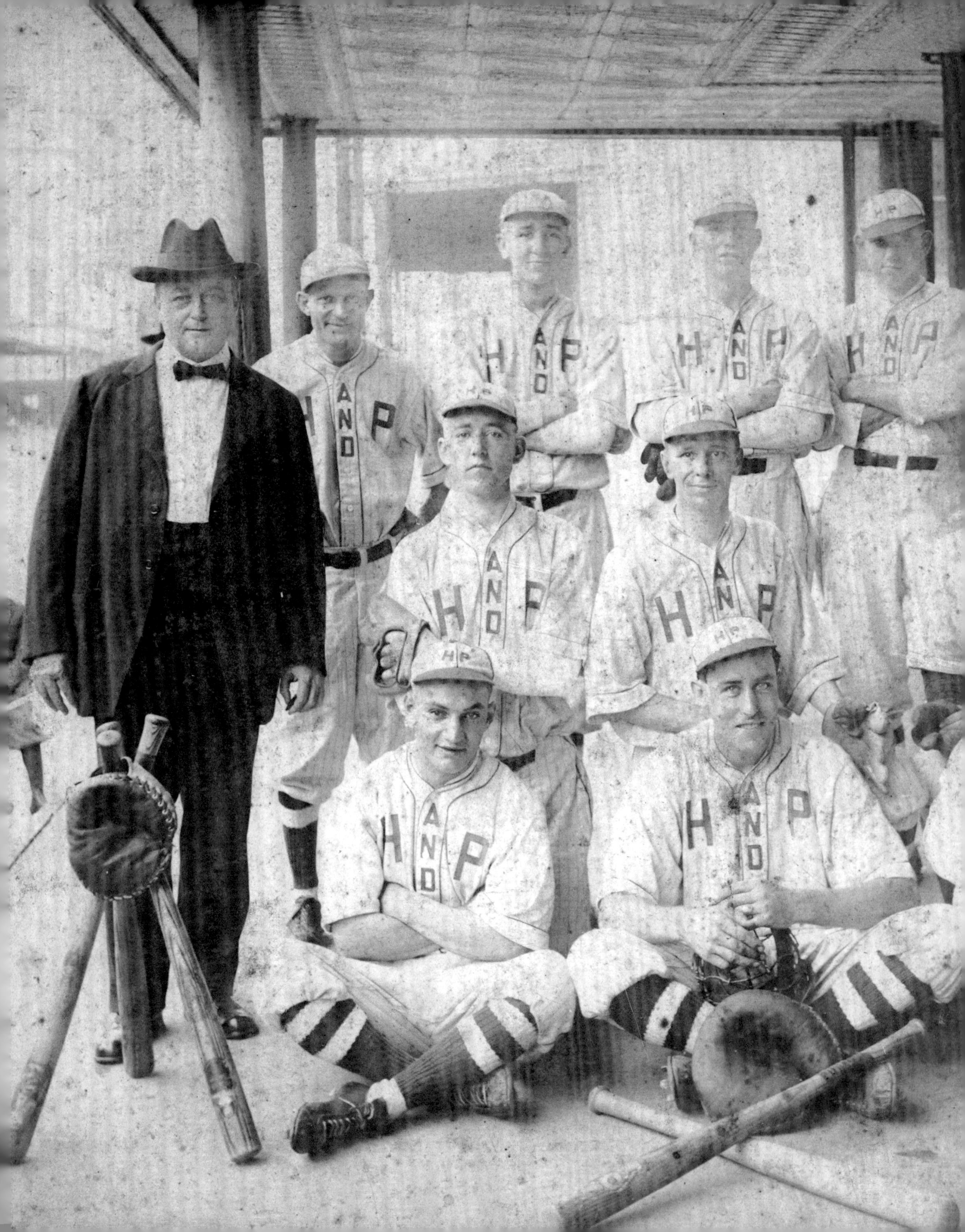
H AND P
HP

CHAPTER TWELVE

AMATEUR & SEMI-PRO BALL

BY MIKE VANCE, MARSHA FRANTY
& JOE THOMPSON

SEMI-PRO BASEBALL

It's difficult to overstate the popularity of semi-pro baseball in Houston prior to 1950. The local papers often gave more ink to a hot semi-pro matchup than they did to the Texas League Buffs. A much anticipated duel between two big oil company teams not only garnered big sports headlines, it often outdrew the local professionals by several thousands. Houstonians loved their sports, and semi-pro baseball was a big deal.

The Henke & Pillot Grocery team pose at their flagship store on Market Square.
Story Sloane's Gallery

The first teams in Texas organized around a profession centered around fire companies and railroads. The Robert E. Lees of Galveston that dated to immediately after the Civil War were made up largely of members of the island's volunteer fire company of the same name. In 1874, the Robert E. Lees of Houston, sporting an obviously popular name in those days, faced the Texas Central team from Waco. The Houston & Texas Central Railroad had reached that city only two years prior. Less than a decade later, railroad sponsored teams were touring regionally as when the Missouri Pacific squad of St. Louis came barnstorming through Houston and defeated the hometown Nationals at the Fairgrounds.[1]

By the time Texas established a professional baseball league, there were a few company teams that could challenge pros. Beer companies were at the top of the list. In Houston it was the Magnolias of Houston Ice & Brewing Company and the Americans of Adolphus Busch's giant American Brewery that stood on

Grand Prize Brewery, owned at one time by Howard Hughes, regularly fielded a top Houston semi-pro team.
Story Sloane's Gallery

the north bank of Buffalo Bayou on the spot occupied today by University of Houston Downtown. In Galveston it was the team representing the island plant of Cincinnati's Christian Möerlein Brewery and another playing under the banner of Pabst, a Milwaukee brewing giant with a facility in Galveston.[2]

In those years when the Texas League went dark due to economic worries, the beer teams became the representatives of the city's honor. Houston's Americans and Galveston's Moerleins each began paying players by the mid-1890s, including some older local favorites like Andrew McGowen and some Texas League talent like Fred Erichson, Will Marmion or Scarborough who had been with the Houston Mudcats and Constantini imported from Dallas. Their frequent home-and-home series was eagerly anticipated by fans in both cities. Several hundred showed up for each contest, and "they looked for great ball playing."[3]

More often than not, players or their sponsors put up money that would go to the winners, higher stakes in the case of the beer teams, and for smaller outfits, it was purses of $25 or $15 a side. In the case of an island matchup between the S.O.R. and Beach Slugger nines, it was five bucks and a keg of beer.[4]

By the 1890s, scores of smaller local companies were getting bitten by the baseball bug. It was team building before the term was invented, and it was also advertising and bragging rights. Kiams clothing store went all out, dressing their ball playing clerks in black uniforms so natty that they warranted a write up in the paper. The Bering's Sporting Goods store outfitted their own Crescents baseball team. Si Packard, a local businessman and politician who was heavily involved with the Houston Buffs, had his own strong semi-pro team that represented his Model Laundry. The local butcher's union had a team, as did Houston's bakers and Galveston's oyster shuckers, and each of the city's wards and suburbs had their own ball club to evoke the neighborhood pride.[5]

The Athletics of the Fifth Ward were one neighborhood club that had a real heyday, going nearly undefeated in 1894. The team was significant enough that an Athletics Junior squad was formed for boys in their early teens, almost like a farm team. When ace pitcher Joe Browne left to attend St. Mary's College six weeks into the season, Houston's sporting press lamented that "his place will be hard to fill." New traditions died hard.[6]

The start of the 1910s brought an explosion of semi-pro baseball in Houston

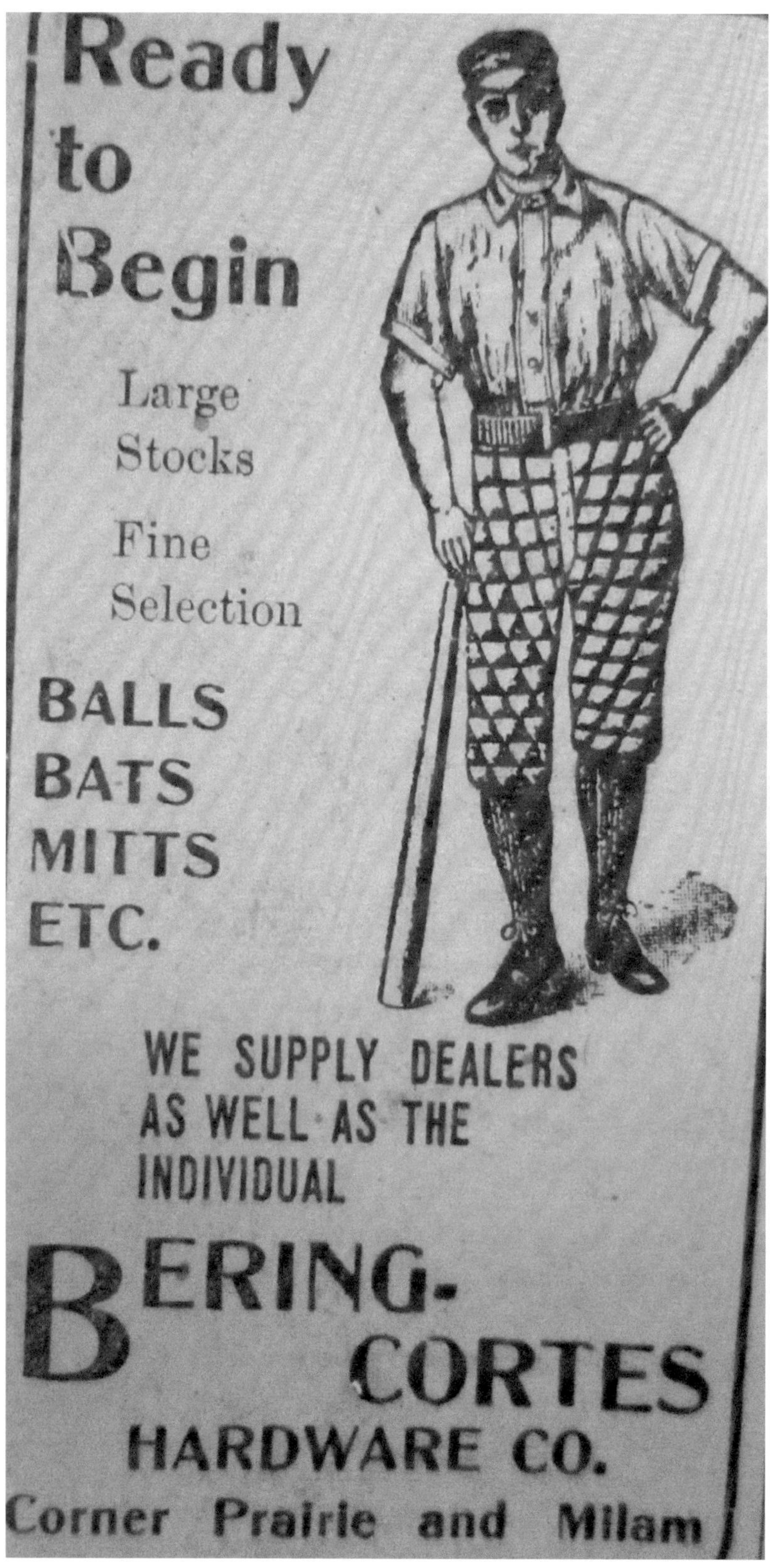

and the appearance of much more organized City Leagues. Oil company teams like Texaco, Sinclair and Gulf represented the newcomers to the local economy. Old standby clubs such as Modern Plumbing, the Houston Drug Pilltossers, Nabisco, men's clothier Leopold & Shafer and the *Houston Post* were highly competitive, too.[7]

The practice of paid ringers was continuing to grow, and it included players with Major League experience. Ed Karger had six years of big league pitching sandwiched by stints with Houston. During his second turn with the Buffaloes, Karger was earning extra bucks throwing for the Sugar Land Blues. Future Houston Buffs GM Fred Ankenman was a sought after semi-pro player who brought management skills with him, even at that stage. He graced the rosters of the Gas Company Hustlers, Adoue-Blaine, Peden Iron & Steel, the Pete Dalies and Barringer-Norton. Ankenman's brother-in-law, Walter Williams, was the leading pitcher for the league champion Baringer-Norton squad whose victories included a win over the professional Buffs in 1915.[8]

During World War I, the many companies at Ellington Field and Camp Logan fielded baseball teams and competed on the base. They also reveled in having their respective best face their special rivals, usually at a neutral site. The aviators from Ellington took on the soldiers, who were coached by Rice's Phillip Arbuckle, at Rice Institute in March 1918, complete with band music from the 108th Army Engineers. As an Ellington publication

The team from Levy's Department Store poses on the roof of their building on Main Street.

Houston Metropolitan Research Center, Houston Public Library

stated it: "Little importance has been attached to developing football and baseball teams. They were chosen at random for just one purpose—to keep Camp Logan in its place."[9]

Many of the early amateur venues were devoid of built structures. Spectators stood along the baseline or sat on the grass. Grota Diamond, located near Woodland Heights, was one such field. The intersection of Live Oak and Texas held another. Many were simply vacant lots at corners such as Austin at Webster and Main at Gray. By the turn of the century, though, two ball fields, Marmion Park in Fifth Ward and Northside Park had been built specifically to accommodate crowds at semi-pro and city league games. Shortly after Marmion Park closed in 1908, Northside Park opened on land off of Pinckney and Fletcher belonging to S.F. Noble. It was a neat wooden ballpark with raised grandstands that held a few hundred.[10]

By 1920, the City League had been joined by the Commercial League, Cotton League, Oil League, Bankers League, Industrial League and others. The

Memorial Park was one of many amateur baseball venues around Houston.
Courtesy Miriam Morris Trost

various leagues then faced each other for a city of Houston championship. In 1921 it came down to a battle at West End Park between Admiration Coffee and an all-star group from Texaco with their respective managers Jim Liuzza and Tex Convery. Texaco featured two big league talents, teenaged pitcher John Berly and Bill Stellbauer who was also an outfielder with the Houston Buffs.[11]

The concept of a consolidated "best of" team representing a company had been commonplace in the decades since the largest employers such as Southern Pacific, Humble Oil and Texaco each had leagues and baseball fields of their own. For the railroad, Houston's largest employer, the ticketers, freighters and shop men had their own teams and strong rivalries. Among the oil companies, it was refining versus transportation versus district sales. A decade and a half later, Hughes Tool would also establish its own baseball circuit.[12]

Semi-pro ball wasn't limited to white players. A city league for African-American teams had sprung up, as well. Southern Pacific was an employer that provided sports opportunities for its many black employees, and the SP Colored team was a good one. The Morgan Shipping Line also fielded a team, but Hughes Tool did not. The Post Office had a crack club of black ballplayers, and Houston's train station Red Caps comprised another. A team called the Monarchs was owned by the Liuzza Brothers, Italian grocers in the Fifth Ward. Another club was sponsored by the Lincoln Theatre, the largest and classiest African-American movie house in town. It was operated by O.P. DeWalt, a local NAACP leader who was gunned down in his own projection room in 1931.[13]

Independence Heights, a brand new city northwest of Houston that was designed solely for African-Americans, had a town baseball team within the first year. The distance from town was bridged by public transportation with "a special car (leaving) Main and Congress at 1:30" to take patrons, black and white, to see the Independence Heights colored team face the Galveston Flyaways. There remained a team in the neighborhood well into the Depression years.[14]

As more and more immigrants came to Houston from Mexico in the wake of revolution, all-Mexican ballclubs came into being. The Aguilas and the Leones, Eagles and Lions, were two of the teams that became prominent during the mid-1920s. By the start of the '30s, a variety of Mexican-American social clubs and neighborhoods were sponsoring ball teams. At least one matchup in 1930 pitted the mostly Mexican Lions against a mostly Italian-American team from Houston's West End. One of the top stars among those first Mexican-American clubs was Hokie Garcia, a top player for years who stayed in the game and became a sought after, and fiery, semi-pro umpire. Dressed in the blue for a South Coast Victory league game in 1945, Garcia got into it with a pitcher named Henry Culp.[15]

"When I told Culp to leave the park,"

Soldiers at Camp Logan in 1917 and 1918 had several baseball teams that played one another. This one belonged to the camp medical unit.

Houston Metropolitan Research Center, Houston Public Library

Houston's Pizzatola family sponsored the Regal Sandwich team.

Houston Metropolitan Research Center, Houston Public Library

A Texaco runner slides home at West End Park. Courtesy Jim Liuzza

This particular Houston semi-pro scene was likely staged for the camera circa 1920. Courtesy Jim Liuzza

said Garcia. "He refused and countered with abusive language. So I hit him."[16]

By the middle and late 1920s, Houston's biggest employers had the city's top baseball teams, as well. Hughes Tool was strong, and Houston Lighting and Power was indeed an electric ball club, almost always in the running for the city championships. Southern Pacific was another powerhouse, with University of Texas pitching star Jubilo Clements on the mound. Clements had played a couple of minor league seasons before moving to Houston for a good-paying day job. He landed with Southwestern Bell, was transferred to Nacogdoches and recruited East Texan Morris Frank to pitch for a team he was managing called the Lufkin Firemen.[17]

Competition in baseball often reflected everyday competition in business. In

Brazoria County, there were two "fast ball clubs" that belonged to rival sulfur companies along the coast. In 1928, Freeport Sulfur and Gulf Sulfur were two of the best entrants in a short-lived semi-pro circuit called the South Coast League. Gulf, managed by the famous Chicago White Sox lefty, Dickie Kerr, had won the first half of the season. Freeport, "tired of getting beat," brought in the famously successful Texas Longhorns coach Billy Disch to manage its team in the second half. They won it to set up a playoff between the two teams. Behind the extremely fast and wild pitching of Longhorns lefty Johnny Railton and a "veteran curve-baller" Johnny Lynum, Freeport eased past Gulf to win the league. The bosses at Gulf Sulfur promptly fired Dickie Kerr.[18]

In 1929, a team called Joe Presswood's All-Stars dominated local semi-pro competition. The ace of the staff was the same Johnny Railton, three time All-SWC hurler who signed with the Yankees organization before developing arm trouble. Presswood's team advanced to San Antonio where they swept a series from that city's Public Service Company team, twice beating their pitching ace, a moonlighting young soldier named Dizzy Dean. A week later they won the state title in Buff Stadium over Employers Casualty Insurance of Dallas.[19]

There were new ball diamonds popping up around town by the start of the 1930s. Houston began to put baseball fields in city parks at Memorial, MacGregor, Mason, Montie Beach Park and Moody. Hermann Park's ball field sat at the corner of Main and Holcombe until it was displaced by the construction of Texas Children's Hospital. Camp Logan was a small diamond in the neighborhood just east of Memorial Park, and the Recreation Fields were located on Louisiana in a spot that would be home to the new YMCA in 1941.[20]

The Mexican-Americans in semi-pro Houston baseball played either alongside Anglos or on mostly Hispanic teams in

Hughes Tool Company (top) and Felix Tijerina's Mexican Inn were two of the dozens of local businesses who fielded semi-pro baseball teams.

Houston Metropolitan Research Center, Houston Public Library

otherwise Anglo leagues. One of the best known of those ball clubs was sponsored by the Mexican Inn, the first restaurant operation owned and operated by Felix Tijerina and his wife, Janie, who would become best known for the local chain called Felix. First fielded in March 1933, the ball team was one of the Mexican Inn's most visible forms of advertising. Like most of the top semi-pro outfits, the ball club travelled. Over their three seasons together, the Mexican Inn played almost every top Anglo team in the Houston area as well as "Mexican teams from Sugar Land, Texas City, Seguin, Bellville" and both a Hispanic and an Anglo team from Refugio.[21]

Felix recruited the best players from the increasingly Mexican Second Ward. The "idol of the Mexican diamond fans" was pitcher Ramon Sustaita, good enough to make a few Texas League appearances. In the team's first year together, Sustaita tallied well over 20 wins and had at least five complete game shutouts. Other top players included pitcher Johnny Cortes and everyday players Lupe Garcia, Miguel "Big Foot" Zepeda, Camargo, Rios and George "Champ" Cordova. One Houston sportswriter called them the "best Mexican team in the state."[22]

The Mexican Inn team was one of the inaugural participants in an event that started in 1935 and would retain a cherished spot on the Houston baseball calendar for a full 20 years. It was the *Houston Post* Semi-Pro Tournament, and it was started by *Post* sports editor Lloyd Gregory and Carey Selph, who within the year after leaving the Buffs had taken over the Houston Amateur Baseball Federation. Needless to say, lines between amateur and semi-pro were sometimes a bit blurry. In the case of the popular *Post* Tournament, the prize money was very attractive.[23]

In addition to Felix's restaurant team, the first year's competition drew the most powerful ball clubs in Southeast Texas: The Texaco Refiners of Galena Park, the Brenham Sun Oilers, Southern Pacific, the Manvel Texaco Fire Chiefs, the Conroe Strake Wildcats and the Barbers Hill Gushers. Soon the *Post* Tournament would be drawing "fast clubs" from out of state. The Halliburton Cementers from Oklahoma and Georgia's Bona Allen Shoemakers would each take home championship trophies before World War II. They also split a winner's share of prize money that often topped $2,500.00, too.[24]

When the 1935 *Post* event got underway, many entrants played an opponent that was not coming to Houston. The Huntsville Prison Tigers was a ball team comprised of men behind bars at the Walls Unit. They played nothing but home games. In spite of a humiliating 28-0 season opening loss to the Houston Buffaloes, the Prison Tigers amassed a very respectable 25 and 8 record against some of the best semi-pro competition in Texas. The prison team's most frequent opponent was the Brenham Sun Oilers with each team winning three contests and one game ending in an 11 inning tie. The burglars, forgers and car thieves made the best of their home field advantage which included "thirty foot outfield walls and 'extra' outfielders carrying guns."

Brenham's Sunoco Oilers team took the inaugural *Post* Tournament by winning the last half of a double-header against the Conroe Strake Wildcats by a tally of 5-3 in front of over 6,000 fans. Jimmy Delmar of the also-ran Grand Prize Brewers offered to furnish all the "beer for a big party at which prize money from the *Houston Post* Tournament will be distributed. All tourney players will be invited." With the tourney concluded, there was one baseball bombshell left. The newspapers announced in bold headlines that the prison team would be coming to Houston to play a two game series against the champion Brenham Sun Oilers. [25]

The interest in the matchup was overwhelming. Prison skipper Albert Moore made bold predictions that they would "wear out" Brenham. The ABC Grocery number 10 put up a "large basket of fruit and cakes" for the first prisoner to score a run. And the Huntsville prison orchestra, under the leadership of convicted theatre holdup murderer Bob Silver, would play at Buff Stadium for the game. The piano-tickling Silver had been granted a pardon by the Governor and would soon be getting released in spite of a notorious escape from the Wynne Unit some years prior.[26]

The prisoners were led by pitcher Army Armstrong a hard case from Dallas who had "a burning fastball and for a change of pace mixed in one still faster." Among the hitters was shortstop Jesse Esparza, "stocky" third sacker Earl Holbrook and the second baseman, Brigham Young. Lawrence Guinn and Arthur McCann were two Houstonian outfielders. Lefty Dalton was a ham-handed right fielder who made up for it with home run power, and Carl Littlejohn held down first base and pitched. Littlejohn was familiar with Buff Stadium since he had played for Houston twice before, hurling the first shutout of the 1925 season and playing on the great 1928 ball club. After winning the Dixie Series that year, he had celebrated with a drive out of town in a car that he forgot was not his.[27]

The twin bill took place on the same day that Huey P. Long was assassinated in Baton Rouge. By the time a reader turned to the sports pages, however, all the news was that the Huntsville Prison Tigers had swept Brenham by scores of 5-4 in 10 and 1-0 in seven. Almost 6,500 customers paid to watch, and the vast majority seemed to be pulling for the convicts. It was the biggest crowd at Buff Stadium since their last Dixie Series four years earlier. Carl Littlejohn had two hits in the opener and was the winning pitcher for the nightcap, knocking in the game's only run with a sacrifice. After the big victory, the prisoners, made temporary trustees for the trip, returned to Huntsville. Their winnings were paid into the prison's recreation fund.[28]

Reflecting the high flying economic engine of the region, the Oilers nickname was everywhere. Humble Oil's Baytown

No company put more resources into semi-pro baseball than Humble Oil which built a top flight complex at its Baytown refinery. Monty Stratton, whose story was made into a movie, is the tall player standing fifth from right in the bottom photo.

Courtesy Sterling Municipal Library, Baytown

Oilers were the most consistent team using that nickname. Humble's Baytown Refinery had sought to hire good baseball players for their workforce since they opened in 1919. They provided multiple diamonds for the employees, eventually building a bona fide stadium. The Humble Oilers represented the pride of the entire community of Baytown, Pelly and Goose Creek, and the company dime paid for the ball players to travel under the Humble Oil banner.[29]

With the Depression lingering and the oil business booming, there was often more money to be made in semi-pro than Texas League ball. Men like Heinie Schuble were retired from pro ball, but they still showed up on rosters for oil company teams in places like Baytown and Barber's Hill. Schuble continued playing semi-pro ball well into his 40s, first with the Grand Prize Brewers, then taking a job with Humble Oil that had him on the infield of the Baytown Oilers and provided an oil industry job that he kept until retirement in 1971.[30]

Houston's own Heinie Schuble found a home playing ball for Humble Oil after seven Major League seasons.

National Baseball Hall of Fame Library, Cooperstown, NY

Another of the perennial betting favorites in the pre-War years was Houston's Grand Prize Beer. The team was known around the country, coming in third in the annual Wichita, Kansas National Semi-Pro Tournament in 1940. Jack Jakucki was a pitcher for that Grand Prize team. He had already put in a brief stop in the bigs and four years of top level minor league ball around Texas and California but had opted to return to Texas, pitching semi-pro and working as a painter and paper hanger. He embodied the fact that it sometimes wasn't a lack of talent but a lack of discipline that kept some men in semi-pro ball. Jakucki's reputation for drinking and rough fun was well-earned. One story had him and teammate Monk Moore jumping into a New Orleans wrestling ring during a "boring match" and beating up both wrestlers and the referee. In Wichita for the national tourney, the stout Jakucki was said to have grabbed a disagreeable umpire by the heels after a game and dangled the poor fellow over the railing of a bridge across the Arkansas River.[31]

Jimmy Delmar managed Grand Prize, owned by Howard Hughes, as well as all the Hughes Tool athletic teams. Delmar was a former boxer who also ran a gym. In later years, he served several terms on the Houston Independent School Board where he was a strong voice for the anti-Communist, pro-racial segregation faction during the 1950s. Jimmy Delmar was honored for his service to HISD and local athletics with the naming of the district's sports complex near Loop 610 and Highway 290.[32]

When the Texas League shuttered its schedule at the end of the 1942 season, the Cardinals organization turned Buff Stadium over to the City of Houston. The city began looking for ways to keep the ballpark occupied, and founded the South Coast Victory League (SCVL), a circuit made up of area semi-pro clubs. The inaugural season in 1943 opened with Hughes Tool, Houston Shipbuilding, Freeport Dow Chemical, the La Porte Coast Guard Station, Ellington Field, Brown Shipbuilding, Humble's Baytown Oilers and a mostly Hispanic team sponsored by Southern Select Beer that featured most of the same roster that had played for Felix Tijerina's Mexican Inn a decade before.[33]

San Antonio, with its slew of Army and Air Corps bases, had recently organized the Service League which was made up of all military teams and boasted players such as Enos Slaughter, Tex Hughson and Howie Pollet. Shipped to the Pacific at the end of the war, Slaughter famously commented that there were "better crowds on Saipan" than there were to see the Philadelphia Phillies." Over the three year life of the South Coast Victory League, more military base teams competed in Houston, as well. Foster Field and Aloe Field, two air bases in Victoria, joined in, as did Bryan Army Air Field. By 1945, the league was rounded out by ball clubs sponsored by Rapid Blue Print and Finger Furniture.[34]

Several players with Major League experience graced the SCVL diamonds. Former Buffs player and future manager, Johnny Keane was the manager at Brown Shipyard. The two oldest players in the league were easily Glenn Myatt and Art Reinhardt, both with extensive Major League resumes. The duo had formed a young battery with the Buffs at the close of the previous World War.[35]

Meanwhile, most of the native Houstonian big leaguers were serving in the military. Johnny Rizzo interrupted his baseball career to join the Navy. Frank Mancuso was training to be an Army paratrooper when a tangled chute caused him to land in some trees, breaking his leg. Red Munger, in the prime of his career, was selected for the National League All-Star team in 1944 thanks to a first half record of 11-3 and a miniscule 1.34 ERA. Drafted by the U.S. Army, Munger instead found himself at Ft. Benning, Georgia. In 1945, he was pitching good ball for the Army. While home on leave in the summer of that year,

Munger pitched in the *Post* Tournament for the Finger Furniture team and was the losing pitcher to Ellington Field in the finals.[36]

All of the teams in the South Coast Victory League had players that were in in the service or were working in a critical war industry job. In many cases, it was true of every player on the squad. Still they found time to play ball as a welcome diversion. Since most all wartime industries were running multiple shifts, there was even experimentation with morning baseball. Galveston tried it for their Service League, scheduling "after-breakfast tilts" so afternoon and evening workers could come watch some baseball.[37]

In June of 1943, the All-Star team from the SCVL beat the Waco Army Air Field Wolves, widely considered to be the best team in Texas at the time. The locals won in large fashion, besting Waco 9-1 behind the four-hit pitching of Sigmund "Jack" Jakucki who was by then toiling on the mound for his war time employer, Houston Shipbuilding.

Based partially on his good work in the SCVL, the talent-starved St. Louis Browns called Jakucki back up for the 1944 and 1945 seasons. He responded brilliantly, winning the only pennant clinching game in Browns history when he beat the Yankees in the season finale. Somewhere during these wartime seasons, the temperamental Jakucki developed difficulties with his one-armed teammate, outfielder Pete Gray. It came to a head when the two had a fist fight with Jakucki holding one arm behind his back. It was the last straw. St. Louis manager Luke Sewell kicked the hard-drinking Jakucki off the club, and he never graced the Major Leagues again. He eventually returned to Houston and Galveston and hard times. Among the friends who stuck by him was his former Browns teammate, Frank Mancuso, who was, by then, a Houston City Councilman.[38]

The team Jakucki bested in the summer of 1943, the Waco AAF bunch, hardly needed any sympathy. They met the SCVL All-Stars again that September and beat them and Jakucki 2-1 with former Washington Senator Sid Hudson on the hill. Waco was managed by Lt. Birdie Tebbetts who would make the All-Army Team that year, and he knocked in both runs for the fly boys in the second matchup. The Waco ball club boasted other former big leaguers on their roster: Hoot Evers, Bruce Campbell and Buster Mills. During the war years, they went 88-16 and won the *Houston Post* Tournament in both 1943 and 1944.[39]

By summer of 1945, Tebbetts was playing his baseball in the Mariana Islands. Buster Mills, Tex Hughson and Sid Hudson were still playing ball, too, but were based in Saipan. There were so many professional ball players with the Navy and Air Corps in the Pacific that there were two American League versus National League All-Star Games played in 1945 on the islands of Tinian and Iwo Jima.

The *Post* Tournament continued

through the war years without missing a beat. Only the teams changed, being made up of mostly service outfits. The big Navy shipyard operation in Orange put together an All-Star team and entered them in the tourney for 1945. Like many wartime clubs, there were guys with big league chops: Wiley Earnsbrother, May Fleming and Tigers pitcher John Tate. In one game they faced the Baytown Oilers who had brought in pitcher Monty Stratton, a top Chicago White Sox pitcher who had lost his leg in a hunting accident. Normally other teams allowed a courtesy pinch runner when Stratton, fitted with a wooden leg, reached base, but with a winner's purse of $6,000 on the line that year, the Shipyard team exercised their right to refuse.

Stratton was making a comeback in semi-pro ball, and it led to several more years in the low minors before he finally retired at age 41. The saddest note in that ballgame, however, came when Shipyard catcher Wayne Carroll was notified in the late innings that his brother had been killed in a Japanese attack on Okinawa. After a moment of silence at Buff Stadium, the game resumed.[40]

Postwar semi-pro powerhouses included several of the teams that had been around for decades like Baytown's Humble Oilers and the Victoria Rosebuds, but new faces soon became familiar at the *Post* tourney, as well. The Pan American Refinery in Texas City, the Huntsville Merchants, Angelo's Café, the Kemah Laundry Sea Gulls and teams from towns like Sinton, Yoakum and Port Arthur joined the usual suspects. The Weimar Herder Truckers, whose home field was the first lighted diamond between Houston and San Antonio, was a strong mix of college players and the best talent from the area's small town teams. They may have set a sibling record for once having a roster that included the three Kana Brothers—Jiggs, Fats and Jack—the three Boeer Brothers—Walter, Hilbert and Werner—and two other sets of brothers in Jimmie and Johnnie Mazoch and Hooks and Cuz Hajovsky. Another post-war entry was Galveston's Turf

The Weimar Herder Truckers from Colorado County, TX were a mainstay at the* Houston Post *semi-pro tournament during the post-WWII years. Their home park was perhaps the first lighted field between Houston and San Antonio.

Courtesy Nesbitt Memorial Library, Columbus, TX

Club, a team sponsored by the Maceo family-owned night clubs on and around the island that included famously illegal gambling.[41]

Hiring college players, technically paying them for an unrelated job while they played baseball for free, was common practice among semi-pro teams in Texas. Conroe was particularly known for its college talent, often being able to boast having an all-Southwest Conference lineup. At one point in the late 1940s, the Conroe Wildcats had an infield of two Longhorns and two Aggies, an all-Baylor Bears outfield, and a Rice pitcher on the mound. Several of the names on the semi-pro rosters were coming off great college success just weeks prior. The Texas Longhorns won back-to-back College World Series titles in 1949 and 1950, and, before the celebration grew cold, players like Gus Hrncir, Frank Womack, Dan Watson, Kal Segrist, Tom Hamilton and Frank Kana were quickly added to team rosters for the *Houston Post* Tournament and more.[42]

Roscoe Ivy, who was a young player for the Lufkin Merchants, recalls that the winners and losers split the game receipts 60/40 with players getting their share in cash on the spot. On a good day that might amount to $25 each per game. For the college players, it worked differently. The Conroe team's winnings were paid to the Conroe Baseball Association, and the college players were employees of the town of Conroe, each with a specific job to do. One of the Baylor players on the Wildcats team, for example, had to "once a week sweep off the apron at one service station down there. That was his job and each one of them had something like that. Go empty the wastebasket in the mayor's office."[43]

Felix Fraga, who played for the Victoria Rosebuds during the summers of his years at University of Houston, recalls that the teams "gave you a job and paid you. You had to show up for practice and the games, but not for work."[44]

The Alpine Cowboys, a West Texas bunch that featured a bevy of college talent, including Ray van Cleef, another College World Series star, came to the *Post* Tournament and was housed at the Buccaneer Hotel on Galveston's Seawall. Team owner Herbert Kokernot gave his team an incentive, though. If they won their third game, he would move them to the new, luxurious Shamrock Hotel. They promptly beat the Baytown Oilers 10-0. Alpine would finish second to the Columbus Redbirds in their first Houston appearance.[45]

Just like high school, Legion or college ball, starring on a semi-pro ball club could occasionally provide a road to the big leagues. Pete Runnels was an easy going young Lufkin native who "had a knack of hitting left-handed and poking into left field." After striking out on earning a contract following time at the Cardinals camp, Runnels returned to East Texas and semi-pro ball. Following a Sunday game with the Lufkin Merchants, Runnels hitchhiked to Henderson, got a tryout with the Class D team there, and was signed. Three years, three ball clubs and a few doubles records later, he was starting for the Washington Senators. Pete Runnels would win two American League batting titles and narrowly miss out on a third. He finished his career with the Houston Colt .45s and retired in Pasadena, Texas.[46]

Bobby Fretz had much success at St. Thomas High School, Texas A&M and on a variety of semi-pro teams. He never fully pursued a career in pro baseball, however, preferring to build his family's construction business instead. He was still a sought after star in semi-pro baseball. During and after his college years, he had playing time with the Conroe Strake Wildcats, Philco, Empire Broom and the Ft. Bend Jay Birds, *Post* Tournament winners in 1952 for whom he pitched and played positions in both the infield and outfield. Like most men in the semi-pro ranks, he just loved to play ball.

Houston claimed three national championships in the early years of the American Amateur Baseball Congress (AABC) tournaments, including the very first one in 1935. The city captured back-to-back titles in 1954 and 1955 behind Jack Schultea's pitching. In those last two, the team was sponsored by Mechanic's Uniform Supply, with trips to games in far off places like Watertown, South Dakota underwritten by Stuart Lange.

Under the rules of the day, up to three players per team could have spent time as a professional as long as they had subsequently been released. After Schultea's great year in 1954, he developed arm trouble. By the time the next tournament came, he had been released by the Cardinals organization. Though he no longer had his naturally sinking fastball, Schultea was again a part of a loaded ball club, defeatingthe Cheney Studs, a team from Seattle-Tacoma, by a score of 7-2 in the finals in Battle Creek, Michigan and finishing the AABC tourney without ever having lost a game. It was a rare feat indeed. They had twice risen to the pinnacle of men's amateur baseball in this country, ending up on top in a tournament that had begun with 3800 teams. Among the items commemorating the second consecutive national amateur title was a resolution of appreciation granted by the city and signed by Mayor Roy Hofheinz, a man who would soon have the biggest hand in bringing the top level of professional ball to Houston.[47]

COLLEGE BASEBALL

Rice Institute opened in the fall of 1912, and by the following spring it sported a competitive baseball team, though at the beginning that might mean only four or five contests with other colleges. The rest of the schedule included semi pro teams and a short series with Houston High School. Led by Phillip Arbuckle, an Amos Alonzo Stagg disciple who also coached football and basketball, the Owls quickly went about building a program at a new campus on the prairie that was almost devoid of any athletic facilities. After one year as an independent, the school became a charter member of the Southwest Conference. They were beginning to make strides in all three sports when campus life was interrupted by World War I. Nonetheless, Arbuckle got Rice athletics off to a solid beginning, and his 58.4 winning percentage in football is still the best in school history.[48]

One of the more unusual baseball opponents for the Owls in their formative years came in 1915 when they entertained the Chinese University of Hawaii for two games, both of which Rice lost rather emphatically. The islanders' pitcher George Bo fanned 14 Owls in game one. The fact was that the ball club had nothing to do with any university. They were really a group of Hawaiian All-Stars who were financed by business interests to promote the Islands. It was no wonder that they played "like seasoned vets." They toured the nation under the moniker of a non-existent school playing mostly collegiate competition. Rice should not have felt alone in their stinging defeats; the Hawaiians also walked away with victories at Texas, Baylor and Southwestern. Nonetheless, when the team returned to the mainland the following year, the Owls refused to play them.[49]

Rice had two baseball coaches of note during the years following Phil Arbuckle's departure. Jack Coombs, a star pitcher for Connie Mack's Philadelphia A's, took over as the school's second coach in 1918. His hiring came only months after Coombs threw his 35th and final big league shutout. Though his time at Rice

Dickie Kerr, best known for two wins in the tainted 1919 World Series, managed both Rice University and regional semi-pro teams during his time in Houston.

Houston Metropolitan Research Center, Houston Public Library

lasted less than one full season, when he left to take a big league managing job with the Phillies, Coombs found his calling in college baseball. He went on to spend over three decades as head coach at Williams College, Princeton and Duke.[50]

The other ex-big league hurler who signed on to mentor the Owls was Dickie Kerr, a little lefty known for his tenacious refusal to go along with the fix during the Black Sox World Series of 1919. Kerr stayed with the school for two seasons in 1927 and '28. Like Coombs before him, he amassed a rather woeful conference record, but he built great goodwill among the city's baseball fans and made Houston his home. A statue of Dickie Kerr from those by-gone days now graces the home park of the Sugar Land Skeeters.

The first mega-star of Rice athletics was undoubtedly Eddie Dyer. He was brought from South Louisiana to South Main on a scholarship, and he did not disappoint. Dyer made multiple All-Southwest Conference teams in baseball and football, in which he was a top-notch halfback. He also excelled in track.[51]

The highest of many high points for the lefty pitcher came in a much anticipated game against Baylor Bears hurler Ted Lyons. In April 1921, the two faced off in a Southwest Conference pitchers' duel. Lyons, who was eventually ticketed for Cooperstown, held the Owls to five hits on the day, even though he had pitched a partial game the day before. Dyer, on the other hand, didn't allow the Bears a single safety, and Rice prevailed 2-1. After tossing his no-no, fans and teammates celebrated by hoisting Dyer to their shoulders and carrying him off the field. He then rested up for a track meet the following day. In a small twist of fate, Dyer's younger brother, Sammy, had gotten his name in the paper only two weeks earlier for throwing a no-hitter against Park Place for his Little Toms team. Eddie Dyer did well all season, and Rice came within a game of winning the conference baseball title. Instead, it went to Texas.[52]

The team on which Dyer played was solid, boasting another all-conference pitcher in Palmer "Peg" Melton, and it was also certified as having been a polite one. After a trip to Sherman where the club lost 3-0 to the Austin College Kangaroos, the manager of the Binkley Hotel took the time to write to Rice Institute president E.O. Lovett and compliment the young men on the baseball team. After a string of visiting squads who "steal the towels, wreck the rooms and cause no end of disturbance thru the house, the boys of Rice were the ONE exception."[53]

Dyer left school in 1922 to accept a signing bonus of $2,500 from the St. Louis Cardinals. He used the money to pay off his father's debts back in Morgan City and cover a year of college for his brother, Sammy. Arm trouble prevented Dyer from fulfilling his potential as a big league hurler, but he made his mark as a manager and executive. During the baseball off-seasons, he came back to campus to work as an assistant football coach. Eddie Dyer finished college at Rice, too, earning his degree in 1936. Along the way, he became friends with wildcat oil man Hugh Roy Cullen who let Dyer invest in some of his successful ventures. He lived out his post-baseball life as a prosperous businessman in his adopted hometown of Houston, bringing baseball friends such as Howie Pollet and Joffre Cross along with him.[54]

Rice had its first All-American pitcher about a decade after Dyer left for the pros. Chester "Smokey" Klaerner was the son, grandson and brother of Gillespie County sheriffs. Growing up in the heavily German Hill Country town of Fredericksburg, Klaerner retained a bit of an inherited Texas-German accent when he dismissively referred to himself in the third person as "Dot Smokey." On the athletic fields along South Main, he was much more assertive.

The six-foot, 210-pound, "strong-armed and stout-hearted" Klaerner had been recruited to play lineman for the Owls football team, a task he handled well for three years. Baseball was where he shined, however. In his banner season of 1932, Klaerner won eight of his 10 starts including two no-hitters, against Baylor and S.M.U.. He skipped baseball his senior year, opting for field events such as javelin instead. After three successful years in the low minors, Smokey Klaerner returned to his hometown where he spent decades as a coach and teacher in Fredericksburg Public Schools.[55]

Three other pre-War Rice ball players would earn their way to the big leagues. Jim Asbell, Joe P. Wood and Frank Carswell played for the Owls in the late 1930s. Outfielder Asbell had come to Houston from Tulane and had four previous stops in the minor leagues. After his turn with the Owls, he spent very little time in the minors before earning a cup of coffee with the Cubs in 1938.[56]

Wood and Carswell were Rice baseball teammates in 1939, but then their career paths diverged. Joe Wood, a native-Houstonian infielder scooped up by the Tigers

Rabbit Reveley, Jack Schultea and Wayne Graham celebrate the final out of an amateur championship.
Courtesy Jack Schultea

organization after only one year of college ball played in Henderson and Beaumont before finally making it to Detroit during the midst of the WWII years. He posted a hefty .323 batting average in 1943 over 60 games before getting the even bigger call to serve Uncle Sam. He never returned to the Majors.[57]

Frank Carswell was a baseball star at Rice who earned three All-SWC basketball nods, as well. After leaving school, his military service was completed before he ever got a whiff of big league cooking. After a partial season at Jamestown, New York, Carswell spent four years in the United States Marine Corps. Returning to baseball, he would see another seven seasons in the minors before the Jeff Davis High School product made it to the show for just 18 plate appearances with the 1953 Detroit Tigers.[58]

Intercollegiate baseball at the University of Houston started in 1947, and the first Cougar player to reach the Majors came off that very first team. Pitcher Bill Henry, out of Pasadena High School, was a portside twirler who ascended to the show as a starter but found his calling in the bullpen. After stops at Clarksdale and Shreveport, Henry got the call to the Boston Red Sox. He stayed four years with a losing record before he found himself back in Triple-A, but by 1958, he was in the bigs to stay. With the Cubs and the Reds, Henry became a closer, posting double digit saves for five straight seasons between 1959 and 1963. Bill Henry finished his career by

Eddie Dyer, seated second from left, was a three sport star at Rice Institute in 1922.

Courtesy Woodson Research Center, Fondren Library, Rice University

making a handful of appearances with his hometown Houston Astros in 1969. He compiled 90 Major League saves.[59]

Although they played some of their bigger games at nearby Buff Stadium, the true home field of University of Houston baseball was a smallish diamond located near Cullen and Wheeler across Cougar Place, south of what was then called Public School Athletic Stadium and Jeppesen Fieldhouse, later known as Jeppesen and then Robertson. UH's conference affiliation fluctuated; they spent years as an independent and single seasons in the Lone Star and Gulf Coast before spending almost the entire decade of the 1950s as part of the Missouri Valley Conference. They didn't make the Southwest Conference until 1973.[60]

The Coogs went through three head coaches in as many years before settling on Lovette Hill who had been coaching and teaching shop at Jefferson Davis High School. Newspaper reports gave top billing to his job as assistant football coach at UH, only mentioning his duty as head baseball coach as a secondary matter. Hill and Clyde Lee, the Cougars head football coach at the time, had been gridiron teammates together at Centenary College in the late 1920s. It turned out Lovette Hill was a natural at baseball, and was especially talented working with pitchers.[61]

In 1951, only a year after taking over, Hill had UH in an NCAA Regional thanks to the hitting of first baseman Felix Fraga, the pitching of Bobby Hollmann and a victory over Texas. Two years later, the team reached the College World Series (CWS). Hill would lead the Cougars to six tournament appearances before he retired after a 24-year tenure. He was replaced

A native of Hawaii, Carlton Hanta, found college baseball stardom at the University of Houston in the early 1950s.

Courtesy Houstonian Yearbook Collection, Special Collections, University of Houston Libraries

by a former player, Rolan Walton.[62]

The 1953 trip to the CWS was earned by a squad that was led by Houston's first All-American. Shortstop Carlton Hanta, the first Japanese-American ever to earn that honor, had approached the UH baseball team as a walk on pitcher, but at 5 foot 6, he was deemed too short. Coach Hill and teammate Foy Boyd worked to turn him into a shortstop. Their patience paid off when Hanta hit .354 the following season. His friend Boyd also alerted coaches to the fact that Hanta was so financially strapped that he often had to skip meals and couldn't even afford shoes to play intramural football. That resulted in a school meal plan. The grateful infielder named two of his sons Boyd and Hill.[63]

The 1953 Cougars finished the regular season by winning 12 of their last 14 and took the Missouri Valley Conference title by beating University of Detroit. The next step was whipping the Oklahoma Sooners in a three-game series to advance to Omaha. Game 2 of that series ended with a tenth-inning walk off homer from Hanta.[64]

Houston's first trip to the College World Series did not end well. They lost their first two games, to Boston College and Stanford, and were then headed home. It came with a small footnote, though. Carlton Hanta later pointed out that the Coogs made the trip with only 14 players out of the allowed 25.

"In the College World Series, you need the pitchers to advance," said Hanta. "Sometimes you play two games in one day. We had a lot of nerve to go in there with only 14 players."

After two seasons around Texas, Hanta returned to Hawaii, and by 1958, he was playing professional baseball in Japan. He played with the Nankai Hawks, who won a Japanese championship, and with the Chunichi Dragons. He remained in Japan to coach for another 10 years.

The oldest college sports program in the Greater Houston area belongs to the Prairie View Panthers. Prairie View A&M University (PVAMU) started in the 1870s as the segregated, state-run counterpart to Texas A&M, and athletic competition soon followed. Regular games were held among all the black colleges that had formed in the state prior to 1900: Wiley College and Bishop College in Marshall, Paul Quinn in Waco, Samuel Huston in Austin and Texas College in Tyler. They were a charter member of the Southwestern Athletic Conference

The PVAMU baseball team was a regular visitor to Houston. They faced the Dillard Colts, a local black semi-pro team, for a three-game series in the very first days of West End Park in April 1905. The contests, split 2-1 in favor of the Colts, were attended by a mixed crowd that included "a cluster of the colored elite of Houston."[66]

By the 1920s and 1930s, the Panthers were yearly opponents of the professional Houston Black Buffaloes, and the games were usually competitive. In 1929, facing one of the best Black Buffs squads ever assembled, Prairie View hurler Asa Hilliard, the son and namesake of a Bay City educator, threw "the greatest game of his career." He scattered five knocks and did not allow an earned run. Negro League stars Red Parnell, Chuffy Alexander, Green Beverly and Dewitt Owens were held hitless. Unfortunately, several errors committed behind Hilliard cost him the ballgame by a score of 3-1.[67]

Texas Southern University began life as a segregated black junior college established by the Houston Independent School District in 1927. Going through a series of name changes, including 14 years as the Houston College for Negroes, the school established a sports program. When the university moved to its own campus, baseball was not yet an official intercollegiate sport. Texas Southern became a member of the SWAC, the home of historically black colleges and universities across the Deep South, in 1954. The conference's first official baseball competition began five years later.[68]

Houston College for Negroes, a forerunner of today's Texas Southern University, fielded this team in the late 1940s.
Houston Metropolitan Research Center, Houston Public Library

RED MAHONEY AND WOMEN'S BASEBALL

When Marie "Red" Mahoney was 15, her knee came out of its socket while she was playing football with her older, bigger brother and his equally big friends. She recalls the anguish that came when the doctor told her that the injury meant the end of all contact sports for the next year.

"It just killed me," Mahoney said. "I just loved to run and play all sports, even though women were not supposed to play sports in the 1930s."[69]

Red's enthusiasm for athletics began at an early age, playing catch with her dad each evening and joining her brothers and young neighbors in ball games of all sorts. Growing up in the Houston neighborhood around the Army's old Camp Logan, she and the other children formed up teams and often played with and against the children at the nearby DePelchin Faith Home. Among her other memories of those years are the hours spent listening to baseball on the radio and making scorecards. She still winces

Southern Pacific held annual games at its athletic complex for employees from around the Texas and Louisiana region. This women's squad poses with a railroad executive.

Houston Metropolitan Research Center, Houston Public Library

at the angst caused when the St. Louis Cardinals summoned the best of the Houston Buffs players to join the major league team.

As a school girl, Red began playing on Catholic Youth Organization (CYO) softball teams, and later at San Jacinto High School, where she participated in every sport offered to female students. After graduation in 1943, Red went to work for the war effort at Gray Tool Company, serving her country as did thousands of other local women. By taking the 11-7 swing shift, she secured time for practice after work.[70]

Her skills on the baseball field gained her a place on the roster of a local fast-pitch softball team as a roving outfielder, where her love of running was given full play. The women's teams played at Sportsman's Park, a field on Houston Avenue that occupied land that had been home to Luna Park, a 1920s-era amusement complex. The city was working hard in those years, and people were more than ready to pay the admission fee of 25 cents. Refreshments and programs were available, and attendance was generally about 1500 people. After that facility closed, Houston Buffs general manager

Marie "Red" Mahoney starred for the Richey's Food Market team (top) before playing for the South Bend Blue Sox of the All-American Girls Professional Baseball League (bottom).

Courtesy Marie 'Red" Mahoney

Noted for being a fast and solid fielder, "Red" Mahoney nonetheless found time for blowing a bubble while in the outfield for South Bend in 1947.

Courtesy Marie 'Red' Mahoney

Allen Russell arranged for the women's teams to play at the Texas League stadium which was then without a primary tenant.

The team on which Red played was sponsored by Richey's Grocery and coached by Mr. Larkin, who was Red's supervisor at Gray Tool Company. In 1941 they were the State Champions.Mahoney recalls that she rode the bus to local games at her own expense but was driven home afterward by the coach. For out-of-town games, the players met at the grocery, and the coach drove the team to the game in the store's van. They travelled widely for games in spite of gas rationing, going to San Antonio, Galveston, Dallas, Fort Worth, Beaumont, and New Orleans.[71]

There were about 15 women on the team, and they played seven-inning games, with the pitcher usually pitching the entire contest. Uniforms, bats and ball were provided by the sponsors while the individual players were responsible for their own gloves and shoes. Mahoney happily remembers her opportunity to go to Oshman's Sporting Goods to select a bat of her choice.

With most of the minor leagues shut down for the duration of World War II, chewing gum magnate Phillip Wrigley had the idea to start a women's league to fill both the void and the fallow ball parks. The All-American Girls Professional Baseball League (AAGPBL) started in 1943 playing softball in contradiction to its name, but it soon changed to overhand pitching and smaller-sized baseballs. The young women, many still in their teens, were expected to be top-notch ball players and to follow high moral standards.In return, their pay ranged from $45 to $85 a week plus some expenses, more than many of the parents were getting.[72]

Though founded in war, the immediate post-war years only increased the popularity of the girls league which was now free to tour without restrictions. After an All-American Girls Professional Baseball League team made an appearance in Houston, one of the players from San Antonio recommended that Mahoney try out. Impressed with her speed and defensive skill, the league signed her, and sent her to play for the South Bend Blue Sox in 1947-48 and for the Fort Wayne Daisies in 1948. For spring training that first year, the ballplayers travelled to Havana, Cuba, which was quite an exotic experience for young American girls accustomed to Midwestern life in Racine and Kenosha.

During the regular season, team members stayed with local families and often developed long-term friendships with these people. For road games, the players stayed two to a room in hotels and were provided a small daily allowance. At all times, they were carefully supervised by suitably grim-faced chaperones who enforced rules which were meant to insure that these young ladies comported themselves in appropriate, feminine ways. Charm School also helped to shape and define their behavior so as to always reflect positively on the team and the league. While with the South Bend Blue Sox, Red was coached by Chet Grant who had played baseball locally at Notre Dame University. One notable game was a 22-inning contest in which respective pitchers Jean Fout and Eleanor Dapkus each went the distance before the ball game was won 4-3 on Red Mahoney's line drive hit.[73]

Like most of the other women playing in the AAGPBL, Red Mahoney was there because of her love for baseball and the chance to get paid for doing something she dearly enjoyed. Over the life of the league, more than six hundred women got their glorious chance to play professional ball. The hundreds of thousands of spectators who paid to watch them play must have enjoyed it, too.

After her time with the All-American Girls Professional Baseball League, Red returned to her home town and worked for Kodak for over 30 years. She continued to play baseball, but her former professional status prevented her team from playing in state and national championships. In subsequent years, Red's love for sports continued with much of her energy directed to golf and bowling. After retirement from Kodak, she ran the New York City marathon and, in her ninth decade at the time of this writing, continues to work on her golf game.

Recognition of the AAGPBL and its players did not come for many years. When Penny Marshall's film *A League of Their Own* was released in 1992. Red was skeptical about the casting of Madonna, but proclaimed upon seeing the movie that Madonna had given a very credible performance and felt that "most of that movie was right." She was even more amazed to find that the chaperone in the movie was a dead ringer for the woman who had rode herd on her South Bend Blue Sox.

With the movie came renewed enthusiasm for the history of women's baseball. On July 2, 2004, Red threw out the first pitch at a Houston Astros game at Enron Field, now Minute Maid Park. Later that month, she joined several of the AAGPBL players to participate in the 2004 FanFest preceding the All-Star Game held that year in Houston. In 2006 Red was inducted into the Texas Baseball

St. Thomas High School hosted an annual tournament for top Catholic boy's schools in Texas.

Private Collection

Hall of Fame along with the only two other Texas women who played in the AAGPBL, Alva Jo "Tex" Fischer and Ruth Lessing, both from San Antonio.[74]

Since the days of her own cherished involvement in the national game, Red Mahoney's enthusiasm for the game of baseball has never waned, and she follows her local ball clubs religiously.

HIGH SCHOOL BASEBALL

At the start of the 20th century, the city of Houston had one high school for whites and one for blacks. There were a handful of other secondary schools scattered around the more rural areas of the county and soon to be in suburban communities such as Brunner and the Heights, and most of them provided baseball as part of their sports activities. Houston regularly faced teams like Beaumont, Huntsville, Port Arthur and Bryan. Most public high schools still fielded teams into the late 1920s, but as the years went on, high school baseball became less prevalent in city schools. It wouldn't be until the end of World War II that consistent competition in baseball would return in Houston.[75]

Part of the trouble was the lack of places to play. The Director of Physical Education for the city stated the obvious: that "if athletics are to prosper there must be adequate grounds provided." Houston High School sat on a block downtown that was bounded by Austin, Caroline, Rusk and Capitol. With the school taking up most of the block, there was hardly room for a good ball diamond. The Tigers played many of their games at West End Park or Rice Institute.[76]

In elementary schools, a popular intermural competition was indoor baseball that was played with something like a large softball and took place in gymnasiums. Austin Elementary School on the east edge of downtown won the city title five out of six years to start the 1910s. The YMCA downtown hosted an indoor baseball season called the Poultry League with the teams sporting monikers like the Wyandottes, Bantams and Leghorns.[77]

One exception to the lack of baseball on the high school level was St. Thomas High School, which had gotten its start under the lofty name of St. Thomas College in 1900 in spite of the fact that most of its students were clearly high schoolers. The Eagles' interest in baseball was constant, and they found opponents wherever they could. In 1925 alone, St. Thomas faced Galveston's Ball High, Houston's South End Junior High and St. Mary's Seminary.

By 1935, the driving force behind St. Thomas baseball was Father James Wilson, a Canadian whom the Basilian Order assigned to Houston. He would remain as baseball coach for over 20 years, molding top teams of varsity, junior varsity and freshman players. In addition to his duties for the Eagles, Fr. Wilson coached other youth teams including the Toms in the mid-1940s and the strong Town House Buffs team that won a city championship in 1950.[78]

During Fr. Wilson's tenure, St. Thomas produced a number of schoolboy heroes who went on to become top players in the college and semi-pro ranks. Among the stand-outs from those years who are now in the school's Athletic Hall of Fame were Burkey O'Rourke, Steve Oggero, Bobby Fretz at A&M, Sam Campise at UH, Johnny Finch at Rice, and Jackie Moore, an all-state catcher who eventually dropped out of school but ended up making the big leagues and later coached for the Astros.[79]

By the 1950s, St. Thomas was hosting an annual tournament that brought together almost every Catholic boys school in Texas. Parochial teams from Dallas, San Antonio, Beaumont, Galveston, Yoakum, Victoria, Ennis and Corpus Christi journeyed to play at the campus on Memorial Drive and the big stadium home of the Texas League Buffs. It generally went quite well for the home team. The St. Thomas Eagles won state parochial school titles in 1953, 1955, 1956, 1960 and 1961.[80]

(TOP)
The team from South End Junior High School puts on their game faces about 1918.
Houston Metropolitan Research Center, Houston Public Library

(BOTTOM)
Reagan Bulldogs pitcher Jimmy Bethea confers with Coach Lee Roy Ashmore, Edwin Butler and Jimmy Ashmore in the mid-1950s.
Courtesy Reagan High School Library

Public schools soon got on board with the more organized programs. The University Interscholastic League began sanctioned high school baseball playoffs in 1948, more than a quarter century after they had established a state championship in football. The first Houston school to take the title was the Reagan Bulldogs of 1952, a powerful team that placed five players on the All-State squad. Pitcher Jack Schultea was a unanimous pick, and he was joined in the honor by Pete Vance, Wayne Tucker, Jimmy Bethea and Vito Marchese, who stole a record four bases in the tournament. Other stars include John Wolda and Don Yeakley.[81]

The title game against Crozier Tech of Dallas did not get off to a flying start. Staff ace Schultea was jittery, and the fielders behind him committed four errors to allow five unearned runs in the first inning. But Schultea settled in, giving up only two hits the rest of the way, while Coach Lee Roy Ashmore's Bulldogs tallied eight runs to take the state championship. Amid the celebration, "Schultea was the happiest of a happy lot. He could not talk coherently."[82]

The most famous player on that '52 Reagan team was a sophomore reserve named Wayne Graham. Though pitcher Schultea and center fielder Bethea starred at UH and went on to a few seasons of minor league baseball, Graham was the sole Bulldog to make it to the show, grabbing brief stints with the Phillies and the Mets. Coaching is where Graham made his biggest mark, however. He learned from one of the best, playing for Coach Bibb Falk at the University of Texas.

After retiring as a pro player following the 1967 season, Graham finished his degree at UT then became the coach at Scarborough High School in Houston. From there he moved to San Jacinto Junior College, where he led the Gators to five NJCAA national titles in a six-year span and earned five awards as national coach of the year. From there he took over a Rice program in 1992 that could count only seven winning seasons in 78 years of Southwest Conference baseball. The school had never been to an NCAA Tournament, but under Wayne Graham, the Owls made the tournament 18 years in a row and had seven trips to Omaha including garnering the first national championship in the history of Rice, a baseball title in 2003. Among the many players that he sent to the pro ranks are superstars such as Roger Clemens and Lance Berkman.[83]

In the segregated world of Texas, African-American high schools played under the separate jurisdiction of the Prairie View Interscholastic League (PVIL) until the late 1960s. Much like their white counterpart, the PVIL sanctioned state football competition for years before they did the same for baseball. When they began awarding a Texas title in 1956, Jack Yates High School of Houston won the first three championships in a row. In fact, the Lions didn't drop a single game in three finals series against Dallas Washington, Waco Moore and Tyler Scott over the three years.

Sammy Taylor was the star hurler on the Lions staff when they captured the first title. He won the District 3 title by throwing a no-hitter and striking out 14. His teammate Joe Cooper blasted a two-run homer in that game. When Yates met Booker T. Washington of Dallas in the final at Houston's Public School Stadium, 1300 attended to see the "first Negro schoolboy baseball championship in history." Once again right-hander Taylor got the start, this time fanning 11. Ivory Jones had five RBIs for the Lions. It didn't hurt that Dallas Washington committed seven errors.[84]

The Yates Lions were led by one of the most remarkable high school coaches in the city's history. Andrew "Pat" Patterson had attended an integrated high school in East Chicago, but opted to come to the segregated South to Wiley College because it was cheap, and it offered him the chance to play some serious baseball. After graduation, Patterson went to the Negro Leagues and became a top player. Though he continued to play during the baseball season, his regular job starting in 1938 was coaching almost every sport at Yates High School. Moreover, he was good at it. In addition to the success in baseball, Coach Patterson led the Lions to five state titles in basketball and three more in football. It was a doubly fitting legacy since Pat Patterson was one of the primary founders of the PVIL in 1939.[85]

Pat Patterson was no jack of all trades reserve in pro ball, either. He was one of the top players with the top clubs in the leagues: the Homestead Grays, Pittsburgh Crawfords and Kansas City Monarchs. He was one of the black players who was recruited to go to Mexico at the start of the 1940s when Jorge Pasqual was recruiting Major League talent. Patterson and his wife Gladys were married in Mexico, and the team threw a big party complete with a roast pig. But when it was time to go back to school, Patterson returned to Houston. In 1946, his Newark Eagles team was in the middle of the Negro World Series with the Kansas City Monarchs, and Othello Renfroe recalls that Pat "had to go back to his high school coaching job in Texas." Pat Patterson ended his career with HISD as a district athletic director and administrator.[86]

The Houston area would claim back-to-back state UIL baseball titles in 1960 and '61. First up were the Bellaire Cardinals who won the championship by beating San Antonio Harlandale 5-4 in the finals. Johnny Crain was the starting pitcher for the Cards, and he got the win by hanging on during a furious Harlandale comeback try. Gary Schessler and Tom Hillary also made big contributions for Bellaire. It would be the first of seven state titles for the school to date.[87]

The Ganders of Baytown brought home the state championship in 1961, shutting out the defending Bellaire Cardinals along the way. The first shot at the final game was rained out, but then Ronnie Kluch and Robert Oliver combined to pitch a tight gem of a ball game. After polishing off Lubbock Monterrey 3-1, Coach Don

Truehardt's team was welcomed back to town by a throng of over 1,000 cheering fans on their home campus.[88]

YOUTH BALL

During the decades prior to World War II, American Legion baseball took the place of high school ball. Though it continues today as a popular supplement to school teams, in Houston of the 1920s and 1930s, it was the bee's knees. Legion rules required that all teams in cities with a population bigger than 50,000 people be made up of boys from the same high school. Mixing was not allowed, so in big cities, they were de facto high school baseball teams in most ways.

One top notch star of American Legion ball in the 1930s was pitcher Clem Hausmann. Playing for the team sponsored by Balshaw's Grocery and managed by Lawrence Mancuso, brother of big leaguers Gus and Frank, he earned local headlines for his mound heroics which included a no-hitter against the All-City Jeeps in 1936. Balshaw's team won the city Legion title that year by taking a hard fought series over the defending state champion Missouri Pacific Bearkats team. They then went on to top the Galveston Rattlesnakes, the island champs. The team captain and Balshaw's other star player was shortstop J.P. Wood who soon headed off to Rice University and eventually the Detroit Tigers. At the same time Wood was playing for Balshaw's junior team, he was also on the infield for the Grocery-sponsored adult entrant in the Community League.

Following that Galveston series, a controversy erupted over Hausmann's eligibility that became big news in the Houston papers. Though Hausmann lived in the neighborhood around Milby High School, he had been attending St. Anthony's Seminary in San Antonio to study for the priesthood. After a much-publicized hearing, he was allowed to continue playing with his childhood teammates from the Southeast side based on the determination that St. Anthony's Seminary was not a high school at all.

Balshaw's Grocery went on to win series over teams from Port Arthur, Austin and Crockett and gain the state title, making it a back-to-back for the City of Houston. It earned them a banquet at the Canton Tea Garden Restaurant on Main and a trip to play ball in New Orleans. In spite of his earlier protestations that he wouldn't play pro baseball if the Yankees asked him and "offered me a million dollars," Clem Hausmann did not enter the priesthood and instead spent 13 seasons in professional baseball including two trips to the Boston Red Sox.[89]

One of the men who coached Hausmann in Legion ball was Billye Miles, a former semi-pro pitcher who wanted to keep a hand in the game after he quit playing in 1927. Over the next 45 years, he coached thousands of boys on a variety of teams, American Legion and otherwise. Besides Clem Hausmann, at least two of his other young charges made it to the bigs, Gus Mancuso and J.P. Woods.[90]

There were several men who believed

in the value of organized youth baseball in those pre-Little League days and spent their time and money making the dream come true in Houston. New Orleans native B.J. Gillan, an old semi-pro player, worked with both youth and men's teams from the 1920s till he retired in 1948 when his "old joints were getting too creaky to hit to the infield, to fungo to the outfield."Jack Nagle devoted so much time to organizing teams and leagues that when he died, the City Parks Department named a ball field in MacGregor Park after him.[91]

The man who brought the most big league credibility to the task was Watty Watkins, Houstonian and hero of the 1931 World Series for the Cardinals. As early as 1938, his first year out of baseball, Watkins teamed up with his old Buffs friend Carey Selph to work with Junior League baseball programs donating bats and helping organize teams. After the war, he worked with Fr. Wilson on the Town House Buffs teams including the 1950 club that won the state Teen Age Baseball title.

"This Teen Age League is just what the kids needed," said Watkins. "There ought to be 13 leagues like this around town. There ought to be enough so's every kid who wanted to could have a chance to play."[92]

Duke Duquesnay was yet another champion of kid baseball, and his close to 60 years of effort might have topped them all. He worked not only in hands-on coaching with teams that included the Heights Rebels of the Ranger League and the American Legion Bearkats, but he made regular phone calls to Houston businessmen asking them for donations to buy bats and balls or clear brush from a potential new ball diamond. Starting

Clem Hausmann, standing fourth from right, led his American Legion team to the Texas State Championship in 1936. He would later reach the big leagues with the Boston Red Sox.

Courtesy Clem Hausmann, Jr.

The Houston Little League All-Stars won the Little League World Series in 1950 behind the pitching of Billy Martin.
Courtesy Little League Museum, Williamsport, PA

his efforts to give boys the wherewithal to play baseball in the first years of the twentieth century, P.E. Duquesnay kept at it through three generations of ball players, many of whom grew up to become his backers.[93]

Buffs president Fred Ankenman said of Duquesnay that "he meant more to youngsters and parents of this city than any other man I know. He worked unceasingly for baseball and kids in the same proportion." Dating to a time when boys were left to their own devices, Duke Duquesnay's final reward came as Little League grew to provide opportunities for almost all kids to get baseball facilities and coaching.[94]

In 1950, Duquesnay was assistant manager for the Houston Team that became Little League World Champions. The team of 11- and 12-year olds from the Bayou City had run through the competition at Williamsport on pitching and defense. Young ace Billy Martin had no-hit the team from Westerly, Rhode Island in the quarter finals, his second no-no of the season. The Texans took Kankakee, Illinois, in the semis and then beat Bridgeport, Connecticut, to capture the title at the Fourth ever Little League World Series. Once again, 12-year-old Martin was masterful, allowing only a single base knock, one walk and fanning eleven. The returning champs were met by a crowd at Union Station that included Ellington Field's brass band.[95]

It represented a meteoric rise for the Little League program in the Bayou City. Only a few years prior, boys from across the city were forced to compete for spots on just a handful of teams. The initial tryouts took place at Canada Dry Field located behind the bottling company of the same name, a company for which Eddie Dyer was a vice president. With so many turned away, it left a few ill feelings, but with a greater capacity and a national title, Houston Little League was off and running.

The homegrown baseball talent of the 1920s and 1930s started getting press in the Houston newspapers in a way reserved today for an exceptional high school quarterback or point guard. As early as 1919, John Berly gained notice for throwing two no-hitters for the Newsboys ball team. His pitching eventually earned him a debut with the hometown Buffaloes at the age of 20 and an 18 year career in the majors and minors.[96]

Sometimes, young baseball hopefuls journeyed to the big city of Houston in search of fulfilling their diamond dreams. Teenager Lon Warneke moved from Mount Ida, Arkansas at the urging of his sister, Kate, and her firefighter husband, Buck. Warneke played semi-pro ball and got a job delivering Western Union telegrams on a bicycle. Eventually, using the convenient connection between his beautician sister and her customer who just happened to be the wife of Houston Buffs president Fred Ankenman, Lon Warneke secured a tryout in front of the local team's manager, Pancho Snyder. Though he proved to be a bust as a first baseman, Snyder liked him as a pitcher, signing him to a contract and farming him out to Laurel, Mississippi in the Cotton States League. Warneke, who came to be known as the Arkansas Hummingbird, went on to win 192 big league games with the Cubs and Cardinals.[97]

The All-City High School Team for 1952 was dominated by players from the Reagan Bulldogs who won the state title that season.

Courtesy Jack Schultea

Today the Houston area is a well-known hotbed of baseball talent, but the much smaller city of earlier days was producing stars from the sandlots, too. Much as the true fans of the 1970s went to watch top high school pitchers like David Clyde, Roger Clemens and Greg Swindell, fans in the early to mid-20th century flocked to get a glimpse of Heinie Schuble, the Mancusos, Clem Hausmann, John Berly, Watty Watkins, Bobby Fretz, Johnny Rizzo and many others.

Youth and high school baseball have continued to grow and thrive in the Houston area. Rice's famous coach, Wayne Graham, himself a former star of the local sandlots, had this to say in 2002: "It's hard to believe the difference in baseball in Houston now from the early 1950s. Then, we had to find ways to play. Now, you have to find ways not to play."[98]

---

1 GDM 25 December 1867; GDN 16 June 1884; Daily Houston Telegraph 21 May 1874; http://www.tshaonline.org/handbook/online/articles/eqh09; History of the Houston & Texas Central Railroad up to the year 1903. Yearbook for 1903.; GDN 23 October 1883

2 HP 22 April 1897; HP 20 July 1896; GDN 4 July 1894

3 GDN 13 June 1896; GDN 14 May 1894; GDN 30 April 1894; GDN 5 September 1892

4 GDN 8 April 1892

5 HP 13 December 1893; HP 20 May 1894; HP 17 April 1898; HP 16 March 1898; GDN 13 March 1893; GDN 28 September 1895

6 HP 16 March 1894; HP 17 March 1894; HP 24 April 1894; HP 2 May 1894;

7 HP 14 May 1905; HP 22 March 1916; HP 6 September 1916;

8 GDN 6 September 1916; HC 26 July 1931; Ankenman, Fred, Sr.. Four Score and More: The Autobiography of Fred N. Ankenman, Sr.. (Texas Gulf Coast Historical Association, 1980)

9 HP 23 March 1918; Vance, Mike. Houston's Sporting Life: 1900-1950. (Arcadi, 2011)

10 HP 18 April 1904, HP 13 June 1904; HP 19 June 1904; HP 8 March 1910; Ankenman, Fred, Sr.. Four Score and More: The Autobiography of Fred N. Ankenman, Sr.. (Texas Gulf Coast Historical Association, 1980)

11 HP 13 March 1921

12 HP 12 May 1894; GDN 13 June 1896; HP 30 July 1930

13 HI 4 June 1932; HI 9 June 1923; HI 9 February 1924; HI 26 April 1924

14 HP 16 May 1915;

15 Houston Arts and Media Collection. Interview with Felix Fraga and Lupe Fraga conducted by Mike Vance. 12 July 2013; Port Arthur News 26 July 1945; HP 30 July 1930

16 Port Arthur New 26 July 1945

17 HP 10 May 1927; HP 4 June 1933; Victoria Advocate 20 April 1980; Evans, Wilbur and Little, Bill. *Texas Longhorn Baseball: Kings of the Diamond.* (Strode, 1983)

18 Gregory, Lloyd. Looking 'em Over. (Gregory, 1968); http://www.baseball-reference.com

19 HC 8 September 1929; HC 9 September 1929; HC 15 September 1929

20 Houston Arts and Media Collection. Interview with Felix Fraga and Lupe Fraga conducted by Mike Vance. 12 July 2013; Houston City Directory ; HP 4 April 1953; HC 7 June 1931; Google Earth 1944 layer accessed 7 September 2013; HP 1 April 1905

21 Kreneck, Thomas H.. *Mexican American Odyssey: Felix Tijerina, Entrepreneur and Civic Leader, 1905-1965* (Texas A&M Press, 2001); HP 3 May 1935; HP 11 July 1935; HP 30 August 1935

22 HP 30 August 1933; Kreneck, Thomas H.. *Mexican American Odyssey: Felix Tijerina, Entrepreneur and Civic Leader, 1905-1965* (Texas A&M Press, 2001); HP 30 August 1935; HP 23 May 1933; HP 11 July 1935

23 HP 14 July 1935;

24 HP 14 July 1935; HP 25 August 1935; HP 26 August 1935; HP 27 August 1935; Seymour, Harold. Baseball: The people's game, Volume 3. (Oxford University Press, 1990); http://www.museumofbuford/shoemakers;

25 HP 3 September 1935; Brown, Gary. *Singing a Lonesome Song: Texas Prison Tales.* (Taylor Trade Publishing, 2001)

26 HP 6 September 1935; Brown, Gary. *Singing a Lonesome Song: Texas Prison Tales.* (Taylor Trade Publishing, 2001); Abilene Reporter-News 14 April 1929

27 Brown, Gary. *Singing a Lonesome Song: Texas Prison Tales.* (Taylor Trade Publishing, 2001)

28 HP 9 September 1935; Brown, Gary. *Singing a Lonesome Song: Texas Prison Tales.* (Taylor Trade Publishing, 2001)

29 http://www.baytownlibrary.org/gallery/index.php/tag/27/refinery; Texas State Historical Marker, Humble Oil and Refining Company;

30 http://sabr.org/bioproj/person/b8f61519;

31 http://www.dvrbs.com/people/CamdenPeople-SigJakucki.htm; New York Times 8 October 1944; http://sabr.org/bioproj/person/763c0a5d ;

32 Kellar, William H.. *Make Haste Slowly: Moderates, Conservatives and School Desegregation in Houston* (Texas A&M Press, 1999)

33 Galveston Tribune 1 April 1943; Freeport Facts 13 May 1943

34 Bullock, Steven. *Playing for their Nation: Baseball and the American Military During World War II.* (University of Nebraska Press, 2004); Freeport Facts 29 April 1945; Port Arthur News 4 June 1945; Port Arthur News 16 July 1945; Corpus Christi Times 28 June 1945

35 HP 18 May 1944; http://www.baseball-reference.com

36 http://www.baseballinwartime.com/player_biographies/rizzo_johnny.htm; http://www.baseballinwartime.com/player_biographies/mancuso_frank.htm; http://www.baseballinwartime.com/player_biographies/munger_red.htm;

37 GDN 6 June 1943

38 Galveston Tribune 22 June 1943; Freeport Facts 17 June 1943; http://www.baseball-reference.com; Neyer, Rob. *Rob Neyer's Big Book of Baseball Legends: The Truth, The Lies and Everything Else* (Touchstone, 2008) http://www.dvrbs.com/PEOPLE/CamdenPeople-SigJakucki.htm

39 Galveston Tribune 16 September 1943; http://www.baseballinwartime.com/player_biographies/tebbetts_birdie.htm

40 Wayne Carroll, *The Stratton Story*, Groesbeck Journal 12 November 2009;

41 Colorado County News 27 August 1948; http://discoverweimar.com/np_history_.html; http://www.weimartx.org/index.php?pageID=3026; JP 30 July 1950;

42 Madden, W.C. and Stewart, Patrick J.. *The College World Series: A Baseball History 1947-2003.* (McFarland, 2004); Evans, Wilbur and Little, Bill. *Texas Longhorn Baseball: Kings of the Diamond.* (Strode, 1983)

43 The History Center, Diboll, Texas. Interview with Roscoe Ivy done by Jonathan Gerland on 7 February 2012;

44 Houston Arts and Media Collection. Interview with Felix Fraga and Lupe Fraga conducted by Mike Vance. 12 July 2013

45 Stout, DJ. *The Amazing Tale of Mr. Herbert and his Fabulous Alpine Cowboys Baseball Team.* (UT Press, 2010)

46 The History Center, Diboll, Texas. Interview with Roscoe Ivy done by Jonathan Gerland on 7 February 2012; http://www.baseball-reference.com; http://sabr.org/bioproj/person/4c82b649

47 Bobby Fretz Scrapbook; Tacoma Public Library Digital Image Archives at http://search.tacomapubliclibrary.org/images/dt6n.asp?krequest=subjects+contains+Baseball%20players%20Tacoma%201950-1960; AABC World Series Results at http://archive.is/qFV9; Baytown Sun 22 September 1954; HP 23 January 1956; Interview with Jack Schultea conducted by Mike Vance. 13 September 2013

48 *Distinguished R Man Awards Program.* 11 November 1975; HP 1 May 1913; HP 7 April 1914

49 http://ricehistorycorner.com/2011/01/05/rice-baseball-vs-chinese-university-of-hawaii-1915/; HP 1 April 1915; Franks, Joel. Asian Pacific Americans and Baseball: A History. (McFarland, 2008); HC 27 March 1916

50 http://sabr.org/bioproj/person/f64fded8 ; Rice Baseball History; HP 5 April 1917; 22 December 1918 http://grfx.cstv.com/photos/schools/rice/sports/m-basebl/auto_pdf/07-mg-baseball-history.pdf

51 http://sabr.org/bioproj/person/b3e94581; *The Campanile.* Rice Institute 1920, 1921, 1922;

52 HP 15 April 1921; HP 16 April 1921; HP 4 April 1921

53 Rice Thresher 29 April 1921; http://ricehistorycorner.com/2010/11/24/eddie-dyer-and-the-polite-1921-rice-baseball-team/

54 http://ricehistorycorner.com/2010/11/24/eddie-dyer-and-the-polite-1921-rice-baseball-team/; http://sabr.org/bioproj/person/b3e94581

55 *Distinguished R Man Awards Program.* 25 October 1974; *The Campanile.* Rice Institute, 1933; HP 5 April 1932; http://www.baseball-reference.com

56 http://www.baseball-reference.com;

57 http://www.baseball-reference.com

58 http://www.baseballinwartime.com/those_who_served/those_who_served_atoz.htm ; http://www.baseball-reference.com; http://www.baseballalmanac.com; Distinguished R Man Awards program. 25 November 1972

59 http://www.baseball-reference.com

60 HP 15 April 1952; GDN 30 July 1949; Houston Arts and Media Collection. Interview with Felix Fraga and Lupe Fraga conducted by Mike Vance. 12 July 2013

61 GDN 30 July 1949; Houston Arts and Media Collection. Interview with Felix Fraga and Lupe Fraga conducted by Mike Vance. 12 July 2013; Interview with Jack Schultea conducted by Mike Vance. 13 September 2013.

62 The Houstonian. University of Houston Yearbook, 1951.

63 Honolulu Advertiser 8 July 2008

64 Houston Cougar Baseball History http://grfx.cstv.com/photos/schools/hou/sports/m-basebl/auto_pdf/08-baseguide-pg105-119.pdf

65 http://www.swac.org/ViewArticle.dbml?DB_OEM_ID=27400&ATCLID=205246152

66 HP 18 April 1905; HP 19 April 1905; HP 20 April 1905

67 HI 19 April 1930; HI 20 April 1929; Bay City Daily Tribune 10 February 1932

68 http://grfx.cstv.com/photos/schools/swac/genrel/auto_pdf/09champs.pdf;

69 Houston Arts and Media Collection. Interviews with Marie "Red" Mahoney conducted by Marsha Franty and Mike Vance. 5 February 2012 and 2 September 2012.

70 Houston Arts and Media Collection. Interviews with Marie "Red" Mahoney conducted by Marsha Franty and Mike Vance. 5 February 2012 and 2 September 2012.

71 Houston Arts and Media Collection. Interviews with Marie "Red" Mahoney conducted by Marsha Franty and Mike Vance. 5 February 2012 and 2 September 2012.

72 http://www.aagpbl.org/index.cfm/pages/league/12/league-history;

73 Chicago Tribune 2 August 1947; Berlage, Gai. *Women in Baseball: The Forgotten History* (Westport, Conn: Praeger, 1994)

74 http://www.tbhof.org/features/feature-20060322.htm

75 HP 9 May 1915; HP 16 May 1915; HP 31 March 1928

76 Report of Houston City Schools, 1909; HP 2 April 1915; HP 7 April 1921

77 HP 15 June 1915; HP 28 April 1901;

78 http://sths.org/hall-of-fame/162-rev-james-f-wilson-csb-; HP 7 July 1944

79 HP 23 May 1956; Paris (Texas) News 5 August 1954; http://www.baseball-reference.com

80 Fifth Annual Texas Catholic High School Baseball Tournament program, 6-7 May 1955; St. Thomas High School Athletic Department. Madelyn Garza.

81 http://uil100.org/archives/athletics/baseball.php; HP 24 May 1952; HP 6 June 1952; HC 10 June 2002; http://www2.uiltexas.org/athletics/archives/baseball/tournament_records.html

82 HC 6 June 1952; HC 10 June 2002

83 http://www.riceowls.com/sports/m-basebl/mtt/graham_wayne00.html; http://www.baseball-reference.com; Conference USA Baseball Media Guide 2013

84 HP 17 May 1956; HP 18 May 1956; HP 24 May 1956' HP 26 May 1956

85 PVIL Collection. PVAMU Libraries; http://pvilca.org/files/2012-PVIL_Banquet_Book.pdf; Rogosin, Donn. *Invisible Men: Life in Baseball's Negro Leagues.* (Kodansha America, 1983, 1995)

86 Rogosin, Donn. *Invisible Men: Life in Baseball's Negro Leagues.* (Kodansha America, 1983, 1995); Holway, John. *Voices from the Great Black Baseball Leagues.* (Dover, 1975, 2010)

87 Lubbock Avalanche Journal 5 June 1960; http://espn.go.com/high-school/baseball/story/_/id/4089569/bellaire-focused-ending-title-drought/;

88 Baytown Sun 25 May 1961; Baytown Sun 11 June 1961

89 GDN 14 July 1936; GDN 15 July 1936; San Antonio Light 14 July 1936; HP 13 August 1936; Clem Hausmann Scrapbook; Pampa Daily News 4 August 1935

90 HC 9 May 1976

91 Houston Press 4 April 1948; HP 19 May 1952

92 Sporting News 1938; Houston Press August 1950

93 Houston Press 23 June 1943; HP 21 June 1942; HP 17 July 1930

94 HP 7 November 1965

95 Wallechinsky, David and Wallace, Irving. The People's Almanac. (1975); Helena Independent Record, 4 September 1950; Vance, Mike. Houston's Sporting Life: 1900-1950. (Arcadia, 2011); Williamsburg Gazette and Bulletin 28 August 1950

96 Houston: A History and Guide. Federal Writers Project. American Guide Series. (Anson Jones Press, 1942); http://www.baseball-reference.com

97 http://sabr.org/bioproj/person/5a2fe3c9

98 HC 10 June 2002

KEY

GDN – *Galveston Daily News*
HI – *Houston Informer*
HP – *Houston Post*
CD – *Chicago Defender*
HC – *Houston Chronicle*

CHAPTER THIRTEEN

SPRING TRAINING & EXHIBITIONS

BY MIKE VANCE

Over two-thirds of all the players enshrined in Baseball's Hall of Fame have played in the ball parks of Houston. For those whose careers were prior to the advent of the our city's Major League entry in 1962, almost all passed through town as members of a ball club here for exhibition games or spring training.

The St. Louis Browns, winners of four straight American Association titles, posed for one of the best team photos in baseball history in 1888.

Courtesy Library of Congress

Today, major league teams gather in Florida and Arizona. Travel distances are short between princely baseball complexes fitted out especially for spring training. One hundred years earlier, however, when things like weight training and conditioning coaches for ballplayers were all but unheard of, a team tossed the ball around, ran a few laps and sweated out the off season's toxins, often while playing exhibitions against mostly minor league competition.

One thing that hasn't changed is the need for hospitable climes in the month of March, and South Texas was one such destination. Many teams in the early twentieth century went to Georgia or the Carolinas, a handful to California or even Cuba. Others preferred resort settings such as Hot Springs, Arkansas, or in Texas at Marlin, Mineral Wells or Hot Wells near San Antonio.[1] The warm mineral waters in those towns were much sought after as an aid to good health.

Texas more than held its own as a place for ball players to warm their bones and get into playing shape and a baseball frame of mind. From 1900, when most

Charles Comiskey and Ned Williamson were two of the earliest baseball stars to visit Houston. Williamson's studio photo features a ball suspended by wire, a common prop of the day.

Courtesy Library of Congress

big league clubs started spending their spring on the road, until 1941 when the St. Louis Browns and Boston Braves each trained in San Antonio,[2] all but two of the 16 major league teams did at least one season of prep in Texas, including towns as far flung as Eagle Pass.

Fifteen times, Major League clubs chose Houston or Galveston as their spring base. With their close proximity and super-convenient intercity train schedules, the locale allowed ball clubs to enjoy the amenities of the area while having two solid minor league teams against which they could play games.

The first teams to "thaw out" in the area were the Chicago White Stockings and Louisville Colonels in 1895, a time when the entire concept of spring training had yet to be universally accepted. A number of team owners saw no need for the expenses connected with travel and lodging. The White Stockings, controlled by Albert Spalding and managed by 43-year-old first baseman/catcher Cap Anson,[3] were among the pioneers of

Adrian "Cap" Anson brought his Chicago charges to train in Galveston with frequent side trips to Houston. Courtesy Library of Congress

training in the South.

At the start of March 1895, they joined forces with John McCloskey's Louisville squad and based themselves in Galveston and Houston respectively. For the Chicago boys, things could hardly have been more convenient. They were lodging at the Beach Hotel and practicing immediately next door at Beach Park, a facility built literally on the sand and where high tide often swept under the fence into the outfield.

As reported by the *Galveston Daily News*, the baseball training sounded fairly basic. On their third day in town, Anson's team, often referred to as the Colts because of their lack of veterans, "put in two good hours of work in the forenoon, followed by a run down the beach, and showed up again promptly at 2 o'clock at the park where a large crowd was waiting for them."[4] The afternoon session consisted of fielding grounders and flies, and a drill modern fans think has fallen by the wayside, laying down bunts.[5]

Two days later, the two began playing games against one another in both Houston and Galveston, a situation that continued for about a month with many of the games being split squad. The first stringers of each club would change cities for alternate games.[6]

Blessed with good weather, the teams put in lots of work, losing only one out of 40 days to rain.[7] Anson's charges did take one day off for recreation. At 10 o'clock on the morning of April 8, all but three of the White Stockings, along with a few guests and reporters, boarded the top cabin sloop Jennie and sailed over to Bolivar to do some fishing. On the afternoon trip back, a freshening breeze and the rougher waves that accompanied it sent at least half a dozen of the players, including Anson, either below deck or to some other place suited to ride out "Neptune's Revenge," all made slightly more nauseating by smoke from pitcher Wild Bill Hutchinson's cigar.[8]

The two teams headed north after expressing much praise and gratitude to the citizens of Houston and Galveston. In the case of Cap Anson, he claimed that the good gates for exhibition games had made his Colts the only club to break even among those National Leaguers who came South, and he promised to return the following year, a pledge that was made good.[9]

Chicago pitcher, Clark Griffith, who would earn his Hall of Fame induction as longtime owner of the Washington Senators, went one step further.

"Some time in the future," Griffith told the News, "when I quit baseball. I'm going to spend a whole summer here so I can get my fill of surf bathing. I did not get enough of it."

The big league team that spent more time training in Houston than any other was the St. Louis Cardinals, establishing a relationship between club executives and local business leaders that would eventually result in Houston becoming a Cardinal farm team.

The Cards first trained here in 1904, the final season for the ball park at the old Fairgrounds. Scheduled for the following

Charles "Kid" Nichols won 361 games during his Hall of Fame career. In retirement, he owned a movie theater and vaudeville house in Kansas City and excelled at his other sports passion—bowling.

Courtesy Library of Congress

season, as well, they were forced into an eleventh hour move to Marlin due to the last minute nature of preparations for Houston's new West End Park.[10, 11] In 1906, however, the Cardinals returned to Houston and would make it their spring home for the next two seasons after that, too.

The latter two springs of that run, St. Louis was joined in the area by the Washington Senators who made their headquarters in Galveston.[12] Much as Chicago and Louisville had done some years prior, Washington scheduled games against the Cardinals and Buffaloes in Houston.[13]

The Senators spent three consecutive

Young Walter Johnson experienced his first spring training in Houston at West End Park.
Courtesy Library of Congress

Marches in the Island City, a span that would include the first two spring training experiences for young Walter Johnson, arguably the most dominant pitcher who ever lived.

Johnson and Sleepy Bill Burns were the pitchers on March 8, 1909, turning in a winning performance over the local squad at West End Park in spite of complaints of general early-spring stiffness. Following the game, Washington manager, Joe Cantillon, allowed Burns to leave the team and go visit his family in San Angelo since he was already in shape.

That game marked a first for area fans, as well. Reporters saw fit to describe a new contraption never before seen locally. Shaped like an overhanging "L" and covered with two-inch mesh, it was called a batting cage, designed to knock down balls that were missed or fouled off.[14]

The young Walter Johnson must have been slightly less stiff when he came to Houston the following spring. He pitched a full game against the Buffaloes on March 7th, striking out 14.[15]

The St. Louis Browns trained in Houston in 1909 and 1910, and the media highlight of the first visit was a story that Houston team owner Otto Sens snuck the Browns star hurler, Rube Waddell, out of the hotel to take him duck hunting in La Porte. Though amended a day later, local papers reported that St. Louis manager Jimmy McAleer was none too pleased to find his pitcher AWOL and ordered

The Browns' Rube Waddell was a hunting guest of Buffs owner, Otto Sens.
Courtesy Library of Congress

Waddell back to Houston forthwith. Rube grudgingly complied, bringing eight ducks with him, one of which he promised in its entirety to teammate Art Griggs who was battling tonsillitis.[16, 17]

Frank Chance and his New York Yankees were here in 1914.[18] Like the Browns, the Yankees chose to stay at the Rice Hotel, but in true New York style, they booked an entire floor of the newly rebuilt version of the city's top hostelry.

The Yankees team that trained in Houston in 1914 was not one of their championship squads, but they were nonetheless feted by the locals.
Courtesy Library of Congress

True to established practice, split squads of regulars and "yannigans"[19] played daily games against the Texas League entries from Houston and Galveston. The New Yorkers also fit in a St. Patrick's Day trip to Texas City to play against the Twenty-Second Infantry stationed at the very large U.S. Army camp there. After giving the Army a sound drubbing, the team enjoyed supper at the officer's mess, took in four boxing matches among the soldiers and caught a late interurban back to Houston.[20]Unlike previous teams' sojourns in Houston, the Yanks time was marked with some complaints about cold, wet weather and a greater than expected number of losses to their minor league competition.[21]

In spite of the slightly less than perfect stay, the athletes were guests of honor at an elaborate banquet at the Rice Hotel featuring a dozen courses, a special Yankee cake, about one hundred guests, and remarks from the Peerless Leader that "Houston suited him from the ground up as a training camp."[22]

The Browns returned to Houston in 1915, and in 1921, the Boston Braves were in Galveston, marking the last time a Major League ball club would hold training in Southeast Texas.

That was not, however, the last big time team to train in Houston. Rube Foster and his Chicago American Giants arrived in Houston on March 3, 1924, with much fanfare among the local African-American community.[23] They were the first black ball team to train in Houston, and they based their practices at the new Scott Street Park in Third Ward.[24]

Packed with top talent such as Cristobal Torriente, Dave Malarcher, Jelly Gardner and Houston native, Leroy Grant, the Chicagoans worked out and played games against Prairie View and Paul Quinn College as well as the professional Houston Black Buffaloes during their two weeks in town.[25] Team owner Foster and his wife also fit in a motor car trip to Galveston.[26]

On their last Saturday night in town, the team was honored with a dinner and smoker given by the Colored Commercial Club at the American Mutual Building on Prairie Avenue. Music was furnished by the Antioch orchestra and praises were spoken by the editor of the *Houston Informer* and the principal of Colored High School. Rube Foster, guest of honor and founder of the Negro National League, gave a rousing speech.[2728]

On their way back to Chicago, the American Giants stopped in Foster's hometown of Calvert, Texas, where stores closed at noon so the locals, both black and white, could come see their most famous former citizen lead his team against the Calvert nine.[29]

The other frequent visitor for spring training in Houston was the most famous Negro League club of all, the Kansas City Monarchs. After playing a huge post season series here in September 1929, the Monarchs returned to Houston for training the following spring, suffering through "the coldest weather ever known in Texas."[30] Rising above the frigid conditions, the city would remain a popular destination for the team, and they would return several times before the downfall of Negro League baseball in the late 1940s.[31]

The more frequent reason for visits from big time ball clubs during the pre-Major League years, though, was for exhibition games or barnstorming tours either before or following their summer season up north.

As early as 1874, the Robert E. Lees of New Orleans paid a heralded visit to Houston and Galveston, taking on multiple local clubs in each city.[32, 33] The Lees had played the famous Cincinnati Red Stockings in 1870. Their fellow New Orleanians, the Southern Base Ball Club, had been among Cincy's opponents in the first all-professional and undefeated tour of 1869, so the visitors offered the first out-of-state, big city legitimacy to the area baseball teams.

Future Hall of Famers Tim Keefe (left) and Mike "King" Kelly (above) were with the great New York Giants tour that barnstormed through Texas in the fall of 1887.

Courtesy Library of Congress

The Indianapolis Blues, a top minor league outfit, came through the area in early March of 1877, though it is unclear whether differences over the Houston venue were resolved in time for them to stop here before heading on to Galveston. Coming only a year after the formation of the National League, Indy represented the next level of professional baseball.

Ten years later, the Bayou City welcomed not one, but three outfits from the National League. The famous New York Giants, heavily laden with future Hall of Famers, passed through both Houston and Galveston in mid-November 1887 on a grand tour to California. Joining Tim Keefe, Buck Ewing and Roger Connor of New York was the even more renowned Mike "King" Kelly.[34] Giants manager, John Montgomery Ward, missed the Bayou City stop when he returned to the Big Apple.

Combative Giants manager John McGraw's fisticuffs in Houston made national news. Courtesy Library of Congress

Christy Mathewson (above) and Bugs Raymond both drew capacity crowds when they pitched at West End Park. Courtesy Library of Congress

Just two days later, the American Association champion St. Louis Browns and a team made up mostly of Chicago White Stockings faced each other at Herald Park, the sponsored name of the park at the old Fairgrounds.[35] The five Chi-town players were joined by two each from Pittsburgh and Cincinnati, including Reds pitcher Tony Mullane who had just finished his fifth straight 30-win season.[36] Demonstrating the city's passion for baseball, over a thousand fans paid 50 cents apiece to watch two top professional teams battle it out.[37]

The Cincinnati Red Stockings toured extensively in Texas in 1888, making every major metropolis in the state. Hitting the state in March, just prior to the start of the Texas League season, the National Leaguers showed the locals up at most every stop.[38][39]Among the Reds was second baseman Bid McPhee, the last regular fielder to play without a glove.

As Houston grew and more ball clubs began to spend their springs in the South, the city became a more and more frequent stop for teams playing their way back up north in advance of the regular season. Not surprisingly, they scheduled games in various towns based on where they might make the most money from a cut of the gate. Though sometimes bypassed for neighboring Galveston as the Boston Beaneaters did in 1894[40], Houston soon became known as a reliable payday for barnstorming ball clubs.

By March 1910, when the St. Louis Browns were already training at West End Park, both the Detroit Tigers and

The first time Ty Cobb's Detroit Tigers came to Houston for exhibition games, the hit king didn't show. It prompted cries of foul from many Bayou City ball fans.

Courtesy Library of Congress

New York Giants came through town to play the Houston Buffs. The Indianapolis Indians of the American Association also stopped at West End.

John McGraw's Giants played two games in Houston with Christy Mathewson starting on Saturday and Bugs Raymond on Sunday. The second crowd broke all local records. Over four thousand people packed the ball yard, hundreds standing behind ropes in right field.[41]As usual, African-American patrons were admitted through the outfield gate to their own segregated section of the grand stands, and it was equally jammed.

Less than a week later, it was the defending American League champion Tigers who came to town for a Saturday tilt. Manager Hughie Jennings had promised that all of his stars would be on hand as the team passed through after training in San Antonio. When they arrived in Houston without batting champ Ty Cobb and three other regulars, local fans accused him of "acting in bad faith." The Buffs extracted revenge for the slight, however, when they defeated the Tigers by a score of 4 to 1.[42]

Though it's a difficult task to even locate mention of every exhibition game played in the Bayou City, let alone find box scores, we know that teams of note continued to pass through town. One such team was the Philadelphia Athletics of 1912. Though some managers fielded

Frank "Home Run" Baker was among the star-filled Philadelphia A's team that visited Houston in 1912. He drew a large ovation, responding with a triple, a single and a walk in five trips.

Courtesy Library of Congress

Connie Mack brought his reigning World Champion Athletics to Houston in late March 1912, thrilling local ball fans.

Courtesy Library of Congress

a lineup of second stringers in these contests, Connie Mack trotted out Home Run Baker, Eddie Collins and every one of his starters from the defending World Champions except Stuffy McInnis. The first two Philly pitchers were Jack Coombs, who was unhittable, and Eddie Plank, who was not, but the A's still beat the Buffs by a lopsided 11-3.[43]

Ty Cobb would eventually make it to Houston in 1916 when the Tigers and Giants made a post-spring training tour together.[44]For the three years that followed, the Chicago White Sox stopped at Houston in early April as they headed back north. In 1917[45] and 1918, Pants Rowland led his team to town. With war raging in 1918, the defending world champion Sox not only played three against the Buffs, all of which they lost,[46, 47] they also journeyed to Fort Crockett in Galveston to face a club from the Eighth Regiment of United States Marines.[48]

The following season, after again training at Mineral Wells, the White Sox returned to Houston. Less than a year later, this team would be derisively known as the Black Sox following a World Series filled with gambling money and accusations of thrown ballgames. Under the leadership of new manager Kid Gleason, the entire squad of Joe Jackson, Eddie Collins, Chick Gandil, Hap Felsch, Eddie Ciccotte, Lefty Williams and the rest started that ill-fated season by playing two in the Bayou City at the start of April 1919.[49]

The 1920 World Series champion Cleveland Indians also played a series of games at West End Park during the spring that followed their big triumph. Much was made of the return of Tris Speaker who had starred for the Buffs in 1907 as a teenaged outfield phenom on his way up. At least one Indian wished he had skipped the trip.

Bill Wambsganss, who had made an unassisted triple play in the World Series the previous fall, broke his arm in the final contest against the Buffs when a snap throw from catcher Dave Griffith to first baseman Jim Bottomley popped baserunner Wambsganss in the forearm.[50]

In 1918, the Brooklyn Robins and the Boston Red Sox, a team with 23-year-old pitcher Babe Ruth, played at Houston.[51] That tandem touring was a practice that became increasingly popular in the 1920s and 30s as the Giants vs. Cleveland,[52] Pirates vs. Yankees,[53] Tigers vs. Giants[54] and White Sox vs. Pirates[55] were among the matchups which came to the city.

One such pairing is particularly noteworthy, a two game series between the New York Giants and the Chicago White Sox on March 21st and 22nd of 1931. The teams made a side trip to the Bayou City to take part in something special.Though it was only exhibition play, the Saturday contest was the first night game ever held between Major League teams.[56]

Before they embarked on a 1919 season that would end in infamy, the Chicago White Sox stopped in Houston.

Courtesy Library of Congress

The game went into the tenth inning knotted at six, but the Sox broke it open with a five spot in the top of the frame, fueled in part by Luke Appling's double. The *Express* of San Antonio reported that "despite the unfamiliar conditions, the players seemed not to be troubled by the floodlights." It's unknown whether the lighting contributed to three Giants errors,[57] but the New York squad was still debating the merits a few days later, with most sentiments being negative.[58]

Another paired tour of significance took place in 1938. The Giants and Indians had been touring together, and Houston was the sight of what at least one newspaper dubbed the "weekly pitching argument" between Bob Feller and Carl Hubbell, two of the best in the game. Hubbell had led his league in strikeouts the year before, and Feller would lead his for the next four straight. Though neither man was left untouched, Feller got the best of things that Sunday in Houston,

Two former Houston Buffs, George "Rube" Foster and Del Gainer sit to the right of their fellow Red Sox George "Babe" Ruth and Ernie Shore.

Courtesy Library of Congress

giving up one run to Hubbell's four in the first three innings.[59]

Not all of Houston's exhibition memories were glorious ones, though. On the final day of March 1914, with the New York Giants about to play the last of a four game series with the Buffs, John McGraw got to West End Park early. As he walked near Buffs player/manager Pat Newnam, with whom he'd exchanged sharp words the day before, Newnam sucker punched McGraw in the mouth, splitting his lip and knocking him on his backside in the stands. Giants shortstop, Art Fletcher, rushed to his manager's aid, and Newnam was soon laid out in one of the boxes that surrounded the field.[60]

Not surprisingly, Buffs owners apologized, fining their manager $50 and suspending him indefinitely, which in this case meant until the Giants were headed back north and the regular Texas League season had started. Papers that week had been reporting that McGraw had discussed buying the Buffaloes from Otto Sens and Doak Roberts, but the discussion never progressed past conversation.[61, 62] As for Newnam, he led Houston to the league title that season.

During the 1930s and 40s, Houston continued to be a prime exhibition location for Negro League teams, as well. The powerful Homestead Grays visited the city for two games in April 1930. Two of the top players in the history of that circuit, Oscar Charleston and Smokey Joe Williams, graced the field at West End Park[63], but the soon to be famous Josh Gibson did not. The 19-year-old wouldn't join the Grays until the following July.[64]

In 1932, the Great Depression caught up with the Negro National League. New leagues formed and disbanded, and many teams, decimated by lagging attendance, resorted moreto a barnstorming model that worked prior to the league's

formation in 1920. Houston remained a profitable destination. The Kansas City Monarchs, New York Black Yankees, Chicago American Giants and Nashville Elite Giants were among the teams that scheduled games in town during 1935 alone.[65] These teams continued to visit even during the heart of WWII, filling a need for quality baseball entertainment in the absence of Texas League ball.[66, 67, 68]

As the postwar boom took hold, many people saw a strong baseball scene as a vibrant reminder of an American culture regained. As for Houston, it was no longer a provincial town. The population had grown from about 79,000 and a national rank of 68th in 1910 to almost 600,000 and being the 14th largest city in the United States in 1950.[69] For touring Major League teams, it was a must stop.

The Boston Red Sox, fresh off an AL pennant, came to Buff Stadium on March 31, 1947. Led by future Hall of Famers Ted Williams and Bobby Doerr, and managed by another in Joe Cronin, Houston kids crowded the rails to see the big league heroes.

Only two seasons after Jackie Robinson broke baseball's color line, he headlined a national post season tour of games between the Negro American League All-Stars and the Jackie Robinson All-Stars, a group that also included Major Leaguers Roy Campanella and Larry Doby. They played two games at Houston at the end of October 1949.[70]

Giants veteran pitcher Carl Hubbell (left) and young Bob Feller (above) provided a premier pitching matchup in a Houston exhibition game in 1938.

National Baseball Hall of Fame Library, Cooperstown, NY

Future Hall of Famer Oscar Charleston was one of the stars for the formidable Homestead Grays when they played in Houston in April 1930. National Baseball Hall of Fame Library, Cooperstown, NY

Similar fall tours came through town for most of the next half dozen years, drawing black and white baseball fans alike.[71, 72]

The city did have one major baseball disappointment. In April 1952, the BoSox returned to town to face the Buffs. Red Sox stories filled the nation's sports pages the day prior and on game

The defending American League champion Red Sox were a very hot ticket in Houston in 1947.

National Baseball Hall of Fame Library, Cooperstown, NY

day, too. The subject matter was not the ballgame, however, it was the fact that Ted Williams, arguably the greatest hitter who ever lived, was in Jacksonville, Florida, taking and passing his physical after being activated from the Marine Corps Reserves.[73, 74]

It wasn't all bad news in the early 1950s, though. Some of the longest-tenured Houston fans still talk about an exhibition game at Buff Stadium on April 8, 1951. Only a day after the Boston Braves and St. Louis Cardinals tangled at the park,[75] the defending champion New York Yankees faced the local Buffaloes.

The crowd was reported as just shy

Brooklyn catcher Roy Campanella played in Houston as part of Jackie Robinson's All-Stars and later returned with top billing and his own touring all-star team. Houston Metropolitan Research Center, Houston Public Library

New York Yankee immortals Joe DiMaggio (left) and Mickey Mantle put on a memorable show before an overflow crowd at Buff Stadium in 1951. National Baseball Hall of Fame Library, Cooperstown, NY

of 14,000, with many lucky ones standing behind ropes in the outfield.[76] They considered themselves fortunate that Sunday afternoon because right in front of them, just a few feet away, Joe DiMaggio stood in center and teenaged rookie sensation, Mickey Mantle, in right. For die-hard Buffs fans, it might have been a day of mixed emotions. The New Yorkers spanked the hometown boys by a count of 15-9 with both Mantle and DiMaggio knocking home runs.[77]

The round trippers were each memorable in their own way, too. Trailing the Buffs into the 5th, phenom Mickey Mantle killed a high drive over the double deck fence in left for the first three Yankee runs of the game. Joe DiMaggio hammered his, a two-run homer to left in the top of the 9th, to put a cap on New York's 15 runs in the game.[78]

The story of Joe D's blast didn't stop there, however. In the middle of the ninth, DiMaggio gave his home run bat to Jerry Witte of the Buffs to fulfill an earlier request. Playing a hunch, Witte came to bat with two runners on base in the final frame and used the gift DiMaggio bat to hit a three-run homer to left. It was no doubt a rare occurrence in organized baseball when two players from opposing teams used the same bat to hit home runs in the same inning.[79]

Since the advent of the Major Leagues in Houston in 1962, the city has been blessed with visits from a myriad of star players including those seen at the three All Star Games hosted here. Life as a minor league town in no way meant that Houstonians of an earlier era missed out on seeing the greats of their day, however, thanks to a steady stream of clubs that saw potential for profit in the Bayou City.

1 baseball almanac.com
2 baseball almanac.com
3 baseball-reference.com
4 GDN 7 March 1895
5 GDN 7 March 1895
6 GDN 9 March 1895
7 GDN 10 April 1895
8 GDN 9 April 1895
9 GDN 10 April 1895
10 HP 10 December 1904
11 HP 3 March 1905
12 baseball almanac.com
13 HC 17 March 1908
14 GDN 9 March 1909
15 *Reach Official American League Guide 1910-11.*
16 GDN 13 March 1909
17 GDN 14 March 1909
18 baseball almanac.com
19 GDN 15 March 1914
20 GDN 18 March 1914
21 GDN 19 March 1914
22 GDN 21 March 1914
23 HI 8 March 1924
24 CD 8 March 1924
25 CD 15 March 1924
26 CD 22 March 1924
27 HI 22 March 1924
28 CD 22 March 1924
29 CD 22 March 1924
30 CD 5 April 1930
31 CD 18 March 1944
32 GDN 3 September 1874
33 GDN 6 September 1874
34 GDN 13 November 1887
35 GDN 14 November 1887
36 http://www.baseball-reference.com
37 HDP 15 November 1887
38 GDN 4 March 1888
39 GDN 11 March 1888
40 HP 18 February 1894
41 HC 20 March 1910
42 HC 27 March 1910
43 GDN 25 March 1912
44 GDN 3 April 1916
45 GDN 30 March 1917
46 San Antonio Light 5 April 1918
47 San Antonio Light 3 April 1918
48 GDN 1 April 1918
49 GDN 29 March 1919
50 HP 3 April 1921; HP 4 April 1921; HP 6 April 1921
51 San Antonio Light 6 April 1918
52 San Antonio Light 8 April 1918
53 GDN 3 April 1929
54 Jefferson City (MO) Post Tribune 29 March 1933
55 Port Arthur News 4 April 1935
56 San Antonio Express 22 March 1931
57 San Antonio Express 22 March 1931
58 Jefferson City (MO) Post Tribune 23 March 1931
59 GDN 4 April 1938
60 New York Times 1 April 1914
61 New York Times 1 April 1914
62 GDN 2 April 1914
63 HI 5 April 1930
64 Brashler, William. *Josh Gibson: A Life in the Negro Leagues.* (, 1978)
65 CD 6 April 1935
66 CD 18 March 1944
67 CD 22 April 1944
68 CD 31 March 1945
69 Campbell Gibson, Population Division, U.S. Census Bureau
70 CD 15 October 1949
71 CD 16 October 1954
72 CD 29 September 1956
73 GDN 2 April 1952
74 Lowell (MA) Sun 3 April 1952
75 Jefferson City (MO) News Tribune 8 April 1951
76 Corsicana Daily Sun 9 April 1951.
77 Abilene Reporter News 9 April 1951
78 HP 9 April 1951
79 Witte, Jerry and McCurdy, Bill. *A Kid From St. Louis.* (Pecan Park Eagle Press, 2003)

KEY

GDN – *Galveston Daily News*
HI – *Houston Informer*
HP – *Houston Post*
CD – *Chicago Defender*
HC – *Houston Chronicle*

CHAPTER FOURTEEN

AFTERWORD: REACHING THE MOUNTAIN TOP

BY MICKEY HERSKOWITZ

Under a sun-splashed sky, with cotton puff clouds and a cool breeze—the kind of day that made Houston feel almost coastal and scenic—Major League baseball reached the Texas prairie. The date was April 10, 1962, and no one seemed to notice that this was the 50th anniversary of the launching of a super ship called the Titanic—a disastrous cruise but an epic and enduring movie.

The great Dizzy Dean never lost his popularity in Houston. He returned several times to appear in Old-Timers Games in the Bayou City.
Houston Metropolitan Research Center, Houston Public Library

Hollywood has shown no interest in the arrival of big league ball in the long neglected Southwest. The event was not a movie, a voyage, a journey, a marathon or a sprint. This was a campaign, partly political and partly personal, the result of sheer persistence, endless phone calls, door knocking, arm-twisting, lunches, secret dinners and large amounts of intrigue.

No one man can be said to have made this ascent possible. The list is as long as a spring training roster. But two, in particular, can be credited with getting the ball, literally, rolling. They were George Kirksey, the human whirlwind, former sportswriter who dabbled in public relations, but confounded friends and clients alike; and Craig Cullinan, Jr., the calm, tall, handsome grandson of the founder of the Texas Company, later Texaco.

Kirksey was the catalyst behind the dream and the drive, the irritant who forged the pearl from the goop in the oyster shell. Cullinan was the voice of reality and reason and provided the seed money.

On their heels appeared the power and the wealth, Judge Roy Hofheinz, the man who imagined the Astrodome, and Robert E. "Bob" Smith, an almost mythical figure, an oilman and rancher who was for decades Houston's largest landholder. In certain respects these two men could not have been less alike. For most of his life Smith operated behind the scenes and had no use for publicity. Hofheinz, a county judge at 26, later a young and controversial mayor, doted on the written word. The word was "Hofheinz."

To honestly describe the adventure that led to Houston going to The Show, it is first necessary to bust a few myths. To begin with, despite a long and distinctive record as a baseball town, dating back to the Houston Babies in the 1880s, and 39 seasons as a training ground for St. Louis Cardinals stars, the city was not a contender, or even an applicant, for a major league team until 1957.

That year marked the true, actual beginning of the mission to bring a big league team to Houston. Although Kirksey had been promoting the idea since he settled here after World War II, and opened a P. R. firm that he basically operated out of his coat pocket, nothing about the effort could be described as organized. Now, in January of 1957, the civic-minded banker, William Kirkland, agreed to invite a few movers and shakers to a meeting to discuss the daring idea of how to move the city from the outback to the Big Show.

A total of 35 businessmen attended the session, held in the board of directors' room at First City National Bank. Kirkland introduced Kirksey, who spoke from notes that covered a three-point agenda: money, people and a stadium. Out of the 35, a handful expressed interest. But a few days later, Kirksey recruited Cullinan, who sought out Bob Smith, who begat Judge Hofheinz, and an entity called the Houston Sports Association was formed. It is still today the parent company of the Houston Astros.

Kirksey enlisted the help of the sports editors of the three Houston newspapers, and now his maneuvering would at least receive some local coverage. Meanwhile, the people who needed to be impressed yawned and picked their teeth.

This disinterest was not unexpected for one critical reason: big league baseball was not a school or fraternity you could join because of good grades or because your daddy was connected. The owners had no incentive—at least, none that they were aware of—to expand or juggle their lineup. Think of it as an almost secret society, with most of the members located on or near the eastern seaboard. Four cities—Chicago, Philadelphia, Boston and St. Louis—had two teams each. New York had three. The other markets were Cincinnati and Cleveland, both in Ohio, Washington, Pittsburgh and Detroit. There was no team below the Mason-Dixon line.

The owners had an anti-trust exemption, written by Chief Justice Oliver Wendell Holmes in 1922, saying that baseball was not involved in inter-state activities or commerce, and was exempt due to its status as a sport.

"Of course, it's a sport," clarified Frank Lane, the general manager of several teams, years later. "No sane person could run a business like this."

Yes, there were rumors and retroactive memories of close brushes with deals that were made by other cities, but for all the financial giants the city could claim and the lovely history as a minor league force the money and tradition never merged

Loel Passe

Loel Passe broadcast baseball in Houston for 26 years, beginning with KTHT broadcasts of the Buffs games in 1950 when station owner Roy Hofheinz brought him from Birmingham, Alabama. Passe would continue with the Houston Major League franchise, staying on through 1976 and partnering with two Hall of Famers, Gene Elston and Harry Kalas. His southern catch-phrases were beloved by the locals even as they sometimes confounded out-of-staters. When a Houston pitcher struck out a batter, Passe shouted "He breezed him!" or "Now you're chunkin' in there." At particularly glorious moments for the home team, it was "Hot ziggedy dog and ol' sassafras tea," or maybe "Peanut butter up and down, jam and jelly all around." Even if a listener didn't understand it, the enthusiasm was contagious. Passe was not above an on-air stunt or two either. Once in Oklahoma City, a nine-run Buffs rally inspired him to call a half inning while hanging on a ledge in front of the press box. When Roy Hofheinz lost control of the Astros, Loel Passe was one of the first to go. It was not a totally surprising move since not everyone liked his style. Longtime baseball executive Bill Giles called Passe "a real cornball." Passe might not have been universally loved as a radio man, but he was a genuine guy, and his home team passion almost always brought a smile.

when opportunities arose. If one were to construct a chronology of Houston's negotiations, it would look like this:

1952 – The Philadelphia Athletics were rumored to be for sale. Among the moneyed class in Houston who enjoyed baseball were George and Herman Brown, foundedrs of the construction giant, Brown & Root; the family of Hugh Roy Cullen, whose fortune established the University of Houston; Gus Wortham, who built American General Insurance; Judge James A. Elkins, and William Kirkland, prominent bankers; and oil wildcatters Glenn McCarthy, who opened the dazzling Shamrock Hotel, and George Strake, supporter of numerous worthy causes.

One or two on this list may have made a phone call, or received one, to inquire about the status of the A's. No one can be sure. Owned by the venerable Connie Mack, who was a big league catcher when they DID NOT WEAR MASKS and also managed the team, the A's later moved to Kansas City in 1954 and eventually landed in Oakland. Mr. Mack was a player/manager when Ty Cobb was a rookie.

1953 – In January, Fred Saigh, the owner of the Cardinals, was sentenced to 15 months in prison and fined $15,000 for tax evasion. Ten weeks later, the franchise was sold to August "Gussie" Busch and the Anheuser-Busch brewery for $3.75 Million. In an interesting footnote, on his way to the penitentiary, Fred Saigh, recognizing that the sales of Budweiser would soar, borrowed $25,000 to purchase stock in the brewery at under $20 a share. With stock splits, his investment was valued 40 years later at nearly $50 million.

Although the details remained vague, Kirksey and Cullinan did have conversations with Saigh when his difficulties became public. However, although his critics charged otherwise, and perhaps to not further prejudice his legal woes, Saigh was committed to keeping the Cardinals in St. Louis.

1953 – At the end of the season, the American League approved the sale of the St. Louis Browns, whose attendance had sunk to 291,000, to Baltimore interests. This was a way for his fellow owners to be rid of the innovative Bill Veeck, who was considered a troublemaker and a maverick because he was, well, innovative. There may or may not have been a phone call from Houston—Kirksey later said he "called around"—but nothing, obviously, came of it.

1954 – The National League approved a request by Lou Perini, one of the brothers who owned the Boston Braves, to move to Milwaukee. Known as "The Three Steam Shovels," a tribute to their construction firm, the brothers had grown weary of sinking attendance and playing second fiddle to the Red Sox and Ted Williams. (No one in Houston saw this coming.)

1958 – Unable to convince the power brokers in New York that he needed a new stadium in Brooklyn, Walter O'Malley cut a deal to move the storied Dodgers to Los Angeles, for the first time bringing the National Pasttime to the western half of the nation. The burly, bespectacled lawyer wanted to build his new ballpark on a site that would later become the Barclay Center, home of the Brooklyn Nets of the NBA. Robert Moses, the land planner whose influence spread across the five boroughs, had offered O'Malley land in Flushing Meadows, in Queens, which later would welcome Shea Stadium and the New York Mets.

St. Louis shortstop Marty Marion was part of the final ownership group for the Houston Buffaloes, but he did not get to have a hand in the new National League franchise.

Houston Metropolitan Research Center, Houston Public Library

Since going west alone made no sense, from a financial or competitive standpoint, O'Malley convinced Horace Stoneham to move the New York Giants to San Francisco. Thus the legendary rivalry moved across the map and relocated on the Pacific Coast. None of this involved Houston, except later and indirectly. By the time O'Malley dropped his bombshell, expansion was on the table—although no sure thing.

Politicians had taken notice and were reviewing baseball's cherished, even sacred anti-trust exemption. And New Yorkers were rendered heart-broken with the losses of the Dodgers and Giants. This was New York, the center of American arts and culture and media, America's most visible and most international city. In today's currency, it would be like selling Broadway to China. The spiritual and emotional loss could not be long ignored.

To address at least two other myths:

1) There was no race between Dallas and Houston for one of the next expansion spots. Judge Hofheinz had rallied support for a revolutionary stadium, the world's first air-conditioned, domed, indoor ballyard and the lords of the flies had bought into it. Dallas had lagged in planning and politicking and, for whatever reasons, would be considered as an American League prospect—when it was considered at all.
2) The most entertaining of the intrigue surrounding the big league push was the emergence of a second bidder, an alternative candidate, in a group led by two St. Louis figures, Milton Fischman, a businessman with baggage, and Marty Marion, a former Cardinal player and manager who, many analysts had argued, was the finest defensive shortstop of his era. There was a catch, however. An opening was created when the Cardinals decided to sell the Buffs in the winter of 1958. And Cullinan would admit later that it was a huge mistake not to purchase the club, as his alter ego Kirksey had stridently urged. But Cullinan, and Judge Hofheinz, both felt that the focus should be on laying the big league groundwork and, secondly, they wished to distance themselves from the bush league image that Houston had once worn with pride.

Marion and his partner lined up a half dozen Houston investors, most prominent among them Eddie Dyer, a former Buff and Cardinal manager who now owned a successful insurance agency. Marty had played shortstop for him. Rusty Rowles and Bill Hopkins added more local credibility. Marion believed they might catch lightning in a thimble and win the big prize, but their fallback position was to cash in on the value of their territorial rights. This was the more realistic option. With Smith bankrolling the Houston Sports Association, the Buffs could have been bought from the Cardinals by the homegrown cartel for $100,000. Instead they passed, and the Marion-Fischman entry paid the fee for a team that no longer had a big league affiliation and was moving into the American Association.

They set the asking price for their territorial rights at $600,000. The price did not seem outrageous, given the potential headaches that might have multiplied as the drama moved forward.

Except for one detail: although few deals are set in Italian marble, and nervousness is a normal state for those closing a transaction within or about baseball, the suspense was only temporary—which doesn't mean it was less than real. But the franchise was wired. No one in Houston was eager to deny Bob Smith and his zillions of dollars. Hofheinz, though not universally loved, was close to Senator Lyndon Johnson, then the leading candidate for the Democratic presidential nomination. And his local political ties were still tight.

Letting the Buffs slip away would cost them time and money; but the franchise was not at risk. Kirksey did not concern himself with clocks, and Bob Smith did not agonize over spending money.

The next and possibly the last myth that needs to be addressed is the Continental League, which the allies in New York and Houston had threatened to organize—and then announced that they had—as a rival to the established two major leagues. In short, the Continental League was a hoax, perhaps the most creative and successful in baseball lore, if you throw out Bill Veeck sending a midget, Eddie Gaedel, to pinch hit for the St. Louis Browns. The 4-foot, 2-inch Gaedel carried a souvenir bat to the plate and drew a walk from Detroit's Bob Cain, as his catcher, Bob Swift, kneeled behind the plate.

The Continental League had one surpassing quality going for it: the magnificent Branch Rickey, who as general manager of the Cardinals had talked the ownership into buying their Texas League farm club in 1922. Rickey had changed baseball, no, he changed the country, when he broke the color line in 1947 by bringing Jackie Robinson to the Dodgers.

The proposed new league was a phantom, with no stadiums, no players, less than eight designated cities and no cash expended other than Rickey's salary as commissioner, believed to be $50,000 and a bargain. The HSA covered the expenses of George Kirksey, who suggested the hiring of the elderly Rickey and served as his assistant for one month.

Rickey was a brilliant man, a pious visionary who had been educated as a lawyer. He had bushy caterpillar eyebrows and a fondness for bow ties and checkered vests and quoting the Scriptures. He was described as looking like a minister, but one capable of cheating at bingo.

He was 80 and moving slowly, but the mind was still quick and the voice strong. Most of all, his former associates had reason to respect and fear him. As the man who ended baseball's most egregious omission, who gave Jackie Robinson the chance that had been refused Josh Gibson and Cool Papa Bell and Satchel Paige for so long, who righted this wretched wrong, Rickey had a cachet no one in the sport could rival.

His role caused much hand-washing and soul-searching and the promise of congressional hearings. In the spring of 1960, Senator Estes Kefauver of Tennessee, who headed the judiciary committee and simply enjoyed raising hell, introduced a bill to re-examine baseball's anti-trust status. He had eager support from Senator Richard Keating, of New York, whose state had lost two teams; and Senator Hubert Humphrey, of Minnesota, whose twin cities, Minneapolis and St. Paul, were on deck as possible Continental League members.

Time out for a small detour: a year earlier, the Buffs had moved to the American Association, under the new owners, Marion and Fischman. It was the last year that the local papers covered any road trips as the surge toward big leaguedom took precedence. Also, the Buffs finished last, the only team to lose more than 100 games.

In 1961, the Senators would move to Minnesota, surfacing as the Twins. The young baseball writer for the *Houston Post* observed this move with special interest. After finishing his story about the first game of the first series the Buffs played in St. Paul, he mentioned casually that he needed a ride back to his hotel. Too lazy to catch the team bus to St. Paul, he was keeping his room in Minneapolis. The Western Union operator, a St. Paul fan, refused to file his copy, out of principle, and another telegrapher had to take over.

The next day, instead of a taxi, he accepted a lift from a fan who had been in the press box. He turned out to be the boss of the local labor union. He thought nothing of it until his host lifted the hood of his car and looked inside before telling him to climb in.

Those were giddy and unpredictable times for fans in Houston. No one knew what to expect or when to expect it.

Cullinan and Kirksey attended the World Series between the New York Yankees and Pittsburgh Pirates in October of 1960. The Series was a strange one, with the Yankees winning three times by scores of 16-3, 10-0 and 12-0—outscoring the Pirates by 35 runs. But Pittsburgh won the seventh game, and the world championship, on Bill Mazeroski's homer in the bottom of the ninth.

Five days later, on Oct. 17, 1960, the National League office confirmed that Houston and New York had been awarded expansion franchises starting with the 1962 season, and were free to begin signing players immediately.

The next meeting was in Chicago, where the HSA accepted the terms laid out by the league's expansion committee: a $5 million deposit for capital costs and $1.75 million for players to be drafted in the expansion pool after the 1961 season. They had a year to hire their front office staff, select a manager, prepare for the draft and—high priority—settle the territorial rights issue and arrange for a ballpark if, as expected, the domed stadium was not yet completed.

This was off-the-charts news for

Houston and the people who had been involved in the perilous effort to achieve big league status. The city celebrated. As Kirksey put it, "This is what it means. Every day, when readers across the country look at the baseball standings in the paper, they will see Houston. And during the season, for half the games, the dateline will read 'Houston,' not 'Dallas.' When people thought of Texas before, they thought of Dallas, Neiman Marcus and the Cotton Bowl. Now they'll think of Houston."

And there was much to be said for that reasoning. If any doubt existed, the question was settled when Walter O'Malley expressed a preference for Houston. The Dodgers needed a stopover on its road trips east and Houston was 1,000 miles closer than St. Louis. The rivalry with Dallas was stopped in its tracks because Judge Hofheinz, who had made his money in real estate and radio, blocked the city from obtaining a franchise for 10 years—until the Senators moved in 1972. He wanted—demanded—that the Houston team's radio network stretch across the state of Texas. For 10 years it did. If anyone in Dallas didn't know why their city was put on hold, now they know.

The triumphant Houston contingent now moved swiftly to meet the National League's mandate. A week after the Chicago meeting, they hired away Gabe Paul, a classy fellow who had been with the Cincinnati Reds for 25 years, as their first general manager. He brought with him Bill Giles, the son of the president of the National League, who became the club's first director of public relations. Giles would in time become president and owner of the Philadelphia Phillies

Another legacy from Gabe Paul was his administrative assistant, Tal Smith, an expert on baseball's Blue Book, who would supervise the construction of the Dome. Tal later served as player personnel director, moved to New York to work for George Steinbrenner, and returned to Houston to run the organization as general manager and, twice, as president.

The 50-year-old Paul was assembling a first rate front office. His early hires included Bobby Bragan, an ex-Dodger backup catcher and former manager of the Fort Worth Cats, and Grady Hatton, a University of Texas product and a popular third baseman with the Reds. Bragan was named the farm director and Hatton was penciled in to head the player personnel office.

Instead, he would be appointed the manager of the team's Triple-A farm club in Oklahoma City and in 1964 would be named the second field manager of the fledgling franchise.

All of them outlasted the man who hired them, Gabe Paul. He signed a three-year contract in October, for an annual salary said to be $80,000, double what he was making in Cincinnati. Judge Hofheinz had reversed two or three of Gabe's decisions and, to a career baseball man, this disrespect was intolerable. Before the start of the 1961 season, he was hired as general manager in Cleveland.

Gabe Paul had been the personal

choice of Kirksey, who had known him since his days with the United Press syndicate in New York before the war. This had to be a dagger of a blow for George, but he kept his silence, aware that allowances had to be made for the temperament of a genius, which was how he appraised Hofheinz. Introducing him to a writer, he said: "The Judge is a man who blows large clouds of smoke—and sees through both sides of it. You can write that down."

Special mention needs to be devoted here to Kirksey, who is not easily explained. As a friend once observed of the writings of Gertrude Stein, "I understand the parts that are meant to be understood. No one understands the rest."

> *In the years since his death, in 1971, a kind of legend has grown about Kirksey. He worked on it while he was alive, and he entrusted the memory of it to friends who had been faithful to the way he was. His will endowed a scholarship program at the University of Houston for journalism students, and he would be proud, and maybe a little stunned, to see how well it has worked.*
>
> *He would purely love the thought that each year more students go into the marketplace of ideas labeled Kirksey Scholars.*
>
> *George was not a man of easily identified talents. He was not a gifted writer, which explains his admiration for those who were. He had a reverence for the language, for the phrase neatly turned.*
>
> *But he had energy, persistence, curiosity, a willingness to commit himself and an eye for the talents of other people—in itself a kind of talent. He was a restless spirit, always looking for his next project, a better restaurant or camera or sports car. Morris Frank, the beloved* Houston Chronicle *columnist and humorist, nicknamed him "Problems, Incorporated." His nature demanded a crisis.*
>
> *Late in life he came into some money, from the sale of his stock in the Astros and a local television company. For a few years, too few, he led the life he had always imagined: bon vivant, world traveler, expatriate writer. He lived the life of a squire, wearing shoes without socks and fleeing to Europe whenever his apartment grew so disordered he could not find the phone.*
>
> *His friends would get letters and cards from Europe or South America. He would show up one day at your door with gifts. You seldom knew he was coming until he got there. He had a hunger for people. He would take you into his confidence and, once in, you never got out.*
>
> *He was this way: George would leave after half an hour, and whatever you had been doing at the time you had to start over again. It was like being interrupted while*

counting beans in a jar. He made you lose count. George had a gift for infuriating people without even knowing it. You would meet someone who knew him from his Army Air Force service in World War II, or as a writer for the top magazines of another age, Collier's, Look *and* The Saturday Evening Post, *and they would get red in the face at the mention of his name. He was married and divorced twice, once to a Broadway actress named Ethel Shutta (Shoo-TAY). Their fights were legendary.*

A dozen friends attended a shipboard bon voyage party for Kirksey in 1971. For a man as impatient as George, it was a curious way to travel. He once sponsored a Mexican racing driver, and he had a passion for fast cars. He died in one later that year, in a two-car collision on a quiet road in a small town in France. It was 3 in the morning and he was on his way to a Grand Prix auto race.

His friends nodded at the news and said it was the way he would have wanted to go. But the truth is, if it were up to George, one suspects he would rather have lived on. He had places to see and plans to keep. He was one of those rare souls who left an impression on every life he touched. Yes, he was a sports writer, and a good one, later a public relations man, and an honest one. He is remembered, by those who won't forget, as the original force behind the drive to bring big league baseball to Houston in the years before 1962.

Where you rank this accomplishment depends on how you feel about baseball, covered stadia and the role of sports in society. The arrival of the Colt .45s created an era of artificial turf and VIP boxes and bringing the great outdoors inside. George thought baseball was mighty important, and it wasn't easy to argue with George.

If there was a comic high point in the transition from the bush leagues to the bigs, it may have occurred on a West Coast trip the Judge organized to court the legislators, county commissioners and city councilmen who held Houston's purse strings. State Senator Searcy Bracewell, once a client of Kirksey's, had drafted a bill that was passed by the legislature in 1957 to approve public money for "parks and entertainment venues." In July of 1958, voters approved a referendum to issue $20 million in revenue bonds for the cost of Houston's covered stadium. But lawsuits had popped up, there were amendments to deal with and Hofheinz needed to firm up their political support.

So in early December of 1961, some 60 politicians and reporters—invited to make the politicians feel important—boarded a Continental Airlines charter for a West Coast trip to inspect the new stadiums in Los Angeles and San Francisco. There would be an unannounced stopover in

Las Vegas on the trip home.

The Judge hauled with him the model of the domed stadium that was close to a work of art. The cost was $40,000 and the details included miniature toilets that flushed. He gave a lecture and demonstration to the executives of both teams, and the baseball writers who worked the beat. A constant refrain was, "This is what it takes for a city to be big league."

Dodger Stadium, built by O'Malley on land donated by the city at a place called Chavez Ravine, and Candlestick Park, overlooking the ocean off San Francisco, were under construction but dazzling to behold. Cocktail parties featured a mixture of Hollywood and sports celebrities: Jayne Mansfield, Clint Eastwood, Marie McDonald, Carl Hubbell and Lefty O'Doul.

Then came the surprise detour to Las Vegas. The visitors checked into the Sands Hotel to freshen up or rest, and then regrouped for dinner in the ballroom, which featured an attraction imported from France called the Folies Bergère. The first several rows of the room had been blocked off for the guests from Texas.

It is safe to say that few of the tourists had seen two- or three-dozen long-legged, topless dancers perform before, and they were transfixed. A runway across some of the tables brought the dancers inches away, spinning and twirling and high kicking. But Kirksey was preoccupied. The team had acquired the rights to a lefthanded pitcher named Hal Woodeshick, and he kept asking the *Post*'s young baseball writer if he thought the pitcher could help the club?

"George," came the frustrated reply, "who cares?"

Well after midnight, the group boarded the charter for the red-eye flight to Houston. The hostesses carefully stored the mockup of the domed stadium, and nearly everyone grabbed a blanket and fell instantly asleep. A little after dawn, the plane landed and taxied on the runway. The irrepressible Morris Frank pulled back the small curtain covering the window by his seat and saw, waiting with the baggage handlers, a small number of wives and friends of the passengers.

"Well," he said, in his East Texas twang, "it was shore great seeing all them big league titties. But it's back to the minors today."

In truth, there was no turning back. You were reminded of the line from the "Music Man," and the promise that "River City is gonna have a band." The rights payment was resolved, without serious bitterness or noise, when the Marion-Fischman group accepted a figure of around $440,000—less than they had asked, but a profit even after deducting the losses they absorbed while operating the Buffs.

The Houston Sports Association was now the operator of the Buffs for what remained of their final season. A working agreement with the Chicago Cubs was still in place, and the manager assigned to the team, Harry Craft, would be held over as the first skipper of the Colt .45s—a name not yet chosen.

Stunned by the sudden exit of Gabe Paul, Kirksey and Cullinan relied on luck and prudent planning. They had a name in mind in case of an emergency, as either the manager or GM, and this development seemed to qualify. Within two months of the blowup, an agreement was reached with Paul "Rapier" Richards, the sage of Waxahachie, a tall, thin catcher who had built championship teams in Chicago and Baltimore, although he left both before the deeds were done.

He was also credited with being uniquely skilled at developing pitchers, including a future Hall of Famer in Hal Newhouser at Detroit. Richards was called up from Atlanta, where he had been the manager, to catch Newhouser during the war year of 1945. He was the hero of the seventh game of the World Series, backing up Prince Hal with two bases loaded doubles, driving in six runs.

As informed and amiable as Gabe Paul was, few exuded or inspired more confidence than Richards. As a younger man, he had pitched for his hometown team in Waxahachie, and had also acted as the sports editor of the local paper. He would climb the rusty stairs to the press box to write his game stories. "We had the greatest masthead in the history of newspapers," he boasted. "It read: 'WE ARE FOR AN EARLY SPRING AND AGAINST THE LOCUSTS.'"

By the time Richards arrived, leaving Baltimore in his rear view mirror, the new franchise had a nickname. Hofheinz had swept aside the early local sentiment to retain the "Buffs." But that hardly

Roy Hofheinz and Houston Radio

Unfortunately, media conglomerates in today's world keep growing, and the public is poorer for the lack of diverse voices. Imagine, though, a major American city where one man controlled the top two newspapers and every single radio station. Such was Houston, Texas, in the 1930s. Jesse Jones, his relatives or his business interests owned both the *Chronicle* and *Post* from 1932 till 1939, and continued to control all three local radio stations for another five years after that. It was a point raised loudly and often by Roy Hofheinz, the young County Judge who had been lobbying the FCC hard to get a radio license of his own. Hofheinz's station, KTHT, finally went on the air in July 1944, just weeks after the D-Day invasion. It began a small explosion of electronic media growth in the Bayou City, some of it fueled by Hofheinz himself. Station KTHT, originally at 1230 on the AM dial and later at 790, made its reputation by concentrating on news through the pioneering use of portable wire recorders. Reporting live from the 1947 disaster at Texas City put Hofheinz on the map. At the same time, the Judge put the city's first FM station on the air. Hofheinz also brought the Mutual Radio Network's Game of the Week onto his station and followed it up in 1951 by bringing live play-by-play of the Houston Buffs road night games sponsored by Ford to KTHT at a time when other local stations were airing re-created contests on tape delay. Baseball was not just a whim for the Judge. He had been a regular patron of Buffs games for many years, and when he was Houston's mayor in the mid-1950s, a reporter revealed that Roy Hofheinz had been practicing his knuckleball in preparation for the Buffs Opening Day first pitch.

Gus Mancuso was an amateur and professional catcher in Houston and a broadcaster following his playing days. His mother was a regular feature in the box seats.

Houston Metropolitan Research Center, Houston Public Library

represented a clean break with the past.

A committee had been selected to judge the nominations submitted by the public, a nicely democratic process, except for the fact that the HSA already had settled on a name: the Colt .45s, after the Gun That Won the West. The Judge initially liked the marketing possibilities, and even more so the price. Kirksey had obtained the rights for free from the Colt Firearms Company.

Among the more popular names submitted were the Ravens, Rangers, Sheriffs and Mavericks. But they were officially the Colt .45s and so they would remain, until the opening of the Astrodome—and a demand by the Colt Firearms Company to be compensated for the use of its product.

In December of 1961, the two expansion clubs selected 23 players apiece out of a talent pool that consisted of discards and rejects from the other National League teams, who were allowed to protect their top 40. "The Mets is great," declared Casey Stengel, the manager of the team. "They give everybody a job, just like the WPA."

Richards did not take so charitable a view. The merchandise so depressed him that he wanted to give it all back, just flat refuse to accept delivery. He might have succeeded if the Mets had agreed to go along. But the New Yorkers were satisfied with their draft, which was deep in old timers familiar to their fan base. Their faith was rewarded by a team that lost 120 games.

The players would not have been heartened by what they were hearing and reading. But most of them were grateful to still be in the majors, and to have a chance to win a regular job. In today's world of air conditioned stadiums, mega-millions contracts and computer scouting, it is hard to appreciate what an oddball blend the original Colt .45s were. It was like the

French Foreign Legion, with every guy on the lam from somewhere else.

Bobby Shantz, who would start Houston's opening game, had been ailing with a sore arm since 1954. Richard "Turk" Farrell had been cast off by the Phillies and the Dodgers as a compulsive playboy and barroom brawler. Norm Larker was labeled a temper case. Hal Woodeshick was the nervous type, who walked in his sleep and had a hard time keeping a roommate. Most of the others were too young or too old. Most of them had jobs in the off-season, working as mail clerks and unloading beer trucks.

Not a pitcher among them had won 10 games in the majors the year before; not a hitter had batted .300 or had slugged 10 home runs. Houston had picked four players out of a blue chip category at a top price of $125,000. They were Farrell, outfielder Al Spangler, catcher Hal Smith and Joey Amalfitano, a flip young second baseman formerly with the Giants. When he heard how much Houston paid for him, Amalfitano quipped: "I better call an insurance agent. I'm worth more than I thought I was."

Joey always regretted that remark. He had to have his phone disconnected because of all the calls from insurance salesmen across North America. Years later he would manage the Chicago Cubs.

There were no great expectations, no inflated promises, about the quality of the team Houston would field in that pioneer season. In spring training, Bill Rigney, the manager of the Angels, took one look at the Houston lineup and predicted, "They'll need three singles to score a run." That judgment, like Milk of Magnesia, would stand the test of time.

Now, after all the twists and turns and trials, all the elements came together for the greater glory of Houston baseball—on April 10, 1962. The Cubs were the opposition the day the city earned its big league dateline. No skepticism, no cold breath of reality, could dampen the city's enthusiasm. The game was played in natural splendor: outdoors, on real grass, in a stadium with no shade. Beautiful Colt Stadium was a temporary ballyard, painted in pastels and rainbow colors, to be replaced sooner or later by the one with the big bubble on top. The cost of the interim structure was said to be in excess of $2 million. At the time, it was hailed as another example of Texas extravagance.

The stadium had the longest dugouts in baseball, because Judge Hofheinz had heard that fans like to buy tickets behind the dugouts. A private club for VIP ticket holders featured a bar even longer than the dugouts, rumored to have been imported from one of the most famous brothels in Paris. Fans were shown to their seats not by ushers, but by Triggerettes, dressed like Dale Evans, the country singer and wife of Roy Rogers.

The last 5,000 general admission seats went on sale at 10 a.m. the morning of the game, priced at a buck and a half. A sellout crowd of 26,000 rose for the national anthem, sung by Frankie Laine, whose big hits were "Mule Train" and "That Lucky Old Sun."

The fact that the grandstand had no roofing, none at all, gave the park a strange, naked appearance. The absence of an overhang made a lot of foul balls available to "lucky fans," as announcer Loel Passe always described them. It also eliminated any protection from that relentless Texas sun, and during day games in July and August the sound of an ambulance siren frequently drowned out the PA system, carrying off another lucky fan who had fainted from too much sun or heat.

But on April 10, 1962, there were no complaints, no problems, no flaws, no nits worth picking. It was the kind of magical day Houston would know infrequently for most of the next two decades. To the unbridled joy of the homefolks, the Colt .45s won big, and won in style, crushing the Cubs, 11-2, on a five-hitter by Shantz and a pair of three-run homers by Roman Mejias. This was a victory for innocence and the underdog and creative landscaping. Aware of his team's lack of punch and lack of speed and other shortcomings, the cunning Richards had let the infield grass grow so tall that one of the Chicago coaches complained, "They planted rice out there."

One of the enduring pictures embedded in the brains of those who were there was the sight of Shantz, twice whipping off his fielder's glove so he could dig in the grass with both hands for a topped or bunted ball. The wispy 5'7" lefthander looked like a kid hunting for Easter eggs.

Shantz was a brief story in Houston, but a marvelous and touching story, the cornball kind they don't seem to make any more. He pitched in pain that day, as he had since he tore a tendon in his shoulder in '54, the last time he had started a season opener. They treated his arm with hot bricks between innings. The 36-year-old artist went the full nine innings, shutting out the Cubs until Ernie Banks homered in the seventh.

During the pre-game ceremonies, Paul Richards stood in the middle of the press box, and said with a smile: "Boys, someday, when Houston is in the World Series and they are raising the pennant in center field, I hope you'll pause and give 10 seconds of silence for ol' Richards."

It was his way of acknowledging that if such a day ever came, he would probably be somewhere else; that the job would take longer than the time he would be given. (He would be fired after the 1965 season.) The lean Texan had left such teams on their way to championships, the White Sox and Orioles. In fact, it turned out that he had used the same line in both cities.

"I saw Richards in 1960," a Chicago scribe told a writer from Houston, "the year after the White Sox got into the World Series. I told him, 'Paul, we gave you your 10 seconds."

APPENDICES

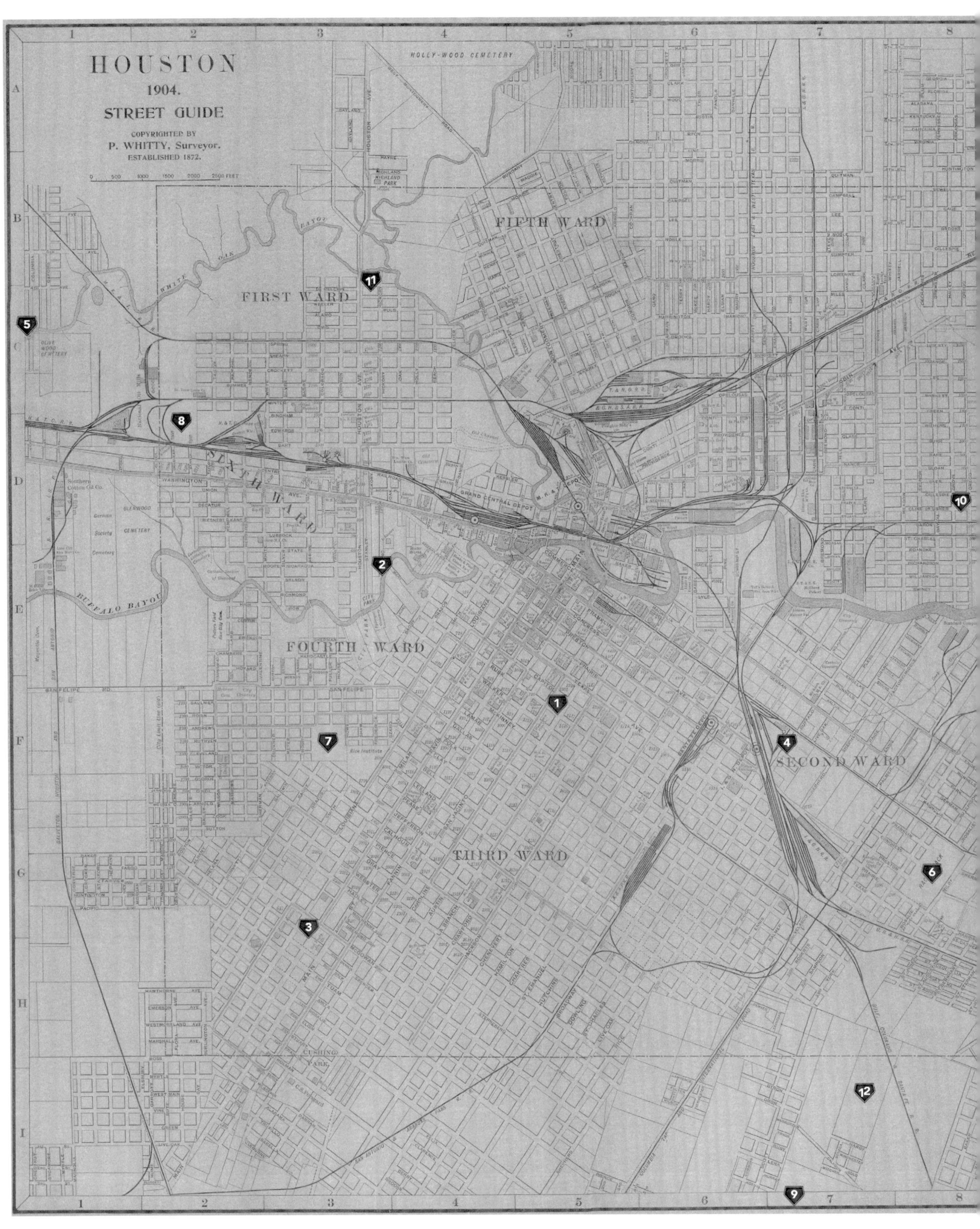

HOUSTON
1904.
STREET GUIDE
COPYRIGHTED BY
P. WHITTY, Surveyor.
ESTABLISHED 1872.
HOLLY-WOOD CEMETERY
FIFTH WARD
FIRST WARD
SIXTH WARD
FOURTH WARD
THIRD WARD
SECOND WARD
BUFFALO BAYOU
GRAND CENTRAL DEPOT
CUSHING PARK

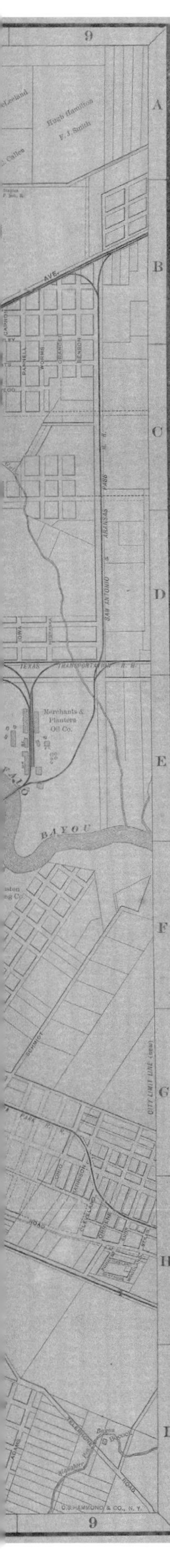

BASE BALL PARKS OF HOUSTON 1859-1961

1. Houston Academy Grounds
   Caroline & Capitol
2. Pioneer Field
   Youngs Old Brickyard
3. Fairgrounds
   Travis & McGowen
4. Union Depot/International
   Near Congress, behind depot
5. Coombs Park
   Heights Blvd. at White Oak Bayou
6. Harrisburg Race Park
   Harrisburg & Milby
7. West End Park
   Andrews & Heiner
8. Southern Pacific Grounds
   Oliver, north of Center
9. Scott Street Park
   Scott & Rosalie
10. East End/Monarch Park
    Cline at Gregg
11. Little Sportsman's Park
    Houston Ave.
12. Buffalo Stadium
    Calhoun & St. Bernard

WHAT IS SABR?

The Society for American Baseball Research (SABR) is an organization of more than 7,000 members, who are dedicated to the history of our national pastime. SABR has more than 57 regional chapters throughout the United States, England, Japan and Latin America. While the emphasis is on baseball research and its preservation, SABR is not just about numbers. Through numerous committees members focus on topics of individual interest, ranging from ballparks, player and executive biographies, Negro Leagues, Scouts, the Business of Baseball, Umpires and Rules to game statistics, Nineteenth Century Baseball, scientific decision-making and many other subjects. Many regional chapters meet monthly and SABR holds an Annual Convention at various locations each year. SABR 44 will be held in Houston, Texas, in the summer of 2014.

For more information, please visit *sabr.org.*

ACKNOWLEDGEMENTS

I first joined SABR back in 1982 and became the Chair for the Larry Dierker Houston Chapter in 2004. Growing up in northern New Jersey during the "Golden Age of Baseball" (the 50's) where there were three major league teams, kids argued over the best team, best centerfielder, best broadcaster and best beer, I fell in love with the sport. My choices were the Yankees, Mickey Mantle, Mel Allen and Ballantine Beer.

In 1960, I graduated from Miami University in Oxford, Ohio, with a BS in Business, and received my commission in the U. S. Navy. I served on active duty at the Naval Communications Station in Norfolk, Virginia, and while in Norfolk, I met and married Peggy, my bride of 53 years. Together we have three children and six grandchildren. After the Navy I jointed the marketing department of Texaco, later Star Enterprise, from which I retired after 35 years of service.

My special baseball interest has always been current and former ballparks where organized baseball has been played. To date Peggy and I have identified and mapped more than 1,000 such ballpark locations and visited and photographed more than 200 of these sites.

Within the chapter, I am the Manager of our vintage baseball team, the Houston Babies, named after the first professional baseball team to play in Houston in 1888. We play at least 4 times a year in regional tournaments using rules established and printed in 1860. We have also been Houston Astros season ticket holders for over 17 years.

When Bill McCurdy first suggested that the chapter write a significant history of Houston baseball, I jumped at the opportunity. Besides assisting in the writing of three chapters within the book, I had the added responsibility for fund raising and the selection of the publisher. It has been a delight and pleasure to work with our accomplished editor Mike Vance and my dedicated friend Bill McCurdy to see the three years of amazing effort come to such a quality conclusion. Thanks, too, to all the other participants, some SABR members, some not, especially Patrick Lopez, who made such valuable contributions. We hope you will enjoy our product.

BOB DORRILL

On the night of May 27, 1954, at old Buff/Busch Stadium in Houston, I was there as a 16-year old fan and soul-inspired witness to the heroic debut of first baseman Bob Boyd as he tripled and doubled his way into Houston Buffs history before a roaring, foot-stomping crowd as the first black player for any locally integrated sports team. All the way home after the game, the thought kept whispering redundantly in my brain: "Somebody ought to write a book about this." Well, it took us sixty years, but we finally did it.

Mickey Herskowitz and I exchanged letters about the need for such a book in 1988, but nothing happened. It wasn't time. We needed more wisdom and the coming together of certain events and people to make it happen just as it needed to be. We also needed some perspective.

The 2005 World Series in Houston finally got the wheels of new work turning. Certain national media types came to town and reminded us that many of them still see Houston as "an ancient football town that only recently has discovered the joys of baseball."

As I began my research in the summer of 2007 with only limited time for the solo project, I wanted to prove them wrong. Finding that proof was not the problem. The problem was finding the manpower hours to get the job done right in a single lifetime. It was not a job for a single researcher/writer who also still held down a day job in an unrelated field.

I took my work on *Houston Baseball: The Early Years, 1861-1961* to my local chapter of the Society for American Baseball Research (SABR) in 2011. Because of the positive, supportive, and dynamic leadership climate that existed in SABR due to good friend and chapter leader Bob Dorrill, a book project took root in May 2011. From under the research and writing wings of SABR members, including iconic writer Mickey Herskowitz, our fine book has emerged in 2014 as our contribution to Houston history.

Our book came to be through the connection of several key people and circumstances over time, a dynamic reflected in the chapters here and in the last oh-so-entertaining and educational piece by Mickey Herskowitz.

In the end, the thing that started in 1954 as an adolescent inspiration now concludes itself as a local baseball history book that we are all joyously happy to have had a humble hand in producing.

Make no mistake, however, the *sine qua non* of all our effort has been a consummate writing professional named Mike Vance. Without Mike's commitment, this legacy-worthy work would not have been possible.

This book has been edited to the bone for the truth alone at every turn of each research corner. It had to be. Good friend and colleague, the indomitable researcher, Mike Vance, has no tolerance for anything that misleads or distorts the truth.

Thanks, too, to Patrick Lopez, the fine artist who gave us eyes to see how the early baseball parks of Houston once appeared, and thanks also to the artful folks at Bright Sky Press who put together our beautiful book in its final package form.

Houston, your early baseball history is in good hands today.

Ours is a book for the ages.

BILL McCURDY

Though as editor, I went over everything in the book, the talented Lucy Chambers of Bright Sky Press combed through each word again after I did. Editing is not the same as writing. Each chapter in this book is listed with the names of those who did the actual writing or at least had a hand in putting that specific information together. That means that these folks also worked at researching the material, as well. You'll see their names at the start of each chapter on which they worked, but it doesn't hurt to mention Bob Dorrill, Bill McCurdy, Joe Thompson, Steve Bertone and Marsha Franty again here.

I'm someone who loves a fun research project. I can also tell you that not everyone is cut out for it. It takes a great commitment of time, focus and patience. We had others who put their efforts into researching certain areas of the book, and that was hugely important. That's why I want to single out a few folks from our research team for particularly special work. Art Spanjer traveled to libraries all over Central Texas in a quest to help me find out the real story behind the early 1920s ownership of the Houston Buffs. Marsha Franty volunteered to go back and hunt down specific articles months after she had turned in the material for which she initially signed up. Tom Murrah gave me great information and then paved the way for some other material on high school and college ball. Steve Bertone worked long hours on a year-by-year breakdown that ultimately got incorporated as a vital part of the narrative of that time period. Darryl and Susan Pittman dug through some 19th century newspapers at the outset of the project. Joe Thompson and the above-mentioned Marsha Franty also put special work into women's baseball. Bill McCurdy answered more than a few calls and e-mails to run down details. Tony Cavender and Lance Carter signed on at the beginning and contributed work on sports media and the Yankees 1914 visit respectively. Finally, Anne Shelton did some searching at the Texas State Library and Archives when I couldn't make a trip to Austin, and my California cousin, Beth Wehrmeister, found some very specific newspaper articles from 1867. A heartfelt thanks to each of them.

When I asked my architectural historian friend, Anna Mod, if she knew of a good architectural artist, she immediately sent me to Patrick Lopez. It turned out to be an absolutely perfect match. Patrick has as much passion for Houston baseball as anyone on the team, growing up in the East End and spending a good deal of his youth at Buff Stadium. His career included illustrating such proposed projects as the Sears Tower in Chicago, and I can't think that our book reached those heights, but he still put in total attention to detail, particularly in his work on the ballpark at Travis and McGowen for which no known image exists. The image that appears in this book was created by Patrick from several written accounts. It truly brings a lost part of Houston history to life.

During over two years of research on this book, I spent a lot of time at various research libraries, and the staffs in each of them deserve recognition and thanks. I must start with the two places that are almost my vacation homes as I work on many fun projects about the history of Texas and Houston: the Houston Metropolitan Research Center of the Houston Public Library (HMRC) and the Harris County Archives. One most deserving friend is Joel Draut, the amazing photo archivist at the HMRC. Other HMRC staff has also been invaluable: Tim Ronk, Caroline Castillo, Jo Collier, Laney Dwyer, Jennifer Nuzzo, Aaron Winslow and of course, HMRC Director Liz Sargent. The other person who needs so many thanks is Sarah Jackson of Harris County Archives. She and Annie Golden have filled countless requests for bringing heavy bound volumes out from the stacks so that I can pore over old pages. And Sarah, I know it's my turn to buy lunch.

I also got help at many other libraries. In no particular order, thanks to Lee Pecht and the staff at Rice University's Woodson Research Center; Miranda Bennett, Pat Bozeman, Mary Manning and Greg Yerke at UH Special Collections; the kind staff at Beaumont's Tyrrell Library; Deborah Dandridge, Kathy Lafferty, Elspeth Healey and Karen Cook at Spencer Library, University of Kansas; Ms. Dennis at the Reagan High School Library (and the nice HPD cop who let me park in a bus zone); Leslie Willis-Lowry at Temple University's

Blockson Collection; Susan Chandler at the Sterling Library in Baytown; Nancy Koehl at the Nesbitt Library in Columbus, Texas; the staff at the Texas State Library and Archives in Austin, staff at the Louisiana Secretary of State's Office in Baton Rouge, Matt Farah of the Historic New Orleans Collection and the Williams Research Center, the Pennsylvania Bureau of Vital Statistics and the staff in the Corporations Division of the Texas Secretary of State's office who likely thought I was crazy for continually ordering pages of 100-year-old business filings.

There were also those who took my inquiries about specific questions and came back with prompt answers: T. Scott Brandon at Out of the Park Baseball; Steve Densa of Minor League Baseball; Brian Finch of the St. Louis Cardinals; Madelyn Garza and Joanie South-Shelley at St. Thomas High School; Tom Kayser at the Texas League and my buddy Bill Bremer at KPRC Television. Thanks go to my local historian pals who are there to help me sort out where a certain railroad depot might have been or some other such minute question. Those good friends include Betty Chapman, Kirk Farris, JR Gonzales, John Nova Lomax, Anne Sloan, Debra Sloan and Story Sloane, none of whom are related believe it or not. Others deserving of specific thanks are: Mike Pede, Orlando Sanchez, Aaron Wendt, Josh Wendt and Larry Wimberly.

Adrian "Pat" Patterson, Jim Liuzza, John Watkins, Frank Mancuso, Jr., Fr. Robert Crooker, Clem Hausmann, Danny Basso, Henry Kana, Bob Fretz and Monique Stoneham all helped with information and/or images about their illustrious baseball ancestors. Likewise, it was invaluable to sit down and talk to people like Marie "Red" Mahoney, Felix and Lupe Fraga and Jack Schultea about their own Houston baseball experiences.

Pat Kelly, photo archivist at the Baseball Hall of Fame in Cooperstown was very easy to work with. I appreciate all the help. Thanks also go to Hall of Fame staff members Freddy Beroski, Bill Francis, Jim Gates, Brad Horn and Tim Wiles.

The staff and some board members of SABR on the national level were most helpful: Marc Appleman, FX Flinn, Deb Jayne, Jacob Pomrenke, Jeff Schatzki and Cecilia Tan. Among the individual, non-Houston SABR members who were helpful are Leslie Heaphy, John Thorn, Larry McCray, Larry Lester and Bruce Allardice. Thanks also to the Pee Wee Reese Chapter in Louisville and the Connie Mack Chapter in Philadelphia for responding to queries posed there.

The team at Bright Sky Press is fantastic. Ellen Cregan and Lucy Chambers are the best publishers that a writer could want. It has been a pleasure. Let's do it again. Marla Garcia is the talented woman who designed our cover and laid out the pages, and everyone else at Bright Sky was most friendly and capable. Kudos also to Sumner Hunnewell for his work and guidance on indexing this book.

The big ticket item comes last. The other two guys on the production trio are Bob Dorrill and Bill McCurdy. They helped with the decision-making and especially with the most thankless and un-fun task of asking other people for money to make this thing happen. I wanted no part of that. The generous, baseball-loving souls who came through with support are these: Harvey Berger, Tony Cavender, Chris Chestnut, Stan Curtis, Bob Dorrill, Gary Eiland, Todd Farquharson, Pat Flynn, Marsha Franty, Bill Gilbert, Phil Holland, Harold Jones, Tom Kleinworth, Andy Lopez, Mike McCroskey, Bill McCurdy, Tom Murrah, Wayne Roberts, Art Spanjer, Joe Thompson, Herb Whalley, Larry Wimberly, Jimmy Wynn and one big donor who wished to be anonymous. When I say that it never could have happened without them, I mean that most literally. Sincere thanks to you all.

This project has been a huge amount of work, but I'm proud of the end result. I hope it adds something to the history record of Houston in general and of Houston baseball in particular. So many of the people involved with this project love both the sport and this city very deeply.

MIKE VANCE
HOUSTON, TEXAS

INDEX

All locales are in Houston, Texas, unless otherwise noted.
(Bold page numbers indicate subject in photograph.)

Fred Ankenman's All-Time Buffs

Few people were around the Houston Buffaloes longer than Fred Ankenman who served as club secretary and club president from 1921 to 1942. After the demise of the franchise, Ankenman told *Post* writer Clark Nealon about his picks for the greatest players at each position over the life of the minor league team. Refusing to pin it down any further, these are what he called "standouts at each position over his span." That means that Major League Hall of Famers like Tris Speaker, Billy Williams and Ron Santo, who came before or after Ankenman's tenure, are not included.

ANKENMAN'S GREATS

Right-Handed Pitchers: Dizzy Dean, Marvin Goodwin and Johnny Grodzicki

Left-Handed Pitchers: Bill Hallahan, Harry Brecheen, Howard Pollet and Frank Barnes

Catcher: Ernie Vick, Harry McCurdy and Frank "Pancho" Snyder

First Base: Johnny Hopp

Second Base: Carey Selph

Third Base: Eddie Hock

Shortstop: Heinie Schuble and Tommy Carey

Outfielders: Chick Hafey, George "Watty" Watkins; Pepper Martin, Joe "Ducky" Medwick, Homer Peel